THE NATURE AND THE EFFECT OF
THE HERESY OF THE FRATICELLI

AMS PRESS

NEW YORK

THE NATURE AND THE EFFECT OF THE HERESY OF THE FRATICELLI

BY

DECIMA L. DOUIE, Ph.D.

LECTURER IN MEDIEVAL HISTORY IN THE UNIVERSITY OF DURHAM

MANCHESTER: AT THE UNIVERSITY PRESS

1932

Library of Congress Cataloging in Publication Data

Douie, Decima Langworthy, 1901-
   The nature and the effect of the heresy of the Fraticelli.

        Reprint of the 1932 ed. published by the University
   Press, Manchester, which was issued as no. 61 of Publica-
   tions of the University of Manchester, Historical series,
   and no. 220 of Publications of the University of Man-
   chester.
        Bibliography: p.
        Includes index.
        1. Franciscans. 2. Fraticelli. I. Title.
   II. Series: Victoria University of Manchester.
   Publications: Historical series; no. 61.
   III. Series: Victoria University of Manchester.
   Publications, no. 220.
   BX3602.D6   1978   271'.3   77-84715
   ISBN 0-404-16121-9

Reprinted from the edition of 1932, Manchester
First AMS edition published in 1978

Manufactured in the United States of America

AMS PRESS, INC.
NEW YORK, N.Y.

TO MY PARENTS

INTRODUCTION

THIS book is an attempt to bring the work of foreign scholars on a very vital and interesting aspect of early Franciscan history to the notice of English readers. Most of those who visit Assisi have been drawn there by the charm of the greatest of her sons, and have been fascinated by the naïve and almost childlike freshness of such writings as the *Fioretti* and the *Speculum Perfectionis*, though they have little knowledge of their historical background, or of the thoughts and aspirations of the circle which gave them birth. My object is therefore to trace the development of the Spiritual movement in the Franciscan Order, as well as to give some account of the intellectual, moral, and religious conceptions which produced it, and which perhaps found their highest expression in such masterpieces as the *Arbor Vitae Crucifixae Iesu* of Ubertino da Casale, and the writings of Angelo da Clareno. Of especial importance in the evolution of the Spiritual party is that versatile and enigmatical personality, " Petrus Iohannis Olivi ", who perhaps did more than any single individual to define and crystallise its peculiar tenets, and yet was no stranger to the philosophic speculations of one of the greatest and most constructive epochs in medieval thought. It may perhaps surprise some readers that such striking figures as Jacopone da Todi and Angela da Foligno are almost entirely ignored in these pages. The reason for this is that they, in spite of their great gifts, played a more secondary rôle in the story of the Zealots, and are, moreover, well known to all students of Franciscan mysticism. The latter part of the book is devoted to the great controversy between John XXII. and the Franciscan Order on the subject of Evangelical Poverty, for this was one of the main sources of that curious body, the Fraticelli, concerning whose origin there was formerly so much controversy among historians, and whose connection both with the Spirituals and with the followers of Occam and Michael of Cesena has now been definitely established through the labours of Cardinal Ehrle, Professor Tocco, and Father Oliger. Much of their history is still obscure, but from the material which has been discovered it is clear that their doctrines have a natural affinity with those of the two circles in which they originated, although their crudeness and exaggerations would have been deeply deplored by such men as Olivi and Clareno. Yet, the heroism displayed in the defence of those by certain members of the sect, even at the time of its greatest degradation, is worthy of the highest admiration. It must not, moreover, be forgotten that the foundation of the Observantines, and other reform movements in the Franciscan Order itself, were a return to the ideals of the Spirituals, and were inspired by the memory of their sufferings and

vii

loyalty. Nor was their devotion entirely the result of a fanatical and misplaced enthusiasm for minor and insignificant details in the teaching of St. Francis, but had at its basis a conception of the meaning of the Christian revelation and of the ultimate regeneration of mankind, which, although containing much which to modern minds seems fantastic and merely sensational, is yet in accord with the highest and noblest aspirations of the human soul. It is for this reason that even to-day their ideas are worthy of careful and sympathetic study, even though we cannot accept their interpretation of history, or understand their strange predilection for the vagaries of apocalyptic speculation.

Yet it is only in the light of this intense preoccupation with allegory and symbolism that it is possible to gain any understanding of the contradiction underlying the attitude of the Zealots towards their own age. Even though they regarded themselves as loyal Catholics and devoted sons of the Church, they could yet as disciples of the Abbot Joachim believe that the world was on the threshold of a new era, in which all outward ceremonies and ecclesiastical organisation would be done away with, and all men would be endowed with the grace of full spiritual understanding. The language in which they denounced the evils of their own period was perhaps no fiercer than that of other medieval reformers, but there was none the less a distinct difference of outlook. To the Spirituals these were not transitory or remediable abuses, but signs of that great flood of iniquity which was to be loosed upon the earth at the time of the coming of Antichrist, whose destruction was to herald the era of peace and righteousness for which they so ardently longed. Their representation of their own age has therefore the intense concentration on one particular centre and the violent opposition between light and darkness which characterise certain pictures of Rembrandt, and none of the mellow sunshine and loving and careful delineation of detail which are so marked a feature of other Dutch art. The latter qualities charm us by their intimacy and their appeal to our sense of objective reality, but they do not exercise the same powerful hold over our imagination as the former. It is only by bearing this fact in mind that we are able to appreciate at its true value the contribution made by the Franciscan Spirituals to the story of religious experience, and to understand their failure to impose their ideal upon the bulk of their Order. Yet it is this very lack of success which has given them a lofty position in the affections and reverence of succeeding generations, for their courage and endurance in the face of ridicule and persecution deserve to be " had in everlasting remembrance ". It is in the hope of interesting English readers in their aspirations and endeavours that this book has been written.

In conclusion, I wish to express my deep gratitude to Professor Powicke and Dr. A. G. Little for their unfailing help, sympathy, patience, and encouragement during the period in which I was engaged on the researches which have now resulted in this book, and to whose kind and helpful criticism are due any merits which it possesses. I also desire to thank the Fathers of the Collegio di San Bonaventura at Quaracchi for their generosity in lending me their rotograph of the letters of Angelo da Clareno, and Mlle. d'Alverny who supplied me with a copy of the summary of her thesis. I only regret that her duties at the Bibliothèque Nationale have retarded the publication of her important and invaluable work. My thanks too are due to Dr. Helen Hughes for allowing me to make use of the last three books of the *De Pauperie Salvatoris* which she has edited in her as yet unpublished thesis. I am also very grateful to S. Pickles, Esq., of Barnoldswick, Yorks, the founder of the studentship which enabled me to spend two years in research work at Manchester, to Dr. Tyson and the other members of the staff of the Rylands Library, and the Warden, Sub-Warden, Lecturers, and Students at Ashburne Hall for their constant and unvarying kindness to me during the same period. Finally, I wish to thank my father for the Index to my book, the Director of the Manchester University Press and all whose business it has been to prepare this book for publication.

DECIMA DOUIE

OXFORD, 1932

CONTENTS

CHAPTER VII

PART I

PART II

CHAPTER VIII

BIBLIOGRAPHY

A. Manuscript Sources

Durham. Bishop Cosin's Library, V. III. 18. " Tractatus Tres Breves " (three treatises on the subject of Evangelical Poverty relating to the controversy between the Franciscan Order and John XXII.).

Florence. Biblioteca Nazionale C. Magliabecchi, XXXIX. *n.* 75 (Rotograph belonging to the Collegio di San Bonaventura at Quaracchi). Letters of Angelo da Clareno.

London. British Museum Roy 6, E VI. and E VII.

Oxford. MS. Bodl. 52 (Treatise of Jean d'Anneux against the Franciscans), MS. New College, 49. Olivi's Commentary on St. Matthew.

B. Primary Sources

Analecta Franciscana (Quaracchi, 1887), II.-V.

Analecta Gallicana (Paris, 1910). Cf. Vidal.

Antoninus (St.). *Hystorialis* (Nuremburg, 1484) ; *Summa Theologica* (Nuremburg, 1477).

Archiv für Litteratur und Kirchengeschichte (Berlin, 1885–   ), I.-IV. ; VI. Cf. Denifle and Ehrle.

Archivio della Società Romana per la Storia Patria (Rome, 1911), XXXIV. Cf. Fumi.

Archivio Storico per le Marche e per l' Umbria (Foligno, 1885). Cf. Faloci-Pulignani.

Archivum Franciscanum Historicum (Quaracchi, 1908–   ), I.-XXIII. Cf. under authors.

Baluze, E. *Miscellanea* (Ed. Mansi, Lucca, 1761), I.-III. ; *Vitae Paparum Avenionensium* (Ed. Mollat, Paris, 1916). 3 vols.

Bartoli. *Franciscus de Assisi, Tractatus de Indulgentia S. Mariae de Portiuncula* (Ed. Sabatier, Paris, 1900).

Baudry, L. " La Lettre de Guillaume d'Occam au Chapitre d'Assise." *Revue d'Histoire Franciscaine* (Paris, 1926), III.

Bergamo, Bonagratia de. " Tractatus de Christi et Apostolorum Paupertate." *A.F.H.* XXII. Cf. also *A.F.H.* VII. and VIII., *A.L.K.G.* II. and III., and *Misc.* III.

Bihl, M. " E documentis ad Historiam Spiritualium nuper per clarissimum virum doctorem Professorem H. Finke editis." *A.F.H.* II.

Bonaventura (St.). *Opera Omnia* (Quaracchi, 1882–   .), VIII.

Brewer, J. S. *Monumenta Franciscana* (Rolls Series), I.

Brown, E. *Fasciculus Rerum Expetendarum* (London, 1690), II.

Bullarium Franciscanum, I.-VII. (Rome, 1759 ; Quaracchi, 1898–1904).

Calendar of Papal Letters (1305–1342).

Carlini, A. " Constitutiones Generales anno 1316 Assisii conditae." *A.F.H.* IV.

Casale, Ubertino da. *Arbor Vitae Crucifixae Iesu* (Venice, 1485).

" Responsio circa questionem de paupertate Christi et Apostolorum facta coram Johanne XXII." *Misc.* II. For pamphlets written in connection with the negotiations at the time of the Council of Vienne, cf. *A.L.K.G.* II. and III. and *A.F.H.* X.

Chiappini, A. " Responsio ' Religiosi Viri ' ad rotulum F. Ubertini de Casali. ' *A.F.H.* VII. and VIII.

xiii

CIVIDALI, P. " Il Beato Giovanni dalle Celle." *Memorie della Reale Accademia dei Lincei* (1907), XII.

CLARENO, ANGELO DA. *Breviloquium*. Edited by Fra Ciro da Pesaro, O.F.M., in *Il Beato Angelo Clareno* (Macerata, 1920).
" Historia Septem Tribulationum." Cf. Tocco, " Le due prime Tribolazioni dell' Ordine Francescano " (Rendiconti della Reale Accademia dei Lincei XVII.). (Rome, 1908.). Remainder in *A.L.K.G.* II.
" Epistola Excusatoria " et " Epistolae " (Extracts). *A.L.K.G.* I. Cf. Ehrle.
Expositio Regulae Fratrum Minorum (Ed. Oliger, Quaracchi, 1912). *Praeparantia.* Cf. *Breviloquium.*

CONYNGTON, RICHARD OF. " Tractatus de Paupertate Fratrum Minorum." *A.F.H.* XXIII. Cf. Heysse.

Corpus Iuris Canonici (Ed. Richter und Friedberg, Leipzig, 1881).

DELORME, F. Constitutiones Provinciae Provinciae. *A.F.H.* XIV.

DENIFLE ET CHÂTELAIN. *Cartularium Universitatis Parisiensis* (Paris, 1891), II.

DENIFLE, H. " Das Evangelium Aeternum und die Commission zu Anagni." *A.L.K.G.* I.
Die abendländischen Schriftausleger bis Luther über Justitia Dei und Justificatio. Luther und Lutherthum (Mainz, 1905), II.

DIGNE, HUGUES DE. " De Finibus Paupertatis." *A.F.H.* V. Cf. Florowsky.

DÖLLINGER, I. *Beiträge zu Sektengeschichte des Mittelalters* (Munich, 1890), II.

ECCARD, J. G. *Corpus Historicum Medii Aevi* (Leipzig, 1723).

ECCLESTON, THOMAS OF. *Tractatus de adventu Fratrum Minorum in Angliam* (Ed. Little, *Collection d'Études et de Documents*, VII. Paris, 1909).

EHRLE, F. " Die ältesten Redactionen der Generalconstitutionen des Franziskanerordens." *A.L.K.G.* VI.
" Die Spiritualen: ihr Verhältnis zum Franziskanerorden und zu den Fraticellen." *A.L.K.G.* I.-IV.
" Petrus Iohannis Olivi, sein Leben und sein Schriften." *A.L.K.G.* III.

FALOCI-PULIGNANI. " Vita di S. Chiara da Montefalco, scritta nel secolo XV per un Francescano suo conterraneo" (*Archivio Storico per le Marche e per l' Umbria.* Foligno, 1885).
" Vita di San Francesco e dei suoi compagni: testo inedito di volgare Umbro del XIV secolo." Todi MS. of Leggenda Antiqua—*Miscellanea Francescana* (Foligno, 1894), VIII.

FINKE, H. *Aus den Tagen Bonifaz VIII.* (Münster, 1902). For eschatological and religious writings of Arnald of Villanova.

FIRENZE, MARIANO DA. " Compendium Chronicarum Fratrum Minorum." *A.F.H.* I.-IV.

Firmamentum Trium Ordinum beati Patris Sancti Francisci.

FITZ-RALF, RICHARD. *De Pauperie Salvatoris.* In appendix to Wyclif's *De Dominio Divino* (Publications of the Wyclif Society, London, 1890).

FLOROWSKY, C. Cf. Hugues de Digne (*A.F.H.* V.).

FRANCIS OF ASSISI (ST.). *Opuscula* (Biblioteca Ascetica Medii Aevi, Quaracchi, 1904), I.

FUMI, L. " Eretici in Boemia e Fraticelli nel Roma," *Archivio della Società Romana per la Storia Patria* (Rome, 1911), XXXIV.

GERSON, JEAN. " An liceat a summo pontifice appellare." *Monarchia*, II.

GOLDAST, M. *Monarchia Sancti Romani Imperii* (Frankfurt, 1614), II.

GUI, BERNARD. *Manuel d'Inquisiteur* (Ed. Mollat, Paris, 1926).

HEYSSE, A. " Descriptio codicis bibliothecae Laurentianae Florentiae S. Crucis, plut 31, sin cod 3." *A.F.H.* XI. Cf. Olivi.
Duo documenta di polemica inter Gerardum Oddonem et Michaelem de Cesena. *A.F.H.* XI. Cf. Ubertino da Casale (*A.F.H.* X.) and Richard of Conyngton (*A.F.H.* XXIII.).

MANSI, D. *Concilia* (Florence, 1759–1798), XXIII. and XXV.
MARCHIA, JACOPO DELLA. " Dialogus contra Fraticellos." *Misc.* II.
MATTHEW PARIS. *Chronica Maiora*, VI. (Ed. Luard, Rolls Series, London, 1878–).
MENENDEZ-PELAYO, M. *Historia de los heterodoxos Españolos* (Madrid, 1880), I.
MERCATI, A. " Frate Francesco Bartoli d' Assisi Michelista e la sua ritrattazione. *A.F.H.* XX.
Miscellanea Francescana (Foligno, 1894–), VIII. Cf. Faloci-Pulignani.
MULDER, W. Gulielmi Ockham tractatus de Imperatorum et Pontificum potestate. *A.F.H.* XVI.-XVII.
MÜLLER, K. Einige Aktenstucke und Schriften zur Geschichte der Streitigkeiten unter den Minoriten in der ersten Hälfe des 14. Jahrhunderts. *Zeitschrift für Kirchengeschichte*, VI.
MURATORI, L. *Scriptores rerum Italicarum* (Milan, 1736), III. Pt. II.
MUSSATO, ALBERTO DE. *De gestis Italicorum post Henricum VII. Caesarem* " (Böhmer, *Fontes rerum Germanicarum.* Stuttgart, 1843), I.
OLIGER L. " Documenta inedita ad historiam Fraticellorum spectantia." *A.F.H.* III.-VI.
" Fratris Bertrandi de Turre processus contra spirituales Aquitaniae (1315) et Cardinalis Iacobi de Columna litterae defensoriae spiritualium Provinciae (1316)." *A.F.H.* XVI.
Cf. Bonagratia de Bergamo (*A.F.H.* XXII.) and Olivi (*A.F.H.* XI.).
"Acta Inquisitoris Umbriae Fr. Angeli de Assisio contra stigmata S. Francisci negantam, contra Fraticellos aliosque." *A.F.H.* XXIV.
" Beiträge zur Geschichte der Spiritualen, Fratizellen und Clarener im Mittelitalien." *Z.K.G.* XLV.
OLIVI, PETRUS IOHANNIS. *Expositio super Regulam.* Printed in *Firmamentum Trium Ordinum.*
Questiones in secundum librum Sententiarum (Ed. Jansen, *Bibliotheca Scholastica Medii Aevi.* Quaracchi, 1922–1926), IV.-VI.
Questio de veritate Indulgentiae Portiunculae (*Acta Ordinis Minorum*, 1895), XIV.
Quodlibeta (Venice, early 16th century).
" De renunciatione Papae Coelestini V., Questio et Epistola." *A.F.H.* XI.
Cf. Denifle, Ehrle, Heysse, and Oliger.
OTTO, H. " Zur italienischen Politik Johanns XXII." *Quellen und Forschungen*, XIV. (Rome, 1911).
PAEZ, ALVARO. *De Planctu Ecclesie.* Liber II. (Ulm, 1474).
PECHAM, JOHN. *Tractatus de paupertate* (B.S.F.S., 1910).
PELZER, A. " Les 51 Articles de Guillaume Occam censurés en Avignon, 1326." *R.H.E.*, XVIII.
PUIR-BURDACH. *Vom Mittelalter zur Reformation* (Berlin, 1912), II.
REICHERT, B. *Monumenta Ordinis Fratrum Praedicatorum historica* (Rome, 1897–), I. and III.
Revue d'Histoire Ecclésiastique (Louvain, 1899–). Cf. Pelzer, Callaey.
Revue d'Histoire Franciscaine (Paris, 1924–). Cf. Baudry.
Sacrum commercium S. Francisci cum Domina Paupertate (Quaracchi, 1929).
SALIMBENE. *Chronica* (Monumenta Germanica Historica Scriptores Rerum Germanicarum. Ed. Holder Egger, Hanover, 1905).
SCHOLZ, R. *Unbekannte kirchenpolitische Streitschriften aus der Zeit Ludwigs des Bayern* (Rome, 1911–1914).
Speculum Perfectionis (Ed. Sabatier, Paris, 1898).
TOCCO, F. *La quistione della povertà nel secolo XIV* (Naples, 1910).
Studii Francescani (Naples, 1909), I. Cf. Clareno.

VANZOLINI, G. " Lettera de' Fraticelli a tutti i Cristiani " (*Sceltà di curiosità letterarie inedite o rare*. Bologna, 1865), 55.

VIDAL, J. " Procès d'inquisition contre Adhémar de Mosset, noble Roussillonnais inculpé de Béguinisme." Analecta Gallicana (*Revue d'Histoire de l'Église de France*, Paris, 1910), I.

WESSELOFSKY, A. *Il Paradiso degli Alberti* (*Sceltà di curiosità*. Bologna, 1867), 86 (1). Letter of Giovanni dalle Celle to Fraticelli.

WINTURTHUR, JOHN OF. *Chronica Iohannis Vitodurani* (Ed. Baethgen, M.G.H., Scriptores Rerum Germanicarum Nova Series. Berlin, 1924), III.

ZAMBRINI, F. S. " Storia di Fra Michele minorità, come fu arso in Firenze nel 1389 " (*Sceltà di curiosità*. Bologna, 1864), 50.

Zeitschrift für Kirchengeschichte, VI. (Gotha, 1877). Cf. Müller.

SECONDARY

Acta Sanctorum. June 15. II.

D'ALVERNY, M. " Les Écrits théoriques concernant la pauvreté évangélique " (*Positions des thèses*. Paris, 1928).

ANNIBALI DA LATERA, F. *Manuali dei Frati Minori* (Rome, 1776); *Supplementum ad Bullarium Franciscanum* (Rome, 1780).

Archiv für Kulturgeschichte (Berlin, 1903–   ). Cf. Grundmann.

BALE, J. *Index Britanniae Scriptorum* (Ed. Poole, Oxford, 1902). *Scriptorum illustrium Maioris Brytanniae quam nunc Angliam et Scotiam vocant Catalogus* (Basle, 1557).

BALTHAZAR, K. *Geschichte des Armutsstreites im Franziskanerorden bis zum Konzil von Vienne* (Münster, 1911).

BELLARMINE, R. *De Romanis pontificibus* (Paris, 1613).

BIHL, M. Review of Callaey's " L'Idéalisme franciscain spirituel au XIVe siècle. Étude sur Ubertin de Casale " (Louvain, 1911). *A.F.H.* IV.

BOULAY, C. DU. *Historia Universitatis Parisiensis* (Paris, 1665), II.

BRETTLE, S. Ein Traktat des Königs Robert von Neapel " De Evangelica Paupertate " (*Festgabe zum 70sten Geburtstag H. Finke*. Munster, 1925).

BURKITT, F. C. " Ubertino da Casale and a variant Reading." *Journal of Theological Studies* (January 1922), XXIII.
Scripta Leonis and Speculum Perfectionis (*Miscellanea F. Ehrle*. Rome, 1924), III.
" The Study of the Sources of the Life of St. Francis " (*St. Francis of Assisi, Essays in Commemoration*. London, 1926).

CALLEBAUT, A. "Acta capituli generalis Mediolani celebrati." *A.F.H.* XXII.

CALLAEY, F. Lambert li Bèges, et les Béguines. *R.H.E.* XXIII.
Les Idées mystico-politiques d'un Franciscain spirituel, Étude sur Ubertin de Casale. *R.H.E.* XI.
L'Influence et la diffusion de l'*Arbor Vitae* d'Ubertin de Casale. *R.H.E.* XVII.
L'Infiltration des idées franciscaines spirituelles chez les Frères Mineurs capuchins au XVIe siècle. (*Miscellanea F. Ehrle*, I.).

CARLINI, A. *Fra Michelino e la sua eresia* (Bologna, 1912).

Catalogus veterum librorum ecclesiae cathedralis Dunelm. (Public. of the Surtees Soc. London, 1835–   ), VII.

CERUT, A. " La Scala del Paradiso " (*Collezione di opere inedite o rare*. Bologna, 1874).

CHIAPPINI, A. *Profilo di storia Francescana in Abruzzo dal secolo XIV al XVI* (Aquila, 1927).

COSMO, U. " Le mistiche nozze di Frate Francesco con Madonna Povertà." *Giornale Dantesco* (Florence, 1898), VI.

DAVIDSOHN, R. *Geschichte von Florenz* (Berlin, 1908), II.
DELORME, F. " L'Œuvre scolastique de Maître Vital du Four " (*La France Franciscaine*, IX.), 1926.
" Pierre de Trabibus et la distinction formelle " (VII.), 1924.
DEMPF, A. *Sacrum Imperium* (Munich, 1929).
Dictionnaire de Théologie Catholique (Paris, 1909), II.
DMITREWSKI, M. Fr. Bernard Délicièux O.F.M., sa lutte contre l'Inquisition de Carcassonne et d'Albi, son procès, 1297–1319. *A.F.H.* XVII. and XVIII.
DULONG, M. " La Vie provençale di Ste Delphine " (*Positions des thèses*. Paris, 1928).
EHRLE, F. Nikolaus Trivet, sein Leben, seine Quodlibet und Quaestiones Ordinarie (*Beiträge zur Geschichte der Philosophie des Mittelalters*, Supplementband II., Festgabe Clemens Baeumker. Münster, 1923).
EUBEL, C. Zu Nicolaus Minorita. *H.J.*, XVIII.
FABRICIUS, J. *Bibliotheca Latina mediae et infimae aetatis* (Hamburg, 1734).
FLACIUS, MATTHIAS (Illyricus). *Catalogus testium veritatis* (Ed. Frankfurt, 1666).
FOURNIER, P. " Joachim de Flore, ses doctrines, son influence " (*Revue des Questions Historiques*. Paris, 1900. 67).
Franciscan Essays, I. (*B.S.F.S.*, 1912). Cf. Gardner and Salter.
Franziskanishe Studien (Münster i. W., 1914–   ). Cf. Jansen.
FUMI, L. *Eretici e ribelli in Umbria* (Todi, 1916).
GARDNER, E. " Joachim of Flora " (*Franciscan Essays*, I. *B.S.F.S.*).
GIBSON, J. P. " Friar Alexander and his Historical Interpretation of the Apocalypse " (*Collectanea Franciscana*. *B.S.F.S.* 1922), II.
GOLUBOVICH, G. *Biblioteca bio-bibliografica de Terra Santa* (Quaracchi, 1906–   ), I.-III.
GRATIEN, P. *Histoire de la fondation et de l'évolution de l'ordre des Frères Mineurs* (Paris, 1928).
GRUNDMANN, H. " Die Papstprophetien des Mittelalters " (*Archiv für Kulturgeschichte*. 1928), XIX.
" *Liber de Flore*, eine Schrift der Franziskaner-Spiritualen aus dem Anfang des 14. Jahrhunderts ". *H.J.*, 49.
Studien über Joachim von Floris (Leipzig, 1927).
HEFELÈ ET LE CLERCQ. *Histoire des Conciles* (Paris, 1869–1878), IX.
HÉLYOT ET BULLOT. *Histoire des ordres religieux* (Paris, 1721), VII. Pt. V.
Histoire littéraire de la France, XXXIII.-XXXVI. Cf. Valois.
Historisches Jahrbuch (Munich, 1886–   ). Cf. Eubel and Grundmann.
HOFER, J. " Biographische Studien über Wilhelm von Ockham." *A.F.H.* VI.
JANSEN, B. " Die Lehre Olivis über die Verhältnis von Leib und Seele." *Franziskanische Studien*, V.
" Petrus de Trabibus, sein spekulative Eigenart, oder sein Verhältnis zu Olivi " (*Beiträge zur Geschichte der Philosophie des Mittelalters*, Supplementband II.). Festgabe Clemens Baeumker. (Münster, 1923.)
JORDAN, E. *Les Origines de la domination angevine en Italie* (Paris, 1909).
KRAUS, F. *Dante, sein Leben und sein Werk* (Berlin, 1897).
La France Franciscaine (Lille, 1912). Cf. Delorme.
LAZZERI, Z. " Un nuovo codice italiano delle Tribolazioni di Fr. Angelo Clareno." *A.F.H.* XI.
LELAND, J. *Commentarii de scriptoribus Britannicis* (Ed. Hall, Oxford, 1709).
LITTLE, A. G. *The Grey Friars at Oxford* (Oxford Historical Society, Oxford, 1891).

LONGPRÉ, E. " Gualtero de Catton." *Studi Franciscani* (1923), IX. Les *Distinctiones* de Fr. Thomas de Pavia. *A.F.H.* XVI.

MAGGIANI, V. " De relatione scriptorum quorumdam S. Bonaventurae ad Bullam ' Exit ' Nicolai III. (1279)." *A.F.H.* V.

MARTINI, A. " Ubertino da Casale alla Verna e la Verna nell' *Arbor Vitae* " (*La Verna*, XI. Arezzo, 1913).

MIERLO, J VAN. " Les Béguines et Lambert li Bèges." *R.H.E.* XXIII.

MOLLAT, G. *Les Papes d'Avignon* (Paris, 1912).

NANTES, RENÉ DE. *Histoire des Spirituels* (Paris, 1909).

OLIGER, L. " De Dialogo contra Fraticellos S. Jacobi de Marchia." *A.F.H.* IV.

" De pueris oblatis in Ordine Minorum." *A.F.H.* VIII. and X.

" De relatione inter observantium Querimonias Constantiensis (1415) et Ubertini Casalensis quoddam scriptum." *A.F.H.* IX.

" Descriptio codicis Capistranensis aliquot opuscula Fr. Petri Iohannis Olivi continentis." *A.F.H.* I.

" Frammenti di un carteggio (1784–1808) per la Conferma del Culto di Angelo Clareno." *A.F.H.* VII.

OUDIN, C. *Commentarius de Scriptoribus Ecclesiasticis* (Leipzig, 1722).

PESARO, CIRO DA. *Il beato Angelo Clareno* (Macerata, 1920).

PITS, J. *De illustribus Angliae scriptoribus* (Paris, 1619).

PLESSIS-MORNAY, P. DU. *Mysterium iniquitatis, sive historia Papatus* (1611).

PREGER, W. " Der kirchenpolitische Kampf unter Ludwig dem Baier und sein Einfluss." Munich, 1879. (*Abhandlungen der Bayerischen Akademie der Wissenschaft*, XIV.)

RAYNALDI, O. *Annales*, XVIII.-XXVII. (Lucca, 1747).

RENAN, E. *Nouvelles Études de l'histoire religieuse* (Paris, 1884).

Revue des Questions Historiques (Paris, 1866–   ). Cf. Fournier and Vidal.

RIDOLFI. *Historiarum Seraphicae Religionis libri tres* (Venice, 1586).

RIEZLER, S. *Die literarischen Widersacher der Päpste zur Zeit Ludwigs des Baiers* (Leipzig, 1874).

SALTER, E. GURNEY. " Ubertino da Casale." *Franciscan Essays*, I.

SCHELLING, F. *Sämmtliche Werke* (Stuttgart, 1858).

SCHNÜRER, G. *Kirche und Kultur im Mittelalter* (Paderborn, 1929), III.

St. Francis of Assisi : Essays in Commemoration of (London, 1926).

TOYNBEE, M. R. *S. Louis of Toulouse* (Manchester, 1929).

TRITHEMIUS, J. *Liber de scriptoribus ecclesiasticis* (Basle, 1494).

VALOIS, N. " Jacques Duèsne, Pape sous le nom de Jean XXII " (*Hist. Litt. de la France*, XXXIV.).

VIDAL, J. " Un Ascète du sang royal, Philippe de Majorque." *Revue des Questions Historiques* (1910), 88.

WADDING, L. *Annales*, III.-VII. and XX. (Rome, 1731); *Scriptores Ordinis Minorum* (Rome, 1806).

LIST OF ABBREVIATIONS

A.F.	*Analecta Franciscana.*
A.F.H.	*Archivum Franciscanum Historicum.*
A.K.	*Archiv für Kulturgeschichte.*
A.L.K.G.	*Archiv für Litteratur und Kirchengeschichte.*
Annales	*Annales Fratrum Minorum.*
A.V.	*Arbor Vitae Crucifixae.*
B.F.	*Bullarium Franciscanum.*
Cart. Univ. Paris.	*Cartularium Universitatis Parisiensis.*
Dict. de Théol. Cath.	*Dictionnaire de théologie Catholique.*
Expositio	*Expositio in Apocalypsim.*
Expos.	*Expositio Regulae Fratrum Minorum.*
Fasc. Rer. Expetend.	*Fasciculus Rerum Expetendarum.*
H.J.	*Historisches Jahrbuch.*
Hist. Litt.	*Histoire littéraire de la France.*
Misc.	*Miscellanea.*
M.G.H.	*Monumenta Germanica Historica.*
Monarchia	*Monarchia Sancti Romani Imperii.*
Post. in Apoc.	*Postilla in Apocalypsim.*
Q. & F.	*Quellen und Forschungen.*
Quod.	*Quodlibeta.*
R.H.E.	*Revue d'Histoire Ecclésiastique.*
R.H.F.	*Revue d'Histoire Franciscaine.*
S.F.	*Studii Francescani.*
Speculum	*Speculum Perfectionis.*
Vade Mecum	*Vade Mecum in Tribulationem.*
Vitae Paparum	*Vitae Paparum Avenionensium.*
Z.K.G.	*Zeitschrift für Kirchengeschichte.*

CHAPTER I

THE ORIGIN AND DEVELOPMENT OF THE SPIRITUAL PARTY IN THE FRANCISCAN ORDER

THE compilers of the *Oxford Book of Italian Verse* [1] have chosen St. Francis' beautiful hymn of praise for the beauty of the Sun and of all created Nature as the first poem in their anthology, thus making him the father of Italian poetry. This may perhaps explain the charm which his character has had for all types of men, whether they are attracted or repelled by the Middle Ages. Many medieval saints chill us by their austerity even while we admire their self-abnegation and singleness of purpose, but the poet turned saint we can both revere and love. In the *Speculum Perfectionis* [2] we read of how St. Francis used to sing in the manner of Provençal troubadours to his first companions, and, like them, he was a lover, though his ideal lady was Madonna Povertà, while the lives of himself and his followers at Rivo Torto and the Portiuncula were the songs he made in her honour. Yet the utter lack of forethought for the morrow, possible in a small community, was impracticable in a great religious organisation which, even before the death of its founder, had spread throughout Christendom. [3] Moreover, as its fame grew, men abandoned great careers both in Church and State to join its ranks, and these naturally considered that the great gifts of learning and eloquence which they brought to the Order could be put to better uses than were afforded by the tending of the sick and the preaching to simple country folk which had satisfied Francis and his early

---

[1] Oxford, 1910.

[2] C. 93. In its present form the *Speculum* probably dates from the early years of the fourteenth century, but much of the matter contained in it is far older, being taken from the " Intentio Regulae " and the " Verba Francisci ", attributed to Brother Leo. These were printed by Father Lemmens in the *Documenta antiqua Franciscana* of 1901 and 1902, together with a shorter and earlier version of the *Speculum* found in the same manuscript (Codex S. Isidore, 1/73) and containing material not found in the two former writings. It is noteworthy that Angelo da Clareno and Ubertino da Casale, who make great use of the authority of Brother Leo, always quote from the " Intentio " and the " Verba " and never from the later version of *Speculum Perfectionis*. These works, and the lives of St. Francis by Celano and S. Bonaventura, are our most trustworthy sources of information concerning the Saint. During the latter part of the thirteenth century many oral traditions grew up, especially among the Zealots, and these generally purported to originate from Brother Leo, or from certain other close companions of the Poverello. For further information upon this fascinating subject, cf. F. C. Burkitt, " The Study of the Sources of the Life of St. Francis " in *St. Francis of Assisi, Essays in Commemoration.*

[3] There were 5000 friars present at the celebrated Chapter of the " Mats " (*Speculum*, c. 68).

companions. Their conception of the means for the salvation of souls included splendid churches and the persuasion of human learning and oratory, and perhaps a feeling of rivalry with the Dominicans increased their enthusiasm. Thus, we find two parties growing up among the Franciscans even during the Saint's lifetime—that of the Ministers or Superiors of the Order, headed by Elias,[1] who desired some mitigation of the strictness of the rule of poverty, and a remodelling of the Order more on the lines of the Black Friars, and another, composed of certain of St. Francis' most intimate companions, men generally drawn more to the contemplative life, who wished to adhere as closely as possible to the strictness and simplicity of the original manner of life. These two bodies were the forerunners of the two later parties, the Conventuals, and the Spirituals or Zealots. It is difficult to know exactly what St. Francis' attitude was to the new developments. His hostility to Elias and his dislike of learning, as well as his prophecies about the decline of the Order from its original purity, have probably been exaggerated by the Spirituals. On the other hand, it is certain that he had many gloomy forebodings about the future, for in his Testament,[2] dictated during the last few days of his life, he commanded his followers to observe the Rule literally and never to seek papal letters authorizing them to make changes or modifications in it. His dying wishes were disregarded, for four years later Gregory IX., who as Cardinal Hugolin had befriended the Franciscans in their humble beginnings, declared the Testament not to be binding,[3] because it had not been sanctioned by any Chapter-General of the Order. This marked the beginning of a long series of papal decretals, which gradually built up a superstructure over the original rule, in much the same way as the stately but cold Church of Santa Maria degli Angeli is constructed over the little

---

[1] The story told in many of the writings of the Spirituals about the attempt made by Elias and the other ministers to prevent the composition of the 2nd Rule, and of the Divine Voice which justified the labours of the Saint, has been accepted as authentic by many modern scholars. The best account is perhaps that given by Ubertino da Casale (*A.V.* l. v., c. v., f. 2 r.), who declares that he obtained his information from the " Rotuli " of Brother Leo. From his description it is clear that the hermitage of Fonte Colombò was high up on the side of the mountain, whereas Elias and his followers were in the valley below. Consequently, the conversation between their leader and St. Francis, must have been conducted in very loud tones. Dr. Burkitt, who visited Fonte Colombò at the time of the celebrations of the quincentenary of St. Francis, discovered that there was a very strong echo, so that the " miraculous voice " admits of a completely rational explanation. According to Sabatier, Giotto's twelfth fresco in the Upper Church at Assisi is probably a representation of this scene. Cf. F. C. Burkitt, " Scripta Leonis and Speculum Perfectionis " in *Miscellanea Francesco Ehrle*, iii. pp. 14-22.

[2] *Bibliotheca Franciscana Ascetica Medii Aevi*, i. pp. 77-84.

[3] " Quo elongati a saeculo," *B.F.* i. p. 68.

Portiuncula. Without this work of alteration and definition the Friars Minor might never have performed their great services to religion and learning, but much of the freshness and spontaneity of the first days of the movement was inevitably lost. It was to save this that the Spiritual party fought so long and so valiantly, and though they were finally defeated, it is their picture of St. Francis which lives for us to-day in the *Speculum* and the *Fioretti*.[1] The history and ideals of the men who produced these are worthy of study by all who are interested in the history of religious experience.

The history of the years succeeding the death of the founder is concerned chiefly with the struggles of Elias, first to secure the generalship, and secondly to enforce his policy upon the Order. It would take too long to describe all the bitterness which arose over the building of the great church of Assisi, and the money collected to make this possible. Elias had the support of Gregory IX., and might have been able to enforce his views successfully but for his tactlessness in dealing with the ultramontane ministers, whom he never summoned to a Chapter-General through fear of their opposition. The first papal decretal, however, "Quo elongati",[2] was obtained by his predecessor, John Parenti,[3] and, although perhaps necessary, marks a decline from the original strictness of the rule. For instance, in it the Pope expressly declared that the friars were bound to obey only those parts of the gospel which were contained in the Rule,[4] and that anybody wishing to give money as alms to the brothers could give it to a "nuncius", chosen either by himself or by the Order, who could buy the goods required.[5] This was to mitigate the severity of the Rule by which the friars were forbidden to receive money either personally or through agents. If any money remained over after the necessary goods had been bought, it was to be kept by a "spiritual friend" to whom the friars could have recourse when it was needed. Finally, the Pope declared that the Minorites had no rights of property, either severally or in common, over the articles which they used.[6]

[1] The Italian version of the latter dates from the middle of the fourteenth century and was taken largely from the *Actus beati Francisci et Sociorum eius*, probably composed about 1322. Cf. Burkitt, *Essays*, p. 47, and Professor Gardner's essay on the "Little Flowers" in the same collection, pp. 97-126.

[2] *B.F.* i. p. 68 *seq.*

[3] General, 1227–32, formerly Provincial of Spain, 1219–27. The English Minorie, Thomas of Eccleston, describes him as "Vir sapiens et religiosus et summi rigoris" (*Tractatus Fr. Thomae vulgo dicti de Eccleston de adventu Fratrum Minorum in Angliam*, ed. Little, p. 79).

[4] *B.F.* i. p. 68.   [5] *Ibid.*

[6] "Dicimus itaque, quod nec in communi nec in speciali debeant proprietatem habere" (*B.F.* i. 69).

It was shortly after this that Elias succeeded in bringing about the deposition of John Parenti and his own election as Minister-General. Angelo da Clareno calls his period of rule " the second tribulation of the Order ".[1] He was deposed in 1239 by the influence of the ultramontane ministers. His two successors, Albert of Pisa and Haymo of Faversham, were both connected with the English Province,[2] and seem to have won the respect even of the Spiritual party. Yet under them the lines of the future development of the Order were firmly laid. Learning was encouraged, and in many cases the convents were removed from the country districts into the towns. Moreover, frequent appeals had to be made for papal protection because of the opposition of the secular clergy to the work done by the friars among their flocks.[3] After Gregory IX.'s death his successor, Innocent IV., cared little about the preservation of the original ideals of the Order, while he realised to the full its usefulness in his struggle with Frederick II. because of its popularity with the masses. An Exposition of the Rule,[4] the first of a long series, drawn up by four leading masters of theology of the Order about 1242, showed the new trend very clearly, for it declared that the friars who were studying were still to say their " offices ".[5] The definition of poverty given by the authors was very strict, but demonstrated clearly that the faithful were already trying to endow the friars with landed property and yearly rents. Haymo died in 1244, and his successor, Crescenzio of Jesi, the Provincial of the March of Ancona, who had been a famous doctor before he joined the Order,[6] was probably already an old man, and had not a strong enough personality for the burden laid upon him. It is possible that his sympathies were definitely on the side of the Conventuals for he obtained many privileges from the Pope, the most important of these being the famous " Ordinem vestrum ",[7] which was really a reinterpretation of the Rule in an even laxer sense than in " Quo elongati ". In it the principle was for the first time definitely laid down that goods left for the use of the friars became the property of the Holy See.[8] In 1247 another decretal, " Quanto studiosius ",[9] gave the Order the right of appointing two proctors

---

[1] Cf. Tocco, " Le due prime tribulazioni dell' Ordine Francescano," p. 68.

[2] Haymo of Faversham (1241–44) was a native-born Englishman and succeeded Angelo of Pisa as Provincial on the election of the latter to the generalship. He and the Papal Penitentiary, Brother Arnulf, had played a leading part in the events which led to the deposition of Elias (*Eccleston*, pp. 82-84).

[3] *B.F.* i. p. 214 (1237), 292 (1241), 343 (1244), 368 (1245).

[4] *A.F.* iii. 247-48. For text cf. *Firmamentum Trium Ordinum beati patris sancti Francisci*, pt. iv. f. xviii. r.–xxi. r.

[5] *Ibid.* f. xviii. v.   [6] *Eccleston*, p. 90.

[7] *B.F.* i. p. 400 (1245).   [8] *Ibid.*   [9] *Ibid.* p. 487.

in each province to manage their financial affairs. The Spiritual party regarded Crescenzio with especial bitterness, and Clareno, writing nearly a century later, called him " a follower of his predecessor brother Elias both in sentiment and manner of life ".[1] The story told by the same author of the seventy-two Zealots who were exiled in pairs to different convents in different provinces, because it had come to the ears of the Minister-General that they were going to Rome to appeal to the Pope against him is probably true, and is typical of the violent measures often employed by a weak personality to quell opposition.[2] In 1247 the Minister-General resigned and the famous John of Parma was elected in his place. His election caused great joy among the surviving companions of the Saint, and brother Giles greeted him with these significant words : " Well and fitly you have come, but you have come late ".[3]

The history of the generalship of John of Parma has been told very graphically by his friend and contemporary, Salimbene,[4] and also by Clareno in the third and fourth parts of his Chronicle.[5] Both pictures given of the man are much the same, though the latter emphasises his austerity and his hatred of the abuses already in the Order, while the former reveals his courtesy and personal charm. The new General felt no hatred of learning,[6] nor of the secular work of the Order, but strove to follow St. Francis' example in the manner of his life. On his journeys to France, Spain, and England, provinces which no Minister-General had ever before visited, he travelled on foot, accompanied only by one friar.[7] Although he was the friend and adviser of St. Louis of France,[8] as well as of the Pope and many of the cardinals, he always shared

---

[1] " Qui predecessoris sui fratris Helie sectatus est affectus et mores," Historia Septem Tribulationum : Tertia Tribulatcio (A.L.K.G. ii. 256). Eccleston, on the other hand, writing from far-away England, describes the minister-general in very different terms (op. cit. p. 90). It must be remembered, however, that Angelo da Clareno passed his early years as a Friar Minor in the March of Ancona and doubtless met many of the victims of Crescenzio's tyranny. Cf. infra, p. 49.

[2] A.L.K.G. ii. 258-260.

[3] " Bene et oportune venisti, sed tarde venisti" (ibid. 263).

[4] M.G.H. xxxii. Scriptores.

[5] A.L.K.G. ii. 262-87.

[6] According to Salimbene (op. cit. 298) he had been lector to the friars at Bologna and Naples. Eccleston declares that he lectured on the Sentences at the University of Paris (Little, Eccleston, p. 91). The same writer tells us that he used to say that the Franciscan Order had been constructed upon the two foundations of piety and knowledge (ibid. 92).

[7] Salimbene, loc. cit. 298. Apparently he was much impressed with the good order of the English province, and exclaimed, " Would that all the provinces were similar to this one ! " Eccleston, pp. 91 and 123.

[8] Salimbene, p. 305.

in the daily routine of the convent where he happened to be staying, and was particularly fond of the society of the younger and less influential friars.[1] Salimbene records his kindness and encouraging words to a young friar whom he had examined for the office of preacher and had found not sufficiently learned.[2] We are not surprised to learn that the Parisian doctors who resented the intrusion of the mendicant orders into the University were completely disarmed by his tact and courtesy.[3] Yet for all his charm, John was a strong man, determined to put down abuses in the Order. At the Chapter-General of Genoa in 1249 or 1251 he carried, in spite of very strong opposition, a decree that the proctors should no longer be appointed and that the Order should make no use of the modifications allowed by " Ordinem vestrum ".[4] It was not surprising that he had many enemies among the laxer friars, and unfortunately a force was at work which was finally strong enough to cause his downfall and the destruction of his work in the Order.

The speculations of the famous Abbot Joachim of Flora can only briefly be mentioned here, but will be dealt with more fully in a later chapter. This strange personality was the son of wealthy parents in southern Italy, who, during a pilgrimage to the Holy Land, was suddenly converted. He bestowed all his money and his rich clothing on the poorer pilgrims and finished the rest of his journey on foot. When he returned to Italy he joined the Cistercian Order, but later retired to a hermitage in southern Italy. Others joined him, and almost against his will he became the founder of a reformed branch of the Cistercians. Joachim believed that the history of the world was divided into three periods —the age of the Father, or the Old Testament ; that of the Son, or the New Testament ; and the final epoch was that of the Holy Ghost, when spiritual understanding of the Scriptures would be given to all men. According to him this new age would begin after the destruction of Antichrist, and would be preached by an order of bare-footed monks. These ideas, which are found in the three chief writings of Joachim,[5] attained great popularity in the thirteenth century. Many pseudo-Joachimite writings were produced, and popular belief identified Frederick II. with Antichrist. Naturally, the Franciscans believed that they were the bare-footed order prophesied by Joachim and became fervent

---

[1] Salimbene, pp. 295-96, 306.   [2] *Ibid.* p. 311.
[3] *Ibid.* pp. 299-301 ; *Eccleston*, p. 92.
[4] *Eccleston*, pp. 52-53. Cf. *A.F.H.* iv. pp. 425-35.
[5] *Concordia Novi et Veteris Testamenti, Expositio in Apocalypsim, Psalterium decem Chordarum.* These were printed at Venice, the first in 1519 and the others in 1527.

exponents of his ideas. Even such an essentially level-headed person as Salimbene was infected by the general enthusiasm, although his former faith deserted him when Frederick II. died and the fatal year 1260, which was supposed to inaugurate the new era, passed away without any significant change taking place in the order of the world.[1] In England Adam Marsh sent Grossetête copies of Joachim's works,[2] while John of Parma passed as a fervent Joachimite. The excitement caused by the new doctrines can best be understood by Salimbene's description of the little group of lawyers, doctors, and other professional men who used to gather in the cell of Hugues de Digne at Hyères[3] and listen to his expositions of the works of the Calabrian Abbot. Hugues was a fervent advocate of strict poverty[4] and a man full of self-confidence, who had little respect for dignity or position. In his sermon before the Curia he rated the Pope and his cardinals as if they had been schoolboys.[5] In its early stages, Joachimism was tolerated and even favoured by the Church, and might have pursued much the same course as most new and sensational religious movements, if an event had not occurred which drew the attention of the Holy See to its inherent dangers.

In 1254 a book called the *Eternal Gospel* appeared in Paris, written by Gerard of Borgo San Donnino, a young Franciscan who had been studying at the University. This treatise consisted of Joachim's three chief works, with an introduction and glosses by Gerard. No copy seems to have survived, so that it is impossible to know the exact nature of its contents,[6] but it is clear that Gerard interpreted Joachim's prophecies in a manner very

---

[1] " Sed postquam mortuus est Fridericus, qui imperator iam fuit et annus millesimus ducentesimus sexagesimus elapsus est, dimisi totaliter ipsam doctrinam " (Salimbene, *op. cit.* p. 302).

[2] *Monumenta Franciscana*, i. (Rolls Series). Epistolae Ade, Marsh, p. 146.

[3] Salimbene, *op. cit.* p. 236.

[4] His exposition of the Rule, and a smaller treatise, " De Finibus Paupertatis ", were very popular among the Spirituals. Ubertino da Casale gives long extracts from the latter in his *Arbor Vitae*, l. v., c. v., f. 2 *r.b*. It has now been printed in the *A.F.H.* v. pp. 277-290. His " Expositio Super Regulam " is found both in the Parisian and Venetian versions of the *Firmamentum*. Cf. ed. Paris, 1512, iv. 34 *v.a*, 54 *r.b*, and ed. Venice, 1513, iii. 32 *v.a*–52 *v.a*. He also probably composed the " Dialogus inter Zelatorem paupertatis et inimicum eius domesticum ", edited in the same collection (ed. Paris, f. 105 *r.a*–108 *v.b* ; Venice, f. 129 *v.b*–133 *v.a*).

[5] He had been asked to preach because of his fame as a Joachimite. Cf. Salimbene, *op. cit.* p. 231.

[6] We are forced to rely on the Protocol to the Commission of Anagni, published by Fr. Denifle in *A.L.K.G.* i. p. 99-142, and on the lists of errors drawn up by the Pari sprofessors, for our knowledge as to the contents of the book. The fullest of these is included by Matthew Paris in the *Liber Additamentorum* (*Chronica Maiora*, vi. pp. 335-39).

favourable to his Order,[1] and also regarded the three writings in question as the new gospel of the age of the Holy Ghost.[2] As the conflict between the mendicants and the University was at its height the appearance of the book gave the Parisian doctors the very weapon they required against their opponents, and a copy was sent to the Pope by the Archbishop of Paris and by William de St. Amour, the bitterest enemy of the friars. Alexander IV. appointed a commission of cardinals to inquire into the matter, and they condemned the introduction and certain of the doctrines of Joachim, but vindicated his personal orthodoxy. The Pope, out of consideration for the Franciscans, ordered the book to be burnt secretly,[3] but the Order was not prepared to deal lightly with one who had brought so much scandal upon them. Gerard was deprived of his lectorship and of the power of preaching and hearing confessions, and later, during the Generalship of St. Bonaventura,[4] he and a certain friar named Leonard were condemned to perpetual imprisonment.[5]

In his fall he had pulled down one much greater than himself. It is very difficult to understand the influences behind John of Parma's resignation in 1257, but a plausible theory suggests that papal pressure was brought to bear upon him because of his known friendship for Gerard and attachment to Joachimism. The Order as a special mark of respect asked him to choose his successor, and he appointed St. Bonaventura.[6] Soon after his accession the new Minister-General, together with Cardinal Gaetani, protector of the Order, and afterwards Nicholas III., held an inquiry into the opinions of his predecessor, and it was only the interference of Cardinal Fieschi, afterwards Adrian V., which saved John from imprisonment.[7] He retired to the little hermitage of Greccio, in Southern Italy, where he lived for thirty years, occasionally visiting the Curia. It is supposed by his admirers that he refused to be

---

[1] Among the errors recorded by Matthew Paris is one declaring that only the bare-footed are fitted to instruct men in spiritual matters (*Chronica Maiora*, vi. 336).   [2] *A.L.K.G.* i. 99.

[3] The letter of the Pope to the Bishop of Paris is given in full in Du Boulay's *Historia Universitatis Parisiensis*, iii. p. 292.   [4] General, 1257–74.

[5] Salimbene, *op. cit.* p. 462 ; *A.L.K.G.* ii. 284.

[6] Salimbene (*op. cit.* 309) and Clareno (*A.L.K.G.* ii. 270) adopt the view that his resignation was due to despair at being unable to control the laxity of his Order. The Chronicle of the 24 Generals which, although not contemporary, makes use of a contemporary writer, Peregrine of Bologna, as its source, declares John's resignation was due to papal pressure (*A.F.* iii. 287). Cf. also *Eccleston*, p. 144 (Appendix), where the actual text of Peregrine of Bologna is given.

[7] *A.L.K.G.* ii. 285 *seq.* After his acquittal John seems to have remained on friendly terms with Cardinal Gaetani, whom he visited at the Curia after his elevation to the Papacy. Nicholas rallied him affectionately about his Joachimism (Salimbene, *op. cit.* p. 302).

created a cardinal.[1] Finally, he sought papal permission for a journey to Greece, where he hoped to heal the schism between the Greek and Latin Churches. This was accorded, but he died at Camerino on his way to the coast.[2] With him perished, for the time being, all the hope of the Spiritual party of controlling the policy of the Order.[3]

Gerard's condemnation, unfortunately, did not altogether destroy the influence of Joachimism in the Franciscan Order. It continued to exercise a fatal fascination over the minds of the Zealots, and thus prevented the veneration which otherwise they would assuredly have aroused through their personal holiness and the strictness of their lives. Their enemies were always able to raise the cry of heresy against them, and thus alienate the sympathy of the moderate party to which the bulk of the Order probably belonged. The ablest representatives of this body were St. Bonaventura and his disciple Pecham, and their views, which are expressed in the " Apologia Pauperum " and the " Tractatus de Paupertate ", became the official tenets of the Franciscans. They held that all the property left to the friars belonged by right to the Church, and that the Order had no legal claim to be allowed to make use of it.[4] The friars were to use the things necessary both for their life and work with moderation, though no exact limits could be laid down.[5] This " usus pauper ", as it was called, became a great matter of controversy between the two parties, for the Conventuals declared St. Francis had meant to put no restrictions on the use of the things expressly allowed to the brothers by the Rule. St. Bonaventura's views received official sanction by the famous decretal of Nicholas III., " Exiit qui seminat ",[6] published in 1279. The Pope, while permitting the former

---

[1] Salimbene, 302 and 304.

[2] *A.L.K.G.* ii. 286 *seq.*

[3] The verdict of Salimbene's friend, Bartolommeo Calaroso of Mantua, is probably just :
" Frater Johannes de Parma turbavit semet ipsum et ordinem suum quia tante scientie et sanctitatis et excellentissime vite erat quod curiam Romanam corrigere poterat et credidisset sibi. Sed postquam secutus est prophetias hominum fantasticorum, vituperavit seipsum et amicos non modicum lesit " (*op. cit.* p. 302).

[4] " Apologia Pauperum ", *Opera Omnia*, viii. p. 312 ; *Tractatus de Paupertate*, ch. x. p. 36.

[5] " Apologia ", ch. vii. 272 and 312 ; " Expositio ", *Opera Omnia*, viii. p. 422. St. Bonaventura goes elaborately into the question of the sandals worn by Christ (A.P. 306), and as to whether he possessed a purse or not (p. 285). In the " Expositio " he declared that Christ was in truth a mendicant (p. 423). (Cf. Pecham, ch. x. p. 37.)

[6] *B.F.* iii. 404-16. There is an interesting article by Father Maggiani in *A.F.H.* v. 3-21, showing the connection between the teaching of St. Bonaventura with regard to poverty and the papal decretal.

mitigations of the Rule granted by his predecessors, expressly declared the friars to be bound to a narrow or restricted use of worldly goods,[1] and maintained that the simple use of fact was based on natural law.[2]   Legacies of land or houses were only to be accepted by the Order if they were converted into money to be spent on articles necessary for its members.[3]   This decretal caused great controversy in later times, for in its conclusion Nicholas had threatened with excommunication all who attempted to put glosses on it.[4]   It was inserted in the Sext by Boniface VIII. who, as papal notary, had assisted at its drafting.   Unfortunately, although Bonaventura's views obtained the approval and support of the Church, he and his successors were unable to secure their enforcement.   The Constitutions of the Chapters-General of this period show that the abuses denounced by the Spirituals, such as the acceptance of landed property,[5] the collection of money from the faithful who attended the services held by the Order,[6] and the absolution of usurers before they had made restitution, were quite common.[7]   The richness of the Church plate and of the vestments used in the services was another ground of complaint,[8] and there were constant enactments against the pictures, reredoses, and stained glass windows, which were infractions of the vow of poverty,[9] as well as various minor abuses, such as the excessive number of habits possessed by each friar and the unnecessary fineness of the cloth of which they were composed.[10]   Olivi draws a pathetic picture of St. Bonaventura at a Chapter held at Paris, weeping over the abuses he was powerless to restrain.[11]   His position was indeed a hard one, as his condemnation of John of Parma had alienated the stricter Zealots.[12]   Nor was there naturally much sympathy between these poor enthusiasts, with their patched habits and passionate mysticism, and one who held the vocation of his Order to be bound up with learning and religious activity among people of all classes, and whose writings display a piety based on moderation and sober reason.

---

[1] B.F. iii. 409.

[2] Ibid. 408.   This is also found in Bonaventura (" Apologia ", 247 and 323).

[3] B.F. iii. p. 412.

[4] Ibid. p. 415.

[5] Constitutions of Narbonne (1260) (Op. Om. viii. p. 464).   This was the first definite collection made of the Statutes of the Order other than the Rule, and formed the basis for all subsequent ones.   Cf. Regulations of Chapter-General of Padua (1310), A.L.K.G. vi. 70.

[6] Op. Om. viii. 452.

[7] Ch.-Gen. of Lyons (1272 or 1274), A.L.K.G. vi. 43 and A.F.H. vii. 680.

[8] Op. Om. viii. 465.   [9] Ibid. 452 and 465.

[10] Ibid. 451 ; Constitutions of Paris (1292) ; A.L.K.G. vi. p. 90, note 5.

[11] A.L.K.G. iii. 517.

[12] Cf. " Hist. VII. Trib.", A.L.K.G. ii. 281.

The history of the Spiritual party during the close of the thirteenth and the opening of the fourteenth century centres in two regions—the March of Ancona and Provence. The movement in Italy is best dealt with in connection with its great historian, Angelo da Clareno, while that in southern France groups itself round Olivi. Here it is necessary to say little about this strange and many-sided personality, who combined original philosophic speculation with a burning zeal for poverty and an equally ardent enthusiasm for Joachimism. The boldness of his theories led to a serious charge of heresy being brought against him by the Chapter-General of Strasburg,[1] and this blackened his reputation during his lifetime and for many centuries after his death.[2] Among his followers, however, both in France and in Tuscany, where he was sent in 1287 as Lector of Sta Croce, he was revered as an uncanonized saint. Perhaps their exaggeration of his doctrines was largely responsible for the sinister memory which he left behind, for his teaching on poverty and the " usus pauper " could easily be reconciled with that of St. Bonaventura and Pecham.[3] At any rate, the Order took advantage of a letter of Nicholas IV., directed against the excesses of certain friars of Provence, to instigate an inquiry against him and his followers.[4] Olivi was acquitted at the Chapter-General of Paris in 1292, but his disciples were less fortunate, and the persecution lasted for over twenty years. Nicholas' letter has unfortunately perished, so that it is impossible to know whether the Zealots were right in contending that it was not intended against themselves but against a small body of heretical friars.[5] The difficulty of accepting this assumption lies in the characters of the three Ministers-General who carried out the Pope's decree, for Raymund Gaufredi was himself very much in sympathy with the Spiritual party, while his successor, John of Murrovalle, was a man of such austerity of life that his enemies accused him of hypocrisy.[6] Of the third

---

[1] Pentecost, 1282.

[2] The reading of his writings was forbidden at the Chapter-General of Marseilles in 1319 (*A.L.K.G.* ii. 149, iii. 451). This prohibition was repealed by Sixtus IV. (1471–84), who exhorted the friars to pluck the roses from Olivi's works and leave the thorns, but was again renewed at the Chapter-General of Terni in 1500 (*ibid.* iii. p. 458); cf. *infra*, p. 94.

[3] *A.L.K.G.* iii. 503-523; cf. *infra*, p. 87. This is the view taken by Olivi in his *Quodlibeta* (f. 47 *r.a*).

[4] *A.L.K.G.* iii. 14, 432; cf. *A.F.* iii. 420.

[5] *Ibid.* ii. 389; iii. 151.

[6] In his " Rahonament ", Arnold of Villanova, the great Spanish physician, who was much attracted by the mysticism of the Zealots, compared him to the ostrich as the most hypocritical of birds. Cf. Balthazar, *Geschichte des Armutsstreites im Franziskanerorden bis zum Konzil von Vienne* (chap. ix. p. 246 and *infra*, p. 34).

general, Gonsalvo di Valboà, little is known, but there is nothing to prove any close connection between him and the Conventual party. It may be that he and his predecessor regarded the excesses of the Zealots as more dangerous to the discipline and integrity of the Order than the lax lives of their opponents. The fierceness of the persecution can be judged by the fact that a learned and pious friar, Pontius Portugati, was sentenced to life-long imprisonment and denied ecclesiastical burial for refusing to surrender certain books written by Olivi which he had in his possession.[1] According to the Spirituals, over three hundred friars were ill-treated and imprisoned during this unhappy period.[2]

In the summer of 1309 the attention of Clement V. was drawn to the sad plight of the Franciscan Order by Robert of Naples,[3] and by the Commune of Narbonne, a city whose inhabitants were very favourably disposed towards the Zealots.[4] He summoned the leaders of both parties to the Curia, and a momentous inquiry began which dragged on for many years, contemporaneously with the Council of Vienne and the destruction of the Templars. All the leading men of the Order were there, the Minister-General, Gonsalvo di Valboà, attended by a large number of representatives from among the Provincials of the Order, including Richard of Conyngton, then Provincial of England,[5] and by many masters and bachelors of theology. Nor were the representatives of the other party less illustrious, for they were headed by the former Minister-General, Raymund Gaufridi, who belonged to a noble Provençal family, by William of Cornillon, Custodian of Arles, and by Raymund of Gigniac, formerly Pro-

---

[1] *A.L.K.G.* ii. 300, 386, 409 ; *ibid.* iii. 184.
Earlier writers have confounded this friar with his namesake, Pontius Carbonelli, Guardian of the Convent at Barcelona (*A.F.H.* ii. p. 139), and have made him the preceptor of St. Louis of Toulouse. Cf. Hélyot et Bullot, *Histoire des ordres religieux*, vii. pt. v. chap. 5, p. 53.
He and another friar, " Raymundus Aurioli ", actually died in prison, while a third, " Johannes Primi ", was only just released in time to save his life (*A.L.K.G.* ii. 386).   [2] *A.L.K.G.* iii. 192.
[3] *Ibid.* ii. 129. Angelo da Clareno says Charles II. of Naples, but this is unlikely, as he was bitterly opposed to the Zealots, and did his best to help the Minister-General against them (*ibid.* ii. 319).
[4] *Ibid.* iii. p. 18.
[5] *Ibid.* ii. p. 356, note 1. At the beginning of the inquiry the Minister-General had only three provincials to assist him, namely, Vidal du Four, then provincial of Aquitaine, Gilles of France, and Alexander of Alexandria, provincial of Naples. The English Franciscan, Martin of Alnwick, was also present as a champion of the Conventual party. Cf. Gratien, *Histoire de la fondation et de l'évolution de l'ordre de Frères Mineurs*, p. 432, and *A.L.K.G.* iii. p. 19 (iv). Eleven more Provincials, amongst whom was Conyngton, arrived for the opening of the Council of Vienne (Gratien, *op. cit.* 458, and *A.L.K.G.* iii. pp. 22 and 39).

vincial of Aragon, all of whom had been friends and companions of St. Louis of Toulouse.[1] Their ablest delegate, however, was Ubertino da Casale who, as chaplain to Cardinal Napoleone Orsini, had just returned from waging a fierce crusade against the heretics of Umbria.[2] The bitterness between the two parties can be seen from a papal bull of April 1310,[3] exempting the Zealots from the jurisdiction of their superiors during the period of the inquiry. The ill-feeling between them was increased by the sudden death of Gaufridi and two other members of his party during the course of the summer. Suspicion of poison was aroused by the rash declaration of one of the Conventuals that their deaths would be to the advantage of the Order.[4] Clement V. had entrusted the question to a commission of cardinals, the members of which were changed repeatedly during the time of the negotiations.[5] A war of pamphlets ensued between both parties, only a few of which have come down to us.[6] The majority of those of the Conventuals,[7] were written probably by

[1] *B.F.* v. 158, p. 65. All three were called as witnesses in the investigations made in 1308 as a preliminary to the canonization of St. Louis of Toulouse. Raymond Gaufridi had known Louis from his childhood onwards, and it was to his hand that the young bishop was clinging at the time of his death. He was also one of the executors of his will, in which he left his Bible and a copy of the Summa of Aquinas to his "companion and friend", Brother William of Cornillon (Toynbee, *St. Louis of Toulouse*, pp. 170, 178, 236, and 237). It is interesting in the light of future events, that another of the witnesses at the canonization process was Pope John XXII., then Bishop of Fréjus, who had been for a short time a member of Louis' household and had helped him in the management of his diocese (*ibid.* pp. 122-123 and 170). [2] *A.L.K.G.* ii. 131-33.

[3] *B.F.* v. 158, p. 65. [4] *A.L.K.G.* ii. 133.

[5] The first two commissioners were the English cardinal, Thomas Jorz, and a Frenchman, Pierre de la Chapelle Taillefer, Cardinal of Palestrina. At a later stage in the inquiry the latter was succeeded by the famous canonist, Bérénger Frédol, and the Pope's nephew, Guillaume Ruffat. Cf. *B.F.* v. 158, p. 65 *n.*, and Gratien, *op. cit.* 440.

[6] These pamphlets are more fully discussed in the chapter on Ubertino da Casale. Only a small portion of these have been printed, but a very full account of the documents produced by both parties to justify their respective positions is given in the catalogue drawn up about the middle of 1318 by Raymund of Fronsac, whose official position at the Curia caused him to be entrusted with the leading part in the defence of the Conventuals. Cf. Gratien, *op. cit.* 453. His work is invaluable on account of his unique knowledge of the documents themselves, and the care taken to record their incipits, and, when it is possible, the names of their authors, as well as to give a brief summary of their contents. This catalogue was discovered by Ehrle and is printed in *A.L.K.G.* iii. pp. 7-31.

[7] The most notable exceptions are the treatises of Alexander of Alexandria, Provincial of "Terra Laboris" and afterwards General (*A.F.H.* x. 116-22), probably composed about 1309 or early in 1310, and of Richard of Conyngton, Provincial of England (*A.F.H.* xxiii. 57-105, 340-60). Cf. *infra*, p. 149. The famous "Petrus Aurioli", afterwards Archbishop of Aix, probably began his literary career at this time with his "Tractatus de paupertate et de usu paupere", in which he comes to much the same conclusions as Alexander of Alexandria.

Raymund of Fronsac, one of the proctors of the Order at the papal court, and by Bonagratia of Bergamo, a young advocate, who had lately become a Minorite and who was employed because of the bitterness and venom of his pen.[1] However, he met his match in Ubertino of Casale, whose treatises are racy reading, particularly in the parts where he describes the abuses of the Order. The policy of his opponents was to endeavour to confine the inquiry to an examination into the reputed heresies of Olivi [2] with the hope of distracting the attention of the papal commissioners from the question of the observation of the Rule,[3] and of proving that the Zealots, as the supporters of a heretic, had forfeited all claim to the protection of the Pope.[4] Moreover, the protracted nature of the investigations allowed the Minister-General time to put an end to the most flagrant abuses and to initiate schemes of reform, with the result that the complaints of the Spirituals seemed exaggerated if not without foundation.[5] Finally, Clement V. decided upon a compromise and issued the decretal " Exivi de paradiso ",[6] which was really a reaffirmation

---

Two manuscripts of this existed in the papal library at Avignon but the treatise is not included in the catalogue of Raymund of Fronsac. It was printed in the Venice edition of the *Firmamentum* (iii. f. 126 *v.a*–129 *v.a*), and also in an earlier copy of the same work, lent to me by the kindness of Dr. A. G. Little. For date and summary of pamphlet, cf. *Hist. Litt.* xxxiii. 481-82 and 489-91. The question in the Quodlibeta of the famous glossator, Nicholas de Lyra, on the nature of the obligation of the " usus pauper " was certainly somewhat later in date, since he quotes from the decretal " Exivi de paradiso ", but was probably composed as the result of the controversy (*A.F.H.* xxiii. 51-56 ; cf. also p. 50).

[1] *A.L.K.G.* ii. 380.

[2] Before December 1309 the Minister-General had presented five as yet unpublished manifestos, condemning the errors of the great Zealot, and justifying the confiscation of his works and the persecution of his followers who refused to surrender them. Amongst these pamphlets is a treatise by the famous Egidius Colonna, Archbishop of Bourges (*A.L.K.G.* iii. 19-20 (vi.-x.) and 453 *s.*).

[3] The four chief questions under discussion were : I. The connection of the Spirituals with the sect of the Free Spirit ; II. The observance of the Rule and the decretal " Exiit qui seminat " ; III. The heresies of Olivi ; IV. The persecution of the Zealots (*A.L.K.G.* iii. p. 18). Raymund of Fronsac's Catalogue shows the eagerness of the Conventuals to establish a connection between their opponents and various heretical sects (*ibid.* pp. 9-11).

[4] Cf. Protest against the Exemption Bull ; *ibid.* ii. 365-74.

[5] Fr. Gratien (*op. cit.* pp. 429 *s.* and 452) sees in the reforms made at the Chapter-General of Padua in 1310 (*A.L.K.G.* vi. 69 *s.*) and in Gonsalvo of Valboà's letters from Pisa to the Provincials of Saxony and Tuscany (*A.F.* ii. 117 *s.* ; Wadding, *Annales*, vi. 172 *s.*) attempts to counteract the attacks of the Spirituals. The Conventuals in their pamphlet, " Sapientia aedificavit ", however, claimed that corrective measures had been taken earlier by the Chapters-General of Genoa in 1302 and of Toulouse in 1307. Cf. *Bibl. Nat. MS. Lat.* 4350, f. 31 *r.*, and Gratien, *op. cit.* 461.

[6] *B.F.* 195, pp. 80-86.

of " Exiit qui seminat " [1] with additions, which left the form and
quality of the habit and the hoarding of grain and wine to the
discretion of the guardian of each convent.[2] This bull was read
in the final session of the Council of Vienne,[3] and despite the
passionate appeal of Ubertino the Spirituals were ordered to return
to their convents and live at peace under the obedience of their
lawful superiors.[4] This command was specially bitter to the
Spirituals, as in 1312 they had withdrawn to an abandoned church
near Malaucène, and to the hermitage of St. Lazare in the neighbourhood of Avignon, for they had been unable to live peaceably
with their enemies in the Franciscan convent within the walls
of the city.[5] On the other hand, although the council condemned
four of the doctrines of Olivi,[6] his name was not mentioned, and
the Pope deposed the superiors who had been proved to have been
most oppressive.[7] He also directed that Bonagratia of Bergamo,
whose violence and insolence had disgusted him, should be imprisoned in a distant convent.[8] His efforts for peace were furthered
by the new Minister-General, Alexander of Alexandria, who
surrendered the three convents of Narbonne, Béziers, and Carcassonne to the Spirituals,[9] so that they might live in quietness
under the rule of their own superiors. A fresh redaction of the
Constitutions of Provence was also made at the Provincial Chapter
of Nîmes in order to prevent a recurrence of the former abuses.[10]

Even if the Pope and the Minister-General had lived it is
doubtful whether they could have enforced their settlement on
both parties, for even before the publication of " Exivi de paradiso "
the Tuscan Zealots were in full revolt. Acting on the advice of
a canon of Siena called Martin,[11] they flung off the yoke of obedience and, with the help of the townsfolk, gained possession of the
convents of Asciano, Arezzo, and Carmignano, paying no heed to

---

[1] *B.F.* iii. 404-16.　　　　　　　[2] *B.F.* v. 195, pp. 82 and 84.
[3] May 6, 1312. *A.L.K.G.* iii. 25, *n.* 4.
[4] *Ibid.* ii. 141.
[5] *Ibid.* 140.
[6] Corpus Iur. Can. Clem. I. 1. " Fidei Catholicae Fundamento " (*B.F.* v.
196, p. 86—May 1312). In the February of the same year a list of rash,
erroneous, and heretical propositions taken from the works of Olivi had been
drawn up under the title of the " Instrumentum duplicis oblationis ". This was
formally presented to the Spirituals, who admitted that the passages condemned
were to be found in his writings, after which the document in question was
presented to the committee of theologians entrusted with the examination of the
doctrines of the great Zealot.—*A.L.K.G.* iii. p. 24 (xxxvii.).
[7] *A.L.K.G.* ii. 158 ; Gratien, *op. cit.* p. 460, note 5.
[8] At Valcabrère, near Cominges, in the province of Aquitaine (*B.F.* v. *n.* 204
—July 1312).　　　　　　　[9] *A.L.K.G.* ii. 161.
[10] Held in 1313. The text of these is given in *A.F.H.* xiv. 426-30.
[11] *A.L.K.G.* ii. 139.

the threat of excommunication launched against them by the Archbishop of Genoa and the Bishops of Bologna and Lucca, who were acting on the instructions of the Pope.[1] Finally, under the leadership of Henry de Ceva, they obtained a refuge with Frederick of Sicily.[2] Further proceedings were put an end to by the death of Clement [3] and the vacancy of the Holy See. Soon after his accession John XXII. took the matter up, and repeatedly during the course of the year 1317 wrote to the king demanding their expulsion.[4] In the spring of the following year he attacked them fiercely in the bull " Gloriosiam ecclesiam ",[5] but Frederick had already arranged for the exile of the Spirituals to Tunis.[6] The sultan of Tunis agreed to allow them a refuge in his dominions on condition that they did not preach to his subjects. It is probable, however, that the whole band did not emigrate, but that certain individuals remained in Sicily under the protection of different landowners.[7] Their subsequent fate is unknown, but they probably swelled the number of the sects which were included under the general name of Fraticelli.[8]

After the deaths of Clement V. and Alexander of Alexandria confusion and anarchy reigned among the Franciscans in the south of France. The Superiors deposed by the Pope secured their election as diffinitors at the Provincial Chapter of Carcassonne, where many of them were restored to their former positions.[9] The Spirituals appealed to the Provincial Minister, but he lacked either the will or the power to protect them.[10] In desperation they took the law into their own hands, and with the active support of certain of the citizens drove their enemies out of the convents of Narbonne and Béziers.[11] Unfortunately, one of the Conventuals, Jacobus Ortolani, was wounded in the scuffle.[12] Their former guardian, Guillelmus de " Sancto Amancio ", was restored to his old position,[13] and they were joined by their adherents from other parts of the province, and even by five friars from Aquitaine. Processes were immediately instituted against them by the expelled

---

[1] B.F. v. 217, p. 96 (July 1313). Cf. Z.K.G. xlv. pp. 219-24.

[2] A.F.H. ii. 158-60. From Finke, Acta Aragonensia, pp. 661-77.

[3] April 20, 1314.

[4] B.F. v. 256, p. 110 (March 15, 1317). Another letter is dated April 5.

[5] Ibid. 302, p. 137 (Jan. 23, 1318). The following year proceedings appear also to have been taken against those members of the Spiritual party who had remained in Tuscany. Cf. letter of the Franciscan Inquisitor, Michael le Moine, to the Provincial of Tuscany and his vicar (A.F.H. xxiii. 120).

[6] A.F.H. ii. 160 ; Acta Aragonensia, 671-72. (May 8, 1317).

[7] Cf. " Gloriosam ecclesiam ", B.F. v. 302, p. 137.   [8] Cf. infra, p. 211.

[9] A.L.K.G. ii. p. 161; iv. pp. 36 and 59.

[10] Ibid. ii. p. 162; iv. pp. 36 and 54.

[11] Ibid. iv. p. 36.   [12] Ibid. pp. 37 and 61.

[13] Ibid. ii. 159. He called himself " vicar ", not guardian, of Narbonne.

guardian, William Astre, in conjunction with the Custodian of Montpellier, Raymund Roverii,[1] and by the Provincial of Aquitaine, Bertrand de Tour.[2] The matter was taken up by the Archbishop of Aix, who gave instructions to the Dean of Maguelonne to declare them excommunicate.[3] The Spirituals, however, had many friends among the Italian cardinals, and the famous James Colonna wrote in May 1316 to the Dean, quashing the sentence on the ground that the matter concerned the Holy See.[4] The reason of this was probably that the so-called rebels had already appealed to the future Pope.[5] Emboldened by the support they had received, they celebrated the anniversary of Olivi's death with great solemnity, the townspeople taking part in the ceremony, and even certain of the cardinals sending gifts to his shrine.[6] They did not, however, wish to separate from their Order, and sent a letter justifying their actions to the Chapter-General held at Naples at Pentecost,[7] but the Conventuals wounded and ill-treated their messenger.[8] Nor did the newly elected General, Michael of Cesena,[9] show them much consideration, as he merely offered them a free pardon on condition that they submitted to their superiors.[10] On the other hand, he sent an encyclical to the different provinces denouncing flagrant abuses of the Rule, and ordering that their perpetrators should be severely dealt with,[11] and drew up a revised edition of the Constitutions of the Order.[12] In August the long vacancy of the pontificate was brought to an end by the election of John XXII., who fully sympathised with the attitude of the new minister-general. The most bitter enemies of the Spirituals flocked to the Curia, among them William Astre and Bonagratia of Bergamo, who had left his prison on the legal quibble that he had been sent to Valcabrère, near Cominges,

---

[1] *A.L.K.G.* ii. 162 *s.*; iii. 27.

[2] Feb. 13, 1315. *Ibid.* For text of process, cf. *A.F.H.* xvi. 339-49.

[3] *A.L.K.G.* ii. 163; iv. 62 (xxi.). Cf. *A.F.H.* xvi. 336.

[4] *A.F.H.* xvi. 350-55. (Feb. 28, 1315.) Cf. *A.L.K.G.* ii. 163.

[5] *A.L.K.G.* iv. 54.

[6] *A.L.K.G.* iii. 443; iv. 58. The honour paid to the memory of Olivi was one of the accusations later brought against the Spirituals by their enemies, who declared that they treated him as an already canonized saint. In their defence the latter alleged that in encouraging popular veneration for the great Zealot they had done nothing unauthorised by the canons of the Church, for it was through such means that certain of the great Franciscan saints had been eventually raised to the altars (*ibid.* iii. 442-43).

[7] *Ibid.* ii. 159-64. Narbonne, May 3.   [8] *Ibid.* iv. 54.

[9] The choice seems to have been a particularly wise one, for Michael, who had lately become a professor at Paris, apparently belonged to the moderate party in the Order and had hitherto taken no share in the controversy (Carlini, *Fra Michelino e la sua Eresia*, p. 55).   [10] *A.L.K.G.* iv. p. 39.

[11] Wadding, *Annales*, vi. 243-45, §§ iii. and v.

[12] Constitutions of Assisi, 1316. *A.F.H.* iv. 269-302, 508-36.

although the papal bull had consigned him to a convent of the name of " Monte Caprario ".[1]   A commission was instituted to inquire into the processes against the Spirituals, and to examine the documents which they had drawn up in their own defence.[2]   To the famous canonist, Berengar Frédol,[3] and Arnald Novelli [4] was entrusted the duty of conveying to them the Pope's commands that they should return to their convents and assume the habits given them by their superiors, instead of the short and skimpy tunics which they had worn at Narbonne and Béziers.[5]   A letter of the Franciscan, Cardinal Vidal du Four, and two of his colleagues to Michael of Cesena and the Provincial of Provence shows that the Zealots turned a deaf ear to this request.[6]   Finally, the Pope instructed the Communes of Narbonne and Béziers to summon the brothers dwelling in their convents to appear before him.[7]   On their way the little band of forty-six Spirituals from Narbonne and fifteen from Béziers was joined by three other friars, one of whom, Bernard Délicieux, was already notorious for his courageous defence of the citizens of Carcassonne and Albi against the Dominican inquisitors.[8]   In his eagerness he had even gone so far as to form a conspiracy for the surrender of the former city to Don Ferrand, the son of the king of Majorca.[9]   They arrived at Avignon very late in the evening of May 22, and in their zeal to defend their cause before the Pope, stayed all night outside the bishop's palace at Avignon waiting for the dawn to break.[10] When at last they were admitted, they put forward Bernard Délicieux as their spokesman, but owing to the clamours of the members of the Conventual party who were present he was hardly able to obtain a hearing, and finally the Pope ordered his arrest.[11]

---

[1] *A.L.K.G.* iii. 40.

[2] *A.L.K.G.* iv. 52 and 60.   No less than five petitions against the Spirituals and their leaders were presented to the new Pope by the official representatives of the Order at the Curia (*ibid.* iii. 27 (vii.)).   Extracts from the documents drawn up by the Zealots in their own defence are printed in *Ibid.* iv. 52-62.

[3] Cardinal of Tusculum.   Cf. *Ibid.* iii. 28 (ix.).

[4] Cardinal of St. Prisca (*ibid*).   [5] *Ibid.*

[6] Avignon, April 2, 1317. *A.F.H.* xiv. 432.   The other two cardinals were Jacques de la Via and Napoleone Orsini.

[7] *B.F.* v. 266 and 267, p. 118 (April 27, 1317).

[8] Cf. Dmitrewski, " Fr. Bernard Délicieux, O.F.M.", etc. ; *A.F.H.* xvii. 183-218; 313-33; 457-88; xviii. 3-32.   Bernard's connection with the Spiritual party does not seem to have begun till about 1310, when he became a diligent student of the Joachimite writings and a fervent admirer of Olivi.   Possibly his generous if somewhat impetuous nature had been deeply stirred by the persecutions suffered by the Provençal Spirituals.   Cf. *ibid.* p. 463-65.

[9] *Ibid.* 323, 325-30.

[10] Hist. vii.; Trib. *A.L.K.G.* ii. 144.   The present papal palace had not then been built.

[11] *Ibid.* 145.   He appears, however, to have obtained a longer hearing than

One of his companions, Franciscus Sanctii, now tried to speak,[1] but his enemies cried out that he must not be heard, for he had used his position as lector to slander the Order, and he suffered the same fate as the former speaker. A similar misfortune befell William of St. Armand.[2] An aged and respected friar, Gaufridus de Cornone, who had no connection with either the band from Narbonne or those from Béziers, tried to defend the Spirituals, but John turned to him scornfully and asked how such an ardent advocate of the strict observance of the Rule could yet wear five tunics. When the unfortunate Gaufridus ventured to protest, the Pope asked roughly, " Then am I a liar ? " and hardly waited for his victim's confused answer before having him arrested.[3] These four were placed in the custody of the papal chamberlain, while the rest were imprisoned in the Franciscan convent at Avignon.[4] In the autumn the Pope issued a new bull, " Quorundam exigit ", the opening words of which show his utter lack of sympathy with the ideas of the Zealots.[5] In this he enacted that the form of the habit was to be left to the discretion of the Superiors of the Order, and commanded the extremists to lay aside their peculiar costume under pain of excommunication.[6] During the course of the following months the Minister-General visited the prisoners at Avignon to induce them to swear public obedience to the new decretal.[7] At the same time he issued stringent instructions to the Superiors that all who wore habits which were not composed of the rough material authorised by the Rule were to be severely dealt with.[8] Only twenty-five of the Spirituals remained obdurate, and these were handed over to the Inquisition.[9]

Clareno's account would lead us to expect, and to have sustained a wordy duel with Michael of Cesena, during the course of which he turned to the Pope and said: " Holy father, if one lying word has passed my lips I am willing to be condemned, for all that I have said must be judged to be false ". He then faced his opponents and declared, " But if they, in all that they have said, have uttered one word of truth I am willing to be condemned, for all that they say is true ". Cf. A.L.K.G. iii. 29 (xviii.-xx.). Our source for the proceedings is a manuscript in the Bibliothèque Nationale (Codex 4350). Cf. Carlini, op. cit. p. 69.

[1] A.L.K.G. ii. 145 ; Codex Bibl. Nat. 4350 contains a long list of accusations brought by Franciscus Sanctii against his opponents, together with the answers made by Michael of Cesena (Carlini, op. cit. 69), so that he probably managed to continue his speech for some time in spite of frequent interruptions from the Conventuals.

[2] A.L.K.G. ii. 146.   [3] Ibid.   [4] Ibid.

[5] B.F. v. 289, p. 128 s. (Oct. 7, 1317): " Quorundam exigit caecae scrupulositatis."   [6] Ibid. 130.

[7] A.L.K.G. iv. 42. Cf. Carlini, op. cit. p. 70.

[8] De Gubernatis, Orbis Seraphicus, i. p. 149, gives the text of this letter. It is dated Avignon, December 5.

[9] A.L.K.G. iv. 42. For proceedings of Inquisition, cf. Baluze-Mansi, Misc. ii. 247-51. The date of the sentence is May 7, 1318.

The case was so complicated that it was referred to a commission of doctors of theology, who decided that their refusal to obey the Pope on the ground that he had not the authority to make alterations in the Rule was definitely heretical. Both Michael of Cesena and the Franciscan, Cardinal Vidal de Four, were members of this body.[1] Finally, four of the twenty-five who continued to assert that to force them to give up their present habits was akin to the action of the Jews in casting Christ out of the synagogue were burnt at Marseilles in May 1318.[2] Another friar, Bernard Aspa, who had recanted only at the very end, was imprisoned for life.[3] The same fate had befallen his namesake, Délicièux, who had been unfrocked and delivered into the charge of his bitterest enemy.[4] Fortunately, death soon put an end to the old man's sufferings. After this an uneasy peace settled on Provence. Olivi's writings were again condemned at a Chapter-General held at Marseilles in 1319,[5] and his body was exhumed and his tomb destroyed.[6] Although during the course of the century there were isolated cases of friars who compared the Pope to Antichrist, on the whole resistance was at an end.[7] This period of calm, however, did not endure for long, for within two years the famous controversy concerning the poverty of Christ arose which nearly created a schism in the Order and turned Michael of Cesena into the Pope's most strenuous opponent. By the irony of fate he and Bonagratia of Bergamo found themselves allied with Ubertino of Casale in the camp of Louis of Bavaria,[8] and John's fulminations against them were even more vigorous than his previous ones against the Zealots. The old Spiritual party seemed for the moment to perish, but their tenets survived in a perverted form among the Béguins in southern France[9] and the Fraticelli in Italy.[10] Moreover, the lives of the saintly Franciscan tertiary, Elzéar, Count of Sabrano, and of his wife Delphine, composed at the end of the fourteenth century, probably at the Minorite convent at Apt, bear witness to the prevalence of

[1] *A.L.K.G.* iv. p. 270. Vidal was created a cardinal in 1312. The attitude of the Spirituals towards him can be realised from the fact that Délicièux declared him to be one of his four bitterest enemies at the papal court. Cf. Baluze, *Vitae Paparum*, i. 676.

[2] *Misc.* ii. 248 s. *A.L.K.G.* ii. 147; iii. 30 (xxiv.).

[3] *Misc.* ii. 250.

[4] *A.L.K.G.* ii. 147; *A.F.H.* xviii. pp. 18 and 19.

[5] *A.L.K.G.* ii. 149.

[6] *Ibid.* 129, 293; iii. 443.

[7] Du Plessis Mornay, *Mysterium Iniquitatis, sive Historia Papatus*, p. 470, quotes an example from the year 1345. In 1354 two friars were burnt at Avignon for holding erroneous views on the question of poverty (*Vitae Paparum*, i. 311).

[8] Cf. *infra*, p. 153 s.

[9] Cf. *infra*, p. 248 s.

[10] Cf. *infra*, p. 209 s.

their influence not only in the Order itself but among certain representatives of the Provençal nobility.[1] A few years later, their spirit and example were to animate the Osservanti, and indeed every later reform movement among the Franciscans has drawn its inspiration from the same source.[2] It is no exaggeration to say that they saved the originality of the foundation of St. Francis, and prevented it from becoming merely a replica of the Dominicans. To the modern mind, their insistence on patched habits and other rather trifling matters seems somewhat ridiculous and unnecessary, but a vital principle was at stake, namely, the true observance of the Rule. If unswerving loyalty to a great ideal in spite of ridicule and strenuous opposition is a noble characteristic the Spirituals certainly possessed it in abundance. They were unsuccessful, but their failure is far more glorious than any victory.

---

[1] Elzéar was canonized in 1370, and it has been suggested that the suspicion of Béguinism, probably incurred through her friendship with Sancia of Naples, prevented the canonization of Delphine. Cf. M. Dulong, " La Vie provençale de Ste Delphine " (Positions des Thèses, 1928), pp. 31-35. For Latin life of St. Elzéar, cf. Acta Sanctorum (Sept. 27), vii. 576-93.

[2] The marked similarity between the petition presented by the French Observantines to the Council of Constance and Ubertino da Casale's treatise, " Sanctitas vestra ", is a striking proof of the influence of the old Spiritual party upon the new movement. Cf. Oliger, " De Relatione inter Observantium Querimonias (1415) et Ubertini Casalensis quoddam Scriptum " (A.F.H. ix. p. 25, and infra, p. 263).

CHAPTER II

THE INFLUENCE OF JOACHIM OF FLORA UPON THE FRANCISCAN ORDER.

Il Calavrese Abate Gioacchino
Di spirito profetico dotato.[1]

IN the august circle of the theologians and in company with the great Christian apologists, St. Anselm and St. John Chrysostom, appears the strange figure of Joachim of Flora, the visionary upon whose fantastic and elaborate speculations the men of the thirteenth century based their hopes of a newer and better age. There is no more striking testimony to the influence of this remarkable personality than his place in the *Paradiso*, for it shows that more than a century after his death he was venerated by one whose work will endure for all time.[2] Yet, if he had lived to-day the Calabrian prophet might have aroused interest and even admiration, both by reason of the romantic nature of his conversion and of his personal holiness, but the educated classes would almost certainly have turned a deaf ear to his message. The modern mind, with its concentration on the present, has some difficulty in understanding the medieval preoccupation about the ultimate fate of the world. At a period, however, when the allegorical interpretation of the Scriptures was the chief concern of the learned, and the coming of Antichrist and the speedy destruction of things temporal were regarded as at least plausible hypotheses,[3] it is not surprising that Joachim's theories soon attained a widespread popularity, their very novelty and abstruseness perhaps adding to their attraction.[4] Even William of St. Amour, the sturdy opponent of the mendicant orders, could describe the friars as the precursors of Antichrist,[5] and the high honour of preaching before the Pope and his cardinals, which was accorded to Hugues de

---

[1] *Paradiso*, xii. 140-41.

[2] The extent of the influence of Joachimism upon Dante is still a matter of controversy among scholars. Dempf, to my mind, goes a little too far in considering that Beatrice is a symbol of the Church of the new age. Cf. *Sacrum Imperium*, pt. iii. chap. iii. p. 487.

[3] This idea is very ably worked out by Balthazar (*op. cit.* p. 151, note 2).

[4] Much work has lately been done on the sources of Joachim's theories by H. Grundmann in his *Studien über Joachim von Floris*. He has come to the conclusion that though somewhat similar conceptions are found both in pre-Christian and early Christian thought, and in the writings of Rupert of Deutz, and Anselm of Havelberg, Archbishop of Ravenna (1155-58), it is difficult to find definite traces of their influence except, perhaps, in the case of the two latter. Joachim is certainly original in applying the scholastic method to the development and exposition of his ideas. Cf. especially pp. 91-95.

[5] "De Periculis Novissimorum Temporum." Printed in Brown's *Fasc. Rerum Expetend.* ii. pp. 18-41. Cf. especially p. 19.

Digne, can be regarded as a proof that an eager curiosity concerning the new doctrines existed in very exalted circles.[1] Innocent IV.'s attitude to the great Franciscan is reminiscent of that of the Athenian philosophers in the days of St. Paul, who were solely interested in the hearing or the telling of some new thing.[2]

Joachim's strange belief in the coming age of the Holy Spirit probably originated in his solution of one of the greatest mysteries of the Christian faith, namely, the question of the Trinity. His views upon this matter were condemned by the famous Lateran Council of 1215.[3] It must not be forgotten that he spent his life in a part of Italy where the remnants of Byzantine culture still lingered, and where the learning and traditions of the Greek Church were kept alive in the Basilian monasteries.[4] Thus it is not surprising that he emphasised the triune nature rather than the oneness of the Godhead, using the similes of a nation and a herd, or, more poetically, of three golden statues, or a fire composed of different elements, to explain its unity.[5] It was easy, therefore, for him to conceive that the action of the three persons of the Trinity could be distinguished at different stages of the world's history, although just as the events of the Old Testament foreshadowed those of the New, so God the Father was the predominant but not the sole agent in the first age, and similarly the Son and the Holy Ghost in the two subsequent epochs. Until the coming of Christ the divine commands were understood literally, and men were ruled by fear, whereas after the Incarnation a more spiritual interpretation was given to the Scriptures and men lived by faith, seeing " as through a glass darkly ".[6] In the coming age, the age of the Holy Spirit, they would be filled with spiritual understanding of both Testaments, the sacraments would be done away with, and faith would be changed into love. Joachim has many beautiful similes for his three periods, as when he compares them to brass, silver, and gold ; starlight, dawn, and full daylight ; and water, wine, and oil. More obvious comparisons are drawn from the great seasons of the Church—Septuagesima, Quadragesima, and Easter—the stars, the moon, and the sun, and nettles, roses, and

---

[1] Cf. *supra,* p. 7.

[2] *Acts* xvii. 21. Salimbene, who, according to himself, was a personal friend of Hugues de Digne, gives the Pope's speech as follows: " Audivimus de te, quod magnus clericus sis et bonus homo et spiritualis. Sed et hoc audivimus quia successor sis abbatis Ioachim in prophetiis et magnus Ioachita. Nunc ergo omnes nos in conspectu tuo assumus audire omnia, quecumque tibi precepta sunt a Domine " (*op. cit.* 231).

[3] *Decretales Gregorii IX.* lib. i. cap. ii.; *Corpus Iuris Canonici,* ii. p. 6.

[4] Fournier, p. 472.

[5] These similes are given in the Protocol to the Commission of Anagni (*A.L.K.G.* i. 137-40).   [6] *Ibid.* i. 132 (1 *Corinthians* xiii. 12).

lilies.[1] By elaborate calculations from the genealogies of Christ Joachim concluded that each age comprised forty-two generations, which, allowing thirty years for each generation, would make the year 1260 mark the conclusion of the age of the Son and the beginning of the period of the Holy Spirit.[2] The Old Testament had been the time of the married, whereas after the Incarnation a celibate priesthood had flourished whose active feet had spread the Gospel throughout the world.   The chief men of the third age would be an order of contemplatives, already foreshadowed by John, the beloved disciple, who was preferred to St. Peter, the chief of the Apostles.[3] In each period there had been three great men —in the first Abraham, Isaac, and Jacob ; in the second Zachariah, John the Baptist, and Christ ; [4] while the prophets of the third age were symbolised by the man clad in a linen robe of the twelfth chapter of Daniel and the two angels, one bearing a sickle and the other having the seal of the living God, seen by the writer of the Apocalypse.[5] Each age was characterised by a beginning, fruition, and decline, and yet there was no violent gulf between them, for one arose out of the other.[6] Uzziah, King of Judah,[7] and Elias had been the precursors of Christ, just as the Benedictines were the forerunners of the new order of contemplatives.[8] On the other hand, by a careful scrutiny of the course of history, it was easy to mark the end of one period and the beginning of the next. Joachim did not claim the gift of prophecy, but merely declared that by a close examination of the Scriptures he was able to foretell the future.   Thus, from the sojourn of the Israelites in Egypt, he conceived the idea of the peace and tranquillity which would be the chief feature of the reign of the Holy Ghost, while their temptations and sufferings in the wilderness were typical of the period of tribulation which was its prelude, for Joachim paid little attention to the chronological order of events.[9] He further subdivided each big era into seven smaller epochs, and believed that the world was now in the sixth stage of the reign of the Son,[10] and that in the seventh the age of the Spirit, or of the Eternal Gospel, would begin.   First, however, Antichrist must come, and

---

[1] A.L.K.G. i. 132 and 100 s.   Cf. Concordia Novi et veteris Testamenti, v. c. 84.

[2] Concordia Tractatus, i. c. 16.   Cf. A.L.K.G. i. 103.   According to Gerard of Borgo San Donnino the spirit and life were to depart from both Testaments in the year 1200.   Ibid. 99.

[3] Ibid. 111.   [4] A.L.K.G. 101 (Concordia, v. c. 71).

[5] Daniel xii. 6; Apoc. xiv. 14; vii. 2.

[6] Concordia, tr. i. c. 4.   Cf. A.L.K.G. i. 102.   [7] 2 Chronicles xxvi.

[8] A.L.K.G. i. 103.   [9] Concordia, v. c. 58 ; A.L.K.G. i. 109.

[10] Fournier, p. 476.   Joachim probably drew his inspiration from the book with the Seven Seals.   Cf. Apoc. v. 1.

from the orthodox interpretation which regarded the seven heads of the dragon who had persecuted the woman girt with the sun as the great empires of the world, Joachim conceived him as a great ruler.[1] He would be vanquished by the rider on the white horse, who was either the Christ returned to the earth, or His Spirit reincarnated in the person of one of His saints.[2] The martyrs belonging to the new contemplative order, who had perished during the short-lived triumph of the former, would ascend immediately as victors to the sky, and a period of peace would ensue which would last for a thousand years.[3] Then would come the greater Antichrist symbolised by Gog, or by the seventh head of the dragon, after which would follow the final destruction of the world and the day of Judgment.[4]

One of the most puzzling problems which arises out of the speculations of Joachim is concerned with the functions of the Church in the new age. The Abbot of Flora was profoundly orthodox in intention, and his writings had been encouraged by the Popes of the concluding years of the twelfth century. Moreover, he possessed all the medieval horror of heresy, and the general belief that he considered the schism of the Greek and Latin Churches to have been inspired by the Holy Spirit arose from a profound misconception of his teaching.[5] Yet, on the one hand, while he never identified the Church with Babylon the harlot,[6] there could be no room for a dominant and elaborately organised hierarchy in an age when the power of interpreting the Scriptures would be granted at least to the order of contemplatives, if not to all the righteous. Joachim appears to have regarded the ecclesiastical order of his day as favourable to the new era, but as playing no part in it. Often he describes the Pope as the aged Simeon who received Christ in the Temple,[7] or as David who, in his old age, had received comfort from the Shunammite woman, but who was succeeded not by Adonijah the man of war, but by Solomon.[8] A rather far-fetched exposition of Genesis led him to accept the butler as a type of Pope Sylvester and his clerks, while Joseph

---

[1] *Expositio in Apocalypsim,* f. 196. *A.L.K.G.* i. 120 and 124. Cf. *Apoc.* xii.
[2] *Expositio,* f. 207 *v. A.L.K.G.* i. 125. Cf. *Apoc.* xix. 11.
[3] *Expositio,* 210 *v. A.L.K.G.* i. 108 and 120.
[4] *Expositio,* 207 *v. A.L.K.G.* i. 125. The Commission probably exaggerated when they concluded that Joachim implied that there would be two days of Judgment.
[5] Such was the view taken by the Commission (*A.L.K.G.* i. 120). Joachim's real meaning was probably " that there were differences of graces but the same Spirit ".
[6] Another misconception of the Commission (*A.L.K.G.* 119). According to Fournier, Joachim intended Babylon to signify evil-doers in general (*op. cit.* p. 476, note 3). Cf. *Expositio,* 194 *r.*
[7] *A.L.K.G.* i. 110.   [8] *Ibid.* 109 (*Concordia,* v. c. 65).

symbolised the new order, by whose teaching grain would be stored up for the barren years during which Antichrist would hold sway upon the earth.[1]   It is probable that during this period of preaching the division with the Greek Church would be healed, and the Jews would be converted to the true faith, but Joachim is not very clear on this point.[2]   The Church organisation of his day obviously had a fast hold over his imagination, for in one passage he described the third great man of the new age, typified by the angel with the seal of the Living God, as a mighty Pope ruling from sea to sea,[3] and he also represented the second Antichrist as a great prelate.[4]   He was very vague about the coming of the new Elias, but possibly identified him with the man clad in white linen.   On the other hand, like most of the moralists of his age, he disapproved strongly of the luxury of the higher clergy, which he felt was stifling the spiritual life of the Church.[5]   Although he does not discuss the question of Evangelical Poverty it is certain that his ideal order would not have possessed temporal riches, and would have obtained the necessities of life by manual labour.[6] In fact, the logical outcome of Joachim's teaching was so clearly subversive, not only of the Church but of the whole existing state of society,[7] that it is surprising that it was tolerated, and even encouraged, for so long by the Holy See.   Perhaps the best explanation is to be found in his great reputation for personal holiness.[8]

The events of the fifty years following Joachim's death must have been regarded by the men of his age as a complete vindication of his theories.   They not unnaturally saw a remarkable fulfilment of his prophecies in the foundation of the two great mendicant Orders, and the life and death struggle between Frederick II. and the Papacy.   Moreover, the Abbot of Flora had been no mere solitary visionary, but the founder of a flourishing branch of the Cistercian Order, comprising no less than forty religious

---

[1] *A.L.K.G.* i. 107 s. (*Concordia*, v. c. 56).   The new order is also described as the angel flying through the heavens carrying the book of the Eternal Gospel (*Apoc.* xiv. 6).   *A.L.K.G.* i. iii.   [2] *Ibid.* i. 113 (*Concordia*, v. 84).

[3] *A.L.K.G.* i. 105 (*Concordia*, iv. 31).

[4] Thomas of Pavia gives a quotation from the *Expositio* which seems to indicate that Joachim regarded the second Antichrist as a great prince of the Church (cf. *A.F.H.* xvi. p. 26).   This is certainly the interpretation given by Gerard of Borgo San Donnino, who describes him as a " Pseudo-papa " (*A.L.K.G.* i. 109).

[5] Cf. Fournier, *op. cit.* 477.   [6] *Ibid.* 465 (*Concordia*, v. c. 81).

[7] Fournier describes him as " un auxiliaire (de l'église) aussi dévoué que dangereux " (*op. cit.* p. 505).

[8] In spite of the condemnation of his views by the Lateran Council, no aspersions were ever cast on his personal orthodoxy even by those who, like Aquinas, were most strongly opposed to his ideas.

houses which acted as centres for the diffusion of his ideas.[1]   The condemnation of his opinions on the Trinity by the Lateran Council of 1215 may even have increased his popularity, and brought him fame as the opponent of the celebrated Peter Lombard.   During the middle years of the century many spurious works ascribed to Joachim appeared, such as the commentaries on Isaiah and Jeremiah,[2] and the visions of Merlin and the Erythraean Sybil,[3] and these were even more widely read than his genuine writings.   They are, on the whole, orthodox in tone, but their criticisms of the Church are much more bitter, for in the Jeremiah she is definitely compared to Babylon, and the memory of Sylvester I., " il primo ricco padre ",[4] is blackened.[5]

The two new religious orders were naturally devoted adherents of the Abbot of Flora, for both regarded themselves as the Contemplatives whose advent he had foretold.   An early Dominican chronicler, Gerard of Frachet, relates that on their first visit to Flora the friars were received by the brethren of the house in procession, with the cross borne before them, an honour generally accorded only to bishops and kings.[6]   The Franciscans were even more enthusiastic, for in their early days they were a far less learned order than their rivals, and therefore were far more liable to be influenced by imaginative speculations.   Moreover, the type of man who had been attracted by St. Francis would have sufficient of the mystic and the poet in his composition to appreciate the ideal of love and the search after a perfection existing nowhere in this world, which lay at the basis of Joachim's somewhat fantastic theories.[7]   Yet, even the most profound minds in the

[1] *A.F.H.* xx. 219.

[2] Many modern scholars regard the Jeremiah as the first fruit of Joachimism among the Franciscans.   It is certainly the work of its kind most frequently quoted by Minorite writers such as Alexander of Bexhövède (cf. *Collectanea Franciscana*, ii. p. 28) and Salimbene (*op. cit.* 236 and 640), the latter of whom, however, obviously regarded it as a genuine work of Joachim (*ibid.*).   Dempf (*op. cit.* p. 332) has suggested as its author the Brother Leonard who shared the fate of Gerard of Borgo San Donnino (cf. *supra*, p. 8).   This would explain the reason of his imprisonment, for which no ground is given by contemporary authorities.

[3] This treatise was much read among the later Spirituals.   Cf. Grundmann, *H.J.* 49, p. 76, and *A.L.K.G.* ii. 289.   [4] *Inferno*, xix. 117.

[5] Jordan, *Les Origines de la domination angevine en Italie*, p. cxix.

[6] Reichert, *Monumenta Ordinis Fratrum Predicatorum historica*; *I. Vitae Fratrum*, p. 13.

[7] Dempf is probably right in considering that the initial mistake of Joachim and his followers among the Franciscans lay in their belief that their own complete alienation from earthly things, and close union with the divine, could be attained by all men at a definite stage in the history of the world.   Such heights of self-renunciation and mystic devotion were only possible for a kind of spiritual aristocracy and could never become a reality for the average man (*op. cit.* p. 282).

order were fascinated by these new ideas, as can be seen from Adam
Marsh's letter to Grossetête, in which he showed that the deep
impression made on him by Joachim's theories was largely due to
the latter's great reputation for sanctity, and begged the bishop to
return the writings he had sent him as soon as he had had them
copied.[1] It is clear from this correspondence that Joachim was
hardly known in England. The extent of their popularity among
the German Franciscans can be judged from a commentary on
the Apocalypse written by a Saxon friar, Alexander of Bexhovëde,
about the middle of the century.[2] Although the writer attributed
his treatise to a divine revelation,[3] he was certainly acquainted with
the " Jeremiah " and perhaps with other Joachimite writings. It
is from the former that he draws his similes for the Dominican
and Franciscan orders, comparing the one to a crow and the other
to a dove.[4] Much of his imagery is worthy of record because of its
poetic beauty, as, for instance, his citation of the twelve foundations
of the new Jerusalem as symbols of the virtues which found their
highest expression in the Franciscan ideal.[5] His devotion to the
honour of his Order sometimes led him to fantastic lengths, as when
he interprets the lack of a temple in the Heavenly City as signifying the smallness of the Franciscan churches.[6] The real centres
of the new ideas, however, were France and Italy. Even so
level-headed a person as Salimbene, who certainly was very little
of a visionary and cared much for the good things of this life, was
proud to proclaim himself a Joachimite, perhaps because it enabled
him to boast of his intimacy with such great men as John of Parma
and Hugues de Digne. It was at the command of the former that
he and his friend " Johannès de Ollis " wrote a commentary on
Joachim's " Concordia Quattuor Evangeliorum ".[7] There is a
delightful naïveté in his belief that the new sect of the Apostles
was certainly sent by the Evil One, since the Calabrian abbot had
not prophesied its foundation as he had clearly foretold that of the
Friars Minor.[8] Yet, even in the early days of Joachimism there
were certain sceptics, who, like the Dominican, Peter of Apulia,
had as little use for the new theories as for the fifth wheel on a
coach.[9] Salimbene's story of his conversion through the exertions

---

[1] *Monumenta Franciscana*, i., Epistolae Ade Marsh, p. 146.
[2] A description of this treatise is given by the late J. P. Gilson in *Collectanea Franciscana*, ii. pp. 20-36. A manuscript of Alexander's Commentary exists at Cambridge (Moore MS. Mm. 5, 31). Cf. *ibid*. 20.
[3] *Collectanea Franciscana*, ii. p. 21. [4] F. 13. *Ibid*. p. 28.
[5] F. 193 *v*. *Ibid*. p. 29. [6] F. 196 *r.b*. *Ibid*. p. 31.
[7] Salimbene, *op. cit*. p. 294. [8] *Ibid*. p. 293.
[9] Peter of Apulia can, perhaps, be taken as an example of the change in the attitude of the Dominican order to Joachimism which took place about the middle of the thirteenth century. A treatise, entitled Epistula de Correctione

of Hugues de Digne, probably gives too favourable an estimate of the eloquence of the great Joachimite.[1] A more interesting example of scepticism was that afforded by the Franciscan, Thomas of Pavia, who had held lectorships at Bologna, Ferrara, and Parma, and was later to become Provincial of Tuscany.[2] In his Distinctiones he came to no very definite conclusions about the value of Joachim's writings, but thought that they contained much that was stupid and erroneous, especially in the matter of dates.[3] When Frederick II. died in 1250, ten years before the time at which the age of the Holy Spirit was supposed to begin, many Joachimites found it difficult to believe the news of his death.[4]

It is probable that the attention of the Church was first drawn to the dangers of Joachimism by the appearance of the Introductorius in Evangelium Eternum. The circumstances which led to its condemnation have been discussed in the previous chapter. At the time of its composition, Gerard of Borgo San Donnino was already lector in theology at the Franciscan convent in Paris,[5] and in spite of his youth had achieved a considerable reputation in the Order, as the result of his personal piety and the sweetness and courtesy of his disposition.[6] His folly lay not so much in the actual writing of his book as in its publication without the knowledge or permission of his superiors.[7] The list of errors drawn up by the Paris Masters [8] is obviously too prejudiced and inaccurate to give

Ecclesie, written about 1248 by a Swabian Dominican named Arnold, shows, however, distinct traces of Joachimism. The author was an adherent of Frederick II., and believed that through his agency a reformation of the Church would be brought about in the seventh age, in which the friars, as the true successors of the Apostles, would take the place of the luxurious and wealthy prelates who were the objects of his most bitter hatred (Dempf, op. cit. p. 330).

[1] Salimbene, op. cit. p. 239 s.
[2] Ibid. pp. 429-30.
[3] Longpré, A.F.H. xvi. pp. 3-33, especially pp. 23-28, where extracts are given showing Thomas' opinions on Joachimism. The Distinctiones were in all probability written shortly after the scandal caused by the condemnation of the Introductorius, for the writer alludes to the strife between the mendicants and the University professors at Paris, which was at its height between 1254 and 1256, and refers to the Summa of Alexander of Hales which was completed about that time. Cf. pp. 16-17.
[4] Salimbene, op. cit. p. 302.   [5] Salimbene, op. cit. p. 236.
[6] " Erat enim familiaris, curialis, liberalis, religiosus, honestus, modestus, morigeratus, temperatus in verbis, in cibo, in potu atque vestitu, obsequiosus, cum omni humilitate et mansuetudine. Vero vir amicalis ad societatem " (ibid. 458).
[7] A.L.K.G. i. p. 67, note 2. Half the book must at any rate have been written before May 1254, for its errors are mentioned in a sermon with the incipit " Qui amat ", preached by William of St. Amour, on St. Philip and St. James' day. Cf. Fasc. Rer. Expetend. ii. p. 51. The references are all drawn from the Introductorius and the Concordia.
[8] Cf. Matthew Paris, Chronica Maiora, vi. 335-39.

us a fair idea of its contents,[1] and this fault is not rectified by the report of the Commission of Anagni,[2] which seems to have concerned itself mainly with the errors of Joachim, for the excerpts given from the Introductorius are few in comparison with those from the works of the famous abbot.   In spite, however, of some minor misconceptions,[3] the verdict of the judges was both just and impartial, and the Pope treated the Franciscan Order with a consideration which he certainly had not displayed in the case of the De Periculis Novissimorum Temporum which had been condemned during the previous year.[4]   Possibly, Gerard himself would have escaped lightly but for his obstinate adhesion to his former opinions, so bitterly deplored by his friend Salimbene.[5]   Even after 1260 his faith was still unshaken, for he confided to the latter in secret that Alfonso of Castile was certainly Antichrist.[6]   When condemned to perpetual imprisonment he entered his cell rejoicing, to endure a confinement which was to last for eighteen years.   After his death his body was denied ecclesiastical burial.[7]   It is sad that such heroism should have had no worthier object than his own exaggerated interpretation of the theories of Joachim.[8]

At first the popular interest in the new apocalyptic speculations was very little affected by the misfortunes of their most ardent exponent, for we know from Salimbene that it was quite possible to be a Joachimite without adopting any of the extravagances of Gerard.   Even the Spirituals, who revered his memory as that of a saint, regarded his commentary as foolish and lacking in any real discernment.[9]   It was a more serious blow when the fatal

---

[1] Such was the verdict of the examiners (Du Boulay, op. cit. 292).

[2] The three cardinals on the commission were Odo of Tusculum, Stephen of Praeneste, and Hugo of St. Sabina. One of the assessors was a former member of Joachim's Order, the Bishop of Banados in Thrace. The actual promoter of the case was Florentius, Bishop of Acre (A.L.K.G. i. 99 and 102).

[3] As, for instance, when they concluded that Joachim had identified the Catholic Church with Babylon the harlot, and had believed that the schism between the Greek and Latin communions was the work of the Holy Ghost (ibid. 119 and 120). Cf. supra, p. 25.   [4] Cf. supra, p. 22.

[5] " Nimis fuit obstinatus in dictis Ioachym et similiter proprie opinioni inseparabiliter adhesit " (p. 236).

" Sed protervitas sue opinionis omnia ista bona destruxit in eo " (ibid. 458).

[6] Ibid. 233.

[7] Ibid. 462. A.L.K.G. ii. pp. 276, 283-84. Some time later another friar, Peter de Nubili, was imprisoned for refusing to surrender a certain treatise, written by John of Parma, which he possessed (ibid. 284).

[8] Grundmann, op. cit. p. 160, note 3, gives it as his opinion that Gerard in reality merely carried Joachim's ideas to their logical conclusion. It is difficult, however, to see how his estimate of these could be reconciled with Christianity, since he regarded the writings of the Abbot of Flora as superseding the New Testament as a final and complete revelation of the will of God.

[9] Clareno describes Gerard's commentary as " sine sale " (A.L.K.G. ii. p. 277).

year 1260 passed away quietly save for the ghastly exertions of
the Flagellants, who strove by such means to turn men's thoughts
to repentance.   Yet even amid the general disillusionment many
were faithful to their former beliefs, for in 1263, at the Council
of Arles, the archbishop [1] complained that Joachim's works were
still studied in secret by many of the religious in his diocese and
did his utmost to secure their final condemnation.[2]   Aquinas,
while ready to acknowledge the piety and good intentions of the
Abbot of Flora, denied to him the gift of prophecy,[3] and declared
that there could be no new revelation of the truth, since the Holy
Spirit had communicated to the Apostles all that was necessary
for eternal salvation.[4]   Although in a general sense the Old
Testament had foreshadowed the New, it was dangerous to search
too closely for parallels between them.[5]   He also controverted
Joachim's doctrine of the Trinity, and his theories upon the
subject of the Divine Essence, which seem to have resembled
those which were later advanced by Olivi.[6]   Perhaps, as the result
of the attacks of the great Dominican, Joachimism lost its foothold
at the universities, and devotion to its tenets came to be regarded
rather as a sign of ignorance and fanaticism than of learning and
scholarship.   As we shall see, the Parisian professors played a
leading part in the condemnation of the apocalyptic writings of
the famous physician, Arnold of Villanova, and the general opinion
of the educated on the *Eternal Gospel* is probably to be found in the
mocking lines of the *Roman de la Rose* :

> Uns livres de par le diable
> C'est l'Evangile pardurable
> Que li Sainz Esperiz ministre.[7]

On the whole, after 1260, the ideas of the Abbot of Flora
had been discredited, partly because of their association with the
Flagellants and with the crude and exaggerated forms of heresy
found among the Apostles [8] and the sect of the Free Spirit,[9]

---

[1] Florentius, formerly Bishop of Acre. Cf. *supra*, p. 30, *n.* 2.

[2] Mansi, *Concilia*, xxiii. p. 1001. As the Council of Arles was only a
provincial synod, Joachim's views were never formally condemned by the
Church.   [3] *Expositio super II*^m *decretalem opusc. XXIV.*

[4] *Summa Theologica*, i. ii. Q. 106, A. 4.

[5] *Ibid.* i. *a*, Q. 39, A. 5. Aquinas was here expressing the general belief
of the Church (Grundmann, *op. cit.* chap. ii.).

[6] *Summa Theologica*, i. *a*, Q. 39, A. 5.

[7] Line 11994. Cited by Renan in *Nouvelles Études de l'histoire religieuse*,
p. 296.

[8] Founded by Gerardo Segarelli of Parma about 1240. Cf. Salimbene,
p. 255.

[9] Its founder, Ortleib, was probably a disciple of Amaury de Bena. The
sect was condemned by Innocent III.

although their doctrines were derived from a popular distortion of Joachim's teaching. A less important but more exciting body were the followers of a certain Guiglielmina of Milan, who was believed to be an incarnation of the Holy Spirit. After her death in 1270, her grave in the Cistercian church at Claircal, near Milan, was visited yearly by immense crowds who were awaiting anxiously for her resurrection. At last the ecclesiastical authorities awoke to the danger of the situation and had her body exhumed.[1] About a hundred years later a similar prophetess arose in the south of France, but was promptly dealt with by the Inquisition.[2] No better means could have been found to discredit Joachimism in the eyes of the intelligent and clear-sighted than these crazy perversions of its true significance.

Yet, the speculations of the Calabrian visionary still had a great fascination for certain highly gifted and imaginative individuals. A striking example of this is afforded by the great physician, Arnold of Villanova, whose skill brought him into close contact with the royal house of Aragon and with the papal court. As early as 1297, before he had any connection with the Franciscan Spirituals, he composed the first version of his *Tractatus de Tempore Antichristi* [3] in which he declared that, by a close examination of the signs of the times, it was possible to foretell the coming of Antichrist as taking place within the next hundred years.[4] This work first appeared at Paris, whither its author had been sent on a diplomatic mission to the French court, and immediately attracted the attention of the university authorities. In spite of the protection afforded by his character as an ambassador, Arnold was arrested and brought before the Bishop of Paris, nor was he released until he had signed a paper accepting the verdict of his judges, who had condemned his treatise as rash and dangerous.[5] His first act on regaining his freedom was to protest against such an infringement of his privileges as the accredited envoy of his master to Philip IV. of France, and to declare that his recantation was a mere empty form, since it had been extorted by force.[6] Nor was he satisfied by the punishment of the royal official responsible for his arrest,[7] but

---

[1] *Dict. de Theol. Cath.* viii. 1447. [2] *Ibid.*

[3] Dr. Finke has printed the *Tractatus de Tempore Antichristi*, together with other of the eschatological and religious writings of Arnold of Villanova, in an appendix to his *Aus den Tagen Bonifaz VIII.* Cf. pp. cxvii.-ccxi. His larger treatises of the same character, the " Introductio in Librum Joachim de Semine Scripturarum " and his " Expositio super Apocalypsim " are still unprinted. Cf. *Dict. de Theol. Cath.* viii. p. 1436.

[4] Finke, *op. cit.* pp. cxxxii., cxxxiii., and clix.

[5] Arnold gives a full account of these proceedings in his protest made in 1304 at Perugia, before the Papal Chamberlain (Finke, *op. cit.* cxci. *et seq.*).

[6] *Ibid.* [7] *Ibid.*

appealed to Boniface VIII. for a revision of the sentence of the university.[1] He issued a new version of his pamphlet, in which he defended his speculations as instrumental in arousing men from a state of sluggish indifference, in turning their hearts to repentance and to the consideration of spiritual things.[2] Moreover, their erroneousness could not be proved since they dealt entirely with future events.[3] The Pope, however, confirmed the decision of the Parisian theologians, but out of consideration for Arnold, to whom he was greatly indebted for his professional services, he allowed him to make his recantation in a secret consistory.[4] The papal condemnation of his treatise did not, however, deter him from further literary activity,and the summer of 1302,spent in the neighbourhood of Anagni, saw the production of various eschatological and religious works. His mind was becoming increasingly preoccupied with the state of the Church, and he dispatched copies of his *De Misterio Cimbalorum* not only to the kings of France and Aragon but to certain of the French and Spanish bishops, presumably in the hope of interesting them in his plans for its reform.[5] Arnold evidently dreaded the effect of his writings upon his illustrious patient,[6] for it was only as the result of a divine command, and after his departure for Provence, that he ventured to send him his *Philosophia Catholica*.[7] During his stay in this region he was brought into a close personal relationship with the Franciscan Spirituals, which was to last for the rest of his life.[8] He also interested himself in the fortunes of the Provençal Béguins, for whose benefit he wrote two short treatises, in one of which he

---

[1] Finke, *op. cit.* p. cxcii.

[2] " Ad officium quoque militantis ecclesie pertinet se ipsam et filios suos adversus astutias demonis premunire, despiciendo terrenam felicitatem et appetitum ad celestia dirigendo " (p. cxl).

[3] " Cum igitur probentur catholice, constat quod nec temeraria, nec falsa, nec erronea possunt dici, set eo ipso, quod futura sunt, possunt ambigua vel dubia nominari. Que tamen dubietas neminem potest ducere in errorem. Nec etiam sequeretur inconveniens aliquod, nocens catholice veritati, vel multitudini si non eveniret futurum " (*ibid.*).

[4] *Ibid.* p. cxciii. Arnold, who had won the Pope's favour by curing him of stone disease, was a member of his household from 1301 to 1302 (Finke, *op. cit.* p. 201 *s.*).

[5] Finke, *op. cit.* p. cxx. This treatise brought about a fierce conflict between Arnold and the Spanish Dominicans, with whom he had previously been on friendly terms (*ibid.* clxxii). Possibly his friendship with Délicieux was partly the result of their mutual hatred of the Friars Preachers.

[6] Letter to Benedict XI. (*ibid.* clxxxii).

[7] The letter sent with this treatise to Boniface VIII. is dated from Nice (*ibid.* p. clx).

[8] The letters which passed between Arnold and Bernard Délicieux after the return of the former to the papal court were later used as evidence that they had conspired together to bring about the death of Benedict XI. The charge was afterwards dropped as unsubstantiated (*A.F.H.* xvii. p. 333).

laid great stress on the Franciscan virtues of poverty and humility.[1] On the accession of Benedict XI., Arnold lost no time in endeavouring to draw his attention to the plight of the persecuted disciples of Olivi,[2] and also in attempting to get a revision of the verdict of Boniface VIII. with regard to the *Tractatus de Tempore Antichristi*. He presented the new Pope with copies of this and of his other works, at the same time writing him a letter in which he declared that the wickedness of the clergy was a sure proof of the advent of Antichrist.[3] Strong in his conviction of his own divine mission, Arnold attributed the pitiful end of Boniface VIII. to his refusal to listen to his advice,[4] and did not scruple to threaten his successor with a similar fate if he also turned a deaf ear to his warnings.[5] Under such circumstances it is not very surprising that Arnold again found himself a prisoner.[6] He must have been released shortly after the death of Benedict XI., for we find him appealing to the papal chamberlain for a further examination of his writings,[7] and in 1305 he made a similar request to Clement V., who was then at Bordeaux.[8] It is probable that the new Pope valued Arnold's medical services too highly to desire a new condemnation of his writings, for he appears to have come to no very definite decision with regard to their orthodoxy.[9] In fact, he was not greatly interested in the apocalyptic speculations of his physician, and once when the latter discoursed on such matters[10] in a consistory his patient thought tranquilly about more important questions.[11] It was in this speech that Arnold made his celebrated attack on the Franciscan cardinals, Gentile de Montefiore and John of Murrovalle,[12] which was afterwards repeated in his

[1] Two treatises written for the Béguins were among the works of Arnold condemned in 1316 (Menendez Pelayo, *Historia de les Heterodoxes Españolas*, i. p. 779). The beginning of one of these, the *Informatio Beguinorum*, written before August 1305, is printed by Finke, *op. cit.* pp. cci-ccii.

[2] Letter to Benedict XI. Finke, *op. cit.* pp. clxxxvi-clxxxvii.

[3] *Ibid.* p. clxxxiii.   [4] *Ibid.* p. clxxxii.

[5] *Ibid.* p. cxci. In his " Interpretatio de Visionibus in Somniis ", Arnold declares that the sudden death of Benedict XI. was to be regarded as an act of divine justice (Menendez Pelayo, *op. cit.* p. 729).

[6] " Protestatio facta Perusii coram domino camerario summi pontificis " (Finke, *op. cit.* pp. cxciv and cxcv).

[7] *Ibid.* pp. cxci-cxcvii.

[8] *Presentatio in Burdegallensem* (Aug. 1305). Finke, *op. cit.* pp. ccii-ccxi.

[9] The Pope referred the writings to a committee of theologians for further examination (*ibid.* pp. ccx-ccxi).

[10] The Rahonament. Only a Catalan version of this work is now in existence. It is printed by Menendez Pelayo (*op. cit.* pp. 753-70).

[11] Letter of Clement V. to the King of Aragon (Grausell, Oct. 21, 1309). *Ibid.* p. 776.

[12] Cf. *supra*, p. 11, note 6. Gentile de Montefiore was attacked probably as the author of a treatise against the Fraticelli. Cf. *H.J.* 49, p. 64.

" Interpretatio de Visionibus in Somniis ", written at the request of Frederick of Sicily.[1] The discourses in question may have been part of a campaign to secure the Pope's intervention in favour of the Spirituals, for Arnold was always ready to use his influence on their behalf.[2] His personal orthodoxy was never called into question during his lifetime, perhaps as a result of his connection with the Curia and with the royal house of Aragon, but in 1316, five years after his death, his memory was finally condemned.[3] This does not seem to have put an end to the study of his works, even in orthodox circles, for in 1345 a gloss to the De Misterio Cimbalorum with the incipit " Ve mundum in centum annis " was made at Paris by a certain " Frater Gentilis ",[4] while among the Franciscan Spirituals and their successors, the Provençal Béguins and the Italian Fraticelli, he was regarded with almost as deep veneration as Olivi.[5]

The influence of Joachimism did not end with Arnold of Villanova, but worked its spell over an even more complex and enigmatical personality, the famous Colà di Rienzi. In his case it is almost impossible to decide whether he was more swayed by motives of self-interest, or by a disinterested passion for the regeneration of the human race through the revival of the former glories of the Eternal City. His celebrated letter to the Emperor Charles IV. shows that he was well versed in the pseudo-Joachimite writings,[6] so that these were possibly the source of many of his dreams for the reorganisation of society. A new zeal for apocalyptic speculation was the natural outcome of the Great

---

[1] Menendez Pelayo, *op. cit.* pp. 720-34. Cf. p. 732 for passages relating to the Franciscan cardinals. This treatise is quoted in the *Catalogus Testium Veritatis* of Flacius Illyricus, p. 358 *s.*

[2] Angelo da Clareno declares that he was one of the persons responsible for drawing Clement V.'s attention to the plight of the Zealots (*A.L.K.G.* ii. 319).

[3] Menendez Pelayo, *op. cit.* pp. 777-81.

[4] Finke, *op. cit.* 218-21. Ceruti, relying on the evidence of a late fifteenth-century MS. in the Biblioteca Nazionale at Florence, ascribes this commentary to the Augustinian hermit, Gentile da Foligno, a friend and disciple of Angelo da Clareno, but the corrupt state of the text and the fact that no mention of Gentile is found in any of the earlier codices makes this theory somewhat doubtful. The MS. in question was transcribed by another Augustinian, Luca of San Gimignano, at the time of the French invasion of Italy (1494), and thus affords valuable evidence of the revived study of the Joachimite and pseudo-Joachimite writings in that Order on the eve of the Renaissance. Cf. *La Scala de Paradiso*, p. xxxviii, and *ibid.* note 1. [5] *S.F.* p. 512.

[6] Puir Burdach, *Vom Mittelalter zur Reformation*, ii. 3, p. 295. From his description in another letter to the Emperor of the beliefs and manner of life of the hermits of the Majella, with whom he lived after his exile from Rome, it is almost certain that they were descendants of the Spiritual Franciscans, and very possibly an offshoot of the Order founded by Clareno. Cf. *ibid.* Letter 49, p. 193.

Schism, and in 1386 the Calabrian hermit, Telesphorus of Cosenza, was directed in a vision to study the writings of his holy compatriot, and those of his friend and contemporary, Cyril the anchorite,[1] and wrote a treatise applying the prophecies to the events of his own time.[2] Two years later, a certain Thomas de Pouille announced in Paris that the age of the Holy Spirit was approaching, and even as late as 1432 another enthusiast, Nicholas of Buldersdorf, was burnt by order of the Council of Basle for proclaiming the end of the period of the New Testament. Nor was the abbot of Flora neglected at the Renaissance, for early in the sixteenth century his three chief works were printed at Venice,[3] as well as certain writings of a similar character, such as the Commentary on Jeremiah and the visions of Merlin and the Erythraean Sybil.[4] This revival of interest, although perhaps partly due to the efforts of the Augustinian hermits,[5] was probably not the result of any deep religious feeling, for a general inclination towards the visionary and fantastic was a very characteristic feature of the age. Yet certain of the pseudo-Joachimite writings were printed in Germany during the first half of the sixteenth century and were known to Luther and Melancthon and to some of the members of their circle.[6] Some Protestant writers even went so far as to regard the seer of Calabria as one of the forerunners of the Reformation,[7] a fact which, perhaps, explains the hostile attitude adopted towards him by Raynaldi.[8] No serious doubts have, however, been cast on his reputation, as can be seen from the writings of the Bolland-

---

[1] The Franciscan Spirituals seem also to have been attracted by this somewhat shadowy figure, for Angelo da Clareno had certainly studied his first prophecy, where he found foretold the life and misfortunes of Olivi (*A.L.K.G.* ii. 289).　　　　[2] *Dict. de Theol. Cath.* viii. p. 1447.

[3] The *Concordia* was printed by Simon de Luere in 1519, and the *Expositio in Apocalypsim* and the *Psalterium* by Bindoni and Pasyni in 1527. Dr. Grundmann is now contemplating a critical edition of Joachim's works.

[4] Printed by Lazzeri in 1517. The early printed editions of the more popular and influential *Liber de summis pontificibus* are dealt with later, since this work almost certainly owes its origin to the Franciscan Spirituals.

[5] The renewed study of the Joachimite and pseudo-Joachimite writings among the Augustinians at the end of the fifteenth and the beginning of the sixteenth century is of especial significance because of Luther's connection with the Order. About 1490 the English Augustinian and Oxford master, John Ergon, composed a commentary on the " Oraculum Cyrilli ", in which he referred to the prophecies of Methodius and of the Sybils, as well as to those of Joachim and John of Rupescissa. Cf. Grundmann, *op. cit.* pp. 194-95.

[6] For German editions of the pseudo-Joachimite writings, cf. Grundmann, *op. cit.* 193-98.

[7] Matthias Flacius, " Illyricus ", the stormy petrel of Lutheranism, mentions Joachim in his *Catalogus Testium Veritatis*, pp. 602-603, as one of the writers who had exposed the errors of the Church of Rome. He even contemplated a new edition of the Jeremiah, which he regarded as a genuine work of Joachim.

[8] *Annales*, xix. 1164, § lii.; 1191, § xxviii.; xxi. 1256, § xx.

ists [1] and the official sanction given to the popular veneration paid to his name. Moreover, the fascination of the theories of the Abbot of Flora has not ceased even in comparatively modern times for minds of a certain stamp. The three great epochs into which the German philosopher Schelling divides the Christian era, namely, the age of Peter or of Catholicism, and the period of Paul, or of Protestantism, both of which in their turn would give place, shortly before the second coming of Christ, to the ideal Church of the Apostle John in which mankind would attain full spiritual freedom, can be taken as a nineteenth-century revival of Joachimism.[2] Perhaps the charm exercised by the Calabrian visionary over some of the younger German historians to-day can be explained by the fact that they regard him as an early exponent of their own ideas of historical progress.[3] Thus, the man who gave voice to the yearnings and aspirations of certain choice spirits of his own age towards a perfection unattainable on earth save by the few, has been in turn hailed as the setter forth of new and strange things, whose prophecies captivated the credulous and polished sceptics of the Renaissance, and as the forerunner of a modern school of philosophical historians.

The real heirs of Joachim, however, were the Spiritual Franciscans, who were yet wise enough to avoid the exaggerations of Gerardo, and never identified the writings of the Abbot of Flora with the Eternal Gospel. The opinions of this circle cannot perhaps be taken as homogeneous, for its members attached many shades of meaning to the idea of the new age, the more moderate believing that its chief outcome would be the triumph of their own party and the reformation of the order they loved so well. The extremists went further and plunged into the vortex of apocalyptic speculations, giving graphic descriptions of the conflict with Antichrist, and entering into details concerning the age of peace and love which would come into being as the result of his fall. The pernicious results of their predilection for these eschatological conceptions have been discussed in the previous chapter, and the different degrees of significance attached to these opinions will be developed in more detail in the chapters devoted to Clareno, Olivi, and Ubertino da Casale. Yet, on the other hand, it is doubtful whether the Spiritual party could ever have endured so valiantly the persecutions and ridicule to which they were subjected by their opponents without the certain conviction of the ultimate triumph of their ideals, and the equally firm belief that they them-

---

[1] *Acta Sanctorum* (May 29), tom vii. pp. 87-143.

[2] *Sämtliche Werke*, ii. 4, pp. 298-344. Schelling acknowledges his debt to Joachim as the originator of his theory (*ibid.* p. 298, note).

[3] This is certainly the case with Grundmann. Cf. *op. cit.* p. 55 s.

selves were the chosen order who should reform the world.   It was Joachimism which inspired those two typical gems of Franciscan thought, the *Arbor Vitae* and the *Historia Septem Tribulationum.*[1] Nor, even among the more orthodox party in the Order was its influence wholly extinct, as can be seen in St. Bonaventura's identification of St. Francis with the angel bearing the seal of the Living God,[2] and in the writings of Bartholomew of Pisa, where a careful collection is made of those prophecies of Joachim which were supposed to foretell the advent and glory of the Franciscan Order.[3]

Perhaps, however, the best picture of the mental and emotional background of the Spiritual party is gained from works which in themselves have little or no literary merit, but yet have value as an expression of the feelings and aspirations of the circle which produced them.   These generally took the form of a series of prophecies reputed to be the work of Joachim, but in reality composed a century or more after his death, when the majority of the events which they foretold had already come to pass.   The most common subjects of these collections were the character and deeds of the various Popes, a visionary element being introduced after the writer had finished describing the events of his own age by speculations concerning the fate of Christendom at the time of the expected coming of Antichrist.   The most famous of these consists of two parts, each containing fifteen revelations, the first group being attributed to Joachim himself, and the second to a fictitious bishop of Marsico called Anselm.[4]   In reality these are two separate works, and almost a century must have elapsed between the times of their composition, for the so-called Revelations of Joachim are certainly a product of the second half of the fourteenth century.[5]   The

---

[1] The whole plan of the chronicle is based on Joachim's theory of the division of each great age into seven smaller periods.   Cf. Ehrle, *A.L.K.G.* ii. 119.

[2] Prologue to " Legenda Maiora " (*Opera Omnia*, viii. p. 504).

[3] *Liber de Conformitate Beati Francisci*, A.F. iv. 33, 53 *s.*, 437 and 563 *s.* Although Proctor of the Order at the Curia, Bartholomew was by no means hostile to the Spirituals, with the exception of Ubertino da Casale.   It is interesting in this connection that there is a mosaic in St. Marco at Venice representing Joachim, St. Dominic, and St. Francis.   Cf. *A.F.H.* xxii. 201-206.

[4] *Revelationes beati Joachim abbatis in monasterio Florensi in Calabria, Vaticinia Anselmi episcopi Marsicani scripta ab eo anno domini 1278, que post obitum Bonifacii pape octavi in lucem data erant Perusii.*   Many copies of these prophecies exist both in manuscript and in early printed editions.   H. Grundmann, in his article " Die Papstprophetien des Mittelalters " (*A.K.* xix. 77-139), has given a critical survey of both works, their sources, their historical background, and their significance both for their contemporaries and later generations.   No bishop of Marsico named Anselm can be traced after 1220 (*ibid.* p. 93).

[5] It was possibly produced in its final form in Florence just before the Great Schism, and was the work of the Fraticelli (pp. 113-17).   Cf. *infra*, p. 216.

Vaticinia Anselmi, described in the title as being written secretly about 1278, but not given to the world until after the death of Boniface VIII., is what concerns us here. With the exception of the first prophecy, a vigorous tirade against the covetousness and nepotism of Nicholas III., which vividly recalls the famous passage on the same subject in the *Inferno,*[1] it proves on closer examination to be a Latin adaptation of the Leo-Oracle, a collection of Byzantine prophecies relating to the future of the Eastern Empire, and popularly attributed to the Emperor Leo the Wise.[2] The translator has simply applied these in a somewhat different order to the Popes of his own period, and even the rude pictures, through which he has striven to make his meaning clearer to his readers, are in many cases the same as in the Greek version with the addition of a figure representing a Pope. It is, however, possible to trace the line of Popes as far as Boniface VIII., and the title of the extract referring to Celestine V. is an exact indication of the sympathies of the writer.[3] This almost solves the question of authorship, for in 1304 Fra Liberato, the leader of a group of Spirituals, who had fled to Greece during the early years of the pontificate of Boniface VIII., was living in the neighbourhood of Perugia with some of his followers, hoping to secure a vindication of his orthodoxy at the hands of Benedict XI.,[4] and it is therefore probable that the book was the work of a member of this circle.[5]

---

[1]   " E veramente fui figliuol dell' orsa,
         Cupido sì, per avanzar gli orsatti."

                                            Inferno, xix. 70-71.
The title of the prophecy in the *Vaticinia* runs as follows : *Genus nequam ursa catulos pascens.* Dante was certainly in Perugia during the summer of 1304, when the book is supposed to have appeared.

[2] Grundmann (*A.K.* xix. p. 91). I verified his conclusions by comparing the papal prophecies with a seventeenth-century Latin translation of the Leo-Oracle and decided that they were substantially correct.

[3] Prophecy 21. *Elatio, paupertas, obedientia, castitas, temperantia, castrimanzia et ypocritarum destructio* (*A.K.* xix. p. 91, note 1).

[4] *A.L.K.G.* i. 530; ii. 319. Cf. *infra,* p. 59.

[5] Grundmann (*A.K.* xix. p. 100), to my mind without sufficient proof, attributes the authorship of the book definitely to Liberato. He considers that Angelo da Clareno was not completely accurate in his *Epistola Excusatoria* when he declared that in their Grecian refuge the Spirituals had used the accustomed prayers for the Church and Pope (*A.L.K.G.* i. 527). If this is so, it is somewhat curious that he should have repeated his former statement in his " Historia Septem Tribulationum ", written for the benefit of his own followers, and not as vindication of his orthodoxy in the eyes of John XXII. (cf. *ibid.* ii. 315 *s.*). Moreover, if Liberato and his followers doubted the validity of Boniface's election why did they return from a comparatively safe asylum in order to submit themselves to his authority. Besides, it would have been the height of folly for their leader to produce such a work as the *Vaticinia Anselmi* at a time when all the hopes of the little community were centred on the recognition of its position by the Church (cf. *infra,* p. 59). My own

After Boniface VIII. the Popes described are purely fictitious personalities, but the conception of the " angelic pastors " is of especial interest as showing the source through which the old Greek belief in the return to earth of a former righteous ruler entered into the apocalyptic speculations of the Spirituals, to become one of the chief features in their schemes for the regeneration of the world, and to be handed on in almost its original form to the Fraticelli.[1] The *Vaticinia Anselmi* seems speedily to have become known outside the author's own circle. It was read by Délicieux and the Provençal Spirituals,[2] and the bitter diatribe against Nicholas III. was known not only to Dante but to the Dominican chronicler, Pippin of Bologna,[3] who was perhaps a stranger to the fierce and uncontrollable indignation which gave it birth. It became the inspiration and model of works of a similar character, such as the Liber de Flore and the Horoscopus, where the writer is described as a certain Rhabanus Anglicus,[4] an error repeated by Telesphorus of Cosenza.[5] Probably it is the treatise mentioned in a fourteenth-century English pamphlet, entitled " The Last Age

---

belief is that the book was written by one of Liberato's companions, perhaps the man whom Ubertino da Casale met at Perugia, to whom he was indebted for the information that the number of the beast in the Apocalypse spelt in Greek letters Benedicti, the Christian name of Boniface VIII., for it is very probable that Angelo da Clareno was not the only one of the little band who knew Greek (*A.V.* lib. v. cap. viii. f. 4 *r.a* ; cf. *infra*, p. 139). Previously, in spite of certain chronological difficulties, Ubertino's informant was held to have been Angelo himself, who was, however, not in Perugia until the following year, when Ubertino was in exile at La Verna.

[1] Although the idea of the " papa angelicus " was known to Roger Bacon (*Op. Minus*, ed. Brewer, p. 86), it played no part in the apocalyptic speculations of Olivi. Ubertino da Casale (*A.V.* lib. v. cap. viii. 5 *r.b*) foretold the coming of a righteous pontiff, but the conception of a series of angelic pastors only became common among the Zealots at the beginning of the fourteenth century.

[2] *A.F.H.* xvii. p. 332, note 3. Cf. Grundmann, *A.K.* xix. p. 108. According to Grundmann, the poorness of the early manuscripts is a sign of their having been the property of the Spiritual Franciscans. The only exception is the fine Codex Vaticanus 3819, which he believes to have belonged to the Colonna family (*op. cit.* pp. 102-106). Certainly the Bodleian MS. (Douce, S. 11, Nr. 88, f. 140 *r.*-147 *r.*) bears out his conclusions, both in the quality of the parchment and writing and in the rudeness of the illustrations. The text differs somewhat from the printed version, and, except in the case of Nicholas III., the popes are not named.

[3] Muratori, *Scriptores Rerum Italicarum*, ix. p. 724 *s.*

[4] " Nam ista (Liber de Flore) et etiam illa, que Horoscopus intitulatur, inter Bonifacium et pastorem Angelicum solum unum pontificem ponere videntur; illa tamen, que Rabano attribuitur (Vaticinia Anselmi) duos intermedios attribuitur." Marginal Gloss to f. 98 *r.* Cf. Grundmann, *H.J.* xlix. p. 40. The Horoscopus is in reality merely an astrological interpretation of the *Vaticinia* (Grundmann, *A.K.* xix. p. 107).

[5] *Ibid.* p. 109.

of the Church ", and formerly wrongly described as a late work of Wyclif, as "Joachim's book on the sayings of the Popes ".[1] In the next century, after it was joined to the so-called revelation of Joachim,[2] possibly it was even more widely read, for its vagueness made it possible to give a contemporary significance to the prophecies by applying them to the Popes of the Great Schism and their successors.[3] The Humanists of the early Renaissance appear to have considered it worthy of study,[4] and numerous printed editions exist under the title of the *Liber de Summis Pontificibus* to show its popularity in the sixteenth and seventeenth centuries.[5] In this form it was known both to Luther and Melancthon, and was used both by Protestant and Catholic writers for purposes of propaganda.[6] The modern age, with its highly developed critical faculty, finds it almost impossible to believe that the cultivated sceptics of the Renaissance could have attached so much significance to a work of so little literary merit or originality.[7]

---

[1] *A.K.* xix. p. 108.

[2] Both sets of prophecies are found in separate MSS. until the end of the fourteenth century. Cf. *ibid.* pp. 102-106 and 124. The ascription of the second series to Anselm, Bishop of Marsico, which appears for the first time after the union of the two collections, can be explained by the fact that the Fraticelli were especially flourishing in that region during the middle and latter part of the century. *Ibid.* p. 126. Cf. also *A.L.K.G.* iv. 95-104, and *infra,* p. 216.

[3] *A.K.* xix. 126.   [4] *Ibid.* 133 *s.*

[5] For the numerous early printed versions cf. Grundmann, *Joachim von Floris,* p. 196 *s.* The best of these is probably that of Paschalinus Regiselmus (Venice, 1589), which afterwards became the standard one and was translated into Italian about the middle of the next century. The "Prophetiae Satyricae", given in the *Corpus Historicum Medii Aevi* (1723), ii. 1845-48, is based on a different rendering, in which the second set of prophecies are not ascribed to Anselm, Bishop of Marsico, for in his Introduction (p. xiv) Eccard mentions that they were sometimes attributed to Malachi, a twelfth-century bishop of Armagh. The *Liber de Summis Pontificibus* was probably the model for somewhat similar collections of prophecies relating to contemporary Popes, a form of literature which was very popular in the sixteenth and seventeenth centuries, and especially at the time of the elections of Urban VII. and Gregory XIV. (1590), for the sudden death of the former, twelve days after his elevation to the papal throne, greatly disturbed men's minds (*A.K.* xix. p. 138).

[6] *A.K.* xix. 136. A commentary upon it was written by Paracelsus, in answer to which a new edition appeared at Cologne in 1570, with a gloss by no less a person than Paolo della Scala, Marquis of Verona. His text and woodcuts correspond almost exactly with those of Regiselmus, but he applies Prophecy XXIII. to the Council of Basle, and XXV., with more justice, to the fall of Constantinople. The last woodcut depicts Luther and Melancthon dressed as monks, the former carrying a miserable-looking devil, greatly resembling a chicken, on his back.

[7] An illustration of the popularity of such prophecies is afforded by a sixteenth-century MS. in the Bodleian, once the property of Archbishop Laud (Laud Misc. 588), which contains both collections of prophecies as well as much similar matter. It is obviously a kind of notebook used by some private individual for transcribing any remarkable revelations which were brought to his

A far more interesting, though hitherto almost unknown, composition is another treatise attributed to Joachim, the so-called "Liber de Flore, de summis pontificibus ab Innocentio quarto usque ad Anti-Christum".[1] Like most works of the same character it is both visionary and historical, for until the end of the pontificate of Boniface VIII. the writer is certainly dealing with matters well known to himself, and it is only afterwards that he plunges into the depths of eschatological speculation. The book consists of a text and a commentary, and was probably written in its present form about the end of 1304 or the beginning of 1305, for it is certainly later than the *Vaticinia Anselmi*, with which its writer is obviously acquainted.[2] There are also allusions to other well-known Joachimite works, such as the prophecies of Merlin and the Erythraean Sybil,[3] and a marginal note, perhaps added at a later date, gives a reference to a curious but very popular work, the Horoscopus, in which astrology is used in the service of the apocalyptic theories of the age.[4] The Liber de Flore is supposed to contain the revelations vouchsafed to an individual described as " the anointed one ", details of whose life, as given in the commentary, correspond very closely with certain incidents in the history of Arnold of Villanova.[5] The earlier part is concerned mainly with the history of the papacy and its connection with the decay of the Franciscan Order. Unlike the more moderate members of his party, the author regarded all papal interpretations of the rule as a violation of the wishes of St. Francis. Gregory IX. was in his eyes not the honoured friend and protector of the Saint of Assisi but the Pope, who, by his

notice. There are several curious diagrams taken from contemporary, or nearly contemporary, prophecies referring to various Popes, and he has even troubled to cut out and paste in illustrations from other books. Grundmann (*A.K.* xix. p. 77) believes that " the book of the prophecies of Joachim the Calabrian abbot concerning the popes", which Montaigne so much desired to possess (*Essais*, i. 11), was none other than the celebrated *Liber*.

[1] Grundmann gives a full and critical description of this treatise and certain extracts from the text in an article entitled " Liber de Flore, eine Schrift der Franziskaner Spiritualen aus dem Anfang des 14. Jahrhunderts ", published in *H.J.* 49, pp. 33-91.

[2] As in the Leo-Oracle Martin IV. is first called a man of blood. Later the writer shows his own feeling by declaring that he was " melior corde quam aspectu " and " bona fide procedat, non astute " (p. 66). Cf. also marginal note to f. 98 *r*. (p. 40) for reference to the " Pastor Angelicus ".

[3] F. 86 *r*. " Merlinus in libro regum."
F. 97 *r*. " Erithrea dicit statim in MCCC. anno superna gloria in fideli populo condescendet."
The latter is probably the treatise in which Angelo da Clareno found foretold the misfortunes of Celestine V. (*A.L.K.G.* ii. 289 ; *H.J.* 49, pp. 74-76).

[4] Probably later than Liber de Flore, since it is cited only in a marginal note to f. 98 *r*. (p. 40).

[5] F. 95 *r*., and f. 102 *r*.-103 *r*. (P. 87 *s*.) Cf. *ibid.* p. 59 *s*.

decretal " Quo elongati ",[1] had taken the first step towards the destruction of the Franciscan ideal,[2] and he writes in much the same strain of Nicholas III., the promulgator of " Exiit qui seminat ".[3] True to the literary conventions of the age, he makes great use of animals as symbols of the leading personalities of the period, but apart from this his attitude towards the mid-thirteenth-century Popes is remarkably tolerant, especially when the narrow but exalted outlook of his particular circle is taken into consideration. Often, as in the case of Martin IV., he shows an unexpected power of characterisation, and an extraordinary degree of understanding of the difficulties which the papacy was called upon to face. He fully recognised the many virtues of Gregory X. in spite of his being the innocent cause of many of the sufferings of his party.[4] In politics he was obviously himself an adherent of the house of Anjou, but could yet be moved by the piteous end of the Hohen-staufen dynasty, and could regard its destruction as a disaster for the Church, since it raised her to the summit of world prosperity.[5] The elevation to the papacy of the Franciscan Nicholas IV. was no cause for rejoicing, for it was a betrayal of the ideals of his Order, and the loss of the Holy Land was to be attributed to an act of divine vengeance for his sins.[6] He writes with tender admiration of Celestine V., " the angelic pastor of whom the world was unworthy ", in every way a complete contrast to his successor, the usurper Boniface VIII.,[7] who is described elsewhere as " the great dragon ".[8] His intimate knowledge of the different stages in the quarrel between his enemy and the Colonna makes it possible that, like Jacopone da Todi, he was an open adherent of the latter and shared in the vicissitudes of their fortunes.[9] He even goes so far as to suggest that the robbery of the papal treasury at Anagni by Stefano Colonna was a proof of God's detestation of the worldliness and luxury of the Church,[10] and it is significant that he regarded the year 1298 as the beginning of better things.[11] He also refers to the proceedings of Philip IV. and the French lawyers against Boniface VIII.,[12] but makes a somewhat veiled

---

[1] *B.F.* i. p. 68 *s.* Cf. *supra*, p. 3.

[2] In the Liber de Flore Gregory IX. is described as " maximus amplexator rerum temporalium " (*H.J.* 49, p. 46).

[3] *B.F.* iii. p. 404 *s.* Cf. *supra*, p. 9 *s.* With reference to Nicholas III. the author of the Liber de Flore quotes an old prophecy of the Tiburtine Sybil, " Ursa omnium malorum inceptrix " (*H.J.* 49, p. 65).

[4] *Ibid.* p. 50.   [5] *Ibid.* p. 49.   [6] *Ibid.* p. 66.

[7] *Ibid.* p. 57. Boniface is described as *perversus, obliquus, pseudo, impius, iniquus,* while the adjectives applied to his predecessor are *simplex, benignus, sanctus, pius, rectus, verus* (*ibid.* p. 67).   [8] F. 95 *v.* (p. 90).

[9] F. 90 *v.*; 92 *r.*-93 *r.* (pp. 57 and 81-84).   [10] F. 92 *v.* (p. 82). Cf. p. 57.

[11] F. 93 *r.* (p. 84). Cf. p. 58.   [12] *Ibid.*

allusion to his terrible death.[1] Save for the fact that only one Pope is predicted as coming between Boniface and the first angelic pastor there is no mention of Benedict XI.[2]

Of even more burning interest to the writer were the fortunes of his own Order. His knowledge of the controversy which arose in the March of Ancona about the obligation of the vow of complete poverty as the result of a rumour respecting the decrees of the Council of Lyons,[3] as well as of the subsequent adventures of Liberato and his companions in Armenia, Cyprus, and Greece, shows his close connection with their circle.[4] Like Angelo da Clareno he divided the order into four classes, the first being the small number of hopelessly relaxed, whose fierce persecution of the Zealots was due to the fear that their strictures would draw attention to their own shortcomings. The bulk of the Order was endeavouring conscientiously to keep its vows, but was prevented through cowardice from siding openly with the Spirituals, and in their final triumph the latter would overcome the sluggishness and inertia of this body by infusing into its members a measure of their own heroic spirit. The fourth class was formed of those who had given up the struggle to observe the threefold vow to the letter and had deserted the order in despair, joining themselves to the followers of Fra Dolcino and other heretical sects.[5] Like the majority of his circle, the writer attached great importance to the " usus pauper ",[6] and felt an especial veneration for Olivi, who like a second Hector had fought in vain to save his Order, and whose prophecies of coming doom had been unheeded.[7] The writer also gives a description of the misfortunes of his comrades in southern France, a matter on which he is excellently informed, even mentioning the fate of Jean de Picquigny, Vidame of Amiens, who as royal reformer in Languedoc had aided Délicièux in his campaign against the Dominican inquisitors, and had died excommunicate as an example of ecclesiastical tyranny.[8] The full vials of his wrath are poured on the two Franciscan cardinals,

---

[1] " Facturus erat mala sed recepturus iniqua: necesse est de calice bibere quem in aliena siti potavit; eodem (MS. idem) gladio, quo innoxum interfecit, eodem gladio perimetur et languidus dolore plenus descendet ad infernos " (f. 94 v. Cf. p. 67, n. 84).

[2] H.J. 49, p. 67 s.   [3] F. 86 r., p. 51.

[4] F. 94 v.-95 r. (p. 53, n. 45). F. 101 r. (ibid. n. 46). It is interesting that he mentions women as accompanying Liberato and his followers on their travels.

[5] Liber de Flore (f. 91 v., pp. 80-81). Like Alexander of Bexhövede (cf. supra, p. 28), he compares the Franciscan Order with a dove, a metaphor adopted by later writers.

[6] F. 87 v. and 99 v. (p. 52, notes 41, 42, and 43).

[7] F. 103 v. (p. 55, n. 50).

[8] F. 96 r. (p. 91). Cf. p. 64 and A.F.H. xvii. pp. 205 and 214.

Gentile de Montefiore and John of Murrovalle. The former thought only of his own advancement and of the means by which he might minister to his own material comfort, and it was for these reasons that he had abandoned the study of divine things for secular learning, and permitted every mitigation of the rule which allowed him to sink himself further in the sea of worldly delights.[1] No fitter epithet than the " dragonolet " [2] could be found to describe John of Murrovalle, the nominee and agent of Boniface VIII., and one who, both before and after his elevation to the cardinalate, had not ceased to show his fierce hostility to the Zealots, for he was the faithful follower in all things of his patron and master.[3] The attitude of the writer towards his opponents is a further sign of his adherence to the more extreme section of the Spiritual party.

In the second part of the treatise its author dwells with much detail upon his hopes and dreams for the regeneration of the Church.[4] These are developed with the greater elaboration because of his firm belief that they would soon become a reality. His plans did not involve the destruction of the ecclesiastical system of his own day, for he was fully convinced of its divine origin, and believed that all its defects were due to the wickedness of the present occupiers of the papal throne.[5] It was through a change in the characters of Christ's earthly representatives that reform would be brought about, and he gives a full description of the personalities and achievements of the four angelic Popes [6] through whose influence a period of peace and holiness would dawn for the whole world. The first of these, a poor and aged monk, chosen through a divine revelation, would heal the divisions

---

[1] Grundmann (*H.J.* 49, p. 62) believes that Arnold of Villanova's unfavourable comments on the two cardinals in the " Rahonament " (cf. *supra*, p. 134) were perhaps derived from the Liber de Flore. The commentary interprets the passages describing the two Franciscan cardinals as applying to the two Popes who were to rule between the death of Boniface VIII. and the coming of the first " angelic pastor " (f. 98 *v*. Cf. *H.J.*, p. 64, *n*. 76). In the Arras manuscript there is a marginal gloss to the passage concerning John of Murrovalle (f. 95 *r*.) which obviously confuses him with John XXII. (p. 89, *n*. 34). Cf. p. 77.

[2] " Primum, quod quidam draconcius inter electos astucia diabolica communitus vexabit. . . ." F. 95 *r*. (p. 89).

[3] Commentary, f. 95 *v*. (p. 90).

[4] F. 97 *r*.-99 *v*. and 104 *r*.-106 *v*.

[5] " Non dico Sancte matri ecclesie in aliquo derogari nec eius verus decor dicitur in aliquo dedecorari; quia decor et decus matris ecclesie ille summus noscitur Jesus Christus; sed eius vicarius non Christi doctrinam sequetur ut convenit." F. 95 *r*.-*v*. (p. 90) ; cf. *H.J.* 49, p. 68.

[6] According to Grundmann it is not quite clear whether the writer believed that the first angel Pope would be the third successor of Boniface VIII., or whether Benedict IX. would be followed by a series of four " ideal Popes ", after whom would come the first angelic pastor (p. 69).

between the different Italian states and cause the King of France to be elected as Emperor. This new ruler would lead an army to the walls of Byzantium and thus would heal the schism between East and West, after which the Emperor would lead his victorious troops to Jerusalem, where, touched by the divine grace, he would lay aside his earthly grandeur to put on the poor habit of a Franciscan friar. Before his death the Pope would be renowned among the heathen, and afterwards his many miracles would be a vindication of his holiness.[1] His successor, a Frenchman, would bring about a reconciliation between Germany and his native land, and would die on an island when returning from a pilgrimage to Palestine. Half a year later an Italian Spiritual would be chosen in his place, whose task would be the regeneration of his own order and a restoration of the wealth of the Church to its lawful possessors, the poor. The conversion of the Saracens and the Jews would be the principal event of his pontificate. The last angel Pope, by race a Gascon, would be met in the Holy Land by the two pagan giants, Gog and Magog, with palms in their hands and with songs of rejoicing. Their act of homage was a symbol of the submission of the heathen to the Vicar of Christ. After this triumph the loosing of the devil and the speedy destruction of things temporal would be made known by the coming of the greater Antichrist.[2] The importance attached to the angel Popes is shown by their incorporation into the works of John of Rupescissa and the later apocalyptic writers of the century.[3] Certain notes in the Arras manuscript of the Liber de Flore show that its prophecies inspired a certain amount of interest even among orthodox writers at the time of the Great Schism,[4] nor does it seem to have been unknown to Rienzi[5] and Telesphorus of Cosenza.[6] No printed version was made at the Renaissance, though two seventeenth-century manuscripts are still extant which show that

---

[1] Liber de Flore, f. 98 v.; H.J. 49, pp. 70-73.

[2] H.J. 49, p. 74.

[3] Cf. infra, p. 47. The belief in a " papa angelicus " was very prevalent among the Fraticelli. One of their mid-fourteenth-century manifestoes gives a description of a reputed work of Conrad of Offida, foretelling the deeds of various Popes (Tocco, S.F. 512 s.). On the strength of a reference to the measures taken by John XXII. against the Franciscan Order, Grundmann (H.J. 49, pp. 77-80) would identify this with the Liber de Flore but rightly rejects its ascription to Conrad of Offida, who was not only a member of the more moderate section of the Zealots, but apparently a personal friend of John of Murrovalle. Cf. A.L.K.G. ii. 312.

[4] This is the only fourteenth-century MS. extant and was used by Grundmann as the basis of his text. For a description of it, cf. H.J. 49, p. 38 s.

[5] Quoted by Rienzi in his letter of August 1350 to Charles IV. Ibid. p. 76, n. 111A. Cf. Puir Burdach, op. cit., Letter 58, pp. 304 and 309 s.

[6] H.J. 49, p. 36.

it was not altogether forgotten.[1] Perhaps its sole claim to be rescued from oblivion lies in its interest to the historian as a typical product of the circle from which it emanated, and an excellent example of the peculiar mental and emotional outlook of a certain section of the Franciscan Order.[2]

Another treatise which throws a vivid light on the hopes and aspirations of the Zealots is the *Vade Mecum in Tribulationem* of the French Franciscan " Johannes de Rupescissa ",[3] who, writing from his prison in Avignon in 1356, gave expression to all the bitterness of his party and the unquenchable belief in the ultimate triumph of their ideals. His powerful imagination had been quickened by the sight of the devastation of France during the Hundred Years' War and the horrors of the Black Death, and he had already established his reputation as a prophet in connection with these disasters. According to John, the iniquity and corruption of the Church would speedily become so intolerable that the laity would rise up against her and strip her of her ill-gotten gains, and restore her to a state of Evangelical Poverty.[4] The flight of the Pope and his cardinals from Avignon would mark the beginning of the regeneration of the Church.[5] In 1356 Antichrist would arise in the East, perhaps in Jerusalem itself, and his coming would be heralded by earthquakes and other portents.[6] He would be able to subjugate Hungary and Poland and parts of Italy and Germany to his power.[7] Meanwhile, in the west, another Antichrist would have arisen in the form of a heretical emperor, resembling Nero in wickedness.[8] He would be finally overthrown by a holy Pope and a saintly cardinal belonging to the Franciscan Order, and after his fall the empire would be reformed under the King of France, the Jews and Moslems would be converted, and the power of the Church would extend from sea to sea.[9] Even the Friars Minor, who had been responsible for all the former iniquities of the world, would be included in the general regeneration.[10] The new age was to last for a thousand years, but men would gradually return to their former ways, and the forces of evil would finally again be loosed under the leadership of God and Magog, after which would come the end of things temporal.[11] It is surprising that John's treatise was written at the

---

[1] Codices Vallicellanae (Rome), J. 32 and J. 33. *H.J.* 49, p. 37.

[2] This is also the verdict of Grundmann (*ibid.* p. 76).

[3] Printed in *Fasc. Rerum Expetend.* ii. pp. 494-508.

[4] *Ibid.* pp. 494, 495, and 499.

[5] *Ibid.* p. 499. [6] *Ibid.*

[7] *Vade Mecum*, p. 500. [8] *Ibid.*

[9] *Ibid.* p. 501 *et seq.* Cf. *supra*, pp. 45, 46, for earlier prophecies concerning the angel Pope. [10] *Ibid.* 503

[11] *Ibid.* pp. 506-507. The year of the coming of Gog and Magog was 2365.

command of a cardinal.[1]   Like most of the Joachimite writings, it is merely an application of the earlier theories to the events of his own age, and it is chiefly important as the last work of its kind produced by a member of the Franciscan Order.   It was among the Fraticelli in Italy and the Provençal Béguins that the dream of a newer and better age survived, carrying with it a fierce hatred of the corruptions of the Church and the luxury and pride of her rulers.[2]   In spite of the distortions due to ignorance and fanaticism, it can be truly said that these humble and obscure men were the heirs of the apocalyptic dreams of the Franciscan Spirituals.

It is a far cry from the crude and fantastic visions of such men as Johannes de Rupescissa and the author of the Liber de Flore to the great poem which will always be regarded as the highest expression of the genius of the Middle Ages, yet all in varying degrees are the fruit of the Joachimite ideal.   Men may differ as to the contribution of the Abbot of Flora to the thought of the *Divine Comedy*, but he and Dante were inspired by the same vision of a world working in harmony with the forces of love which moved the sun and the stars, though the poet sought to make his dream a reality through the agency of an earthly monarch.   It must ever be a source of pride to the Franciscan Order that Joachim probably owes his lofty place in the *Paradiso* to Dante's love for that famous book which is perhaps the finest product of the Spiritual movement, the *Arbor Vitae Crucifixae* of Ubertino da Casale.[3]

[1] *Vade Mecum*, p. 496.
[2] Cf. *infra*, pp. 209-58.
[3] Cf. Professor Gardner's essay on Joachim in *Franciscan Essays*, i. p. 67. More detailed works dealing with the connection between Dante and Ubertino da Casale are Umberto Cosmo's " Le mistiche nozze di Frate Francesco con Madonna Povertà " in *Giornale Dantesco*, vi.; Davidsohn, *Geschichte von Florenz*, 2, Pt. ii. pp. 275-78; and Kraus, *Dante, sein Leben und sein Werk*, the last named being especially suggestive. Although Ubertino was certainly in Florence during Dante's early manhood, there is very little evidence to show that they were personally known to each other. To my mind the curt and somewhat derogatory reference to the famous Spiritual in the *Paradiso* seems rather to point in the contrary direction. This and kindred questions are more fully dealt with in Chapter V.

CHAPTER III

ANGELO DA CLARENO

THE story of the sufferings of the Zealots and their fierce loyalty to the ideals of the " poverello " will live for ever in the " Chronicle of the Seven Tribulations ",[1] written by one who took an active share in the doings of his party, and thus was well fitted to record their lofty aspirations and bitter and continual disappointments. Angelo begins his book with the closing years of the life of St. Francis and ends it with the beginnings of the quarrel between the Order and John XXII. Thus, his account is concerned mainly with the first century of Franciscan history, and we meet many familiar figures in its pages. We see the founder himself, wearied out with his hopeless struggle to save his dream from the shackles of officialdom and secular learning, which were eventually almost to stifle it, and haunted with gloomy forebodings concerning the future. By his side hovers the sinister shadow of Elias of Cortona, the destroyer of his work, determined to model the Order after his own plan, and willing to use any weapons, whether of craft or violence, to carry out his aims. His successor, Crescenzio of Jesi, is more slightly drawn, as befits his weaker personality,[2] and then in contrast with him comes the portrait of John of Parma, perhaps less human and attractive than in Salimbene, but nevertheless a majestic figure in his lonely and heroic struggle for the preservation of the true spirit of St. Francis against the elements of decay and corruption which were slowly destroying it. We follow him on his lonely road towards the little hermitage of Greccio, an old man borne down by the forces of evil, which had proved too strong for him, and in his heart all the bitterness of failure. Then the scene shifts to Provence, and we are shown the picture of " the man of God ", Olivi, whom Angelo probably never saw but whom he loved so well. Rougher and less finished studies are given of the friends and disciples of the great Spiritual leader, Ubertino of Casale, and the saintly lay brother, Conrad of Offida. In fact, as we wander through this gallery devoted to portraits of Lady Poverty's most ardent lovers there is only one who is missing, namely, Angelo himself. The

---

[1] Unfortunately the only complete edition of the " Historia Septem Tribulationum " is in the second volume of Doellinger's *Beiträge zu Sektengeschichte des Mittelalters*, ii. pp. 417-526. A far better version, however, of the later part is contained in *A.L.K.G.* ii. pp. 125-55, 256-327. Professor Tocco has edited the first two tribulations in the *Rendiconti della Reale Accademia dei Lincei* of 1908.

[2] There were two generals, Angelo of Pisa, 1239-40, and Haymo of Faversham, 1240-44, between Elias and Crescenzio, but Angelo hardly mentions them. His description of the latter as " a disciple of Elias in feeling and mode of life " is hardly just. Cf. *A.L.K.G.* ii. 256.

author of the "Historia Septem Tribulationum" possessed a modesty which was perhaps rarer in the Middle Ages than it is to-day, and which sprang from a total lack of egoism. To his mind his own deeds in the service of her he loved so faithfully were as nothing compared with those of her other suitors. Fortunately in the "Epistola Excusatoria",[1] written to justify himself and his followers in the eyes of John XXII., he is forced to relate more of the story of his own life ; yet even in this, his "Apologia pro vita sua", it is the sufferings of others and not his own upon which he dwells. It is this humility which lends a gracious charm to the somewhat austere figure of this leader of the Zealots and arouses our interest, for we long to know more about a man who was so reticent as to his own deeds. Yet, it is with reverent fingers and a feeling of awe that we strive to remove the curtain, and gaze upon the figure of one who would always have been desirous of avoiding the prying eye of future generations.

So little has Angelo told us about his early life that, until recently, even his name and birthplace were matters of uncertainty. Now, through the testimony of the Inquisition records [2] and of a contemporary chronicle [3] it has been established that during his early days in the Order he was known as Peter of Fossombrone, and only assumed the name of Angelo after his separation from the main body of the Franciscans. As many writers of the fourteenth century and later [4] call him Angelo of Cingoli, it is generally supposed that he was born at Fossombrone, in the March of Ancona, and became a novice in the Franciscan convent at Cingoli in 1270. As his death did not take place till 1337 he was probably not very old when he took this momentous step. Possibly he was opposed by his family, for in certain of his letters he writes with great bitterness of the carnal love which leads parents to put

---

[1] Edited by Cardinal Ehrle in the first volume of *A.L.K.G.*, pp. 521-33. In his introduction he gives a very sympathetic account of Angelo.

[2] *A.L.K.G.* iv. p. 9. "Frater Angelus Clarani de Fossabruno, qui alias fuit vocatus frater Petrus de Fossabruno."

[3] Chronicle of Paulinus Veneti, O.F.M., Bp. of Puteoli (1324-44), 1294: "Petrus de Macerata et Petrus de Forosinfronio apostate fuerunt Ordinis Minorum et heretici. . . . Et mutaverunt illi duo sibi nomina, primus vocavit se Liberatum, secundus Angelum, quia angelicas se fingebat revelationes habere ". The whole passage is quoted by Golubovich in *Biblioteca bio-bibliografica della Terra Santa*, ii. p. 80, and this extract in Father Oliger's Introduction to Angelo's Commentary on the Rule, p. xxi, *n.* 1. Before this discovery was made Angelo's authorship of the "Historia Septem Tribulationum" was sometimes doubted on the ground that in it certain actions were ascribed to Peter which in the "Epistola Excusatoria" were said to have been performed by Angelo himself.

[4] Bartolommeo di Pisa. *Liber de Conformitate*, "Locum de Cingulo, in quo fuit ille predicator insignis frater Angelus" (*A.F.* iv. p. 518). Cf. also Mariano of Florence, *A.F.H.* i. 469-70.

obstacles in the way of their children's true advancement.[1] His sympathies must soon have drawn him towards the stricter party in the Franciscan Order, for his native province was one of the chief centres of the Zealots, whose strongholds were to be found in the smaller convents or hermitages hidden among the folds of the Apennines rather than in the more sumptuous friaries generally built in the midst of the populous towns. Moreover, the nearness of Assisi brought the brothers into close relationship with the surviving companions of St. Francis, certain of whom the young novice appears to have met and talked with.[2] Perhaps he even saw Brother Leo, for the former secretary [3] and confidant of the seraphic father did not die till 1271. We can imagine that the old stories of the " poverello " and the bitter complaints about the degeneracy of the present state of the Order sank into attentive ears. It may have been from these men, many of whom despite their religious zeal were simple and unlettered, that Angelo derived his marked distaste for secular learning. In many places he writes with great bitterness of " the evil pursuit of the arts of Aristotle and of the sweet seductions of Plato's eloquence comparable only with the plagues of Egypt for the disasters which they had brought upon the Church ".[4] We do not know if he himself had been tempted by the charms of these " sirens ", but his writings show few traces of scholasticism, though they bear witness to a surprising knowledge of the fathers of the Church. He was certainly in deacon's orders,[5] but was prevented from attaining to the dignity of the priesthood by his unwillingness to assume the responsibility of hearing confessions.[6] It was probably at this time that Angelo made the acquaintance of the saintly hermit, Peter of Murrone, afterwards Pope Celestine V., who was then living in the region watered by the river Chiaro which lies between Ascoli and the

---

[1] Codex Magliabecchiana, xxxix, *n.* 75, 147 *r.* In a letter to two novices (f. 31 *r.*) he gives a quotation from St. Jerome's epistle to Heliodorus (Migne, *P.L.* xx. 348), showing the violent opposition which must be expected from parents.

[2] " Vidi ego fratrem qui audivit eum Bononie predicantem " (Tocco, *op. cit.* 42).

[3] Secretary is a bad translation, for the " socius " of the General of an Order was in a far more independent and confidential position than the modern secretary. In monastic orders he was often appointed by the brothers, and was not responsible to his master.

[4] *A.L.K.G.* ii. 265 : " aut Aristotelis artium malam industriam vel Platonis eloquencie dulcem seductionem, qui in ecclesiam nostram male et corrupte introducti sunt tamquam egipciace quedam plage ". Cf. *Expos.*, pp. 210 and 212. The quotation is from St. Gregory Nazianzene (Migne, *P.G.* 36, p. 202).

[5] Codex Magliabecchiana, xxxix, *n.* 75, f. 10 *v.* In the beginning of this letter instead of the usual " Frater Angelus " we have " P. dyaconus ".

[6] *A.L.K.G.* ii. 143 *s.*

Nursian Alps, and began his friendship with his future leader and fellow-sufferer, Peter of Macerata.[1] It seemed possible at this time that his life might have passed in the same peaceful and retired manner as that of his friend and contemporary, Conrad of Offida, who, after enduring a certain amount of persecution and ridicule for his strict adherence to the footsteps of St. Francis, succeeded finally in winning the veneration and love of the Minister-General of the Order and of all with whom he came into contact.[2] Unfortunately, a storm was about to break over the March which was to bring long and bitter tribulation to Angelo and his friends, and finally even to separate them from the Order they loved so faithfully.

During the sessions of the Council of Lyons [3] the fate of the Dominicans and Franciscans, as well as that of the other less powerful mendicant orders suppressed by that assembly, appears to have hung in the balance. It is not surprising, therefore, that wild rumours spread through the different provinces of the Order, and that the future seemed veiled in uncertainty. In the March of Ancona a widespread belief prevailed that the Pope was about to force the two great mendicant orders to hold property in common.[4] The Conventual party, who were powerful in the towns which lay along the sea-board and through the membership of the Superiors of the province, saw their opportunity and declared openly that they were prepared to obey the will of Christ's Vicar in all things. The Zealots, on the other hand, protested passionately against such a breach of the vow of evangelical poverty. So heated were the passions of all concerned that the matter was brought up at the next meeting of the Provincial Chapter in 1274.[5] By this time the subject was merely of academic interest, so that only three of the Zealots, namely, Peter of Macerata, a certain Traymond, and Thomas of Tolentino, who afterwards died a martyr's death in India,[6] clung fiercely to their former opinions. They were imprisoned in distant hermitages,[7] but the following year were again

---

[1] In the " Historia " (*A.L.K.G.* ii. 308) Peter of Macerata " et socius eius " (Angelo) were sent to Celestine because they already knew him. Did Angelo's connection with the districts near the Chiaro, from which he drew his name, belong to this period in his history and not, as Wadding supposed, to a later date? Cf. *Scriptores Ordinis Minorum*, p. 15.

[2] *A.L.K.G.* ii. 312. Even writers belonging to the Conventual party, such as the author of the Chronicle of the 24 Generals, speak of him with reverence (*A.F.* iii. 422-30).   [3] Held in 1274.

[4] *A.L.K.G.* ii. 301 *s*.   [5] *Ibid.* 302.

[6] In 1321. Cf. Wadding, *Annales*, vi. p. 353 (1321), § 1 ; Golubovich, *op. cit.* iii. p. 221; *A.L.K.G.* ii. 303, " Qui nunc in Tana Indie cum sociis palmam martyrii adeptus ". This passage shows that the " Historia Septem Tribulationum " in its present form must be later than 1320.

[7] *Ibid.* 302.

brought before the Provincial Chapter. This time an old and respected friar named Benjamin [1] was able to mediate between the two parties and the Zealots were left in peace for three years. At the end of this period, however, the leaders of the Conventuals, who had been pursuing an active policy in the acquisition of new building sites in the bigger cities, in the acceptance of legacies and the accumulation of books, began to dread the growing influence of the Spirituals.[2] The Provincial Minister and four of his colleagues from the neighbouring provinces held a secret meeting,[3] the result of which was that the three former leaders of the Zealots, together with Angelo and certain other friars,[4] were arrested as schismatics and heretics and condemned to perpetual imprisonment, and deprived of the use of books and of the sacraments.[5] The horror of their imprisonment can best be realised by taking the prison at Assisi as a type of medieval prisons in general. This is sixty feet under the earth,[6] and we read in Angelo's account of the sufferings of himself and his friends that they were fettered to the wall of their cells.[7] Their opponents so dreaded the effects of their example that even the friar who brought them food was strictly forbidden to speak to them. Every week their sentence was read in the chapters of the different convents, and it was known that any brother who made any reflections upon its justice would share the same fate.[8] This did not, however, deter a brave friar named Thomas of Castro Mili from protesting that their punishment " was cruel and unjust, and lacking in the fear of God and in all charity, and displeasing to God and the Saints ". A few months later he died in prison, and his cruel enemies even went so far as to deny his body ecclesiastical burial.[9]

For eleven years the imprisonment of the Zealots lasted without a break, except perhaps for an occasional change of place.[10] In

[1] *A.L.K.G.* ii. 302 *s.*   [2] *Ibid.* ii. 303.   [3] *Ibid.*

[4] Probably they were the same friars who were afterwards sent to Armenia. Besides the three mentioned before there were three others—" Angelo of Tolentino, Marco di Montelupone, and another, Peter (of Fossombrone) ". *A.L.K.G.* ii. 306. Cf. " Epist. Excus." (*ibid.* i. 524).

[5] *A.L.K.G.* ii. 304. Cf. " Epist. Excus." (*ibid.* i. 524).

[6] I owe this interesting fact to the kindness of Father Longpré of the Collegio di San Bonaventura, Quaracchi.

[7] *A.L.K.G.* i. 524; ii. 304.   [8] *Ibid.*

[9] " Ego certus sum, hanc sententiam esse iniquam et iniustam et sine timore dei et caritate factam et deo displicibilem et omnibus sanctis " (*A.L.K.G.* ii. p. 304).

[10] In a letter written to his followers from the papal court, Angelo mentions Ancona, " Forani " Rome, Viterbo, and Assisi as some of his prisons. The passage would seem to imply that he was arrested in Rome and finally imprisoned in Ancona, stopping at the other places on the way, but the reference is too obscure to be accepted with any certainty (*A.L.K.G.* i. 548). Cf. Oliger, Intro. *Expositio*, xxv.

1289, however, the newly elected General, Raymund Gaufridi,[1] held a provincial chapter in the March, during the course of which he held an inquiry into the causes of their imprisonment. When he learned that the sole charge against them was their strict observance of poverty, he exclaimed indignantly, " Would that we ourselves and the whole Order were guilty of such a crime! "[2] and ordered their immediate release. He received them with marked kindness, but realising that to leave them in the March would involve exposing them again to persecution the instant his back was turned, decided to send them to the court of the Pope's new ally, the King of Armenia, who had written asking for the services of friars of good reputation and holy life to instruct his people in the faith of the Roman Church. The missionaries soon won the esteem and affection of the king and his barons, and it was probably through their influence that the former, although still performing the duties of his position, assumed the Franciscan habit.[3] Letters were sent to the General highly commending the work of the friars whom he had sent, and these were read in a Chapter-General held at Paris in 1292, to stifle the complaints of the Conventuals against Gaufridi.[4] The success of their labours in Armenia, however, was not slow in arousing the jealousy of the friars in the province of Syria, and especially of a certain Paul who had been secretary to the Provincial of the March and was now guardian of Acre.[5] They prevailed upon the Provincial minister to write to the king warning him against Zealots as heretics and schismatics. Hayton summoned a council of his barons and the missionaries were able to satisfy him concerning their orthodoxy.[6] The Provincial was afterwards honest enough to withdraw the charge, and summoned Peter of Macerata and Angelo to Cyprus in order that the former might clear the reputation of himself and his followers by preaching before the king and his court. Yet even he was unable to prevent the guardian of Nicosia from detaining

---

[1] Elected at Chapter-General of Assisi. He belonged to a noble Provençal family, and was the first French Minister-General.

[2] *A.L.K.G.* i. 524; ii. 305.

[3] Hayton of Armenia is mentioned by Wadding, who got his information from Marino Sanuto's *Secreta Fidelium Crucis*. Like Godfrey of Bouillon he always refused to use the insignia of his office, preferring to be known as "Brother John ". He succeeded in defeating a rebellion of his brother Senibat, who was aided by the Tartars, but afterwards had to make use of their services himself in order to defeat an invasion of the Saracens (*Annales*, v. p. 324, § x.). Hayton was buried in the church of the convent of the Friars Minor at Sis, the capital of Armenia, founded about the year 1289 by the Franciscan missionary, John of Monte Convino, afterwards Archbishop of Pekin (*B.F.* v. 85, p. 37 (1307)). Cf. Golubovich, *op. cit.* i. p. 339, and Oliger, *op. cit.* p. xxv.

[4] *A.L.K.G.* i. 525; ii. 306.

[5] *Ibid.* i. 525; ii. 307.   [6] *Ibid.*

them as excommunicates and further insulting them by forbidding them to take part in the services held by the brethren, although they were permitted to share their meals.[1] Finding their work hampered in Armenia by the malice of the Syrian friars, the Zealots decided to return to Italy and lay their case before the General. It was thought wiser to separate, so it was arranged that Peter of Macerata and Angelo should seek Gaufridi while the others went back to their native provinces. While the former were passing through the March, sick and weary from their journey, they received a brutal message from Fra Monaldo, the vicar of the Provincial, forbidding them to halt anywhere on their way, and declaring that he would rather receive fornicators in his province than friars such as they.[2]

When the Spirituals reached Italy, widespread enthusiasm had been aroused in their immediate circle by the election of the saintly ascetic, Peter of Murrone, to the papal throne. It seemed therefore good to the General and to the leaders of the stricter party, among whom were Conrad of Offida and Jacopone da Todi, that Peter of Macerata and Angelo, who were already known to the new Pope, should go to him at Aquila and seek his protection for themselves and all who wished to observe the Rule and Testament of St. Francis in their original strictness.[3] Celestine received them gladly and willingly granted their request.[4] He absolved them from the promises of obedience which they had made to their former Superiors, and declared that they were no longer to be called Franciscans but poor hermits serving God in remote places.[5] The Pope appointed Peter of Macerata, or, as he was now to be called, Brother Liberato, as General of the new Order,[6] and placed it under the protection of Cardinal Napoleone Orsini,[7] and of a certain abbot of his own Order to whom he sent letters, instructing him to put certain hermitages in southern Italy at the disposal of the brothers.[8] In fact, the mystic strain so prominent in the beginnings of the Franciscan Order was to receive official recognition, by the separation of those of its members who felt drawn to a contemplative life from the main body who were engaged in the work of securing the welfare of the souls of others and in the

[1] *A.L.K.G.* ii. 307-308.
[2] *Ibid.* Fr. Oliger dates their return about 1294. Cf. *op. cit.* p. xxv. Perhaps this Fra Monaldo was afterwards the Bishop of Città di Castello who died in 1306. Cf. " L' Umbria Seraphica " in *Miscellanea Franciscana,* iii. 122.
[3] *A.L.K.G.* i. 525; ii. 308: "quod ad summum pontificem frater Petrus de Macerata et socius eius accederent, eo quod familiarem eum ante papatum habuissent". In the "Epistola Excusatoria" Angelo uses the 1st person plural.
[4] *Ibid.* 526; ii. 309.   [5] *Ibid.*   [6] *Ibid.*
[7] *Ibid.*   [8] *Ibid.* i. 526.

pursuit of learning. Unfortunately, the hopes of the Zealots were soon crushed by the renunciation of Celestine, which exposed them to the full fury of their enemies. Even before this event took place they had tried to gain possession of the persons of Liberato and Angelo by force of arms.[1] Their position was further endangered by the repeal of all Celestine's decrees by his successor, Boniface VIII. The Spirituals, under the leadership of their new General, resolved therefore to seek safety in flight.[2] They eventually succeeded in reaching Greece, perhaps after a period of imprisonment,[3] and for two years (1295–1297) lived on the island of Trixonia,[4] in the Gulf of Corinth, under the protection of Thomas of Sole,[5] the lord of one of the Latin principalities established after the Fourth Crusade. Even there they were not free from the pursuit of their enemies, who discovered their refuge through the report of certain merchants, and spread rumours among the people of the district that they were Manichaeans and denied the validity of the sacrament of the altar and the claims of the Pope.[6] The neighbouring bishops and feudatories sent spies to the island, who found the brothers holding the usual services of the Church and never omitting the name of the Pope from their prayers.[7] In order to prove the falseness of the slander, they were invited to celebrate Mass before the bishop and his clergy, and after the ceremony a public banquet was held, at which they showed that, unlike the Manichaeans, they had no scruples about the eating of meat.[8] The Conventuals, however, were not yet defeated, and determined to appeal to Boniface VIII.[9] Their petition was supported by the new General, John of Murrovalle,[10] a man of

---

[1] *A.L.K.G.* i. 527; ii. 309.   [2] *Ibid.* i. 527; ii. 310.
[3] Cf. *A.L.K.G.* i. 549. As we stated above, p. 53, *n.* 10, this passage is very vague, and Angelo alludes to no period of imprisonment at this time in either his Chronicle or his " Epistola Excusatoria ". The only evidence which seems to favour the latter is that of Paolino de Venetiis, who declares that they made their escape from Sicily to Greece. Cf. Golubovich, *op. cit.* pp. 80–81 and 96–97.
[4] *A.L.K.G.* i. 527; ii. 313. Cardinal Ehrle suggests Trixonia as the island in question and there is no occasion for doubting his hypothesis. Cf. *ibid.*, *n.* A.
[5] *Ibid.* ii. 316. Cf. p. 313, *n.* A. Salona or Sole belonged to the family of de Stromoncourt.
[6] *Ibid.* i. 527; ii. 314 *s.* According to the " Epistola Excusatoria " they enjoyed two years of peace before their refuge was discovered by their enemies.   [7] *Ibid.*
[8] *Ibid.*   [9] *Ibid.* i. 528; ii. 315.
[10] *Ibid.* ii. 315. In 1295 Boniface had deposed Raymund Gaufridi, after trying to remove him more tactfully from his position by offering him the bishopric of Padua. The reason for his deposition was probably his leniency to the Spirituals, or, perhaps, as Father Gratien suggests (*op. cit.* p. 365), his friendship for Philip IV. of France. His successor was created a cardinal in 1302, and later became Cardinal Protector of the Order. He died during the last Sessions of the Council of Vienne.

austere life and an admirer of Conrad of Offida,[1] but bitterly prejudiced against the Spirituals. At first Boniface VIII. was disinclined to interfere, and turned angrily on the petitioners, telling them not to meddle with men whose deeds were better than their own.[2] It was only when the accusers devised the cunning slander that Liberato and his followers were adherents of Celestine and did not recognise him as the lawful Pope,[3] that his anger was roused against them, and he wrote to the Patriarch of Constantinople and to the Archbishops of Patras and Athens ordering their excommunication and arrest.[4] The Patriarch was at this time at Venice, and his colleagues refused to take any steps against the fugitives, being convinced of their innocence. In vain did Liberato and his followers repeatedly seek the archbishops, for they were anxious to be cleared from the charges brought against them. Their servants had strict injunctions to deny them admittance,[5] and in order further to divest himself of responsibility the Archbishop of Athens prevailed upon Thomas of Sole to expel them from Trixonia.[6] Their hardships were further increased by the fact that their ejectment took place at a time of famine, when even the rich had great difficulty in obtaining food.[7] Finally, the little band settled in southern Thessaly, which at that time formed part of the territory of a Greek prince, the Sevastocrator of Epirus.[8] Here they lived securely for some years, suffering less molestation from men belonging to the orthodox Church than they had experienced from their fellow-Catholics, but their poverty was extreme, though this does not seem to have affected their happiness.

[1] *A.L.K.G.* ii. 312.

[2] *Ibid.* i. 528. "Sinite eos quia ipsi melius quam vos faciunt." Cf. ii. 316.

[3] Such at least was Angelo's view. It is necessary to distinguish between the friars in Greece and the Superiors of the Order in Italy. John of Murrovalle possibly believed that Liberato and his followers as adherents of Celestine did not recognise the validity of his abdication, for this was a common attitude among extreme Spirituals such as Jacopone da Todi and Ubertino da Casale. Even in those days, however, it would have been easy to make investigations before taking action against them.

[4] *Ibid.* i. 528. In the "Historia Septem Tribulationum" (*ibid.* ii. 316) Angelo first mentions the Archbishop of Athens and then changes to the Archbishop of Thebes. Possibly he was confusing him with Isnardus, Archbishop of Thebes, who, as papal vicar at Rome in 1310, released him from the sentence of excommunication launched by the Patriarch of Constantinople. Cf. *infra*, p. 60. According to the Catalogue of Raymund of Fronsac (*ibid.* iii. p. 12) the incipit of the papal bull was "Sepe sacram ecclesiam". Its tenor is found in the letters written in January 1300 by Charles II. of Naples to his sister, Isabella of Villeharduin, and to the representative of his son, the Prince of Tarento, in Albania, Athens, and Achaia, informing them of the processes against the Spirituals, and ordering them to help the Patriarch and archbishops to put them into effect (*ibid.* ii. 334-36).

[5] *Ibid.*

[6] *Ibid.*   [7] *Ibid.*   [8] *Ibid.*

It was at this time that Angelo acquired his knowledge of the Greek tongue, which was regarded by his contemporaries as due to a miracle. The story ran that during the midnight office he suddenly asked Liberato's permission to read the lesson in Greek.[1] In spite of the privations they endured they seem to have been happy in their solitude, for they laughed heartily when Angelo, or another member of the community, who was reading to them from the commentaries of St. Justin the Martyr on the Apocalypse, came to the place where the number of the beast was interpreted in Greek letters as " Benedicti ", for their persecutor, Boniface VIII., before his assumption to the Papacy had been known as Benedict of Anagni.[2] Meanwhile the Patriarch of Constantinople had returned to the East in 1301 and had lost no time in proclaiming them excommunicate.[3] According to Angelo this measure only served to increase the unpopularity of the Franciscans in the Latin principalities, and the death of the Patriarch, which followed shortly after his sentence, was looked upon as the act of God.[4] The Conventual party sent Girolamo, the future Bishop of Kaffa, as a spy to discover their retreat. He pretended to be the bearer of a letter from the great Provençal Spiritual Olivi, but they were warned against him by a priest called Don Henry.[5] More congenial visitors were Giacomo del Monte,[6] and their old friend Thomas of Tolentino, who had been sent with certain other friars on a mission to the East. The former, through his authority as vicar of the General in those parts, absolved them *ad cautelam* from the sentence of excommunication and wrote to John of Murrovalle asking his permission to take them with him on his journey, thinking in this way to restore peace to the Order.[7] Although this request was supported by Conrad of Offida and the General's own secretary, Brother Thadeus, it was refused, and Giacomo was too loyal to disobey the head of his Order in spite of a private letter from Thadeus giving him this

---

[1] Bodleian MS. Canon Ital. 155. This is an Italian version of the *Scala Paradisi* of St. John Climacus. It is quoted by Tocco in *S.F.* i. 293-94, and by Oliger (*op. cit.* xxxv.).

[2] *A.V.* lib. v. cap. viii. f. 4 r. Cf. *supra*, p. 39, *n. 5.*

[3] *A.L.K.G.* i. 528; ii. 317.

[4] *Ibid.* i. 529; ii. 317 *s.*

[5] *Ibid.* Provincial of Romania between 1300 and 1310, Bishop of Kaffa, 1316(?)-24. Angelo's account of him is probably distorted. Cf. Golubovich, *op. cit.* iii. 38-57 and *infra*, p. 154, *n. 5.*

[6] *A.L.K.G.* i. 529 and ii. 318. This was probably the famous Giacomo da Monte Rubbiano who had been one of the seventy-two Spirituals imprisoned by Crescenzio of Jesi (Golubovich, *op. cit.* iii. 59). His expedition to the East with eleven companions had been planned by Conrad of Offida, who, however, was not able to accompany them (*ibid.* ii. 312-13).

[7] *Ibid.* i. 530; ii. 318.

advice.[1]   He departed on his way, and Liberato and his followers
decided to take the bold step of returning to Italy and appearing
personally before Boniface.[2]   Leaving Angelo behind to make
the final preparations for their departure, the General of the poor
hermits returned to his native land accompanied by certain of
his companions.   When he reached Perugia, Boniface was no
longer alive and his successor, Benedict XI., was on his death-bed.[3]
Liberato decided to settle among his followers in southern Italy
and await the election of the future Pope.[4]   There he was arrested
by the Dominican Inquisitor, Thomas of Aversa, acting on instructions received from Charles II. of Naples.[5]   Fortunately, his
captor had an even greater dislike for the Franciscans than the
majority of the members of his Order,[6] and was quite prepared
to vent his spite by secretly releasing his victim.[7]   He advised
Liberato to proceed to the Curia, travelling by night so as to avoid
the snares of his enemies, and even gave him letters to certain of
the cardinals.[8]   However, the old man never succeeded in reaching his destination, for he was overtaken by sickness at Viterbo,
and died two years later at the little hermitage of St. Angelo di
Vena in the neighbourhood of the town.[9]   Meanwhile the Inquisitor, repenting of his former kindness and perhaps fearing the
wrath of the king at the escape of Liberato, arrested as many of
his followers as he could find, and subjected them and certain
heretics belonging to the sect of the Apostles to such cruel tortures
that even the neighbouring bishop was disgusted.[10]   Finally, after
being publicly beaten and branded, they were expelled for ever
from the kingdom.[11]   It was said that Thomas of Aversa was
haunted on his death-bed by the memory of his victims, of whose
innocence he had always secretly been convinced.[12]

Meanwhile Angelo had reached Perugia in 1305.[13]   There,

[1] *A.L.K.G.* ii. 318.

[2] *Ibid.* i. 530; ii. 319.   According to the " Epistola Excusatoria " Liberato
twice sent two friars with letters to Boniface VIII., but they were seized by his
enemies and so never reached their destination.

[3] *Ibid.*   [4] *Ibid.*   [5] *Ibid.*

[6] He had been suspended from preaching for seven years for casting aspersions
on the stigmata (*ibid.* ii. 319, *n.* D).

[7] *Ibid.* i. 531; ii. 320.   He gave Liberato a very friendly warning about
the eagerness of his enemies to destroy him.

[8] *Ibid.*

[9] *Ibid.*   He was ill for two years.

[10] He had to remove his victims to another place because of the protests of
the Bishop and the chief men of Trivento at his proceedings.   The description
of the tortures given in *A.L.K.G.* ii. 321-27 is almost too terrible to read.

[11] *Ibid.* ii. 326.

[12] *Ibid.*

[13] *Ibid.* i. 531.   He had certain followers with him when he arrived in
Perugia, as the first person plural is used.

more fortunate than Liberato, he found Cardinal Napoleone Orsini, who took him under his protection.[1] It is possible that at this time he met the famous Ubertino da Casale, who afterwards became one of the cardinal's chaplains.[2] It was perhaps from him that he derived his passionate admiration of Olivi.[3] Orsini was on his way to join the new Pope, Clement V., at Bordeaux and was anxious for Angelo to accompany him, but the latter fell sick.[4] In fact, from now onwards his health seems permanently to have been affected by the privations which he had undergone, and there are numerous references in his letters to his weakness and bodily infirmity. When he recovered sufficiently he succeeded to the position of Liberato, and possibly visited his scattered followers in different parts of Italy. Wadding attributes his sojourn in the neighbourhood of the little river Chiaro, from which he drew his name, to this part of his career.[5] Between 1308 and 1310 he was certainly in the neighbourhood of Rome, for he was released from the sentence of excommunication laid upon him by the Patriarch of Constantinople by Isnardus, Archbishop of Thebes, then papal vicar in the eternal city.[6] Finally, he set out for Provence and reached the papal court in 1311, the year of the Council of Vienne, little thinking that his stay there would last for over seven years.[7]

[1] *A.L.K.G.* i. 531.

[2] Cf. *A.V.* v. cap. viii. f. 4 *r.a.*, and *supra*, p. 39, *n. 5.* Angelo speaks of Ubertino's famous book, and his preaching against the heretics in Umbria in his Chronicle (*A.L.K.G.* ii. 130-33).

[3] Father Gratien (*op. cit.* 383) suggests that Olivi and Angelo da Clareno met after the release of the latter and his friends and before their departure to Armenia as missionaries. He bases his assumption on a passage from a letter of Angelo to his friend Robert of Mileto, written, as he believes, during the closing years of the life of the former.

It runs as follows: " Et quia Christo docente, cognovi, iam fere sunt anni XL. elapsi, quod pater misericordiarum et luminum decreverat in homine Dei Petro Iohannis Olivi ponere spiritum fundatoris, ideo subesse, sequi et confirmare me ei tanquam nuntio signato primi lapidis angularis Francisco integre et cordialiter amo " (*A.L.K.G.* i. 554 ; Codex Magliabecchiana, xxxix. *n.* 75, f. 118 *r.*), but seems to me somewhat insufficient evidence on which to base his fascinating theory. Angelo and his companions must have departed for Armenia shortly after their release, since letters from King Hayton, thanking the Minister-General for their services, were read at the Chapter-General of Paris in 1292, at which Olivi himself was present. It was therefore presumably shortly after his own election as Minister-General that Raymund Gaufridi sent Olivi back to his native province as lector at Montpellier. Moreover, the letter cited is one in which Angelo writes of his approaching death, which did not take place till 1337, so that the dates do not correspond. He knew Olivi well by reputation through his friendship with Ubertino da Casale and Conrad of Offida, both of whom were his disciples.

[4] *Ibid.* i. 531.

[5] Wadding, *Scriptores Ordinis Minorum*, p. 15.

[6] *A.L.K.G.* i. 531 *s.*

[7] *Ibid.* 532.

In his "Epistola Excusatoria" Angelo wrote with passionate sincerity that he had found his stay at the Curia more irksome than any of his former sufferings,[1] and we can well believe it. His retiring and meditative temperament made it difficult for him to endure the bustle and intrigue of a courtly existence, nor did a life of privation spent in the loneliness of the Italian mountains, or in the still wilder solitudes of Thessaly, fit him for the luxury of palaces. His impatience to be gone was further heightened by his fears for his followers in Italy, who were wearied by his long absence, and by the insecurity and continual dread of persecution to which they were exposed.[2] Angelo's lieutenants, Francesco di Fallirone and Giovanni di Bologna, gave repeated offence, the former by too much strictness, and the latter by an excessive laxity, with the result that their leader was often forced to intervene in support of their authority.[3] Yet there must have been compensations at least during the early years of his stay at the Curia, for his host, Jacopo Colonna, the elder of the two cardinals chiefly known to history by their rather discreditable opposition to Boniface VIII., had a real love of holiness and had known and reverenced John of Parma.[4] He treated Angelo more as a friend than as a dependent[5] and consulted him about many things.[6] Moreover, the questions at issue between the two parties in the Franciscan Order were being decided at the papal court, so that Angelo could renew his friendship with Ubertino da Casale, and through him be brought into relationship with the other leaders of the Spirituals.[7] The hopes of the stricter party were very high, for the Pope was known to sympathise with their aspirations. Angelo followed the negotiations with great interest, and with his usual moderation could even accept the compromise affected by the decretal, "Exivi de paradiso", as a possible settlement of the controversy.[8] The canonization of Celestine V. in 1312 made him feel confident that Clement

---

[1] *A.L.K.G.* i. 532. "Et licet semper odiverim toto corde esse in curia, plusquam aliam aliquam penam, quam nunc usque in mundo isto probaverim."

[2] Codex Magliabecchiana, xxxix. 75, f. 1 *v*., 12 *r*. (*A.L.K.G.* i. 555, 13 *r*.). Cf. f. 211 *v*.

[3] Cf. Codex Magliabecchiana, xxxix. 75, f. 159 *r*. (*A.L.K.G.* i. 556), where Angelo writes that in spite of his youth he would rather obey the commands of Brother John than those of St. Bonaventura, if he were still alive.

[4] Balthazar, *op. cit.* 125 *s*. [5] F. 63 *r*. (*A.L.K.G.* i. 543).

[6] F. 63 *r*. Angelo wrote from the Curia in the Cardinal's name to Gentile da Foligno on business connected with a certain girl who was purported to have visions.

[7] F. 46 *r*. (*A.L.K.G.* i. 548). Cf. f. 64 *r*. (*A.L.K.G.* i. 545).

[8] F. 63 *v*. (*A.L.K.G.* i. 544). In his Chronicle (*A.L.K.G.* ii. 139) he describes "Exivi de paradiso" as exceeding the other papal commentaries on the Rule "sicut aquila volans".

would eventually legalise the position of himself and his followers.[1] His hopes were dashed to the ground by the schism of the Tuscan brothers and the death of the Pope in 1314. During the three years' vacancy of the apostolic see Angelo followed Cardinal Colonna and his colleagues in their wanderings round different cities of Provence, realising to the full the danger caused both to the Church and to the Franciscan Order by the continued interregnum. In Provence itself there was open warfare between the Conventuals and Zealots, and Angelo followed the vicissitudes of his party with fervent sympathy. He could even commend the Italian cardinals to the prayers of his followers because they favoured the way of God.[2] Angelo was present at the abortive conclave of Carpetras, but was very despondent as to its result. It was not, however, till the summer of 1316 that the long vacancy was brought to an end by the election of John XXII. His only comfort during this anxious time was in the friendship of Philip, the younger son of the King of Majorca,[3] who was visiting the Curia at this time. Always enthusiastic in his affections, Angelo described this young prince to his followers as a second St. Francis.[4] Nor was Philip slow in returning his admiration. He was already in minor orders [5] but was fired by Angelo with the idea of founding a new Order whose mode of life should be based on the Rule and Testament of St. Francis. Two visits paid by his new friend to Majorca in the summers of 1316 and 1317 only strengthened his determination,[6] and he applied to John XXII. for his sanction.[7] The new Pope, however, refused his request and retained him in Majorca as regent for his nephew.[8] No worse choice could have been made, for Philip's essentially monkish virtues did not attract the feudatories or the communes of the little kingdom, while he lacked the strength of character which would have won their

---

[1] *A.L.K.G.* i. 543 (f. 102 *r*.).

[2] *Ibid.* i. 545 and 547 (f. 64 *r*. and f. 41 *v*.).

[3] The best account of Philip of Majorca is that given by Vidal in the *Revue des Questions historiques*, lxxxviii. 361-403.

[4] F. 18 *v*.; 176 *v*.; 199 *r*.

[5] Philip already held certain canonries, together with the office of Treasurer of Tours (Vidal, p. 367). In an undated letter Angelo congratulates him for refusing a bishopric (*A.L.K.G.* i. 564, *n.* 1, f. 114 *r*.). This was the bishopric of Mirepoix, one of the new sees created by John XXII. (Coulon, *Lettres secrètes*, i. p. 367, *n.* 456). Philip had already been a candidate for the archbishopric of Tarragona. Cf. Vidal, *op. cit.* p. 369.

[6] 165 *r*. Vidal thinks he visited Majorca again sometime after 1325. Cf. *op. cit.* 372.

[7] In 1317 (*A.L.K.G.* iii. 29) and again in 1328 (Wadding, *Annales*, vii. p. 90 (1328), xxx. and xxxi.

[8] Philip's brother, Sancho the Good, died in 1324 and was succeeded by his nephew, James II. Cf. Vidal, *op. cit.* p. 378.

respect. He did not even succeed in gaining his nephew's love, and the young king disliked him heartily.[1] The dealings of John XXII. with the Spirituals have been described in an earlier chapter. As might be expected, the Conventuals lost no time in presenting petitions against the Zealots of Provence and against Angelo and his followers.[2] The former appeared in Consistory to answer the charges brought against him.[3] At first John refused to let him speak, but his sense of justice was aroused by the bold defence of the humble prisoner. "Holy father, you have listened to the falsehoods of the friars, but will not hear the truth which I speak to you."[4] The hearing was finally adjourned and Angelo was placed in the custody of the Papal Chancellor until it was proved whether his old excommunication was valid.[5] During his imprisonment he wrote his "Epistola Excusatoria".[6] His trial probably took place after the arrival of the deputation of sixty-two Spirituals at Avignon in the Pentecost of 1317, for his description of their reception by an openly hostile Pope, surrounded by their bitterest enemies, reads like that of an eye-witness.[7] He himself was more fortunate, for John XXII. was finally convinced of his innocence and released him from the old sentence of excommunication.[8] Angelo returned to the house of Cardinal Colonna,[9] and hoped that the Pope might be induced to recognise his Order, but John ordered its suppression in the bull "Sancta romana ac universalis ecclesia" of December 1317.[10] He tried to prevail on Angelo to return to the Franciscans,[11] or to join another of the approved orders, and at last he was persuaded to adopt the white habit of a Celestinian hermit.[12] He remained at the papal court till the death of his friend and protector, Cardinal Colonna, in the spring of 1318 and then returned to his followers in Italy.

---

[1] As soon as he got the power into his own hands the young king instituted an inquiry into the orthodoxy of his uncle's favourite, Adhémar de Mosset, to whose charge he had once committed him. Cf. Vidal, "Un Procès d'Inquisition contre Adhémar de Mosset" in the *Revue d'Histoire de l'Église de France*, i. p. 555 and *infra*, p. 253 s.

[2] *A.L.K.G.* iii. 12.   [3] *Ibid.* ii. 143.   [4] *Ibid.* 144.

[5] *Ibid.* ii. 144. Cf. *ibid.* i. 548 (f. 42 r.-49 r.), a letter which Cardinal Ehrle considers was written by Angelo to his followers from prison; and f. 65 v.-66 r. (*ibid.* i. 549), which gives an account of his release, and was sent to Gentile da Foligno from the Curia by "Frater F. de Nursia".

[6] He sent a copy of the accusations brought against them and his answer to his followers in Italy. Probably the version of the "Epistola Excusatoria" in Codex Magliabecchiana, xxxix. 75, was copied from this. Cf. *ibid.* i. 546 (f. 190 v.).

[7] *Ibid.* ii. 144 s.

[8] *Ibid.* i. 549, 550 (f. 201 r.); *ibid.* ii. 144.

[9] *Ibid.* i. 549.   [10] *B.F.* v. 297, p. 134.

[11] *A.L.K.G.* i. 550, ii. 144.   [12] *Ibid.*

During the years which followed his return to his native land, Angelo settled in the neighbourhood of Rome under the protection of the powerful Abbot of Subiaco, and devoted himself to the organisation of his Order upon the Franciscan model.[1] The chief settlements of the poor hermits were in the country round the Eternal City, in the March of Ancona, and in the kingdom of Naples, but they possessed scattered hermitages in Umbria and other parts of Italy.[2]   In Rome itself, by some strange irony, they were living at the Convent of St. John, before the Latin gate,[3] once the home of the Franciscans at Rome.   Angelo divided the settlements into different provinces, each under a provincial, and the old titles of custodian and guardian were revived.[4]   In some places the bishops and priests took the hermits settled in their district under their protection,[5] and the Inquisition records show that in Rome and in other places they won the affection of the common people and even of some of the nobility.[6]   At first, probably, Angelo was able to visit the different provinces himself,[7] but as he grew increasingly infirm he was forced to delegate this duty to his secretary, Nicholas of Calabria,[8] and to content himself with letters.   These were sealed with a seal engraved with the figure of St. Francis espousing Poverty, and beneath was the picture of a kneeling friar,[9] for Angelo remembered the instructions of his master, that a General Minister should possess a breviary for his own use and a seal and pen case to be employed in the service of his followers.[10]   The gradual deterioration of the Order was perhaps due to the withdrawal of his personal influence. The Inquisition Records of 1334 show that the members often displayed a violence and intolerance in their language with regard to John XXII. and the secular clergy of which their General would hardly have approved.[11]   What was worse, men were occasionally admitted who wished to use outward sanctity as a

---

[1] The best source for Angelo's organisation of his Order is to be found in some Inquisition Records for 1334, edited by Cardinal Ehrle in *A.L.K.G.* iv. pp. 10-15.   [2] *Ibid.* p. 22.

[3] Cf. Codex Magliabecchiana, xxxix. 75, f. 1 *r.* and 16 *v.*

[4] *A.L.K.G.* iv. p. 10.

[5] Codex Magliabecchiana, xxxix. *n.* 75, f. 134 *r.*   The bishops of Fermo and Camerino were accused in 1336 of favouring the Fraticelli, as Angelo's followers were called.   Cf. Letters of Benedict XI. to his nuncio, the Archbishop of Embrun (*A.L.K.G.* iv. 73 *s.*)

[6] *Ibid.* 19.

[7] One of Angelo's letters to Philip of Majorca is written in the neighbourhood of Rome (f. 106 *v.*).

[8] *A.L.K.G.* iv. 10 and 14.   Nicholas of Calabria was still Angelo's secretary at the time of his death (Codex Magliabecchiana, xxxix. *n.* 75, f. 215 *v.*).

[9] *Ibid.* iv. p. 15.

[10] *Expos.* p. 187.   [11] *A.L.K.G.* iv. pp. 9, 10, and 12.

cloak for looseness of life.[1] The bulk of the Order, however, were probably simple-minded enthusiasts, far below the level of their chief both in learning and in elevation of character. Angelo's personal influence, however, extended far beyond the circle of his own followers. He kept up an active correspondence with Philip of Majorca,[2] who had thrown up the regency in disgust and had settled at his brother-in-law's court at Naples.[3] The darling wish of his heart was still to found his Order, but John XXII. still withheld his permission and tried to persuade him to join one of the older religious bodies.[4] When the quarrel between the Pope and the Franciscans was at its height Philip took up a fiercely hostile attitude, and preached publicly against the Pope.[5] Angelo strongly disapproved of this step, for although he regarded John as the pastor uncanonically elected, foretold by St. Francis, who should preach heresy against the poverty of Christ and enforce his views on the Church, he believed that prayer and patience were more truly Christian than violent opposition,[6] and had no illusions about the character of the antipope, Peter of Corbara. In his later letters he calls his friend " Brother Philip ",[7] so that perhaps in the end Philip carried out his plan without waiting for the papal consent,[8] for some years later certain men described as the " fratres domini Philippi " [9] were found in Naples. Angelo also had correspondents among the Augustinian hermits, two of whom, Gentile da Foligno and the blessed Simon of Cassia, were perhaps his closest friends. His friendship with the former began before his stay at the Curia,[10] while through the latter, who was one of the most popular Italian preachers of the day, the influence of the recluse of Subiaco reached many who had never heard his name.[11]

[1] Cf. Process against Paulus Zoppus of Rieti (A.L.K.G. pp. 78-82).

[2] Codex Magliabecchiana (xxxix. n. 75, f. 83 r.-98 v.; 105 r.-116 r.) contains no less than nine letters to Philip, certain of which were written during Angelo's stay at Avignon and others later.

[3] Probably in 1329. Cf. Vidal, op. cit. 389. B.F. v. n. 894, p. 490.

[4] A.L.K.G. iv. p. 67; B.F. v. n. 894, p. 490.

[5] A.L.K.G. iv. p. 89 ; B.F. vi. 123, p. 77.

[6] A.L.K.G. i. 567 (f. 89 v.).

[7] C. Magliabecchiana, xxxix. n. 75, f. 83 r., 105 v., 106 v., 107 v., 109 r.

[8] He tried again after John's death, but Benedict XI. made his famous sermon and love for the society of heretics an excuse for refusing (B.F. vi. n. 123, p. 77).

[9] A.L.K.G. iv. 100. Cf. infra, p. 212.

[10] (F. 66 r.-66 v.); A.L.K.G. i. 545 (65 v.-66 r.). Both of these letters were written from the Curia.

[11] Ibid. i. 552 (f. 135 r.). Cf. ibid. p. 537.
Shortly before his death in 1348 Simon of Cassia, according to the Fraticelli, preached openly in Florence on the subject of the poverty of Christ in a sense very different from that contained in the decretals of John XXII. The Signory protected him against the Dominican inquisitors (Tocco, S.F. i. pp. 516-17).

Always anxious that his friends should use their gifts to the full in the service of God, he rejoiced when Gentile was made the " socius " of the General of his Order,[1] though the latter shrank from the responsibility and publicity of such an office. The Abbot of Subiaco also loved Angelo well,[2] and was often ruled by his advice. Another of his correspondents was a certain abbot belonging to the new Order of Monte Uliveto, recently founded by Bernardo Tolomei of Siena.[3] He seems also to have known the papal penitentiary, Alvaro Paez, afterwards Bishop of Silves and author of the famous " De Planctu Ecclesiae ".[4] Their opinions were not always the same, though Angelo made efforts to be courteous in his criticisms of Alvaro's writings.[5] Perhaps his most beneficial influence over the Franciscans was exerted through Giovanni di Valle,[6] the originator of a movement which was to end in the foundation of the Osservanti, a reformed branch of the Order, whom tradition asserts to have been his admirer and disciple. Nor were secular persons excluded from his friendship. The dearest of these was probably Robert of Mileto, perhaps a scion of the great house of San Severino and afterwards a Franciscan friar,[7] but there are references to other men and women, often of high rank, scattered through his letters. In spite of the claims of his correspondence and of the organisation of his Order, Angelo was able to devote the early years of his stay at

---

In the Life written by his secretary, John of Salerno, in Codex Marciana (Venice), iii. 107, we learn that he often stayed up the greater part of the night writing to his spiritual sons (*A.L.K.G.* i. p. 537).

Perhaps the two short treatises by Angelo, which are found in the same Codex, were also written for their benefit. Cf. *infra*, p. 77.

[1] *A.L.K.G.* i.

[2] " Quod dictus abbas nichil faciat sine consilio dicti fratris Angeli " (*A.L.K.G.* iv. p. 11).

[3] *A.L.K.G.* i. 554 (f. 136 *v*.-138 *v*.). Only the initial of the abbot is given.

[4] Their connection may have been due to the fact that Paez was at one time Confessor to the Claresses at San Lorenzo in Panisperne, a convent founded by Cardinal Colonna (*De Planctu Ecclesiae*, ii. cap. 51). Angelo was in correspondence with the abbess (f. 55 *v*.).   [5] *A.L.K.G.* i. 551 (f. 66 *v*.).

[6] Angelo's trying habit of giving only the initial of the persons to whom his letters were addressed makes it impossible to trace Giovanni de Valle among his correspondents.

[7] Two letters are directed to him (f. 116 *v*.-f. 117 *v*. ; f. 118 *r*.-f. 120 *r*.), extracts from which are given in *A.L.K.G.* i. 554. Ilaria, Countess of San Severino, and her son Roger, Count of Mileto, both appeared as witnesses at the trial of Fr. Andreas " de Galiano " at Avignon in 1338 (*B.F.* vi. Appendix I. pp. 606 and 616-17. Cf. *infra*, p. 185), while the squire of Robert of San Severino was healed of a sore on his foot at the intercession of the dead Angelo whose tomb he was visiting (f. 219 *v*.). The " Fr. Rubertus de Mileto ", who was Sancia of Naples, executor, is generally identified with Angelo's friend (Wadding, *Annales*, vii. p. 315, 1344, § x.). The papal letters connected with the will are printed in the appendix to this volume.

Subiaco to his " Historia Septem Tribulationum ", and to his more weighty Commentary on the Franciscan Rule. Probably he was able to make use of the monastery library for the citations from the early fathers of the Church, which are so marked a feature of the latter work. It is difficult to know whether his presence at Subiaco was generally known. Between 1320 and 1330 the papal power was greatly shaken in Italy by the invasion of Louis of Bavaria, and the Franciscan authorities probably did not wish to risk a quarrel with one of the most powerful of the Italian abbots, supported as he was by the Pope's most faithful ally, Robert of Naples.[1] One of Angelo's letters shows that certain precautions had to be taken when his friends visited him, but this was written after 1331 when the Inquisition was again active in Italy, and just before the old man's departure for the hermitage of San Michele in the Basilicata.[2] The guardian of the Franciscan convent at Ara Coeli had been taking active steps to induce the abbot of Subiaco to surrender him, and perhaps Angelo was afraid of bringing trouble to his friend and protector by remaining. He probably left Subiaco in 1334, but we do not know how long he remained in the Basilicata, for only one picture of his life there has come down to us. In the list of miracles collected after his death, we learn that a certain Fra Petruccio de Roccha Montis Draconis [3] visited him there, and finding the old man busy mending a Greek manuscript, lent him his needle to perform this work, for Angelo's own was too fine.[4] In June 1337 he died at the little hermitage of Sta Maria del' Aspromonte, among the mountains overlooking Sicily. The privacy which he had courted all through his life was denied him in death, for the rude peasants from the districts round came in multitudes to be present at the end of one whom they regarded as a saint. Robert of Mileto was forced to place guards at the doorway of the hut in order to keep them from crowding in and disturbing the last moments of the dying man.[5] As his is the only account of Angelo's death

---

[1] Robert of Naples was brother-in-law to Philip of Majorca. There is a letter from John XXII. to the guardian of Ara Coeli, dated February 1334 (*B.F.* v. *n.* 1058, p. 567), blaming him for not taking active steps to capture Angelo. In the Inquisition records (*A.L.K.G.* iv. 14) one of the prisoners declared that the guardian had asked the abbot to surrender him, but the latter had replied that he would not do so if they were to make him pope. It is not certain if the bull of November 1331 (*B.F.* v. *n.* 948, p. 513), directed against " Angelus de Valle Spoletane ", refers to Angelo or to another leader of the Fraticelli.

[2] *A.L.K.G.* i. 553 (f. 67 *v.*).

[3] Perhaps a monk in the new monastery of Sta Anna, founded by Angelo's friend the Abbot of Subiaco (*Scriptores Rerum Italicarum*, xxiv. fasc. 6, p. 44).

[4] Codex Magliabecchiana, xxxix. *n.* 75, f. 215 *v.* Oliger, *op. cit.* xxxviii.

[5] Codex Magliabecchiana, xxxix. *n.* 75, f. 216 *v.* Cf. *A.L.K.G.* i. 534.

which we have, we know nothing of what passed inside the rude building. An observant chronicler of the fifteenth century, " Bernardinus Aquilanus ", related that his last instructions to his followers were that they were to return to the Franciscan Order if ever they found that the Rule and Testament of St. Francis were being faithfully observed in its ranks.[1] Such a story is not improbable, for Angelo had always believed that after bitter tribulation the Friars Minor would return to their original state, and his hopes had further been raised by the lives of Giovanni da Valle and his followers. It may, however, have been invented by some later admirer, anxious to safeguard his reputation for orthodoxy. The crowds who surrounded his death-bed, however, had no doubts on such a subject, and his reputation for holiness was further enhanced after his death by the miracles wrought by his intercession.[2] These were diligently collected by his friends, and, although most of them are among the commonplaces of hagiology, some even raise a smile, as for instance the story of the peasant woman who had had one of her teeth knocked out by an enraged husband. She fell on the floor weeping bitterly, and her husband lit his lantern and began looking for the missing tooth. When he found it he fixed it again in his wife's mouth, at the same time vowing that he would take her to visit Angelo's grave. The tooth remained stuck fast in the gap, and the couple caused a great sensation when they arrived at the place of pilgrimage, for the woman showed her tooth to everyone and declared that it was firmer than any of her others.[3] An office was composed in Angelo's honour by Thomas the Englishman, prior of the neighbouring Celestine monastery of Marsico.[4] For centuries popular veneration hailed him as " beato ", and the Bollandists of the seventeenth century placed his name in the *Acta Sanctorum* for June 15,[5] the anniversary of his death. The Church, however, has never officially recognised his right to this title. But more precious by far than the empty reverence of future generations was the feeling of desolation and emptiness left in the hearts of those he had known and loved. It was no common devotion which made Simon of Cassia feel when the news of Angelo's death reached him that " the light of life had departed never to

---

[1] *A.F.H.* iii. 254.

[2] These were collected and sent by Robert de Mileto to Gentile of Foligno and are contained in the Codex Magliabecchiana, xxxix. *n.* 75, f. 214 *v.*-219 *v.* They were printed by the Bollandists in the *Acta Sanctorum* for June 15.

[3] F. 218 *r.*

[4] F. 68 *v.*; *A.L.K.G.* i. 534.

[5] Codex Magliabecchiana, xxxix. *n.* 75, was discovered through the researches of Papebroch, who drew the attention of Father Harold, Wadding's nephew and literary executor, to it (*ibid.* i. 515).

return ", or which made him order the collection and transcription of his letters and other sayings, "being unwilling that his memory should altogether be forgotten ".[1]

The Mind of Angelo da Clareno as reflected in His Writings

Our estimate of the value of the writings of Angelo differs profoundly from that of his contemporaries. To-day, every serious student of Franciscan subjects has read extracts from his great chronicle, while even the great scholars whose labours have contributed so much to our knowledge of his works have never done more than glance at his translation of the *Scala Paradisi* of St. John Climacus.[2] Yet, for the first two hundred years after his death, his Latin works were ignored except in the immediate circle of his followers, but every Franciscan chronicler, from Bartolommeo of Pisa onwards, records with pride his knowledge of the Greek tongue, and gives a rather inaccurate list of his translations from the Fathers.[3] It is probable that Angelo himself would have accepted their verdict without hesitation, for he was fascinated by the asceticism of the Greek hermits, and desired to bring their writings to the notice of his countrymen. In a letter written to Robert of Mileto he begs him to guard carefully his translation of the rule of St. Basil which he had sent him, and to return it as quickly as possible, for there were other servants of God to whom he wished to lend it and he had no other copy.[4] Unfortunately, in spite of all his precautions, it is uncertain that any manuscript of this work survives to-day.[5] The same fate has befallen the " Dialogues of St. Macarius ", but there are numerous copies

[1] Simon's letter to his secretary, John of Salerno, is quoted by Ehrle (*A.L.K.G.* i. 536) and by Oliger (*op. cit.* xxx.).

[2] Father Oliger has compared the passages of the *Scala Paradisi* quoted in the *Expositio* with the codices supposed to contain Angelo's version of this work, but has not made a detailed study of the treatise in question. Cf. *op. cit.* pp. xli-xlviii.

[3] *Liber de Conformitate* (*A.F.* iv. 340). Cf. Mariano da Firenze, *A.F.H.* ii. 469-70, and Prologue to MS. (Bodl.) Canon Ital. 155. Golubovich (*op. cit.* i. 429), relying on the authority of Bartolommeo of Pisa (*A.F.* iv. 513), mentions a Greek grammar among Angelo's works. Father Oliger, however, believes that in the Middle Ages " grammatica graeca " was sometimes used to denote any piece of writing in the Greek tongue. Cf. *op. cit.* l. *n.* 3.

[4] *A.L.K.G.* i. 554 (f. 117 *v.*).

[5] Father Oliger thinks it may be contained in Codex 227 of the Library at Subiaco. His Introduction to the *Expositio*, pp. xl-xlviii, gives a splendid summary of the codices containing Angelo's translations from the Greek.

of the *Scala Paradisi* still in existence, both in Latin [1] and in an Italian translation made from Angelo's version by Gentile da Foligno.[2]   The book seems to have been very popular in the later Middle Ages, for a new translation was made from the Greek at the end of the fifteenth century by the Carthusian, Ambrogio Traversari.   In his introduction he writes very scornfully about the roughness of Angelo's style and his slavish following of the original,[3] but his judgment was not always accepted by later scholars. The question is one which can only be decided by the expert, and whatever the verdict the value of Angelo's work would not be greatly lessened.   The learned men of the fourteenth century were indebted to him for much of the knowledge they possessed of the writings of St. Basil and Climacus, for his versions were practically the only ones in existence.[4]   He is also credited by Bartolommeo with the translation of a treatise by St. John Chrysostom, but this is believed to be an error by certain modern scholars.[5] When we realise what a door to the study of patristic literature he opened for his contemporaries we are not surprised that they believed his knowledge of Greek to be the result of a miracle.

For us, however, to-day it is Angelo's original works which are the most worthy of study.   Most of the writers on Franciscan subjects, from Wadding onwards, have used his chronicle as their chief source for the history of the Spirituals.   It was probably written in its final form during the early years of his stay at Subiaco, for although he refers to the great question which arose between the Dominicans and Franciscans over the poverty of Christ, he gives no detailed description of John XXII.'s decretals on the subject, but dismisses it with the brief remark that " the friars minor stood firm for the truth ".[6]   His trustworthiness as a historian has often been called into question by scholars, but it is generally admitted that although writing as a partisan and often

---

[1] Among these is one in the Bodleian, Cod. Canonicianus Lat. 333.

[2] Numerous Codices remain of this version, including four in the Bodleian Library, MSS. Canon. Ital. 155 (xiv. c.); 249, 271, 295 (xv. c.).   The name of the translator is only given in Codex 1351 of the Riccardiana at Florence. The book was printed at Venice in 1477 and 1478, 1492, and 1517.   The Bodleian has copies of the versions of 1478, 1492, and 1517, and the British Museum of the version of 1492.   A modern edition has been made by Ceruti in *Collezione di opere inedite o rare*, Bologna, 1874.   The popularity of the work is further shown by the fact that there is a Sicilian version in the Royal Library at Turin (Ceruti, p. xlii).

[3] Prologue to Translation quoted by Oliger, *op. cit.* li.   A later translator, the Jesuit Matthaeus Raderus (1633), warmly defended Clareno's version (Ceruti, *op. cit.* xx. s.).   Cf. the verdict of Gradenigo, Oliger, *op. cit.* lii.

[4] There was an earlier version of the rule of St. Basil by Rufinus.

[5] It is not mentioned by Raderus, or accepted by Fr. Oliger (*op. cit.* xlix.).

[6] *A.L.K.G.* ii. 149.

prejudiced and hasty in his judgments, as in the case of St. Bonaventura,[1] he never wilfully distorts or suppresses facts.[2] Moreover, he was an eyewitness of many of the events which he describes, and for the early part of his chronicle made use of the lives of St. Francis by Celano and St. Bonaventura, as well as one by the papal notary, John of Ceperano.[3] He also knew the writings of Brother Leo, and received some of his information from contemporaries of the Saint, who had been actually present when certain incidents which he mentions took place.[4] Yet, his partiality makes him a bad portrayer of character, and his St. Francis has none of the naïve and almost childlike charm of the "poverello" which we find in the *Speculum* and the *Fioretti*. Instead, we see a gloomy and austere fanatic, whose mouth is filled with terrific denunciations of the wickedness of his Order, and with fearful prophecies of its impending doom. Even when he comes to his own age Angelo is hardly more successful. In spite of his love for Olivi he cannot make him live, while John of Parma is merely an abstraction of a righteous man in a wicked age, and not a fullblooded human being as in Salimbene. Perhaps his veneration for his heroes prevented him from realising that it was their kinship with their fellows and not their superhuman qualities which won for them the hearts of men. He is more successful in his portraits of sinners, often getting his effect in a few words. Boniface VIII.'s single remark to the Conventuals when they petitioned him against Liberato and his followers, " Leave them alone, for their deeds are better than yours ", is a wonderful summary of the Pope's character, revealing his cynical knowledge of the men around him, and his indifference to everything which did not affect his own claims.[5] Yet, if Angelo's ardent sympathies made him in many ways a bad judge of character, they gave him a power of description which has seldom been surpassed. Even when he is recording incidents which he only knew through hearsay, as, for instance, in his account of the writing of the second Rule,[6]

---

[1] According to Angelo and many of the Spirituals, who never could forgive Bonaventura's treatment of John of Parma, Bonaventura had first shared in the Joachimite views of his great predecessor, and had afterwards turned against him in order to win the favour of the Conventual party in the Order (*A.L.K.G.* ii. 277).

[2] This question is decided in Angelo's favour by Cardinal Ehrle in his Introduction to the Sixth and Seventh Tribulations (*ibid.* p. 123).

[3] Tocco, " Le due prime Tribolazioni ", p. 1.

[4] *Ibid.* 42, 72, and 81.

[5] *A.L.K.G.* ii. 316. Cf. *supra*, p. 57.

[6] Tocco, *op. cit.* pp. 55-58 ; *Expos.* p. 127. The account given by Ubertino da Casale (*A.V.* l. v. cap. v., f. 3 *r.b*) is perhaps even more vivid and realistic, since it includes a description of the topography of Fonte Colombò. Cf. *supra*, p. 2.

his readers can see the whole scene as clearly as if they themselves had been present: the barren mountain-side and St. Francis kneeling in ecstasy, awaiting the divine inspiration. Up the steep path come the figures of the Superiors of the Order, led by Elias, dreading the austerity of the new Rule and determined to interrupt the saint at his labours. Then we hear the thunder of the voice of Christ proclaiming his servant's work as his own, and finally St. Francis' triumphant cry, " Are ye now convinced, or do ye wish that the Lord should speak to you again? " Perhaps Angelo's most poignant picture of all is that of the little band of Zealots, standing all through the hours of darkness outside the papal palace, waiting for the dawn to break and for the doors to open. The contrast between the peace of the short summer night, and that morning when they were to appear before an openly hostile Pope, surrounded by their bitterest enemies, and feel their dearest hopes perish before the bitter sarcasm of his mocking gibes, is almost heart-breaking.[1]   Angelo's power is due to his simple directness, and his avoidance of a single unnecessary word. When Wadding tried to clothe his Chronicle in a seventeenth-century dress his grandiloquence deprived it of half its force.[2]   It is only those who write from a full heart, and live over again the incidents which they describe, who can hope to achieve the same affect.

The " Epistola Excusatoria "[3] must be taken in conjunction with the " Historia Septem Tribulationum ", for although written during Angelo's stay at the Curia, at the command of John XXII., it describes the fortunes of Liberato and his followers, which are also recorded in the Chronicle. In order to justify himself and his friends in the eyes of the Pope, Angelo begins his story with an account of their imprisonment in the March of Ancona, and ends it with his own arrival at the papal court. He dwells especially on the accusations which had been brought against them by their enemies, to wit, that they were apostates from their Order, and did not recognise the authority of Boniface VIII. and his successors, besides holding erroneous views about the sacraments, and daring to preach and hear confessions without the permission of their lawful superiors.[4]   His attitude towards the Pope is deferential and at the same time independent. His position gives him the responsibility and the power of deciding between truth and falsehood, and God will require the blood of his poor servants at his hands if he fails to do them justice and to free them from the fury of their oppressors.[5]

---

[1] *A.L.K.G.* ii. 144 *s.*
[2] *Annales*, iv. p. 89, 1307, § ii.   Cf. *infra*, p. 272.
[3] *A.L.K.G.* i. pp. 521-33 ; Codex Magliabecchiana, xxxix. *n.* 75, f. 138 *v.*-
147 *r.*   [4] *A.L.K.G.* i. 522 (f. 139 *r.*).   [5] *A.L.K.G.* i. 533 (f. 147 *r.*).

An interesting question arises in connection with the Chronicle, namely, how far was Angelo a Joachimite? Like most of his party he had read the works of the Calabrian Abbot, for he quotes from his Commentary on the Apocalypse in his Exposition of the Rule.[1] He had also studied many of the pseudo-Joachimite writings, such as the prophecies of St. Cyril and of the Erythraean Sybil, and regarded them as certain revelations of future events.[2] It is obvious, moreover, that he believed Joachim to be a perfectly orthodox writer, for he declares that it was not his teaching on the Trinity which was condemned at the Lateran Council, but his misunderstanding of the doctrine of Peter the Lombard.[3] The title and scheme of his book, moreover, recall the seven periods which, according to the Abbot of Flora, were to elapse between the death of Christ and the coming of the age of the Holy Spirit.[4] There are certain passages also which seem to be inspired by the apocalyptic speculations of the age,[5] and Angelo was obviously familiar with the identification of St. Francis with the Angel having the seal of the living God, which was so common among the Franciscans.[6] Yet he had no sympathy with the extravagances of Gerard of Borgo San Donnino, and describes his book as being " without salt ".[7] On the whole, he was more interested in the prophecies of St. Francis than in those of Joachim, and in one of his letters declares that self-love is a far more serious enemy to the soul than Antichrist with his hosts.[8] His scheme for the regeneration of the world does not seem to have gone further than the reformation of his own Order, and even of that he was sometimes doubtful. The alpha and omega of religion to him lay in the personal union of the soul with God, and his mind was in many ways too simple and direct to busy itself with fantastic theories about the future state of the world. For Angelo himself, as he declares in another letter, the worst hell of all was the sin which separated man from Christ,[9] though he shared the beliefs of his day with regard to the physical torments of the place of eternal punishment. One of his descriptions of its perpetual

[1] *Expos.* p. 227.

[2] *A.L.K.G.* ii. 289. According to himself he had found the life and suffering of Olivi in the prophecies of St. Cyril, the friend of the Abbot Joachim, and the career and fate of Celestine V. in those of the Erythraean Sybil.

[3] *A.L.K.G.* ii. 276.

[4] Cf. Ehrle, Introduction; *A.L.K.G.* ii. 119.

[5] Cf. *ibid.* 125-27, 137-38; *Expos.* 234-36.

[6] *Expos.* pp. 78 and 226.

[7] *A.L.K.G.* ii. 277. Cf. *supra*, p. 30, *n.* 9.

[8] Codex Magliabecchiana, xxxix. *n.* 75, f. 22 *v.* Cf. 82 *v.* There are other passages, however, which show that he was influenced by the general views of his age on this subject.

[9] *Ibid.* f. 42 *v.*

disorder and confusion is reminiscent of Dante's *Inferno*,[1] and his story of the wicked abbot who was allowed to return for a few short hours to the earth as a warning to his monks is a delightful example of medieval crudeness. The visitor wisely took refuge in the convent stream to cool his burning pain, and when the monks by his instructions threw in their iron candlesticks they melted as if they had been wax.[2] It is descriptions such as this which reveal the difference between the mysticism of the Middle Ages and that of a later date. The central vision can never change, but its details are inspired by the theology of its own era.

At the same time as he was writing his " Historia Septem Tribulationum ", Angelo had probably embarked on his *Expositio Regulae Fratrum Minorum*. Possibly he had conceived the idea of this work during his stay at the papal court, when he had been pestered by messengers from his followers asking for his advice on various points connected with the observation of the Rule. In the manuscript which preserves his letters there is a small treatise, headed "De Verbis et Consiliis Fratris Angeli", which deals with the reception of novices, and discusses such matters as prayer and obedience, but its title would lead us to suppose it to be a collection of his sayings written down after his death by one of his followers.[3] The *Expositio* itself gives us many incidents in the life of St. Francis which also occur in the " Historia ",[4] and this, together with the numerous citations from the fathers used to prove the utter poverty of Christ and his Apostles, makes it probable that it was written about 1321, when this question was causing so much agitation at the papal court.[5] It is noteworthy too that Angelo never refers to the decretal, " Cum inter nonnullos ", of 1323,[6] which declared that it was heretical to hold that Christ and his disciples had possessed nothing of their own, either severally or in common. Angelo probably made use of the library at Subiaco while writing his treatise on the Rule, for few books of its size contain so many quotations from the early Fathers of the Church.[7]

---

[1] Codex Magliabecchiana, xxxix. 75, f. 6 r. " nam si omnia folia arborum et herbarum et gucce plumarum essent lingue tormenta infernorum, cruciatus et dolores explicare nequirent. Terra miserie et tenebrarum ubi umbra mortis et nullus ordo sed sempiternus horror inhabitat ".

[2] *Ibid*. 35 r.   [3] *Ibid*. f. 78 r.

[4] Sermon before the Cardinal of Ostia (Gregory IX.) at the Chapter-General of Assisi, p. 46. Prophecies, p. 54 ; cf. Tocco, pp. 17, 73, and 25. Story of writing of Second Rule, pp. 127-28. Cf. Tocco, 55-58.

[5] Pp. 141 onwards. Cf. Letter to Philip of Majorca (*A.L.K.G.* i. 566), written about 1329. Cf. Oliger, *op. cit.* lv-lviii.

[6] *B.F.* v. 518, p. 256.

[7] Oliger, *op. cit.* lxx-lxxii.

Many of the passages from the Greek Fathers, and notably the numerous citations from the Rule of St. Basil, must have been derived from his own translations of their works. It is interesting as showing his attitude towards the learning of his day that he never makes use of the writings of any of the great schoolmen,[1] or mentions St. Bonaventura's numerous treatises on the question of poverty. His information about St. Francis is drawn from the same sources as in the " Historia Septem Tribulationum ", and he gives us both versions of the Rule as well as examples from the " Admonitions " and other writings of the Saint which throw light upon his interpretation of it.[2] Treatises well known in Spiritual circles, such as the " De Finibus Paupertatis " of Hugues de Digne, are extensively employed, and there is an interesting passage which is also found in the so-called " Verba Conradi ", generally ascribed to Conrad of Offida,[3] and many quotations from Olivi's Commentary on the Rule, and also from his other works.[4] The whole question of Angelo's sources is, however, a very knotty one until we know more about the early traditions which grew up around the name of St. Francis, and especially the part played in their formation by the writings of Brother Leo.

Perhaps the most striking feature of Angelo's Commentary is its marvellous interpretation of certain aspects of the mind of St. Francis. As in the " Historia Septem Tribulationum " he is perhaps prone to exaggerate the austerity of the " poverello " and his dislike of learning and culture, as well as dwelling overmuch on his depression and dissatisfaction with the development of his Order during the period immediately preceding his death. Yet possibly no other writer has ever so completely succeeded in catching the spirit which lurks behind the curt simplicity of the Rule of the Friars Minor as this man, whose mind had been nurtured in all the learning of the first centuries of the Christian Church. When we read the *Expositio* of St. Bonaventura we realise that it is the learned scholar and doctor of the University of Paris who is speaking to us and not the humble Francis, but in Angelo's case it is different, and his numerous citations from the fathers are only used as illustrations and explanations of the Rule, and do not crush it beneath their weight. Yet, he never loses his originality, and the character of his book is far more due to his close resemblance to St. Francis in

---

[1] Cf. Oliger, *loc. cit.*

[2] Cf. Oliger, pp. lix-lxx, for a discussion of the Franciscan sources of the *Expositio*.

[3] Pp. 44-47 and 127. The " Verba " was edited in *Miscellanea Franciscana*, vii. p. 135 s. The information about St. Francis contained in it is definitely stated to have been derived from Brother Leo, but he was the general authority for all the traditions which were common among the Zealots.

[4] Pp. 172-4, 231-3. For " Expositio in Apocalypsim " cf. 231-33.

spirit than to any conscious effacement of his own personality. For both men the central fact of their lives was their close union with their Master,[1] and they even welcomed suffering as a means of bringing them yet nearer to one " who was despised and rejected of men ".[2]   Angelo regarded the Rule as inviolate because it was a summary of the counsels contained in the gospels,[3] and believed that the whole of Christ's teaching could be concentrated in the three-fold vow of poverty, chastity, and obedience.[4]   In a letter to his followers, he declares that St. Francis had wished his foundation to be called not the " Ordo Minorum " but the " Vita Minorum ",[5] thus showing how much his mind had been permeated by its spirit. Guardians, minister, and even the Cardinal Protector himself, existed merely for the sake of the Rule, and were subservient to it. If they were swept away the Rule would still remain, just as the Church had not perished in that dark hour when even the Apostles' faith had failed and only Christ's mother had remained true to him.[6]   The same sanctity surrounded the Testament of St. Francis, for without it the Rule was " as the crown of stars in the Apocalypse but with no head to encircle, or like a good deed done unwittingly, a bride without bridegroom or bridal ornaments, an heir deprived of his inheritance through disobedience ".[7]

Angelo's conception of the Rule affected his whole attitude towards his superiors, and indeed towards the whole ecclesiastical system of his age.[8]   He had no doubts on the subject of the papal claims, and in his eyes all authority and power was derived from God, whatever might be the character of its possessor.[9]   Even " the pastor uncanonically elected " was an instrument of the divine vengeance.   Like St. Francis he forbade his followers to sit in

---

[1] Cf. Codex Magliabecchiana, xxxix. *n.* 75, f. 21 *r.* " qui habet Iesum habet omne bonum et vivit in deo ".

F. 167 *r.* " nam Christi Iesu inhabitatio est illa (verbalis) nostri interioris hominis ignota inexpertis resurrectio, per quam omnis boni beata susceptione dotamur, sine qua viventes mortui sumus, et operantes otiosi, et loquentes muti, et videntes ceci, et audientes surdi, et ambulantes homines immobilia et insensibilia idola ".

Cf. f. 168 *r.* It is impossible even to give references to the numerous passages in the letters on this theme. Cf. *Expos.* pp. 13, 29, 69.

[2] F. 1 *v.*, 120 *r.*, 183 *v.*, 200 *r.*   Cf. *Expos.* p. 27.

[3] *Expos.* pp. 15 and 33.   Cf. Letters, f. 17 *r.*, 36 *v.*, 186 *r.*, etc.

[4] *Expos.* p. 34.

[5] Codex Magliabecchiana, xxxix. 75, f. 43 *v.*; *A.L.K.G.* i. 563.

[6] *Ibid.*

[7] *Expos.* p. 234.

[8] The best exposition of his views on this subject are found in a letter written to his followers from the Curia (f. 7 *v.*-10 *v.*). Extracts from this are quoted in *A.L.K.G.* i. 563.

[9] " Ex Christi dono est auctoritas et potestas clavium ecclesie " (*A.L.K.G.* i. 564).   Cf. 59 *r.*, 188 *r.* (*A.L.K.G.* i. 555).

judgment on the characters of the secular clergy,[1] for their office entitled them to respect whether they were saints or sinners. Obedience was in his eyes one of the greatest of the typically Franciscan virtues, and a friar was bound to carry out the commands of his Superior, even at the risk of his own life, as long as these did not involve any violation of the Rule.[2] That indeed was sacrosanct and no pope could alter one word of it, any more than it was lawful for him to change the gospel itself.[3] It is noteworthy that in his Commentary he only mentioned one papal decretal, the " Quo elongati a saeculo "[4] of Gregory IX., and he sternly rebuked Philip of Majorca, who was still hesitating whether to adopt the Rule and Testament as his manner of life in the teeth of the papal prohibition, with the words, " I have not found that any of Christ's disciples sought the counsel of a priest or a ruler of the synagogue ".[5] The morbid scrupulousness of his friend found no echo in his simple and straightforward mind. Yet at the same time Angelo was no rebel. Persecution and suffering did not release men from the obedience which they owed to their superiors, for neither the Church nor the Pope could prevent men from doing good or from fulfilling the promises they had made to God.[6] Undeserved punishment for such acts must be received with due meekness and submission as a means of purification.[7] Perhaps, occasionally under the sting of calumny and misrepresentation, Angelo fell short of his own high standard, yet generally he taught his followers to respect the ecclesiastical authorities of his time by example as well as by precept. It is sad that his moderation was not imitated by other members of his party.

Besides the *Expositio* and the " Historia " three smaller treatises written by Angelo have come down to us. The " De Verbis et Consiliis "[8] has already been mentioned. The other two, the *Breviloquium*[9] and the *Preparantia*,[10] were probably written at the request of Simon of Cassia, as they were discovered in a manuscript containing a contemporary account of his life. The first, as its prologue tells us, was written chiefly for men and

---

[1] *A.L.K.G.* i. 561 (134 v., 177 r., 205 v.). Cf. *Expos.* ix. pp. 193-7.
[2] *Expos.* p. 201. Cf. *A.L.K.G.* i. 555.
[3] *A.L.K.G.* i. 560.
[4] *B.F.* i. p. 68 s. Cf. *Expos.* pp. 51, 52, and 189.
[5] Codex Magliabecchiana, xxxix. n. 75, f. 105 v.
[6] *A.L.K.G.* i. 560.　　　[7] *Ibid.*
[8] Codex Magliabecchiana, xxxix. 75, f. 78 r. Cf. *supra*, p. 74.
[9] This has been printed by Fra Ciro da Pesaro at the end of his book on Clareno, published at Macerata in 1920, pp. 401-12. He took it from the codex in the Marciana at Venice, containing a life of the blessed Simon of Cassia, and his letter written on receiving the news of Angelo's death.
[10] Ciro da Pesaro, *op. cit.* pp. 401-403. The version found among Angelo's letters is contained in f. 28 r.-29 v. of the Codex Magliabecchiana.

women living in the world, and deals very simply with such matters as the doctrines of the Catholic faith, prayer, and the mode of acquiring the essential Christian virtues. The whole object of the treatise was to draw its readers nearer to Christ. The other little work, called from its incipit the *Preparantia*, is found also in the manuscript containing Angelo's letters, but from its contents was obviously intended for those who desired to separate themselves from the world. Such essentially Franciscan counsels as manual labour and the care of lepers are given to the would-be religious. In a letter to his follower, Andrea da Rieti, Angelo mentions another treatise dealing with certain virtues and their contrary vices,[1] which he had written during his time in Greece, but this has not yet been discovered. On the whole, Angelo's shorter works are more akin to his letters than to his two great books. The lack of any formal or detailed scheme enabled his pen to run freely from thought to thought.

It is very difficult to give any description of Angelo's letters, for they are the most intimate and personal of all his writings. In his Chronicle he was recording the sufferings and endurance of others, and in his *Expositio* he was striving to interpret the mind of St. Francis, but his letters were not meant for the outside world at all. They were written for an inner circle of faithful friends and disciples from whom he had no secrets, and he shares with them all the weariness and disappointment of those years at the papal court,[2] and the wonder and freshness of the first days of his friendship with Philip of Majorca.[3] Yet, although Angelo writes freely of all the things nearest to his soul, his object is always the profit of his followers, and not the more egotistical pleasure of self-expression. Many of his instructions are practical, and are concerned with such matters as the reception of novices,[4] the question of manual labour,[5] and the relation of his disciples to the neighbouring clergy.[6] Often he rises to heights of mysticism not reached in any of his other writings, and there are few letters which do not dwell on the fact that it is only in God that man can find his real life. No man can serve two masters,[7] so that the only way to union and fellowship with Christ lies along the bitter and narrow path of self-renunciation and the abandonment of all merely human learning.[8] Few religious writers have surpassed

---

[1] Codex Magliabecchiana, xxxix. 75, f. 149 *r*.

[2] *Ibid*. f. 103 *r*. (*A.L.K.G.* i. 543); 168 *v*. (i. 556); 207 *r*. (i. 557).

[3] F. 18 *v*., 147 *v*. (i. 566) ; 176 *v*., 199 *r*.

[4] F. 45 *v*., 134 *r*., 160 *v*., 190 *v*., 192 *v*., 204 *v*. (i. 554).   [5] F. 177 *r*.

[6] F. 134 *v*., 177 *r*., 204 *v*. (i. 554) ; 205 *v*.

[7] F. 161 *r*.

[8] 161 *r. seq*., 221 *r*. Cf. 194 *v*., " plurimum litterati ad inferna descendunt ".

the sublimity of Angelo's description of the wisdom which is truly Christian. " It despises the savour of present things and seeks only the celestial, releasing its lovers from the desire of all that is visible and filling them with peace and the divine light. Through poverty it makes men rich and transforms them into God by the operation of perfect love. He who has wisdom has Christ, and he who has Christ desires to know nothing and to have nothing except him, and, rejoicing in misfortune and glorying in derision, passes through the prison of this life." [1] Angelo's letters are also full of beautiful passages about love, which to him was the passion which drew men to God, and to each other, for its supreme manifestation was found in the life and death of Christ.[2] All the other virtues, and even Lady Poverty herself, were handmaids [3] to this supreme one, which was no mere attribute of God, but the very core of His being. Earthly means, and especially the Sacraments, were to be used as a means of seeking this mystical union of man with his Saviour, but there came a time when all outward forms were merely a hindrance to the soul. Thus, although it was good for the religious to make use of all the services established by the Church, they could be omitted without sin if they were found a distraction from mental prayer.[4] Confession to a priest was beneficial whenever possible, but in cases when such a means of grace could not be had God freely forgave the sins of the true penitent.[5] Angelo dwells long and fondly on the Franciscan virtues of humility [6] and obedience,[7] but most of all on Poverty,[8] " the bride of Christ and the companion of angels ",

---

[1] Codex Magliabecchiana, xxxix. *n.* 75, 39 *r.*

[2] " Veritas caritatis . . . est legis plenitudo et evangelium et fons gratie et mater glorie et virtutum omnium radix et perfectio et deus et dei spiritus et vita eterna" (f. 9 *v. seq.*).

" Amator enim hominum Christus non sibi placuit sed impropria nostra se tulit, ut et nos qui vero displicibiles et natura filii ire sumus, nobis ipsis penitus displicamus et sanctificantia obprobria eius ardentissima caritate diligamus " (f. 38 *r.*).

[3] " Caritas ex vero numquam excidit quia caritas deus est " (f. 51 *v.*). Cf. 136 *v.*

" Sed omnia tantum sunt vera virtuosa et bona quantum caritati veritatis serviunt" (f. 96 *r.*).

[4] " Cum quis super mentem et intellectum sursum actus ex fruitione veritatis caritatis, omnibus cogitationibus et intelligentiis movitur, et ex tali fruitione finem verborum et virtutem breviatam in caritate verbi unione et multipharie, primo sine verbis, secundo in verbis super verba in verbo speculatur. Huic non est imposita tali tempore lex horarum, qui ad speculationem et visionem verbi in enigmate archanum medium est, silentium et non dicere verum et summum dicere est, et non orare orare, et esse sine cogitatione et intellectu in memoria eterna super memoriam et intellectum esse " (f. 32 *v.*).

[5] F. 106 *v.* (*A.L.K.G.* i. 564), f. 205 *r.* (*A.L.K.G.* i. 554).

[6] F. 114 *r.*, 44 *v.*   [7] F. 81 *r.*

[8] F. 149 *v.* Poverty was the subject of the first beatitude (f. 20 *r.*).

without which no real self-surrender was possible.   No better example of Angelo's spiritual kinship to St. Francis can be found than his constant and affectionate allusions to " domina paupertas ".[1]

In order to ascertain Angelo's exact position in the history of the Zealots, it is well to compare him with the two other great Spirituals whose personalities also form part of the subject of this little treatise. He possessed perhaps a less many-sided and versatile mind than Olivi, and lacked the burning passion and the immense creative force of such a poet as Ubertino da Casale.   It is not that he fails either in feeling or in imagination, but it never runs riot, and while the greatest passages in the *Arbor Vitae* gleam with the fire and radiance of innumerable precious stones, many of Angelo's remind us of a sunny garden full of fragrant herbs.   There is room here for only two examples, namely, his beautiful description of Obedience taken from the *Expositio*, and some striking metaphors taken from one of his letters, which reveal as by a flash the whole meaning of the Franciscan Rule.   " Obedience through the mortification of our own wills is the salvation of the soul, the life of faith, the mother of all virtues, the key of knowledge, a gentle fire bearing men ever upwards, the crown and support of the perfections of the saints, the fruit of the cross, a highway of safety leading to the unspeakable rest of the peace of Christ." [2]   " For it is the tree of life and the unconquerable fortitude of the soul, a city for the strong, filled with all the fairness of wisdom, of the law and of grace, the throne of the house of David, the dignity of the Apostles, the long suffering of the martyrs, the wisdom of the fathers, the justification of the saints, and the very life, peace, and reflection of all who strive to know and to follow Christ." [3]

Angelo is the only one of the three great Spirituals who can rightly be termed a saint.   In spite of his misfortunes and perplexities he was a happy man, for he had gained the calm serenity of soul which comes from union with Christ and an utter surrender of self.   Long before that summer day at Aspromonte, when the spirit was at last set free from his worn-out body, he had entered into " the peace which passeth all understanding".

[1] Cf. especially Codex Magliabecchiana, xxxix. 75, f. 175 *r.* and f. 205 *v.*
[2] *Expos.* p. 62.   Cf. *infra,* p. 100.
[3] Codex Magliabecchiana, xxxix. 75, f. 23 *r.*

CHAPTER IV

OLIVI

" PETER, the son of John Olivi, who was the leader of the rebels in Provence, in the schools and elsewhere, both in the Order and outside, was called Antichrist." [1]

" Again, they (the Béguins) commonly call the said brother ' Petrus Iohannis ', the holy but uncanonized father. . . . Moreover, they say that since the days of the Apostles and the evangelists there has been no doctor greater than he. . . . Again, certain among them declare that there has been no teacher in the Church of God save St. Paul and the said brother Petrus Iohannis, whose words were not in some manner refuted by the Church, but the whole doctrine of St. Paul and brother ' Petrus Iohannis ' must be kept always by the Church, nor can one jot of it be changed." [2]

The memory of this famous leader of the Spirituals has been darkened both by the calumnies of his enemies and the ill-judged enthusiasm of his friends. In the eyes of the former he was a pestilential heretic and the main cause of sedition and disturbance within the ranks of his Order, while to the latter he was an object of veneration second only to St. Francis himself. Even to-day it is well-nigh impossible to form a just estimate of this complex but fascinating character because of the clouds of prejudice and partiality which still hide his figure from our view. Often the events of his life have been so distorted by contemporary accounts that it is exceedingly difficult for the modern historian to sift the mass of contradictory evidence, and it is sometimes possible only to guess at what actually took place. When we come to examine the writings from his pen which have come down to us the same bewilderment prevails, for the stern enthusiast, to whose teaching upon the question of poverty were ascribed all the wildest excesses of the Zealots, writes with the moderation of a Bonaventura or a Pecham.[3] Moreover, the tongue which denounced with such

---

[1] " In secunda parte huius voluminis continentur capitula infrascripta. In primo capitulo ponitur thema ' Antichristus venit ', quia frater Petrus Iohannis Olivi, qui caput fuit rebellium in Provincia, in scolis et alibi in statu et in ordine vocabatur Antichristus." From the Catalogue of Raymund de Fronsac (*A.L.K.G.* iii. p. 10).

[2] " Item, eundem fratrem Petrum Iohannis communiter vocant sanctum patrem non canonizatum . . ." (Bernard Gui, *Manuel de l'Inquisiteur*, i. p. 138).

" Item dicunt ipsum esse ita magnum doctorem quod ab apostolis et evangelistis citra non fuerit aliquis maior eo. . . . Item, aliqui ex eis dicunt quod non fuit aliquis doctor in ecclesia Dei, excepto S. Paulo, et dicto fratre Petro Iohannis, cuius dicta non fuerint in aliquo per Ecclesiam refutata; set tota doctrina Sancti Pauli et fratris Petri Iohannis est tenenda totaliter per Ecclesiam, nec est una littera dimittenda " (*ibid.*).

[3] Extracts from Olivi's questions on poverty have been published by Cardinal Ehrle in *A.L.K.G.* iii. pp. 503-33.

energy the wickedness of the " carnal " Church, and called upon
the elect to withdraw from all contact with her members,[1] rebuked
in no measured language the presumption shown by the followers
of Liberato and Angelo da Clareno in separating themselves from
the Franciscan Order.[2] Yet, although the outlines of the
portrait are faint and blurred, we can at least be certain that
Olivi was no nonentity, for only a man of powerful personality
and one possessing a strange and magnetic attraction could
have exerted such a decisive influence over the destinies of his
party, or could have inspired on the one hand such ardent and
deep-rooted devotion and on the other such intense and enduring
hatred.[3]

Like his great forerunner, Hugues de Digne,[4] Olivi was a
native of Languedoc, although the scope of his activities extended
far beyond the boundaries of his own province.   He was born in
1248 or 1249 at Serignan, or at Castel Ste Marie in the neighbourhood of Béziers,[5] a district in which the French form of his name is
still common.[6]   We know nothing about his parentage or of his
life before he joined the Franciscan Order,[7] but it must always
be remembered that he came from a region which had been
profoundly influenced by the teaching of his famous compatriot.
Perhaps his own father was one of the little band of lawyers and
doctors who had gathered in Hugues de Digne's cell at Hyères
to hear him expound the prophecies of the Abbot Joachim.[8]   Such
an atmosphere would explain the fatal spell which such speculations cast over his keen and subtle intellect, a charm which was
to prove dangerous both to himself and his followers.   Tradition
asserts that he joined the Franciscan Order when only twelve

[1] Post. in Apoc. p. 263. The condemnation of 1319 is printed in Baluze-
Mansi Misc. ii. 258-70, and gives extracts from the original. Since it was
Olivi's last book it must have been written shortly before his death, which took
place in 1298. Cf. A.L.K.G. ii. 384.

[2] Letter to Conrad of Offida (A.F.H. xi. 366-73). The date of this letter is
1295. Olivi accuses Liberato and his followers of justifying their separation
from the Order by Apoc. xviii. 4, and makes use of this same text in his "Postilla"
to urge the segregation of the elect from the rest of the Church.

[3] This is also the opinion of Davidsohn (Geschichte von Florenz, ii. 275).

[4] Cf. supra, pp. 7 and 22.

[5] Codex Laurentianus, S. Crucis, Pl. 31, sin cod. 3, f. 206 r. (margin).
Cf. A.L.K.G. iii. 411. On f. 205 of the same manuscript he is described as
" Magister Petrus Iohannis de Castro Sancte Marie dyocesis Biderrensis ".
Cf. A.F.H. xi. p. 264.

[6] The French form of Olivi is Olieu. Cf. A.F.H. xi. 310.

[7] His father's Christian name was probably John, for whatever the case of
Petrus, Iohannis is nearly always found in the genitive (A.L.K.G. iii. 410).

[8] Salimbene, op. cit. p. 236. By his enemies Hugues was reputed to be the
founder of the Saccati, a mendicant order suppressed at the time of the Council
of Lyons (ibid. pp. 254-55).

years of age,[1] and it is almost certain that he spent his student days at the University of Paris.[2] The years which he spent there profoundly affected his outlook, especially with regard to the question of poverty, and left their mark upon his whole life. Although the first generation of Franciscan thinkers was no longer teaching, its place had been taken by such men as John Pecham and Matthew of Acquasparta, while the great Aquinas and Gerard of Abbéville were also lecturing in the schools.[3] Moreover, the mendicant orders, which had formerly presented a united front against the fierce onslaughts of the professors, drawn largely from the ranks of the secular clergy, had now begun their bitter rivalry and were divided over the question of poverty. It is clear that Olivi followed the strife with eager interest, for among his writings on the subject is an attack on the theory of the Angelic Doctor that a life of complete poverty was only a means towards attaining perfection, and was not necessarily the highest mode of existence.[4] He was also present at the Chapter-General held by St. Bonaventura at Paris, where the great Minister-General lamented bitterly over the abuses which he was powerless to check.[5] It must have been at the same Chapter that he identified St. Francis with the angel having the seal of the living God.[6] Bonaventura even went so far as to accord a personal interview to the young student, in which he told him that the decline of the Order was due to the multiplicity of duties which had fallen to its lot.[7] Olivi probably left Paris without receiving his master's degree, perhaps from humility,[8] although his subsequent career would lead us to

[1] Codex Laurentianus, S. Crucis, Pl. sin cod. 3, f. 206 *r*. Quoted *A.L.K.G.* iii. 411.

[2] *Ibid.* Cf. Bartholommeo of Pisa, " Liber de Conformitate " (*A.F.* iv. 339). He probably passed his novitiate at Béziers (*Histoire des Ordres religieux*, vii. 58).

[3] *A.L.K.G.* iii. 413.

[4] Postilla in Mattheum, cap. x. (MS. New College 49, f. 77 *r.b*-81 *v.b*). This is found as a separate treatise among Olivi's questions on Poverty in Codex Vaticanus 4986, and extracts from it are printed in *A.L.K.G.* iii. 517-23. Cf. M. D'Alverny, " Les Écrits théoriques concernant la Pauvreté Évangélique " (*Positions de Thèses*, pp. 5-6).

[5] *A.L.K.G.* iii. 516. Perhaps Olivi's estimate of St. Bonaventura is far more favourable than that of the majority of his party because of his personal contact with the great Minister-General.

[6] Cf. *A.V.* lib. v. cap. iii. f. 1 *v.a*; Olivi, " Quaestio de Veritate Indulgentiae Portiunculae ", p. 142 ; and St. Bonaventura, " Legenda Maiora ", *Opera Omnia*, viii. p. 504.

[7] Olivi, " Defensio et Expositio articulorum quorundam ab infrascriptis magistris damnatorum " (*Quod.* f. 46 *v.a*).

[8] *A.L.K.G.* iii. 412. Cardinal Ehrle thinks that Olivi fulfilled all the conditions necessary for his master's degree but for some reason never actually received it. Bartholommeo da Pisa (*loc. cit.*) calls him " bachalarius formatus Parisius ".

suppose that he might already have put forward opinions which were regarded as dangerous by the university authorities. We know very little about the following years of his life beyond the fact that they were probably spent in his native province, where he appears to have gathered round him a little band of followers. He probably attained to the dignity of the priesthood, as many of the " questiones " in his *Quodlibeta* are concerned with matters which would only affect one who was in the habit of administering the sacraments and hearing confessions.[1] Moreover, Angelo da Clareno in one part of his chronicle speaks of him as celebrating Mass.[2] During the generalship of Jerome of Ascoli, afterwards Pope Nicholas IV., certain views which he had held concerning the Virgin Mary were condemned as erroneous, and he was ordered to burn the treatise containing them, which he did with an unmoved countenance, a fact which left a deep impression on the mind of his Superior.[3] This condemnation does not seem to have affected Olivi's reputation in the Order, where he was gradually gaining fame both for his theological and philosophical doctrines and for the holiness of his life. In 1279, when Nicholas III. held the celebrated inquiry into the closely connected questions of poverty and the " usus pauper ", which was to result in the bull " Exiit qui seminat ",[4] he was not only requested to give his opinion in writing on these subjects but was probably actually present at Soriano when the decretal was promulgated.[5] It must have been during this visit to Italy that he visited Assisi, and wrote his little " Quaestio de Veritate Indulgentiae, vulgo dictae de Portiuncula ".[6] Since his own views had been largely embodied in the papal exposition of the Rule, Olivi must have returned to his native province with high hopes both for the reformation of his Order and for his own future career. If such was the case they were soon to be frustrated, for within a few years a storm was to break forth which, except for a few brief interludes, was to last for the remainder of his own life and then rage with redoubled fury over the heads of his devoted followers.

At a Chapter-General, held at Strasburg in the Pentecost of 1282, Olivi was denounced as a setter forth of strange and erroneous

---

[1] Cf. *Quod.* v. f. 33 *r.*-37 *r.*

[2] *A.L.K.G.* ii. 288.

[3] *Ibid.* Cardinal Ehrle believes that at this time a general inquiry was held into Olivi's doctrines. Cf. *ibid.* iii. 13 and 414. Jerome was General from 1274 to 1278 and was created a cardinal in 1278 by Nicholas III. He became Pope in 1289 and died in 1292.

[4] *B.F.* iii. p. 404 *s.*

[5] Olivi mentions in the sixth chapter of his exposition of the Rule that his opinion was asked through his Provincial. Cf. *A.L.K.G.* iii. 415.

[6] Printed in *Acta Ordinis Minorum*, xiv. pp. 139-45.

doctrines.[1] By a strange irony of fate the letters of the Minister-General [2] directed to this chapter contain recommendations concerning the observation of the " usus pauper " in the sense laid down by the decretal " Exiit qui seminat ", and also a solemn warning against the opinions of Olivi and his followers.[3] We can only make conjectures as to the cause of the accusations. Just at this time Olivi had been attacking the doctrines of a certain " Frater Ar ",[4] whom scholars have identified either with the future General, Arlotto of Prato, or with Arnald " de Roccafolio ", later Provincial of Provence.[5] Perhaps the latter suggestion is the more probable, for Arlotto was already a doctor of theology and highly esteemed in the Order, so that it would have been presumptuous for a young and still comparatively obscure " bachelor " to take exception to his opinions, and although Olivi was by no means devoid of self-confidence he rarely failed in deference towards his superiors. Arnald, on the other hand, was his equal in rank, and if he were the man attacked his bitter hostility towards both Olivi and his disciples can easily be explained.[6] Perhaps he and his followers drew up the charges against his rival as a kind of counter-attack. Certainly, the Minister-General seems to have received both denunciations but only concerned himself with the one directed against Olivi.[7] The committee of Parisian theologians whom he appointed to examine his doctrines was carefully chosen, but its procedure was open to censure, for the accused was not heard in his own defence.[8] Furthermore, when he applied to his Provincial for permission to go to Paris where the inquiry was being held this was expressly denied him.[9] In his letter [10] to his judges, Olivi complains bitterly that in many cases they had entirely misunderstood his views. Moreover, the extracts from his writings quoted in their report did not give a true conception of his

---

[1] *Chronicle of the 24 Generals (A.F.* iii. p. 374).

[2] Bonagratia di San Giovanni in Persiceto, General 1279–83.

[3] *A.L.K.G.* iii. 415 ; cf. *ibid.* ii. 385 and 387.

[4] *Quod.* f. 42 *r.*-53 *r.* Mentioned by Olivi in his letter to Frater R. de Camliaco (*ibid.* f. 52 *r.b* and f. 52 *v.a*).

[5] *A.L.K.G.* iii. p. 478. Cf. *A.F.H.* vi. 593. Another suggestion is Frater " Arnaldus Galhardi ", and this is supported by the somewhat doubtful evidence of the Catalogue of Raymund de Fronsac. Cf. *A.L.K.G.* iii. 16.

[6] He was Provincial of Provence in 1300, and made use of his position to persecute the Zealots. Cf. Ubertino da Casale's Defence of Olivi (*A.L.K.G.* ii. 388).

[7] " In explicatione eorum que contra aliqua dicta sua (fratris Ar) scripsi, credens quod per generalem tam sua quam mea examinaretur." Letter to Frater R. de Camliaco (*Quod.* f. 52 *v.a*).

[8] " Letter to Judges " (*ibid.* 54 *r.*). Quoted in *A.L.K.G.* iii. 419-21.

[9] *Quod.* f. 54 *r.*; *A.L.K.G.* iii. 420.

[10] *Quod.* f. 54 *r.*-50 *v.b.* At f. 54 the numeration of the leaves suddenly goes back to f. 43.

teaching because of their divorce from their original context.[1]   It was for this reason that he wrote his famous apology, which is in reality a justification of all his teaching.   This document is an invaluable source for estimating the extent of the examination, for it shows us that it was not mainly concerned with Olivi's teaching on poverty but also with his theological and philosophical theories. Such questions as his denial of the " Rationes Seminales ",[2] and his belief that the Rational, or Intellectual, Soul was not the "form" of the body but was only connected with it by means of the sensitive soul,[3] as well as his views concerning the Divine Essence,[4] were also censured.   His judges, moreover, took exception to the fact that he had taught that matrimony, having existed under the old law, conferred less grace than the other sacraments which had been instituted by Christ,[5] and that baptism bestowed the same " character " to the soul as dedication gave to the Church.[6]   It is very difficult to understand the precise meaning of this last tenet. Finally, thirty-four excerpts were taken from the writings of Olivi and were set out in a roll, together with the verdict of the commission upon each.   Some were judged as definitely heretical, while others were merely stigmatised as rash.   Not content with this document, the judges drew up another, to which they appended their seals, containing opinions exactly opposed to those drawn from the works of Olivi.[7]   This is generally known as the " Littera VII. sigillorum ", and was sent to the Minister-General at Avignon along with the conclusions of the Commission.[8]   The accused was now summoned to hear the sentence of his judges, but when he arrived Bonagratia was too ill to direct the proceedings himself, so that his authority devolved on his secretary, Gerard of Prato, Arlotto's brother.[9]   Olivi was ordered to sign both documents, thus being faced with the terrible alternative of accepting the verdict of the Commission without question, and of subscribing to doctrines exactly contrary to those which he had formerly held and taught, or of being regarded as a stubborn heretic, disobedient to the commands of his superiors.[10]   He chose the latter, but at the

---

[1] *A.L.K.G.* iii. 419-20.   [2] *Quod.* f. 45 *v.a.*

[3] F. 45 *v.a* and 51 *v.b.* Cf. Q. 51 of *Questiones in II. Sententiarum*, ii. 101-36.

[4] *Quod.* f. 43 *r.b*-45 *r.b*, and a special treatise written for his judges (*ibid.* f. 53 *v.a*-61 *v.b*).

[5] " Letter to Judges " (*Quod.* f. 45 *v.a*-46 *r.b*).

[6] Letter to " R. de Camliaco " (*ibid.* f. 51 *v.b*).

[7] F. 54 *r.a*-54 *v.a* ; *A.L.K.G.* iii. 419.

[8] *A.L.K.G.* iii. 419.

[9] *Ibid.* 417; from the *Chronicle of the 24 Generals* (*A.F.* iii. p. 376.)

[10] " Qua causa modus ita perplexus et captiosus circa me est habitus, et si vellem fugere Scyllam, inciderem in Charybdim, aut si eligerem maris profunda vitare, eo ipso caderem in Bithalassum " (" Letter to Judges ", *Quod.* 54 *r.a*-54 *v.a* ; *A.L.K.G.* iii. 419).

same time tried to justify his attitude by his dignified letter to his judges [1]—no easy task since all copies of his writings had been removed from him.[2] When we read it we are struck both by his moderation and by his sturdy independence. Olivi believed firmly that the ultimate decision on matters of faith lay with the Holy See,[3] and that to accept the opinions of any body of men, however learned, without being intellectually convinced of their truth, savoured of the error of the Corinthians, who had boasted of belonging to the faction of Paul or of Apollos, or of the theologians of his own day, who proclaimed themselves the disciples of Aquinas or of Aristotle.[4] For his own part he was prepared to submit if only the falsehood of his former theories was proved to him by reason, and, moreover, to show his respect for the wisdom and reputation of his judges, he would subscribe without further ado to their verdict upon purely philosophical questions,[5] but to do so with regard to his theological beliefs would involve him in the sin of idolatry. After this he gives a reasoned exposition of certain of his doctrines, with frequent references to matters already touched upon in his " questiones ". The most significant of these is perhaps his defence of his teaching with regard to poverty.[6] There is a wonderful ring of defiance in his contention that if they condemned his views on this subject, they might equally denounce those of Pecham and St. Bonaventura.[7] The theory of the generation of the divine essence was evidently regarded by Olivi as being of paramount importance, for he discusses it in a separate treatise, justifying his attitude by many quotations from the Scriptures and the Fathers and the decrees of the Church.[8] Finally, he ends with a passionate plea to his judges, as his fathers and brothers in the Order, to take pity on one who was labouring under such a weight

[1] Written from Nîmes in 1285 (*Quod.* 54 *r.a*-50 *v.a*).

[2] At the actual time of writing he had miraculously obtained a copy of his " questiones " as well as one of the verdicts of his judges (*Quod.* 54 *v.a* ; *A.L.K.G.* iii. 420).

[3] " Ex hoc tamen a me obedientiam talem exigere aut exigendam consulere non debetis, ut vestris dictis, quamvis solemnibus quamvis reverendis, tanquam Catholicae fidei, aut velut scripturae sacre eloquiis, aut tanquam determinationi Romani pontificis vel concilii generalis omnino debeam subdi, nisi enodatione luce clariori primitus innotescat, vestrum dictum esse vere dictum catholicae fidei et scripturae sacrae" (*ibid.* 418).

[4] In letter to " R. de Camliaco," f. 52 *v.b.*

[5] *Quod.* 54 *v.a* ; *A.L.K.G.* iii. 420.

[6] F. 46 *r.b*-48 *r.b.* Cf. his question on the " usus pauper " in *A.L.K.G.* iii. 507-14.

[7] " Item, quare tunc non damnat dicta fratris Bonaventura. . . . Quare etiam non damnat dicta fratris Ioannis de Pachano. . . . Ulterius, quare non condemnant omnia illa que declaratio, seu decretalis, domini Nicolai dicit de paupere usu ? " (f. 47 *r.a*).

[8] F. 53 *v.a*-f. 61 *v.b.*

of calumny and detraction, and his eagerness is further shown by the fact that he implores them to send him a reply by the bearer of his own letter.[1]   This remarkable piece of writing is dated from Nîmes in the year 1285.   A similar letter, directed from Montpellier to a certain Frater " R. de Camliaco " and others of his disciples whose faith in their master had been shaken by the judgment of the Commission, was probably written earlier, for in it Olivi mentions that he had been deprived of every copy of his writings.[2]   The matters dealt with in it are often different from those defended in his letter to his judges,[3] and are on the whole less important, though it is interesting to note that he had already incurred suspicion because of his predilection for apocalyptic speculations.[4]   We see from this letter how bitterly his proud and sensitive nature was tortured by the loss of his reputation, and particularly by the fact that he was regarded by many in his Order as a spreader of sedition.[5]   His only consolation lay in his consciousness of his own innocence, and he believed that this chastisement had been sent by God as a punishment for his secret sins.[6]   In the days of his prosperity he had thought too much of gaining fame as a teacher, thereby imperilling his immortal soul by dwelling constantly upon earthly vanities.[7]   There is something infinitely touching in the proud submission of his attitude.

The two years following the death of Bonagratia di San Giovanni in Persiceto are very confused, especially as his successor was not elected till 1285.[8]   Gerard of Prato seems to have continued the proceedings, by issuing stringent ·instructions to the authorities in the various Franciscan convents that they should prevent the friars under their charge from reading Olivi's books pending the election of the new General.[9]   At the Chapter-General of Milan in 1285, where Arlotto of Prato was elected General, a decree was passed ordering the confiscation of these until the will of the new head of the Order was known.[10]   We know nothing of the fate of Olivi during these years, for he does not even tell us in his letters whether he was in prison or at large. The new General appears at once to have resumed the inquiry

---

[1] *Quod.* f. 50 *v.a.*

[2] " Omnibus denudatus, etiam scriptitationibus meis " (53 *r.b.*).

[3] It is interesting that in his letter to his followers Olivi was mainly concerned with the defence of his philosophical doctrines.   [4] F. 53 *r.a* and f. 53 *r.b.*

[5] *Quod.* f. 51 *r.a* and 51 *v.a.*   [6] F. 53 *r.b.*   [7] F. 51 *r.a.*

[8] By the constitutions of Narbonne no Chapter-General could be held at the Pentecost following the death of the Minister-General. Thus the long delay in electing a successor to Bonagratia. Cf. Callebaut, " Acta Capituli Generalis Mediolani celebrati " (An. 1285, *A.F.H.* xxii. 273-4).

[9] *Quod.* f. 54 *r.a* ; *A.L.K.G.* iii. 418.

[10] *A.L.K.G.* iii. 429 ; *A.F.H.* xxii. p. 289.

by arranging for a meeting between the accused and certain of his judges, but it is difficult to know whether any settlement had been reached before the death of Arlotto in 1286. According to the Spirituals, Olivi had already succeeded in defending himself from the charges brought against him,[1] but, as the matter was again brought up at the Chapter-General of Montpellier in 1287, it is by no means certain that such was the case.[2] The *Chronicle of the 24 Generals* declares that Olivi eventually accepted the decision of his judges in every particular, but this is not a very trustworthy source of evidence owing to the antipathy of its author for the Zealots.[3] It is difficult, moreover, to see how Olivi could have taken such a step and yet have retained the respect and devotion of his disciples. It is also utterly inconsistent with the resolutions underlying the dignified moderation of his letter to the commission at Paris. Besides, at the Chapter-General of Montpellier he was again questioned concerning his doctrine of the " usus pauper ", which did not in fact materially differ from that contained in the official policy of the Order as embodied in " Exiit qui seminat ".[4] Arlotto's successor, Matthew of Acquasparta, has even to-day some renown as a speculative thinker,[5] and for this reason perhaps was favourably disposed towards Olivi. To show the latter's innocence of the heresies of which he had been accused he sent him as lector to Sta Croce, one of the largest and most important of the Franciscan " studia ".[6] With this appointment a new phase in Olivi's life began.

Matthew of Acquasparta may have hoped to restore peace to Provence by sending Olivi to Italy. The result of his action, however, was merely to extend the storm to another region, for the new lector at Sta Croce had too much magnetism not to inspire either ardent affection or vehement hatred in the hearts of those who surrounded him. Scholars have scrupled to attribute the origin of the Spiritual movement in Tuscany to his influence, but he is certainly responsible for its later developments, and ultimately for the schism of the Tuscan Zealots in 1313.[7] In Florence, moreover, he met one who was to be the greatest of his followers and was to play a leading part in the doings of his party for many

---

[1] According to the " Chronicle of the Seven Tribulations ", Arlotto arranged a meeting at Paris between Olivi and Richard of Middleton and John of Murrovalle, both of whom, like himself, had sat on the commission of 1282 (*A.L.K.G.* ii. 296). Ubertino da Casale, in his defence of Olivi, declares that he definitely quashed the process instigated by his predecessor (*ibid.* 387).

[2] *Ibid.* 400. At any rate, he made a declaration concerning his doctrine of the ' usus pauper " which was accepted by the Chapter (*ibid.*).

[3] *A.F.* iii. p. 376.   [4] *B.F.* iii. p. 404.

[5] Cf. de Wulf, *Histoire de la philosophie médiévale*, i. pp. 358-61.

[6] *A.L.K.G.* ii. 389.   [7] *Ibid.* iv. 25 *s.*

years after his leader's death. Ubertino da Casale has left us a vivid picture of the devotion which Olivi inspired in his heart,[1] and tells us that the time of his intercourse with him was the turning-point in his life. Moreover, this new disciple was no un-lettered fanatic but a graduate of Paris,[2] able to enter into all the philosophic speculations of his master, though by temperament more interested in his moral teaching and his studies upon the " Apocalypse ".[3] We do not know how far the influence of the great Spiritual extended beyond the borders of Tuscany. In the letter to Conrad of Offida, written during the closing years of his life,[4] Olivi expresses himself almost as if he had a strong claim to the obedience of the Italian Zealots. Angelo da Clareno, moreover, although he had probably no knowledge of him, save what he gained through his friendship with Ubertino and certain leaders of the stricter party in Provence,[5] never mentions him except with reverent awe. It is a strong testimony to the force and vitality of Olivi's personality that during his short stay in Italy he should have gained such a position for himself.

Soon after his election to the Generalship of the Franciscan Order, Raymund Gaufridi appointed the great Spiritual to a lector-ship at Montpellier, an even more important " studium " than Sta Croce.[6] Olivi's return to his native province was merely a pre-lude to further troubles, for in 1290 the general was instructed by Pope Nicholas IV., formerly Jerome of Ascoli, to take proceedings against certain Friars of Provence who reputed themselves holier than their fellows and were exciting schism in the Order.[7] As the papal letters have been lost,[8] it is not certain that these men were in fact followers of Olivi,[9] especially when it is remembered how deeply the south of France had been impregnated with the Albigensian heresy, and how prone the Provençal temperament was to religious excesses. The inquiry was entrusted to Bertrand of Sigottier, the Franciscan Inquisitor in the county of Venaissin,[10] but Olivi was again forced to justify and expound his doctrine with regard to the " usus pauper " at the Chapter-General of Paris in 1292,[11] so that it is likely that the action of the rebels

---

[1] *A.V.* Prologue, i. f. 2 *v.b.*   [2] *Ibid.* f. 2 *r.a.*

[3] *Ibid.* f. 2 *v.b.*   [4] Published in *A.F.H.* xi. pp. 366-73.

[5] *A.L.K.G.* i. 466 ; ii. 288 *s.* " Sanctus homo dei." Cf. *supra*, p. 60, *n.* 3.

[6] *A.L.K.G.* ii. 389 and iii. 431. Raymund Gaufridi was General from 1289 to 1295.   [7] *A.F.* iii. p. 420.

[8] These letters are recorded in the Catalogue of Raymund de Fronsac. Cf. *A.L.K.G.* iii. 14.

[9] Ubertino da Casale declared that the friars in question had no connection with Olivi (*ibid.* ii. 389; iii. 192).

[10] *A.F.* iii. p. 420 ; *A.L.K.G.* iii. 15 and 435.

[11] *A.F.* iii. p. 421 ; " Historia Septem Tribulationum " (*A.L.K.G.* ii. 295 ; iii. 191).

may have originated from a garbled version of his theories. He spent the last years of his life at Narbonne, much beloved by the brethren of the convent but still mistrusted by his Superiors. So great was his reputation for holiness that Robert, Louis, and Raymund Berengar, the three sons of Charles II. of Naples, wrote to beg him for his company during their imprisonment in Aragon. Olivi's answer [1] shows how greatly touched he was by the invitation, but he refused it on the ground that he had made it his rule to silence his detractors by accepting no worldly honour. [2] Moreover, he had heard a report that his attendance would not be pleasing to the king of Naples, who feared that he might corrupt the faith of his sons. [3] This letter is a proof that Olivi fully understood the suffering which lies at the basis of all existence, and without which man cannot hope to attain perfection or render himself pleasing to God. His own last days were far from cloudless, for he was deeply wounded by the stigma of heresy which still clung to his name, and which his loyalty and devotion to the Church rendered even more insupportable. Moreover, his generous and affectionate nature [4] must have been deeply troubled by the persecution of those who mistakenly regarded themselves as his disciples. His last book, the Commentary on the Apocalypse, shows that he brooded long and bitterly over the evils of his age, and that he reluctantly came to the conclusion that the only safety for the faithful lay in separation from the " carnal " Church, just as at the beginning of the second great epoch in the history of the world Christ's disciples had withdrawn from all contact with the synagogue. [5] On his death-bed he called the Brothers round him, and, again repeating those opinions on the question of poverty to the defence of which he had devoted so large a portion of his life, he declared himself to be a loyal son of the Church, to whose judgment he committed all his written works. [6] He passed away at the sixth hour on the fourteenth of

---

[1] *A.L.K.G.* iii. pp. 534-40. This letter was written from Narbonne in May 1295. The invitation to Olivi was probably due to the fact that Frater Petrus Scarerii, lector to the young princes, and afterwards Bishop of Rapolla, was his personal friend (Toynbee, *op. cit.* p. 76).

[2] *A.L.K.G.* iii. 538.

[3] " Nam et michi a fide digno aliquo dictum fuit, quod eciam dominus pater vester timuerat vos imbeguiniri, seu ut proprius loquar in divinis infatuari per eloquia oris mei " (*ibid.* p. 539).

[4] His question on the Freedom of the Will (Questio LVII. ii. 305-94) contains some fine passages upon friendship.

[5] *Misc.* ii. p. 263.

[6] *A.L.K.G.* ii. 409 and 411 ; iii. 411. This confession may possibly be the one contained in the Codex Laurentianus, S. Crucis, Plut 31, sin cod 3, f. 206 *s.*, and now printed in *A.F.H.* xi. 267-9. It was used by Wadding in his *Annales*, v. p. 378, § xxxiii. Cf. *infra.* p. 119, *n.* 1.

March, in the year 1298, having lived fifty years in the world, thirty-eight of which had been spent in the Franciscan Order.[1]

Olivi's death rather increased than diminished the sufferings of his disciples. For ten years more the persecution continued in the south of France, and over 300 friars were punished for refusing to surrender his books, and for declaring that the " usus pauper " formed part of the substance of the vow of poverty.[2] Many of the victims were men of high character and attainments, though it is possible that the bulk of them were simple-minded enthusiasts who laid more stress on ragged and patched habits than on weightier matters. In the case of a certain Raymund Aurioli, who had been imprisoned in Aragon, the persecution ended fatally, while his companion, " Johannes Primi ", was only just released in time to save his life.[3] The events in Provence also had repercussions in Tuscany.[4] When Clement V.'s attention was at last drawn to the condition of the Franciscan Order,[5] the subject of the doctrines of Olivi was one of the most important questions at issue between the two parties.[6] These were ably defended by Ubertino da Casale, who was able to confute his opponents by long quotations from the works of his beloved master. For the most part the heresies attributed to Olivi were the same as those which had been condemned in 1282. Unfortunately, the works from which Ubertino drew his information have in many cases not come down to us, although parallel passages can be found in certain other writings of Olivi, and notably in his own defence of his doctrines. The early part of his " Summa " on the sentences which contains the statement of his theory of the divine essence has never been found,[7] but we gather that he believed that the essence was the same in the three persons of the Trinity, the only difference being that it was generating in the Father, generated in the Son, while in the case of the Holy Spirit it emanated from the other two conjointly.[8] His opponents, on the other hand, declared these distinctions to be rather personal than essential.[9] Only certain fragments of the

[1] *A.L.K.G.* iii. 411.
[2] *A.L.K.G.* ii. 300, 384, 386, and 409 ; iii. 184. Cf. *supra*, p. 12.
[3] *A.L.K.G.* ii. 386. Cf. *supra*, p. 12, *n.* 1.
[4] *A.L.K.G.* ii. 384.
[5] Cf. *supra*, p. 12.   [6] Cf. *supra*, p. 14, *n.* 3.
[7] *A.L.K.G.* iii. pp. 464 and 474 *s.*; ii. p. 392; and Jansen, Introduction to Olivi's *Questiones in II. Sententiarum*, p. xiv.
[8] *A.L.K.G.* ii. 389, 392-93.
[9] " Et quod eadem sacrosancta ecclesia diffinivit et in concilio generali posito, extra de sum. trin. et fide cath. firmiter tenendum et simpliciter confitendum quod essentia in divinis, sive sumpta in communi, prout est communis tribus personis, seu sigillatim, prout videlicet est in patre et filio et spiritu sancto, non generans, nec genita, nec procedens, et quod nulla est distinctio ponenda in essentia divina, cum pater et filius et sanctus spiritus eandem omnino

Tractatus de Sacramentis alluded to by Ubertino have ever been discovered.[1] The only new heresy was taken from a passage in Olivi's exposition of St. John's Gospel, where he gave it as a possible opinion that Christ had been pierced by the lance before his death, but, according to Ubertino, did not state definitely that such a view was either true or false.[2] Finally, this was declared to be erroneous, and, together with Olivi's doctrines with regard to the rational soul, baptism, and the divine essence, was condemned by the Council of Vienne, though the name of their originator was not mentioned in the definition which declared the opposite dogmas to be more in accordance with the Catholic faith.[3] This in the eyes of the Zealots was tantamount to an acquittal,[4] and they believed that soon the Church would vindicate the fame of their great leader by enrolling him among her Saints.[5] During the anarchy which prevailed in Provence after the death of Clement V. and the Minister-General, Alexander of Alexandria, his tomb at Narbonne became almost a centre of pilgrimage, and even certain of the cardinals sent offerings to his shrine.[6] But the triumph of his friends was short-lived, and after the accession of John XXII. the Franciscan authorities destroyed his grave[7] lest it should become an object of popular devotion. At the Chapter-General of 1319 the reading of his works was again forbidden,[8] and the same year a papal commission examined his Commentary on the Apocalypse[9] though it was not finally condemned till 1326.[10] Save for certain of his most faithful followers, who often vindicated their devotion with their lives, the only persons who remained true to the memory of Olivi were the Béguins. They regarded him as their founder, and accorded him a veneration even greater than that which they paid to St. Francis,[11] but the fanatical zeal of these

---

habeant substantiam indivisibilem et indistinctam, utpote omnino simplicem, sed est pater qui generat, filius qui generatur, et spiritus sanctus qui procedit, ut distinctiones sint in persona et unitas in natura."

" Accusations of the Conventuals against the doctrines of Olivi of March 1, 1311 " (*A.L.K.G.* ii. 367).

[1] *A.L.K.G.* iii. 476. Cf. *infra*, p. 112, *n*. 3.   [2] *A.L.K.G.* ii. 368, 402 *s.*

[3] In " Fidei Catholicae fundamento ", passed during third Session of Council (*A.L.K.G.* v. 379). Decree given in Mansi, *Concilia*, xxv. 411. Cf. *B.F.* v. *n.* 196, p. 86.

[4] *A.L.K.G.* iii. 449.   [5] *Ibid.* ii. 129, 293 ; iii. 443.

[6] *Ibid.* iii. 443. Cf. *supra*, p. 17.

[7] *A.L.K.G.* ii. 293 ; iii. 443. Ehrle thinks the early tradition that his body was burnt at Avignon is unfounded. Cf. *ibid.* iii. 457.

[8] *Ibid.* ii. 149. This Chapter was held at Marseilles.

[9] Probably in 1319. For Report of this Commission, cf. *Misc.* ii. 258-70.

[10] Possibly John XXII. requested the opinion of Franciscus Silvestri, Bishop of Florence, before finally condemning it. Extracts in Raynaldi, *Annales*, xxiv. 1325, xx.; and *B.F.* v. 297, *n.* 2.

[11] Bernard Gui, *op. cit.* i. p. 110.

poor and ignorant men served only further to blacken his reputation, and to cause him to be regarded by the orthodox as the originator of a heretical sect. There is no fate that Olivi would have
more deeply deplored.

On the whole, the judgment of the Franciscan chroniclers of
the fourteenth and fifteenth centuries was more favourable towards the great Spiritual than might have been expected.[1] The
ban laid upon his writings, however, was not lifted until late in the
fifteenth century, though a certain amount of laxity seems to have
existed concerning its observance,[2] at least among the higher ranks
of the Order. Finally, Sixtus IV. gave the friars permission to
study his works upon condition that they plucked the roses and
left the thorns,[3] but the prohibition was again renewed upon pain
of imprisonment at the Chapter-General of Terni in 1500.[4]
Possibly, this time it did not last very long. At any rate, in the
following century, Olivi found a zealous champion in the Franciscan
historian, Wadding, who defended him valiantly against the attacks
of the famous annalist, Baronius.[5] His true vindication, however,
has had to await the publication of certain of his writings which
has only taken place in recent years.[6] Now it is seen that the saintly
fanatic of earlier writers was in reality a keen and subtle thinker
dominated rather by his intellect than by his feelings, and one,
moreover, who made use of both moderation and good sense in his
solution of the moral problems which affected his Order. Olivi
was not merely like Angelo and Conrad of Offida, a lover of poverty,
but like Bacon and Duns Scotus, a seeker after knowledge.

THE WRITINGS OF OLIVI

"Qui totam Bibliam, tam vetus quam etiam novum Testamentum postillavit, nichil dimictens intactum. Opus utique
prolixum et laboriosissimum. Scripsit super IV. Sententiarum
libros et opuscula et questiones quam-plurima multum profunde".[7]

---

[1] Cf. Bartolommeo de Pisa (*A.F.* iv. 340); and Glassberger's Chronicle
(*ibid.* ii. 100).

[2] It was probably always possible to obtain permission to read his works.
Cf. *A.F.H.* xx. 301. They were certainly known to Bartolommeo of Pisa and
S. Bernardino. Cf. *infra*, p. 262.

[3] *Chronologia historico-legalis Seraphici Ordinis* (Naples, 1650), i. p. 178.
Cf. *A.L.K.G.* iii. 458.

[4] *Ibid.*

[5] *Annales*, pp. 381-93, 1297, §§ xxxvii.-li.

[6] Especially of the extracts from his Questions on Poverty in *A.L.K.G.* iii.
503-33, and his *Questiones in II^m Librum Sententiarum* in the *Bibliotheca
Franciscana Scholastica Medii Aevi*" (vols iv.-vi.).

[7] Mariano da Firenze, "Compendium Chronicarum Fratrum Minorum"
(*A.F.H.* ii. 462).

The above summary of the writings of Olivi, written over two hundred years after his death, is on the whole not greatly exaggerated. He was renowned even during his lifetime for the wide range of his works, which, as his disciple Ubertino da Casale proudly boasts, were seventeen times as extensive as those of the famous Peter Lombard.[1] Certain have not survived and are only known to us through the catalogues of the libraries of Urban V. and Benedict XIII.,[2] but Cardinal Ehrle's description of the manuscripts which still exist occupies at least thirty pages of his article.[3] The contents of perhaps the majority of these are almost unknown, even to scholars, but sufficient of Olivi's work has now been printed to allow us to form a general conception of the most characteristic features of his thought, and an estimate of its value as a contribution to the solution of the problems which have baffled the mind of man throughout the ages.

When we first study the writings of Olivi we are forced to stifle a strong feeling of disappointment. His subject-matter is abstract rather than personal, and he is altogether lacking in the imaginative power of Ubertino da Casale, nor does he possess that sense of the magic of words which gives a haunting fragrance to Angelo's shortest letter. His style is clear and lucid, and he aims at convincing his hearers rather by the force of his arguments than by the strength of his personal convictions. The calm atmosphere of the lecture-room pervades even his discussions of subjects very near to his heart, such as the kindred questions of poverty and the " usus pauper ", which were wont to raise Angelo to heights of mystic ecstasy, and arouse in Ubertino hot and bitter indignation against the abuses in the Franciscan Order. We must always remember that much of what has come down to us was intended primarily for the "schools", and thus originally received warmth and colour from the close personal contact between master and pupils. How great a spell this must have been we know from the fact that men preferred to face torture and imprisonment rather than surrender the writings of one whom they revered as a saint.[4] Probably, at no time in his life had Olivi sufficient leisure to do more than roughly revise his lecture notes, so that it is not surprising that his work is lacking in finish. Yet, it is never slovenly in execution, for his meaning is generally clearly and concisely given, while he devotes much time to the

[1] *A.L.K.G.* ii. p. 406. " Et sciat sapientia apostolica, quod quantitas librorum fratris P(etri) . . . ascendit plusquam X. et VII. vicibus ultra, ut credimus, quam textus libri sententiarum in lictere quantitate."

[2] *Ibid.* iii. 459-65.

[3] *Ibid.* 465-97. The whole article is only 132 pages, 43 of which are taken up by extracts from Olivi's works.

[4] *Ibid.* ii. 384, 386, and 409; iii. 183.

statement and solution of the arguments of his opponents. Moreover, the whole discussion is methodically arranged, after a logical and well-devised plan, and he seldom yields to the temptation to wander off into bypaths. On theological and philosophical subjects especially he is an original, if not a very profound, thinker, and even on more practical matters his opinion is usually worth consideration. If his work is destitute of fire and imagination, it is none the less remarkable because of its wide and varied range. Almost every social, moral, or political problem affecting the diverse and manifold phases of medieval life is a subject for eager speculation on the part of this Franciscan, who had renounced the world before he had tasted of its cup, and he brings all the subtlety of his keen intelligence to his help when engaged upon their solution. Nor are his answers those of the typical religious enthusiast, but show both a complete grasp of the issues involved and a practical ability which is even more surprising when we remember how very little experience he can have had of the ordinary affairs of life.

Perhaps the most influential part of Olivi's teaching is his exposition of his views on poverty and kindred questions, which is to be found in his commentaries on the third book of the Sentences. Extracts from this have been printed by Cardinal Ehrle, but it is not certain whether they have been taken from his Summa[1] or if they are simply redaction of his lecture notes.[2] Their actual date is a matter of uncertainty, but some of them must have been delivered, though perhaps not in their present form, as early as 1279.[3] For instance, the famous discussion of the " usus pauper "[4]

---

[1] St. Bernardino in his dialogue with his disciple Paul quotes from Questions 11 and 12, which he declared were to be found in the third part of the Summa. Cf. *A.F.H.* xi. 312 ; *infra*, p. 262.

[2] Ehrle uses Codex Vaticanus, 4986. It is noteworthy that Codex Capistranensis, xxvi., which gives a totally different order for certain of the questions on Poverty, refers on f. 83 *r.* to the arrangement of the Vatican Codex as if it were the official one. It also gives a totally different ending to the Tractatus de Usu Paupere (cf. *A.L.K.G.* iii. pp. 514-17), which corresponds exactly with the one given by Ubertino da Casale in his defence of Olivi (*A.L.K.G.* ii. 400 *s.*). For description of the Capistrano codex, cf. *A.F.H.* i. pp. 617-22.

[3] Ehrle believes that Questions 1-10 in C. Vat. 4986, which form a little group by themselves, were probably composed during Olivi's stay in Rome, for in Q. 15 he refers to matters already dealt with " in questionibus quas Rome feci " (*A.L.K.G.* iii. p. 507, *n.* 1). The remaining eight are all later than 1279, the 13th (*ibid.* 525-28), dealing with the lawfulness of the renunciation of Celestine V., being as late as 1294 (*ibid.* 497-502 ; cf. also, M. D'Alverny, *op. cit.* p. 6). The reference in C. Capistranensis, xxvi. f. 83 *n.*, is to the earlier section of questions."

[4] Q. ix. (*A.L.K.G.* iii. pp. 507-14). This must not be confused with the treatise on the same subject, written not only after the papal pronouncement but after the letter of Bonagratia di San Giovanni in Persiceto, enforcing its provisions (*ibid.* 514-17 ; cf. *supra*, pp. 84-85). For Olivi's defence of his doctrines, cf. *Quod.* f. 46 *v.a*-48 *r.b* and *supra*, p. 855.

to which his judges took such exception was, as we learn from another question,[1] composed before the promulgation of " Exiit qui seminat ".[2] For Olivi, the only path to perfection lay in the complete renunciation of possessions, after the example of Christ and his apostles, and in a small treatise attached to his " questio " devoted to this theme he shows that the Franciscan rule embodied the means necessary for leading such a life.[3] Nor had he any patience with those who would deny so complete an abandonment of temporal things to the Claresses, for it was equally suited to women as to men.[4] The " usus pauper " was inseparably bound up with the Franciscan vow of poverty, for a free and lavish use of worldly goods turned possessionlessness into a mere fiction.[5] The importance which he attached to this point is shown by the fact that he discussed its implications in connection with many matters contained in the Rule, such as the wearing of coarse tunics and the restrictions upon riding and the use of shoes.[6] According to Olivi, certain matters fell indeterminately under the vow, and often cases arose in which the individual was forced to make use of his own discretion. In times of urgent need it was permitted to ride and wear shoes, and, since men's estimates of necessity differed, every breach of the rule was not mortal sin, but only flagrant and repeated offences, as, for example, making it a matter of habit to go on horseback or wear shoes.[7] In the same way, every infringement of the " usus pauper " could not be judged severely, but only such an unrestricted use of temporal goods as might be termed free rather than limited.[8] Olivi goes on to discuss certain abuses which had crept into the Order, such as the proctorial system,[9] and the popularity of the Minorite Churches as burial-places for the wealthy, a custom which led to endless disputes with the secular clergy over the mortuary dues. In fact, only in cases of extreme need could the burial of the dead be termed a religious duty, and even then it must always be abandoned when it conflicted with higher claims.[10] Olivi's essential moderation is

---

[1] Q. xv. (*A.L.K.G.* iii. p. 531).   [2] *B.F.* iii. p. 404 *s.*

[3] Q. viii. (*A.L.K.G.* iii. 505-507). Cardinal Ehrle thinks that perhaps this may be the treatise Olivi wrote at the request of his Provincial. Cf. *ibid.* p. 505, *n.* 5, and *supra*, p. 84, *n.* 5.   [4] *A.L.K.G.* iii. 506.

[5] *Ibid.* 508. " Non enim invenies aliquam paupertatem altissimo modo valere ad altissimam virtutum perfectionem nisi ei adiungatur usus pauper." " Sicut forma se habet ad materiam, sic usus pauper se habet ad abdicationem omnis iuris."   [6] *Ibid.*   [7] *Ibid.* 510.

[8] " Unde non omnis deviatio a paupere usu in professoribus suis mortale inducit, sed quando est talis et tanta, quod pensatis hinc inde circumstantiis potius debet censeri dives usus quam pauper " (*ibid.*).

[9] *Ibid.* 513. Cf. *Quod.* 47 *v.b*-48 *r.b.*

[10] *Ibid.* 46 *r.b*-46 *v.a.* Cf. Ubertino's Defence of Olivi (*A.L.K.G.* ii. pp. 391 and 402).

H

clear when he treats of the question of debt.   As long as no legal obligation was involved and the sum needed was small, it was quite permissible for the representatives of the Order to raise the money, by promising to do all in their power to repay it within a given period.[1]   On the other hand, the friars could in no case contend in the law courts if they suffered wrong, but could only petition their injurer to do them justice.[2]   Olivi's confutation of the opinions of Aquinas is a further proof of his keen sensitiveness with regard to any reflections on the Franciscan ideal.[3]   Moreover, although a staunch supporter of the papal authority, he believed that even the Pope could not dispense from the vow of poverty, for his power had been given him for edification and not for destruction, and he therefore could not justly permit a man to abandon the path of perfection.[4]   He supports his argument by declaring that it was for this reason that St. Francis in his Testament had forbidden his followers to seek for any decretals from the Curia which would alter their manner of life.[5]   He prudently avoids dealing further with the vexed question of the papal expositions of the Rule, but there can be no doubt that he loyally accepted " Exiit qui seminat ", which indeed was merely a restatement of the doctrines of St. Bonaventura.[6]   Olivi believed that the obligation of poverty rested also upon bishops as the successors of the Apostles, and suggested that they should entrust the management of the temporalities of their sees to discreet men who would administer them in the interests of the poor, while they devoted themselves to their spiritual duties.[7]   His austere nature was deeply shocked by the luxury of many of the prelates of his day, and especially of those who had been members of the Franciscan Order. He protests with vehemence that if one friar dared to live in the manner affected by the majority of the dignitaries of the Church the whole world would be scandalised, and yet the vocation of the

---

[1] *A.L.K.G.* iii. 513.   [2] *Ibid.* 512.

[3] Postilla in Mattheum, MS. New Coll. 49, f. 77 *r.b*-81 *v.b* ; *A.L.K.G.* iii. 517-23 ; cf. *supra*, p. 83.

[4] " Non potest in destructionem sed in edificationem." " Non potest cum aliquo dispensare ut de statu simpliciter perfectiori descendat ad statum imperfectiorem. . . . De statu evangelico qui proprie est et dicitur status Christi non potest per dispensationem, aut per quamcunque aliam viam facere, ut professor eius ad quemcunque alium statum descendat." Q. XIV. (*A.L.K.G.* iii. p. 529).   [5] *Ibid.*

[6] In his expositions of his beliefs at the Chapters-General of Montpellier and Paris and upon his death-bed he declared that he accepted the interpretation of poverty and kindred questions which was given in this decretal (*A.L.K.G.* ii. 400 ; cf. *A.F.H.* xi. 265).

[7] Q. IX. (*A.L.K.G.* iii. 511-12) ; *Quod.* (f. 47 *r.b*-47 *v.b*). Defence of Ubertino (*A.L.K.G.* ii. 391). Cf. Occam, " Opus Nonaginta Dierum " (*Monarchia*, ii. pp. 1128-29). Cf. *infra*, p. 192.

latter was equally high.[1] This section of his teaching provoked
bitter opposition on the part of his judges, and in his "apologia"
he went so far as to admit that a bishop's duties might prevent him
from putting so strict an interpretation upon the obligation of
poverty as was possible for a member of a religious community.[2]
The Church had so far come to no decision as to how far a Friar
Minor who was raised to episcopal rank was still bound by his
vows, but Olivi had no doubt as to what her final verdict would be.[3]
In minor questions, such as the value of study as opposed to that of
manual labour,[4] or the lawfulness of a knowledge of other subjects besides the Scriptures to men who had renounced the world,[5]
he inclined rather to the attitude of St. Bonaventura than to that
of the extreme Zealots. Only the friars who possessed neither
intellectual ability nor spiritual gifts should be forced to work with
their hands, and although the supreme object of all learning was
union with God, any knowledge which rendered a man fitter for
this fellowship was certainly good. Philosophy, and what we
should now term science, were merely the handmaids of theology,
and ought not to be pursued as ends in themselves. Fortunately,
much that is now regarded as metaphysics was looked upon in the
Middle Ages as a part of this highest of all studies. Like the majority
of the Spirituals, Olivi considered the contemplative life as perhaps
on the whole nobler than the active, and less dangerous to the
individual.[6] The excessive preoccupation of the Franciscan Order
with the spiritual welfare of others had been regarded by no
less a person than St. Bonaventura as one of the chief causes of
its decline,[7] and its members gained great unpopularity by their
interference in many matters which by rights fell to the charge
of the secular clergy. Olivi, however, was no selfish ascetic, and
realised that there were occasions when a man was forced to imperil the peace of his own soul for the sake of the spiritual welfare
of others. Yet the world was benefited by prayer as well as by
preaching, and men were often led by vanity and ambition to concern themselves with the souls of others, thereby endangering their
own without profiting those whom they mistakenly believed that
they were guiding along the paths of salvation.[8]
    Olivi's final examination of the questions affecting the welfare

    [1] " Quia unus frater minor vivens ita laute et otiose et pompose, et in tot
et tantis passionibus ire et concupiscentie, et in tot solatiis et trufis seu ludis et
fabulis sicut unus episcopus secularis, qui tamen hodie iudicabitur communiter
esse in statu salutis, credo communi omnium iudicio iudicaretur esse in statu
damnationis " (*A.L.K.G.* iii. 512).
    [2] *Quod.* f. 47 r.   [3] *Ibid.* and *A.L.K.G.* iii. 512.
    [4] Q. x. *ibid.* 522.
    [5] Q. III. *ibid.* 503.   [6] Q. I. *ibid.*
    [7] *Quod.* 46 *v.a.* Cf. *supra,* p. 83.   [8] Q. I. *A.L.K.G.* iii. p. 503.

of his Order is his exposition of the Franciscan Rule,[1] probably written towards the close of his life.[2]   It is therefore valuable as embodying the results of a long experience of the problems involved in the Franciscan manner of life, and combines idealism with a profound sense of practical realities.   The dissimilarity between his interpretation of the Rule and that of his younger contemporary, Angelo da Clareno, is all the more striking when we remember that the latter shows his admiration for the views of the elder writer by numerous citations from his Commentary.[3]   This comparison is in some ways detrimental to Olivi, for, when contrasted with the depth of poetic feeling and the mystic fervour of Clareno, his treatment of the Rule seems dull and almost prosaic.   For example, one of the finest passages in Angelo's Commentary is his marvellous description of the obedience, where his power of imaginative intuition and his soaring splendour of language raises the reader to the very foot of the throne of grace.[4]   Olivi, in commenting on the same passage, confines himself to a consideration of the obedience owed by his Order to the Pope.[5]   Nor, what is stranger still, does he display the same profound and varied knowledge of the writings of the Fathers, or dwell with the same loving insistence on the life and sayings of St. Francis, as the best illustration of the meaning of his Rule.   In fact, his Commentary might more justly be termed an adaptation of the " Expositio quattuor magistrorum " to meet the needs of his own generation than an interpretation of the actual rule drawn up by the saint of Assisi.[6]   Although these

[1] Printed in the 1513 or Venetian edition of the *Firmamentum Trium Ordinum* (f. 106 *r.a*-124 *v.b*). Through the great kindness of Dr. A. G. Little I have been able to make use of an early copy of the *Firmamentum*, the date and place of which is unknown, although the foliation corresponds to the Venice edition of 1513. The Paris edition of the previous year contains only extracts of Olivi's Commentary, dealing with such matters as Fraternal Charity, Learning, Prayer, Chastity, Confession, and Sin. The fact that his work is described as " Tractatus, sive expositio super regulam beatissimi patris Francisci secundum divinum doctorem fratrem Petrum Ioannis " (Venice edition, 106 *r.a*) shows the high esteem in which he was held among the Observantines.

[2] His frequent references to his earlier writings may be taken as a proof that the Commentary was composed during the later years of his life. Cf. f. 110 *r.a*, f. 111 *r.a*, f. 112 *v.b*, f. 113 *r.a*, f. 115 *v.b*, f. 116 *r.a*, f. 116 *v.b*, and f. 123 *v.a*.

[3] Cf. especially *Expos.* pp. 226 and 231-33. Frater Hilarius Parisiensis, a nineteenth-century Franciscan writer who had studied both works, gave his verdict in the following terms : " Petrus Ioannis paulo minus extensus videtur quam B. Angelus et magis theologus " (*Regula Fratrum Minorum iuxta Romanorum Pontificum decreta et documenta Ordinis . . . explanata* (Lyons-Paris, 1870), p. 790). Quoted in *A.F.H.* xi. 316.

[4] *Expos.* ch. i. p. 62. The passage is given *in extenso* in the previous chapter. Cf. *supra*, p. 80.   [5] Cap. i. f. 107 *v*.

[6] From the second chapter onwards he quotes and comments on passages from the "Expositio quattuor magistrorum". With the exception of one reference

differences are mainly due to dissimilarity of temperament and outlook, it must not be forgotten that Angelo and Olivi belonged to very different circles, the former being the superior of a number of small and scattered communities, passing their lives in retirement and meditation, while the latter had been lecturer at Florence and other big convents, whose inmates would be mainly occupied in the work of study and preaching. For such men his treatise is admirable both in its lucidity and its sterling good sense. Olivi never compromises upon the ideals which form the basis of the Franciscan Rule,[1] but he realises that a certain measure of modification and development was necessary to meet the needs of his own day. For this reason he recognises, and even welcomes, the decretals of Gregory IX. and Nicholas III. as authoritative decisions on matters left undefined by the founder of his Order.[2] For him, like the rest of the Spiritual party, the Rule of St. Francis was sacred, being founded entirely on the gospels, and thus enabling the Friars Minor to follow literally the example set by the Saviour of the human race.[3] With a rare flight of imagination he compares its twelve chapters to the number of the apostles,[4] and declares that even the constitution of the Order was revealed in the gospel.[5] Mendicancy was to him no onerous obligation but a rare and highly valued privilege, shared not only by Christ and His disciples [6] but by the prophets Elijah and Elisha,[7] and by the angels who had visited Lot at Sodom.[8] Moreover, such a mode of life was beneficial to the faithful, for it stimulated them to charity and good works.[9] Although he discusses it more briefly, Olivi is just as emphatic upon the subject of the " usus pauper " as in his earlier writings,[10] and only on very rare occasions did he think it lawful

---

to the Rule of St. Basil and another to St. John Chrysostom's Commentary on St. Matthew, his few citations from the Fathers are somewhat hackneyed. Only two incidents from the life of St. Francis are mentioned in the whole treatise, namely, his answer to the novice who desired to possess a breviary (f. 123 *r.a*) and the psalm which he was heard to murmur on his death-bed (f. 116 *v.a*). Cf. Clareno, *Expos.* p. 174.

[1] For instance, his insistence on evangelic poverty and on mendicancy. " Qui igitur abiectionem et humilitatem evangelice mendicitatis negant, negent et humilitatem crucis Christi et martyriorum omnium martyrum suorum (f. 119 *r.b*).

[2] F. 106 *r.b*, f. 112 *r.b*. Actual quotations from the decretal, " Exiit qui seminat ", occur on f. 110 *v.b* and f. 113 *v.a*.

[3] F. 107 *r.a* and f. 107 *r.b*. Cf. " Exiit qui seminat ", *B.F.* iii. p. 404.

[4] "Notandum quod tanquam apostolica et in Christi XII. apostolis exemplata, XII. continet capitula " (f. 106 *r.b*).   [5] F. 107 *r.b*.

[6] F. 118 *v.a*. Cf. f. 119 *r.b*.   [7] F. 118 *v.b*.

[8] "Et idem contigit de duobus angelis coram Loth, seu potius de deo in eis " (*ibid.*).   [9] F. 112 *v.b* and f. 119 *r.b*.

[10] "Ipsius negatio et precipue tam explicata et expressa esset in maxime exterminium fidei Christiane et regule nostre et totius evangelici status " (f. 116 *v.b*).

for the friars to take thought for the morrow.[1] It is possible that he would have admitted that the friars through the medium of the " amicus spiritualis " might receive money for other necessities besides clothing and the care of the sick brethren, but he dreaded an extension of this principle even to such works as the building of convents and the encouragement of literary activity, lest these should give rise to greed, cupidity, and cause his Order to be defamed.[2] His bitter indignation was aroused by the *bursarii*, or small boys who accompanied friars on their journeys in order to collect the alms given to their masters, though he discusses this matter with more moderation than his disciple, Ubertino da Casale.[3] Perhaps the most interesting part of the Commentary is his interpretation of the views of St. Francis on the subject of learning, for in it we see the struggle of a sensitive conscience anxious to obey the rule to the letter, and a keen intelligence eager to absorb all the knowledge within its reach.[4] While pointing out that the Saint of Assisi was fully aware of the need for eloquent and learned preachers,[5] Olivi fully admits that all mental activity which did not lead to an increase of spiritual vigour, and which was not undertaken under the inspiration of the Holy Ghost, was vain and even dangerous, for it fostered the vices of ambition and arrogance.[6] With a wistful humility he declares that many simple and devout men reach a higher measure of understanding of divine things than those who have passed long years in study, and for such learning was of no service, but rather a distraction, since they had already attained to the highest wisdom.[7] He gives a new and characteristic touch to the story of St. Francis and the novice who desired a breviary, for according to him the seraphic father himself had longed to become learned, but it was revealed to him in a vision that by divine illumination he had been raised to a height of spiritual experience unattainable through mere worldly knowledge.[8] Great scholar as he was, Olivi realised that there were peaks in the life of the Spirit to which he himself could never climb, and it is perhaps for this reason that he laid such stress on prayer as the foundation of all religious aspiration.   The passages devoted to this theme are perhaps the finest in the whole commentary.[9] With

---

[1] *Firmamentum,* f. 112 *v.a.*   [2] F. 112 *r.b.*

[3] F. 112 *v.b.*   Cf. *infra*, p. 145.

[4] F. 122 *v.a.*-123 *r.a.*   Cf. especially f. 122 *v.b.*

[5] F. 122 *v.b.*   [6] F. 123 *r.a.*

[7] " Unde et sepius sum expertus quosdam fratres laicos soli mentali studio et devotioni vacantes in divinis longe perspicatiores et peritiores fuisse quam quosdam fratres clericos parum de sola albugine seu cortice littere suos oculos vellatos habentes " (f. 122 *v.b.*).   [8] F. 123 *r.a.*

[9] " In oratione autem puri cordis non solum communem abstinentiam a delitiis carnis inclusit, sed etiam omnem abstersionem et depurationem a quibus-

regard to the different forms of work to be undertaken by the friars, he believed that the temperament and abilities of the individual should be carefully considered.[1]   Manual work was no more obligatory for the Franciscans than for other religious bodies,[2] but no honest form of labour was to be shunned [3] unless it was harmful to the soul, in which case even the commands of the superiors of the Order could be disregarded.[4]

Unlike many of the Zealots, Olivi was profoundly interested in all questions concerning the organisation of his Order, and discusses at length the constitutional position of the General with regard to the General Chapter.   Somewhat reluctantly he admits that by the Rule the former was subject to the latter, and that in the case of a clash between the two authorities the friars were bound to obey the decrees of the chapter.[5]   On the other hand, its acts were invalid unless the General himself were present, or had given his consent to the holding of such an assembly.[6] Olivi heartily approved of the new method of election, by which the Minister-General was chosen by the provincials and one custodian from each province, instead of by the whole body of custodians, as was enjoined by the Rule.[7]   In spite of his vindication of the supremacy of the Chapter-General he regarded the constitution of his Order as a monarchy, which, on the authority of Aristotle, he accepted as the best form of government, for it was more easy to discover one wise and good man than a body of such men.[8]   Moreover, a single ruler was more capable of combating the forces of anarchy and decay.[9]   A certain consideration for the heavy responsibilities of the General is shown by the fact that he would only allow individual friars access to him if they knew for a certainty that they had been placed in situations in which it was impossible for them to keep the Rule.[10]   The morbid over-scrupulousness of many of his party, who made use of this provision as a justification for schism and rebellion, met with scant sympathy at his hands.   He is also emphatic about the direct submission of the friars minor to the Holy See, regarding it almost

---

cunque illecebris et fantasmatum nebulis : ut sic serene oculo et mundo corde semper, ac si in celis videant faciem dei sui " (*Firmamentum*, f. 123 *r.a*).

" In oratione est primitus divini cultus et obsequii virtualis actus et exercitii sapientialis studii et seculi " (f. 123 *r.b*).   " In hoc vero primatus omnis studii et desiderii ; quia per ipsam et in ipsa pie et sapidissime tenetur gustatum et cernitur summum bonum " (*ibid.*).

[1] *Firmamentum*, f. 114 *r*.   [2] F. 114 *v.a*.
[3] F. 113 *v.a*.   [4] F. 113 *r.b*.
[5] F. 120 *v.b*.   [6] F. 121 *r.b*.
[7] F. 120 *v.a*. Clareno, on the other hand, thought it would be wiser to abide by the Rule. Cf. *Expos.* p. 189 *s*.   [8] *Firmamentum*, f. 121 *r.b*.
[9] F. 121 *r.b*.   [10] F. 122 *r.b*.

in the light of a privilege bestowed on them as a mark of especial sanctity.[1]   On the whole, the Commentary shows a remarkable insight into the difficulties to be faced by the superiors of the Order, and it is strange that its author should have been considered as a stirrer up of discord and revolt; yet, even in a work concerned mainly with practical questions of administration, Olivi could not altogether refrain from Joachimite speculations.   To him the Franciscan missionaries of the thirteenth century were the heralds of the coming age, in which both Jews and infidels should be converted to the faith of Christ, and he draws a parallel between their labours and those of Barnabas and Paul, who, thirteen years after the death of Christ, had been sent to preach to the Gentiles.[2] The mystic significance of the comparison is emphasised by the fact that St. Francis' first visit to the country of the Saracens took place in the thirteenth year after his conversion.[3]   In fact, there is nothing very new and original about the opinions expressed in the " Expositio ".   They are the natural outcome of his earlier teaching on similar subjects.   There is, indeed, a greater caution, an increased reliance on the authority of the earlier Franciscan thinkers, and an avoidance, as far as possible, of controversial questions.   His preoccupation with problems of administration rather than with the great ideals which form the basis of the Rule can be partly explained by his anxiety not to do more than touch upon questions already dealt with in his earlier writings.[4]   He can in no way be said to compromise in vital matters, such as the obligation of complete poverty, or the literal observation of the Rule,[5] though, as always, he was prepared to admit the legitimacy of modifications in matters of organisation and detail.   Indeed, the " Expositio ", although interesting as the final development of its author's views on the ethical questions affecting the life of his Order, and as a striking testimony to his essential moderation and reasonableness of outlook, lacks the force and vigour of his earlier writings.   We feel that it is the work of a man worn out before his time, who, in spite of his thorough grasp and adequate discussion of the matters with which he deals, seldom rises above the level of a somewhat prosaic mediocrity.

[1]   " Quid mirum si regula evangelica in supererogativo zelo fidei Christi plantata debuit sicut principali sede Christi suum statum infigere ; ut nullus stipes vel surculus, sive ramus rectius vel firmius staret in illa " (*Firmamentum*, f. 106 *v.a*).

[2]   F. 124 *r.a.*   Cf. Clareno, *Expos.* p. 226.   [3]   *Firmamentum*, f. 124 *r.a.*

[4]   For instance, he dismissed the question of the inviolability of vows with the following words, " De hoc in questione an in votis evangelicis cadat dispensatio (cf. Q. XIV. *A.L.K.G.* iii. p. 528) prolixiora sunt dicta " (f. 110 *r.a*).   Cf. also f. 111 *r.a* for reference to Postilla in Mattheum.

[5]   *Firmamentum*, f. 107 *r.b* and f. 119 *r.as*

Olivi's Postilla in Mattheum [1] is also an important source for his opinions on poverty and kindred subjects. After a somewhat cursory investigation,[2] however, I have found little which throws any fresh light upon his views on poverty, though it is interesting that he classes both St. Jerome and Plato together as advocates of the advantages of bare feet.[3] On the whole, perhaps, Olivi may be regarded as belonging rather to the school of Pecham and St. Bonaventura than to that of St. Francis and Brother Leo. Had he belonged to an earlier generation of Franciscan thinkers his opinions would have been accepted without question or comment. His originality of outlook is more patent in the realm of metaphysics than in that of ethics.

Olivi is perhaps the only one of the Zealots who interested himself in philosophical questions. Amid the vexations and trials of his stormy life his mind must have found relief in the solution of abstract and impersonal problems, and he regarded any matter not already decided by the Church as a proper subject for discussion and argument.[4] During his student days at Paris he had been nurtured in the tradition of Bonaventura and Alexander of Hales, and his philosophy always remained definitely Franciscan, although he had far too much individuality to be classed as the disciple of any master. He was teaching at a time when the older scholasticism was being profoundly modified by the Thomistic interpretation of the doctrines of Aristotle, but, like most of his Order, he was more in sympathy with the Neo-Platonism of St. Augustine. The latter was perhaps his favourite authority, but he was no slavish follower of his opinions, and even opposed him in certain matters.[5] Although he often cited the theories of Aristotle and of his Muhammadan commentators, he obviously accepted their conclusions with much misgiving, and had serious

---

[1] Two manuscripts of this work exist in England, one belonging to Corpus Christi College, Cambridge, and the other to New College, Oxford. The Oxford MS. has the following note : " Erat quidam Petrus Joannis hereticus unus ex complicibus Joachimi abbatis heresiarche, cum ergo non constar cuius Petri Jo hoc opus sit, non alienum putavi ab offitio meo in prudentiam lectorem admonere ne . . ." The rest is erased.

[2] I have not investigated this Commentary at all thoroughly, as it has been used by Mlle. d'Alverny as one of the main sources for her thesis entitled " Les Écrits théoriques concernant la pauvreté évangélique ".

[3] Interpretation of " Neque Calceamenta " (Matt. x. 10), f. 77 *r*. Olivi's Commentary is also very interesting as showing that the question of the authorship of the Gospels was not ignored by the medieval theologian (f. 3 *v.b*). Traces of Joachimism are also to be found. Cf. cap. xx. f. 121 *r*.

[4] This is seen from his letter to the Paris doctors (*Quod.* f. 54 *r.a*), quoted in *A.L.K.G.* iii. 519. In his confession made at the Chapter-General of Montpellier, and perhaps renewed on his death-bed, he defended free speculation as beneficial to the faith (*A.F.H.* xi. 269).

[5] Cf. Q. LIV., " De Potentiis Animae ", *Questiones in II. Sententiarum*, ii. 230-83.

doubts as to the wisdom of an extensive study of their works. By far the most interesting and complete of the philosophic writings of Olivi which has come down to us are his commentaries on the second book of the Sentences, which have recently been published.[1] These in all probability do not form part of his Summa, but are a freer and more general exposition of the metaphysical and ethical questions which had been dealt with by the Lombard.[2]   It is doubtful at what period in his life these lectures were given, for many of the subjects discussed are found in other manuscripts besides the Vatican Codex, though in a less detailed form.[3]   Traces of certain of them can be found even in his *Quodlibeta*.   More-over, in his defence of his doctrines and in his attack on the opinions of Frater Ar he makes frequent references to his *questiones*, but this cannot be taken as implying that he did not afterwards make considerable alterations and enlargements.   Father Jansen be-lieves that the Vatican Codex which he used as the basis for his text is an early copy of Olivi's final revision of his lecture notes.[4] However, his actual doctrines are in reality far more interesting than any question of date or place, and do not seem to have varied very greatly since the date of his condemnation by the Parisian doctors.

Olivi makes use of the same arrangement in all his lectures. After stating the problem to be solved, he gives the arguments of his opponents, which in the end he answers one by one, after a careful exposition of his own views.   It is unfortunate that his theory of the divine essence is contained in his Commentary on the first book of the Sentences,[5] which has not yet been discovered, but it is at last possible to understand his conception of the union

---

[1] Olivi's *Questiones in II. Sententiarum* have been edited by Father Jansen for the *Biblioteca Scholastica Medii Aevi*, vols. iv., v., and vi.   As I was unable to study them in any detail, I used De Wulf's *Histoire de la philosophie médiévale*, i. 364-70, as a guide to the parts to be consulted.   Father Jansen's article, entitled " Die Lehre Olivis über das Verhältnis von Leib und Seele ", in *Franziskanische Studien*, v. (1918), 153-75, 233-58, which I have also read, gives a very com-prehensive study of his most important philosophical opinions.

[2] Such is Jansen's view (*op. cit.* iii. p. xiv.).   Olivi uses the matters already dealt with by Peter the Lombard as a basis for an exposition of his own views, but gives no commentary on the actual text of the Sentences.

[3] Codex Vaticanus, 1116.   This manuscript dates from the early part of the fourteenth century, and was obviously carefully revised from some standard text.   I do not know if the fact that Olivi refers to himself as being at Narbonne (cf. i. 633) can be taken as evidence that he revised his lectures during the concluding years of his life.

[4] *Op cit.* iii. xxvii.

[5] "Videantur dicta sua de hoc in questione de divinis productionibus prima et secunda et littera Magistrorum " (*Quod.* f. 43 *r.b*-45 *r.b*, and Special Treatise sent to Judges, *ibid.* 53 *v.a*-61 *v.b*), " et in prima parte summe ". Ubertino da Casale's Defence of Olivi (*A.L.K.G.* ii. p. 392).

of the rational soul with the body.[1] The former being spiritual
could not be the form of the latter without conferring upon it its
own immortality. It was, however, incomplete unless united to
the body, of which it became an essential part through the medium
of the sensitive soul, to which it was joined in a kind of spiritual
matter. The hindrances to freedom of action found in children,
idiots, and those under the influence of sleep were due rather to
the deficiencies of the senses than to any defect of the intellect
itself.[2] The chief seat of the sensitive soul appears to have been
the brain, which co-ordinated the impressions received through the
different senses. Olivi fully realised the interaction of the intellect
and the will as well as of the other potentialities of the mind, and
regarded them not as separate entities but as parts of one whole.[3]
Unlike Aquinas he was a staunch upholder of the freedom of the
will, confirming his position by many psychological arguments.[4] So
strongly did he stress the spiritual nature of the mind that he refused to believe that an external object could be the cause of any
mental process. Rather, the intellect and the will were already
working in unison, and their concentration upon some outward
entity was merely the final stage of their activity.[5] His conception
of the species differed from that of Henry of Ghent, who regarded
it as a material reality existing somewhere in the space between the
object seen and the eye of the observer. Olivi, on the other hand,
believed that it was the result of a purely subjective process, for
the different senses combined together to form images of the world
surrounding the individual, and these they afterwards transmitted
to the mind.[6] He was, however, no Neo-Platonist in his doctrine
of the Universal, for he believed that it existed only in the mind

---

[1] Q. LI. vol. ii. 101-36 ; LIX. *ibid.* 537-42. If the three sets of *questiones*
found in the Todi manuscript (MS. Todi, 95) which contains three of his
quodlibets are, as is almost certain, the work of Vidal du Four, the latter is probably the unknown opponent whose attacks on his own views concerning the
soul Olivi replies in the Appendix to Q. LI. (*ibid.* p. 136 *s.*). The controversy
was apparently carried on in a friendly spirit, for Olivi describes his antagonist's
objections to his theory as " zelo veritatis, ut aestimo, facte ". In the same
manuscript (f. 22 *r.*-24 *v.*) there is a résumé of four of Olivi's questions (XXI.,
XV., XXXI., and LI.), perhaps made by Vidal with a view to the refutation
of the arguments which they contain.

Cf. Delorme, " L'Œuvre scolastique de Maître Vital du Four ", in *La
France franciscaine*, ix., pp. 421-71. It is also of interest that the future cardinal
was possibly Olivi's successor at Montpellier, where he was lector in 1295. Cf.
Langlois, " Vidal du Four, Frère Mineur ", in *Hist. Litt.* xxxvi. p. 296.

[2] In the " Impugnatio quorundam articulorum " (*Quod.* 47 *v.*) Olivi denies
that the will or the intellect could be injured by any mishap which might
happen to the body

[3] Q. LIV. ii. 230-83.

[4] Q. LVII. ii. 305-94.

[5] Q. LXXII. iii. 1-51.

[6] Q. LXXIII. iii. 52-106. Cf. especially 82-89.

and not in the outside world or even in the heavens.[1] In the same way he broke from the Franciscan tradition by denying the " Rationes Seminales ",[2] or the doctrine that the essence of every form was to be found potentially in inanimate· matter and owed its being to some outside agency.   Possibly he approached more nearly to the attitude of Aquinas, who held that matter was without form, but possessed an endless potentiality or inclination towards the forms which it afterwards received, though in general he was prejudiced against the theories of the great Dominican.[3]   Since matter had no existence apart from form it could not be conceived as being limited in quantity.[4]   It is strange that Olivi should have denied that man received any separate form which set him apart as an individual from the human species,[5] especially as he admitted that the proportions of the forms imprinted varied in different persons, some receiving more of certain of these and others less.[6] The lower forms rendered the matter in which they subsisted more fit to receive the impress of the higher ones, and an organism was the more perfect according to the number of forms which it was capable of accepting.   It is doubtful if, like later thinkers, Olivi held that the different species were derived from any one paramount form, though he was completely orthodox in believing that it was his spiritual and reasoning faculty which separated man from the animal creation.   Nothing was devoid of matter save God alone—even the angels possessing a spiritual variety of it,[7] the potentialities of which differed from those of the matter which formed the basis of all finite life.   In his theory of motion Olivi anticipated Galileo [8], for he believed that its cause was a force entirely external to the object moved, and in this he was opposed to the idea prevalent in his age, which made motion depend upon the co-operation between the agent and its patient.[9]   Like his great contemporary, Bacon, he was keenly interested in scientific experiment, and devoted part of one of his Questions to an account of the structure and faculties of the human eye.[10]   Moreover, many of his theories are based on deductions from his own observations rather than on abstract reasoning.   He was certainly much fascinated by mathematics, and especially by the science of number.   To

---

[1] Q. XIII. i. 231-55.   Cf. especially p. 235.

[2] Q. XXXI. pp. 508-70.   Cf. letter to Paris doctors (f. 45 *v.a*) and to Fr. R. de Cambiaco (*Quod.* 52 *r.a*, Q. XXI. i. 379-88).

[3] He certainly held that there were different potentialities in spiritual and corporal matter.   Cf. Q. XX. i. 370-79.

[4] Q. XXI. i. 379-88.   [5] Q. XII. i. 210-31.

[6] Q. XXII. i. 388-421.

[7] Q. XVI. i. 290-355.   [8] Cf. Jansen, *op. cit.* p. xii.

[9] Q. XXIV. i. 434-38.   Olivi's theory of motion forms the subject of Q. XXIII-XXXI.   [10] Q. LXXIII. iii. pp. 89-97.

his mind the finite nature of the world was closely connected with the human conception of time, for in eternity there could be no past, nor present, nor future.[1] The verdict of Jansen must perhaps be respected when he declares that Olivi does not stand in the first rank of medieval philosophers,[2] and yet nobody who has even glanced at his works can fail to be struck by his sturdy but not aggressive originality. He was content to follow the guidance of his own judgment in accepting, or rejecting, the opinions of previous or contemporary thinkers, and he was never afraid of following the dictates of his reason, so that his philosophy is the outcome of his own personality.[3] Standing as he did between the older and newer scholasticism, and suffering from the discredit cast upon his work by the most learned men in his Order, it is not surprising that, with the exception of Peter " de Trabibus ",[4] he possessed few disciples. His importance in the history of Franciscan thought lies in the fact that he bridges the gulf which divides the school of Bonaventura from that of Occam and Duns Scotus.

Perhaps Olivi's most fascinating work is his *Quodlibeta*, which was printed at Venice during the early years of the sixteenth century. Copies of this are unfortunately very rare, there being

---

[1] Q. III. i. 35-86.   [2] *Op. cit.* p. xii.

[3] The verdict of De Wulf is of great interest : " Malgré son respect pour Augustin, Olivi recuse ses doctrines sur plus d'un point ; il n'est pas augustinien. Il combat Thomas d'Aquin sans le nommer ; il s'élève contre l'émanatisme néoplatonien, et bien qu'il se réclame d'Alexandre de Hales et de Bonaventura, il est avant tout personnel " (*op. cit.* i. 370).

[4] Author of the late thirteenth-century Commentary on the Sentences, for which Father Delorme suggests 1285-95 as a possible date (*La France franciscaine*, vii. p. 262). Peter, who either derived his name from the convent of " Trabe Bonatis ", now Ponte della Trave, near Camerino, or from Le Trau in Médoc, tells us in the prologue to his Commentary that at the time of writing he was exercising the office of lector, " in loco solemni " (*ibid.* 260), so that it is possible that he was one of Olivi's assistants at Florence (*ibid.* 262). The similarity of their doctrines is so marked that Cardinal Ehrle suggested that " de Trabibus " might be merely a Latinisation of Olivi (*A.L.K.G.* iii. 459). Father Jansen, however, after making a special study of both thinkers, proved conclusively that although Peter " de Trabibus " accepted the most important of Olivi's philosophical theories, such as the relation existing between body and soul, his treatment of these is often more decisive than that of his master. In certain other problems, as, for instance, the question of free will, he shows a certain measure of independence of thought, and his method of exposition is different from that employed by Olivi. Cf. " Petrus de Trabibus, sein spekulative Eigenart, oder sein Verhältnis zu Olivi ", in *Festgabe Clemenz Bäumker zum 70. Geburtstag*, pp. 243-54. This verdict is apparently endorsed by de Wulf (*op. cit.* 370). Olivi also appears to have influenced Roger Marston and Nicolas of Occam (Ehrle, *op. cit.*). His letter to " R. de Camliaco " shows that at any rate one group of his followers were interested in philosophy, but the majority of them were in all probability profoundly indifferent to such studies, or, like Ubertino da Casale, regarded them as a peculiarly subtle snare of the evil one to detach men from higher matters. Cf. Prologue to *A.V.* f. 2 r.a.

probably only three or four in existence.[1] Its special interest is due
to the fact that it is one of the few examples we have of a bachelor
playing a leading rôle in this particular form of academic exercise,
which in its early stages was generally reserved to masters of theology.[2] The great charm of the book lies in the variety of matters
discussed. The philosophical questions, although cruder and less
finished, are reminiscent of his later work both in technique and in
the nature of the problems with which he deals. The beginning
of the second section is devoted to scriptural exegesis, and it is
amusing to notice the author's lively interest in Biblical personages,
and his eager endeavours to understand the psychological and moral
situations with which they were faced. In a period when a belief
in sorcery was almost an article of faith, the question as to whether
the witch of Endor actually raised the spirit of Samuel at the request of Saul, or only a demon in his likeness, must have aroused
burning interest. Olivi compared the king of Israel to the scholars
of his own age, who sought for the divine wisdom in the writings

[1] In the eighteenth century copies existed in the Episcopal Library at
Seville, and in the convent of the Observantines at Madrid, as well as in the
Sorbonne. Sbaralea, the eighteenth-century collector of papal bulls relating
to the Franciscan Order, also found a copy in the convent of SS. Apostoli at
Rome, but none of these can now be traced. After a long search Cardinal
Ehrle learned from Father Jeiler that a copy printed at Venice by Lazarus
Soardo in 1509 had been discovered in a convent library. Two copies absolutely
corresponding to this in foliation and in the kind of type used, but lacking
any printer's mark, are in the former Royal Library at Munich. Another
copy was exhibited at Rome by the Bibliopola Samonati, and there was some
talk of bringing out a modern edition. Cf. *A.L.K.G.* iii. 466-70 ; *A.F.H.* xi. 313.

The Bodleian copy corresponds perfectly, as far as I can judge, with those
at Munich, and is bound up in folio form with the *Quodlibeta* of a certain
John Bacon, presumably John Baconthorpe, and other treatises printed at
Venice by the heirs of Octavianus Scotus of Modena between the years 1521
and 1527. The contents are as follows :
  i. f. 1 *r.*-42 *r.*, *Quodlibeta* ; ii. f. 42-53 *v.*, " Attack on the doctrines of
Fr. ' A '." ; iii. f. 54 *r.*-51 *r.*, " Letter to Judges " ; iv. 51 *v.*-53 *r.*, " Letter
to R. de Camliaco " ; v. f. 53 *v.*-61 *v.*, " Treatise on the Divine Essence ".
The curious fact that after f. 54 the numeration of the pages suddenly changes
to f. 43, is found in every known copy of the book.

[2] This was the general rule in the thirteenth century, but it is possible that,
in the first few years after the invention of the Quodlibet, a certain laxity of
practice prevailed in the " studia " of the two great mendicant orders, and that
even bachelors were allowed to give the final solution or " determinatio " of
the questions brought forward by those who took part in the debate. It was
not until 1280 that a Dominican General Chapter, held at Oxford, limited the
Quodlibet with certain exceptions to masters (Reichert, *Acta Capitularum
Generalium Ordinis Fratrum Praedicatorum*, i. p. 208). It is probable, therefore,
that Olivi's Quodlibets were delivered some time between his return from Rome in
1279 and the Chapter-General of Strasburg in 1282, especially as they are found
in the printed version with the documents relating to the condemnation of his
opinions. Internal evidence would point in the same direction.

of Aristotle rather than in the Scriptures, and thus received truth
mingled with falsehood. As Saul had recognised the prophet and
had learned from his lips the doom awaiting him and his race, so
Christ was revealed in the midst of the errors of pagan writers.
The Arians had been led astray by the doctrines of another false
magician, namely, Plato, while the flesh of the calf upon which
Saul feasted symbolised the errors of Antichrist.[1] Olivi certainly
did not lag behind his contemporaries in the freedom of his expositions of the Scriptures.

The *Quodlibeta* is a striking testimony to the versatility of its
author, for it is concerned with the religious and ethical aspects of
almost every side of medieval life. This eager interest in the world
around him is another trait which separates Olivi from the other
great Zealots. In spite of his utter lack of egotism, Clareno is only
really concerned with the questions of his age in so far as they
affected the spiritual welfare of his own friends, while Ubertino's
universe would appear to be peopled only by a wealthy and corrupt
ecclesiastical hierarchy, and by the members of the Franciscan
Order. Neither of them would ever have been prepared to discuss
the moral aspects of usury,[2] or the question as to whether it was a
grievous sin for a man to use unjust weights, if such was the general
custom of the town in which he lived.[3] Olivi was, moreover,
keenly alive to the political aspect of the papal claims, and gave his
opinion on the donation of Constantine with much of his customary moderation. Although he would have preferred the Church
to remain without the incumbrance of temporal riches, he did not
deny the legitimacy of the gift, but regarded it as revocable at the
whim of the secular power by whose authority it had originally
been bestowed.[4] Unlike most medieval writers he attached little
importance to the two swords produced by St. Peter in the garden
of Gethsemane.[5] It was obvious from the context that Christ did
not intend them to be used defensively, and if they had any symbolic meaning it would rather be found in the spiritual authority
of the Church than in its claims to any earthly greatness. On the
other hand, Olivi was prepared to admit that men might be called

---

[1] *Quod.* ii. Q. v. f. 12 *v.*

[2] *Ibid.* i. 7 *v.*-8 *r.*   [3] *Ibid.* v. 35 *v.*

[4] " Ad 4ᵐ dicendum quod quantumcumque terrenam potestatem Constan-
tinus pape dederit ex ipsamet donatione constat quod potestas illa non sibi
prius inerat ex sola Christi commissione, seu ex sola potestate spirituali. Quod
autem et quantum dederit non est nobis nunc cum re, quia potestas temporalis
sicut temporaliter est acquisibilis sic et amissibilis et hoc multiplicibus modis "
(*ibid.* i. f. 9 *r.*). The latter part of this " Questio " is found in C. Laur. S.
Crucis, Pl. 31, Sin. Cod. 3, f. 183 *v.* Cf. *A.F.H.* xi. p. 260.

[5] Olivi even believed that Christ was deriding the simplicity of his disciples
when he answered " It is enough " (*Quod.* i. f. 9 *r.*).

upon to defend the possessions of the Church, but in that case they must be quite certain that they were fighting in a just war.[1] A bishop who suffered death in the defence of the temporalities of his see might rightly be termed a martyr provided that his motives were good.[2] His mind was obviously much preoccupied by questions connected with the Sacrament of the Mass, and the intention of the officiating priest.[3] There is a very modern ring about his contention that the sanctity of the ten commandments lay rather in the spirit than in the letter, though he illustrates his meaning by an allusion to form and matter.[4] Even in medieval times the observance of Sunday was apparently a serious problem. Olivi was much preoccupied as to whether it was worse for men to plough or dig, as was customary on week-days, or to waste their time in gambling and feasting, or in the telling of improper stories. The first alternative was a direct insult both to God and His Church, while the second was clearly mortal sin.[5] Eventually, like many modern reformers, he came to the conclusion that innocent relaxations were permissible provided that men devoted some part of their time to hearing Mass. His great literary activity is partially explained by the fact that he regarded writing as quite a suitable employment for Sundays and feast days as long as it did not interfere with the paramount duty of worship, and the scribe gained no personal profit from his labours.[6] The *Quodlibeta* is a proof that although his chief interests were philosophical and theological, his eager sympathy with his fellow-men gave him power to envisage many of the problems which affected the everyday life of his age. Nor did the abstract and impersonal quality of his solutions diminish their value, for his natural good sense was unclouded by the mists of passion or prejudice.

Olivi's *Expositio in Apocalypsim* is the only one of his Biblical Commentaries which exists except in manuscript, and even this is known chiefly through the extracts given in the report of the Papal

---

[1] *Quod.* i. f. 9 r.

[2] *Ibid.* iv. f. 32 r.-33 r. One of the examples which he gives is St. Thomas of Canterbury.

[3] Cf. especially *Quod.* iv. Q. XXI.-XXVIII. The numbering of the questions almost gives rise to the supposition that this is a separate treatise, and we know from Ubertino da Casale (*A.L.K.G.* ii. 394) that Olivi wrote a Tractatus de Sacramentis, fragments from which are found in various manuscripts (*A.L.K.G.* iii. 476. Cf. *supra*, p. 93), but I can find no correspondence between his references and the matters dealt with in the *Quodlibeta*. In Question XXII. Olivi discussed the efficacy of the Sacraments when administered by an evil priest, and came, like the later Fraticelli, to the conclusion that it was in no way diminished. [4] *Quod.* v. f. 34 r.

[5] " An minus malum sit fodere vel arare in festis quam ludo alearum et taxillorum aut coreis et poculis et fabulis vitiose vacare " (*ibid.*).

[6] *Ibid.* v. f. 34 r.

Inquiry of 1319.[1] Since the whole work has not yet been studied in any detail, it is a moot point as to how far these give any just idea of its contents.[2] The verdict of the Commission of Anagni [3] upon the writings of the Abbot Joachim shows that even an impartial body was liable to misconceptions, and bitter prejudice had been aroused against Olivi by the disturbances in Tuscany and Provence, for which he was held responsible.[4] No exception can be taken to the Committee appointed by John XXII.,[5] nor had they anything to gain by an unmeasured condemnation of the work in question, for their functions were purely advisory, and the Pope prided himself too much on his theological knowledge to be greatly influenced by their decision.[6] A study of the sixty excerpts from the " Postilla " is very disappointing, for they possess little literary merit, and it is surprising that a man possessing such a fine intelligence and keen critical faculty as Olivi should be led into such barren and unprofitable speculations. Nor, although this Commentary is his last work, can its exaggerations be attributed to the failure and anxiety of the closing years of his life, when he brooded over the evils so rampant both in his Order and in the Church, and strove so earnestly to prevent a final breach between the Spirituals and the remainder of the Franciscans. Even in 1282 his judges had taken exception to his prophecies concerning future events,[7] and such early writings as the *Quodlibeta* [8] and the treatise on the Indulgence of the Portiuncula [9] show distinct

---

[1] *Misc.* ii. 258-70.

[2] Professor Tocco verified the extracts by comparing them with MS. Laur. Conv. Sopp. 397, 31, and Mlle. Florowsky has been for some time engaged on a special study of the " Postilla," the results of which have not yet been published (*A.F.H.* xi. 314, *n.* 4). Fabricius alludes to a copy, with a French translation, printed at Amsterdam in 1700. Cf. *Bibliotheca Latina Mediae et Infimae Aetatis,* v. p. 478. Döllinger's version (*Beiträge,* ii. pp. 526-85) has been almost entirely ignored by historians.

[3] *A.L.K.G.* i. 99-142. Cf. *supra,* p. 30.   [4] Cf. *supra,* p. 15 s.

[5] Only two Franciscans were represented—Bertrand de Tour, Provincial of Aquitaine, raised to the Cardinalate in 1320, and Arnald Roiard, later Bishop of Salerno. There were two Englishmen on the Commission—a certain " Laurentius Anglicus ", whom Mr. Pantin, lecturer in Ecclesiastical History at Manchester University, thinks may possibly be identified with a Benedictine monk of Gloucester, and a Carmelite called Simon. The whole proceedings were entrusted to Nicholas de Albertis, Cardinal of Ostia, who had played a leading part in the Inquiry into the state of the Franciscan Order held at the time of the Council of Vienne.

[6] The book was not finally condemned till 1326. The functions of the Committee are shown by their letter to John XXII. to have been purely advisory. Cf. *Misc.* p. 258, and Denifle, *Chartularium Universitatis Parisiensis,* ii. *n.* 790.

[7] Cf. letter to " R. de Camliaco ", *Quod.* 53 *r.a s.,* where Olivi defends his speculations, and *supra,* p. 88.   [8] *Quod.* ii. Q. ix. f. 16 *v.*

[9] *Acta Ordinis Minorum,* xiv. cap. i. pp. 141 and 142.

traces of Joachimite influence.   Perhaps modern opinion is apt to
be unfairly prejudiced against the medieval love of symbolism,
which naturally strove to interpret the vision of St. John the Divine
in terms of the events of its own age.   It must also be remembered
that Olivi was a Provençal, and endowed with all the ardour and
passion of the Southern temperament.[1] In the face of all the wickedness and injustice of the world around him he turned eagerly to
the prophecies of the Calabrian seer, which supplied an adequate
explanation of the present miseries and also depicted a future in
which all men would be drawn to God by the twofold bond of
knowledge and love.

Judged by the extracts given in the report of the Commission,
Olivi's Commentary is not a very original work.   He produces all
the chief ideas of the Abbot of Flora, and it is only in details that
he allows himself to follow the dictates of his own fancy.   He dwells
less on the three main epochs of the history of the world than on
the seven subdivisions of the second period,[2] the sixth of which
was marked by the coming of St. Francis, the founder of the new
Order which was to combat and finally to triumph over the forces
of Antichrist.[3] Without going to the extremes of Gerard of
Borgo San Donnino, Olivi definitely established the founder of
his Order as the Messiah of the new age, although his mission was
rather the renewal of the life of Christ upon earth than the pro-
clamation of any new doctrines.[4] By the stigmata God had set
him apart from all other men, and had made him His chosen instrument for the conversion of the world.[5] Like St. Bonaventura,
Olivi regarded his master as the angel of the sixth seal, whose right
foot being planted on the sea symbolised the conversion of the
Saracens.[6] The Franciscan Rule was possessed of the same sanctity as the Gospel, and would be rejected by the carnal church
just as Christ's teaching was scorned by the synagogue.[7] There
can be little doubt that he identified the Church of his day with
Babylon [8] the great harlot, while the new congregation of the

---

[1] Cf. *supra*, pp. 82 and 90.   [2] Article I. *Misc.* ii. p. 258.   [3] *Ibid.*

[4] Article IX. *Misc.* ii. p. 260. " Sicut etiam in sexta aetate, rejecto carnali
Iudaismo et vetustate prioris saeculi, venit novus homo Christus cum nova lege,
vita, et cruce, sic in sexto statu, rejecta carnali Ecclesia et vetustate prioris
saeculi, renovabitur Christi lex et vita et crux.   Propter quod in eius primo
initio Franciscus apparuit, Christi plagis characterizatus et Christo totus con-
crucifixus et configuratus."   [5] *Ut supra.*

[6] Article XXII. *ibid.* pp. 261 and 266. We know from Ubertino that Olivi
had heard this from St. Bonaventura's own lips. *A.V.* L. V. cap. iii. f. 4 *a.*

[7] Article XXIV. *Misc.* ii. p. 262 ; XXX. p. 263.

[8] Articles III., VI., and XIX. *ibid.* pp. 259 and 261. Allusions to the
wickedness of the Church are to be found in Articles XX., XXI., XXVII.,
XLVI., XLVIII., LIII., and LIV. The Commission were more horrified by
Olivi's identification of the Church with Babylon than by any of his other errors.

elect was the holy Jerusalem.[1] The passage where he describes the mystic intuition which would characterise the new age is really poetical.[2] The great crime of the Church had been the denial of the twin doctrines of poverty and the " usus pauper ", and the persecution of those who adhered to them.[3] The darkening of the sun symbolised the general wickedness of her rulers,[4] while the locusts from the abyss might be taken as signifying the majority of the laity.[5] Just as the Church of the apostles had embodied all that was noblest in Judaism, so the good in the old Church would pass into the new, while its wickedness would be embodied in Antichrist and his followers.[6] The spiritual superiority of the elect of the sixth age over former generations resembled the predominance of man over the animal creation.[7] During the fiercest days of persecution, when the power of Antichrist was at its height, St. Francis would rise from the dead and lead his faithful followers to their final triumph.[8] Olivi was very guarded in his references to the former and refused to identify him with any definite person. According to him there was to be both a mystic and an open Antichrist, the one a great king, and probably a descendant of Frederick II., and the other a false Pope.[9] The former by his might was to set the latter in the place of Christ, and he and his followers would spread the pernicious doctrine of the duty of unquestioning obedience to the papal decrees.[10] After their overthrow an era of peace and righteousness would ensue in which it would appear that the new Jerusalem [11] had indeed descended from the heavens. Finally, even this golden age would degenerate, and so the way would be prepared for the second coming of Christ to

---

[1] Article XII. *Misc.* ii. p. 260 ; XXXIII. p. 264.

[2] " Ergo in tertio tempore Spiritus Sanctus exhibet se ut flammam et fornacem divini amoris et ut cellarium spiritualis ebrietatis et ut apothecam divinorum aromatum et spiritualium unctionum et unguentorum, et ut tripudium spiritualium jubilationum et jucunditatum, per quam non solum simplici intelligentia, sed etiam gustativa et palpativa experientia videbitur omnis veritas sapientie verbi Dei incarnati et potentia Dei patris " (*ibid.* Article XIII. p. 260).

[3] Article XXX. p. 263.   [4] Article XXIV. p. 262 (*Apoc.* vi. 12).

[5] Article XXXIV. *Misc.* ii. p. 265 (*Apoc.* ix. 3).

[6] Article XIX. *ibid.* p. 261.

[7] Article VIII. *ibid.* p. 259.

[8] Article XXVIII. *ibid.* p. 263. Olivi cites as his authority for this a certain holy man who had heard it from the lips of Brother Leo. This is very probably a reference to Conrad of Offida.

[9] Article XLIV. *ibid.* p. 267. Olivi's interpretation of the two Antichrists is not always very clear. Probably, as in the *Arbor Vitae,* they were symbolised by the beast ascending from the sea (*Apoc.* xiii. 1) and the beast ascending from the earth (*ibid.* v. 11). The worship paid to the pseudo-Pope was symbolised by the adoration of the image of the former. Cf. *Misc.* ii. p. 260.

[10] *Ibid.*   [11] Article I. *ibid.* p. 258.

judge the world.[1] Such were the main outlines of the teaching of Olivi which aroused such enthusiasm among his followers. They were found in a still more exaggerated form among the Provençal Beguins.[2] This predilection for his apocalyptic theories rather than his philosophic speculations is not surprising, for religious enthusiasts would naturally be drawn to the more sensational parts of his teaching. Unfortunately, owing to their influence it became the only one which was generally known, and thus Olivi came to be credited with a system of beliefs with regard to the future of the world which were not peculiarly his own but were the common property of the circle in which he moved. The baleful fascination of the doctrine of Joachim of Flora for the Zealots can best be understood when we consider the extent of its influence over the mind of their ablest representative.

Olivi's Commentary on the Epistle to the Romans was studied by Father Denifle in connection with his great work upon Luther.[3] He was very highly impressed with it,[4] and cites certain extracts in his second volume which contains a general survey of the opinions of medieval writers upon the question of justification by faith.[5] If Olivi's views were not given in medieval Latin it would be possible to imagine that they were those of a modern theologian. His general orthodoxy can be judged by the fact that his Commentary on the Canticles was generally attributed to St. Bonaventura, and thus found its way into the Tridentine edition of his works.[6]

Perhaps the most interesting of his shorter writings is his justification of the Renunciation of Celestine V.,[7] in which he answers twelve arguments against its validity, four of which were found in the Colonna manifesto of 1297.[8] Olivi's little treatise was probably written shortly after this date in reply to one of the numerous pamphlets written by the enemies of Boniface VIII.,[9] and shows a remarkable grasp of the situation. To the contention of his opponents that men could be released from their office only

[1] Article XVIII. *Misc.* ii. p. 261.
[2] Cf. *infra*, p. 250 s.   [3] *Luther und Lutherthum.*
[4] While working on the Codex in the Convent at Assisi, Denifle informed Father Oliger that Olivi's treatise was one of the best of the medieval commentaries upon the question. Cf. *A.F.H.* xi. 315.
[5] *Die abendländischen Schriftausleger bis Luther über Justitia Dei und Justificatio,* pp. 156-60.
[6] In *Supplementum S. Bonaventurae,* Trent, 1772, vol. i. 50-282. In a fourteenth-century manuscript (C. Vat. 918) it is also attributed to the Seraphic doctor. Cf. *A.L.K.G.* iii. 485. A *Principia generalia in sacra scriptura* which is attributed to Olivi in the catalogue of the Library of Urban V. (*A.L.K.G.* iii. 460) is printed in the same edition as a work by St. Bonaventura (*Supplementum,* i. 23-43, 283-374; and ii. 1038-1115; and cf. *A.L.K.G.* iii. 495).
[7] Edited by Father Oliger in *A.F.H.* xi. 309-73.
[8] *A.L.K.G.* v. 493-529.   [9] Oliger, *A.F.H.* xi. 331.

by the sanction of their superiors, and that the Pope was responsible only to God,[1] he answers that the cardinals as electors had power to accept Celestine's renunciation.[2] Moreover, although except in the doubtful case of St. Clement there was no precedent of a Pope having surrendered his authority, this did not necessarily mean that such an abdication was unlawful, for throughout the ages the Church had possessed the power of giving authoritative pronouncements on matters formerly undefined.[3] According to Olivi the Pope could freely decide on all matters which were not contrary to the law of Christ or the decretals of his predecessors,[4] nor was it necessary for him, except in matters of vital importance, to await the decision of a General Council.[5] He distinguished clearly between the sacramental and judicial capacities of the Pope. The former, which he shared with the humblest priest, could never be lost, but the latter was merely part of his office, and thus could be alienated in the same way as a deposed bishop no longer exercised any authority over his see, although he was still able to perform his priestly functions.[6] If the Pope could dissolve the ties which bound his subordinate to his diocese, he had surely the same authority over himself. Yet although Olivi recognised the Pope's right to renounce his office, and even to appoint his successor,[7] he believed that it should be exercised only in cases of grave crises,[8] for constant abdications would imperil the authority of the Church. The same arguments are used in a less developed form in one of his *questiones* [9] and in his letter to Conrad of Offida, written from Narbonne in 1295.[10] In this he separates himself from the extreme Spirituals by defending the papal interpretations of the Franciscan Rule, contained in the decretals " Quo elongati " [11] and " Exiit qui seminat ".[12] Such constitutions in no way infringed the dying command of St. Francis, for they were merely decisions upon doubtful points and were in full accord with the spirit of the Rule.[13] Olivi also deplored the folly shown by the extremists of his party in interpreting literally every counsel found in the Gospels.[14] The moderate tone of this letter makes it difficult to understand why his teaching aroused such vehement opposition among the Conventuals.

A word must also be said about the " Questio de veritate

---

[1] *A.F.H.* xi. 341.　　[2] *Ibid.* p. 353.　　[3] *Ibid.* p. 364.

[4] *Ibid.* p. 347 *s.*　　[5] *Ibid.* p. 365.　　[6] *Ibid.* p. 357.

[7] *Ibid.* p. 358.　　　　　　　　　　[8] *Ibid.* p. 363.

[9] Q. xiii. Incipit : " Quia propter renunciationem Celestini nuper factam quidam dubitant, an papa possit renuntiare papatui " (*A.L.K.G.* iii. 525-28).　　[10] *A.F.H.* xi. 366-73.

[11] *B.F.* i. p. 68.　　[12] *Ibid.* iii. p. 404.　　[13] *A.F.H.* xi. 370.

[14] *Ibid.* p. 371. On p. 372 Olivi speaks bitterly of the foolish and obstinate insistence of the Spirituals upon the question of the Franciscan habit.

Indulgentiae Portiunculae ",[1] for it is a very curious little treatise. The more famous work on the same subject by Fra Francesco Bartoli of Assisi [2] deals with the question in its historical aspect, confirming this testimony by a long record of the miracles and visions vouchsafed to the faithful who availed themselves of the Indulgence. Olivi, on the other hand, treats the whole matter almost as if it were a philosophic question, and strives to establish the position that the all-embracing character of the graces accorded were due to the merits of St. Francis as the renewer of the evangelic life and the herald of a new age. Even at this early stage in his life the writer was obviously an adherent of the apocalyptic theories which were to have so much influence upon his own future and upon the destinies of his followers.[3]

The charge of inconsistency has often been brought against Olivi by those who, by their long and devoted studies of his personality and teaching, have perhaps the best right to speak on such a matter.[4] Here I hope I am not presumptuous in opining that a change of outlook is often rather a sign of intellectual advance than of any moral instability. A man of Olivi's acute intelligence must have realised that many of the problems which he discussed were matters for speculation among thinkers about which no final and definite conclusion could easily be reached.[5] The acuteness of the situation with which he was faced is sometimes not realised. A loyal son of the Church, and yet from the austerity of his own temperament fully alive to the evils which he believed were corroding her spiritual life, it is not surprising that he turned from the darkness of the present to dream of a future in which goodness and holiness should reign upon earth, without perhaps fully realising that his ideal was utterly incompatible with the claims of the ecclesiastical system of his own age. He also felt with an even greater desolation of spirit the difficulties of his position in his own

---

[1] In *Acta Ordinis Minorum*, xiv. 139-45. Now published separately by the Collegio di San Bonaventura at Quaracchi. The end is unfortunately missing.

[2] *Fratris Francisci Bartholi de Assisio, Tractatus de Indulgentia S. Mariae de Portiuncula*, edited by Sabatier in *Collection d'études et de documents sur l'histoire religieuse.*   [3] Cf. *supra*, p. 113.

[4] Both Cardinal Ehrle and Father Jansen are among these. Cf. *A.L.K.G.* iii. 435, and Jansen, *op. cit.* iii. xxvii. This is also the verdict of Father Oliger (*A.F.H.* xi. 335).

[5] " Dico etiam utile esse contrarias opiniones conscribere et recitare, absque tamen assertione pertinaci, ut ex hoc plenius appareat quod neutrum tenetur ut fides, et quod neutrum immobiliter asseritur, et ut etiam ex mutua eorum collatione provectorum aut provehendorum intelligentia possit plenius exerceri, et ut ad defensionem et elucidationem fidei viis multiplicibus possimus manduci. Intelligo autem de illis opinionibus que videntur posse subancillari seu subservire defensionibus aut manuductionibus fidei nostre."

" Confessio ", *A.F.H.* xi. 269 ; Wadding, *Annales*, pp. 378-80, 1297, § xxxiv.

Order, for he conceived it his duty to denounce its abandonment
of the ideals of its founder, and yet dreaded and strove to avert a
schism. At least there is little ground for believing that he ever
compromised upon vital questions, for he died affirming those
views upon poverty and the " usus pauper " and the right of the
individual to follow the dictates of his own judgment in matters
not yet defined by the Church,[1] for the defence of which he had
laboured for so many years under the twofold weight of calumny
and persecution.

Olivi's personality and achievements are the more difficult to
judge because he was first and foremost a teacher, and his writings
when divorced from the spell cast by his personality seem cold, and
perhaps even colourless. His was certainly a complex nature,
formed of various elements not always at union with one another,
for his two chief characteristics—namely, a careful and yet acute
reasoning faculty, and a powerful and vivid imagination, strongly
attracted towards the visionary and fantastic—seem to have had
little interaction upon each other.[2] If he had not been a man of
great charm, as well as of passionate sincerity, it would be difficult
to understand the secret of his influence. Even his enemies could
cast no aspersions on his personal holiness. We may not be justified in accepting without question the estimate of his disciples, who
placed him on an equality with the early Fathers of the Church, and
believed that one day his name would stand beside that of Francis
and Clare in the long roll of Franciscan saints.[3] Yet it is impossible to deny great qualities to the object of such ardent devotion.
How deep this love and reverence must have been can be gathered
from the letters and other works of Angelo da Clareno, who,
although he probably never felt the magic inspiration of close personal contact with his hero, could yet describe him as " the corner-
stone of the foundation laid by the Saint of Assisi ", and declare
that for forty years he had striven to follow humbly in his footsteps.[4]

[1] A declaration of Olivi's views concerning the " usus pauper " made at
the request of a certain Chapter-General is found in C. Laur. S. Crucis, Plut. 31
sin Cod. 3, and has been printed in *A.F.H.* xi. 264-67. It is followed in the same
manuscript by a confession declared to have been made on his death-bed
(*A.F.H.* xi. 267-69). This is cited by Ubertino da Casale in his defence of
Olivi (*A.L.K.G.* ii. 411). At the end of the manuscript, however, and in
Ubertino's citation Olivi professes his loyalty to the Church, "of whom the
governor is now Pope Martin ", whereas the reigning Pope at the time of his
death was Boniface VIII. Possibly Olivi made his confession at one of the
Chapters-General held during the pontificate of Martin IV. (1281–85), and
renewed it on his death-bed. This theory is corroborated by the fact that the
variant version printed by Wadding in his *Annales*, p. 378, 1297, § xxxiii.,
gives the name of the Pope as Boniface. Cf. *A.F.H.* xi. 263-64.

[2] Cf. Oliger, *A.F.H.* xi. 323.

[3] *A.L.K.G.* iii. 443. [4] *Ibid.* i. 554. Cf. *supra*, p. 60, *n.* 3.

CHAPTER V

UBERTINO DA CASALE

IT is customary to begin all accounts of this famous leader of the Zealots with the well-known lines from the *Paradiso* :

> Ma non fia da Casal, nè d' Acquasparta,
> Là onde vegnon tali alla Scrittura,
> Che l' un la fugge, e l' altro la coarta,[1]

nor is this a mere convention, for it is through Dante that Ubertino gains his chief title to renown. Scholars and historians may be interested in his valiant efforts to secure for himself and his friends the right of observing the Rule and Testament of St. Francis in their primitive simplicity, and may follow with heartfelt sympathy the vicissitudes of his tragic and eventful life. Yet to many who love and ponder over the work of the great Italian poet he is only a name, and they care little for his failure in the service of a great and soul-mastering ideal. We do not know if Dante ever sat in the shadow of the old Franciscan church outside the Porta San Gallo [2] and listened to the words of one whose eloquence was the more moving because it came straight from the heart.[3] Perhaps it was only the rumours of the proceedings of the Council of Vienne which led the exile of Verona to regard Ubertino as the typical representative of his party. All we can say with certainty is that Dante read and brooded over the *Arbor Vitae Crucifixae*, for its imagery inspired certain passages in his great poem. Possibly he was indebted to Ubertino for his knowledge of the Joachimite prophecies and for the reverence which led him to place the Calabrian abbot among the doctors of the Church.[4] Even if all the passion and struggle of the long and stormy life of this leader of the Zealots were vain and futile, it is no mean achievement to have influenced the thought of one whose work contains all that is best and noblest of the speculations and ideals of the Middle Ages, and will be an inspiration and delight to mankind as long as the world endures.

In the first prologue of his great book Ubertino has given us

---

[1] *Paradiso*, xii. 124-27.

[2] The old Franciscan convent where Olivi and Ubertino lived and taught was outside the Porta San Gallo. Sta. Croce was not yet built.

[3] Davidsohn (*op. cit.* ii. 176 *s.*) believes that Ubertino was personally known to Dante, and that the poet may have been much influenced by his sermons. It is with the utmost humility that I venture to disagree with this eminent authority on Florentine history, but these few rather disparaging lines do not seem to me to betoken any very great intimacy with the famous Zealot, especially as they are not supported by any other evidence. Moreover, there is no direct allusion to Ubertino's great master Olivi in the whole of the *Divine Comedy*.

[4] *Paradiso*, xii. 140. Cf. *supra*, p. 22.

the story of his life up to the year 1305. The chronology of this account has given rise to many disputes among historians, for its author was only interested in the spiritual significance of the events which he records, and cared little for the actual order in which they took place. We gather that he was born about 1259, in the little town of Casale, which at that time formed part of the diocese of Vercelli. From a later papal bull we learn that he belonged to the family of de Ilia,[1] representatives of which are still to be found in the neighbourhood.[2] When he reached the age of fourteen his parents yielded to his ardent desire and allowed him to join the Franciscan Order as an oblate.[3] The only relation whom he mentions is a young brother, or stepbrother, called Joanninus, who was fired by his example to join the Friars Minor and at whose prayer he wrote his famous book.[4] Perhaps Ubertino was permitted to serve his noviciate in his native town, for Casale probably at this time possessed a Franciscan convent.[5] At any rate, it is probable that he did not leave his native province of Genoa until he was sent to the Studium Generale at Paris.[6] During the period of probation the novice was supposed to eschew all secular learning and devote himself to prayer and meditation.[7] Ubertino seems to have abandoned himself to the practices of the contemplative life with all the ardour of his passionate temperament. Under the guidance of able and pious instructors he devoted each

[1] *B.F.* v. 287, p. 127.

[2] Cf. Father Martini's article on Ubertino in the 1913 (centenary) number of *La Verna*, p. 195, *n.* 1.

[3] Prologue, f. 2 *r.a*. Although it had been ordained by the Constitutions of Narbonne that novices were not to be received into the Franciscan Order till they reached the age of eighteen, unless for some special cause, the practice of oblation still persisted and was warmly defended by Pecham (cf. *A.F.H.* viii. 406-409, 414-39). The custom, however, had by the thirteenth century been shorn of its worst features, for by canon law when the oblate reached the age of fourteen he was allowed to decide whether he would take the final vows or return to the world. It is perhaps for this reason that Father Oliger does not mention the case of Ubertino in his article, " De Pueris Oblatis in Ordine Minorum ", in *A.F.H.* viii. 389-447 ; and x. 271-88.

[4] Prologue, f. 3 *r.b*. He may have been a stepbrother, as he is described as " frater uterinus ", and must have been much younger than Ubertino, who looked upon him as a son. If he can be identified with the Fra Giovanni da Casale, a doctor of theology, who wrote a treatise upon Inequality about the year 1346 (*A.F.H.* i. 116), and also Commentaries on St. Paul's epistles to the Galatians and the Philippians (Denifle, *op. cit.* 198-203), his outlook must have changed greatly from that of the eager youth who was so anxious to share in the mystic dreams of his famous brother (cf. Martini, *op. cit.* p. 202, *n.* 1).

[5] There was a convent at Casale at the end of the thirteenth century (Martini, *op. cit.* p. 196).

[6] " Nam novem annorum spacio quibus legi et Parisius fui " (Prologue, f. 3 *r.a*).

[7] Constitutions of Narbonne. Cf. *A.L.K.G.* vi. 89.

day of the week to pondering over the different incidents in the life of Christ, and such was the force of his imagination that sometimes he conceived himself to be transformed into the penitent Magdalen, at others into John the beloved disciple, or the dying thief, or even into the Mother of God herself.[1] When he rose at dawn on Sunday it seemed as if heaven and earth sang,[2] yet looking back on these early experiences he realised that he still stood on the threshold of the mystic life and had not yet entered into its fuller perfection.[3] At the end of his noviciate he was sent to study at Paris, and there amid the seductions of scholastic philosophy he abandoned his former pursuits.[4] But he was still haunted by the memories of his old life, and his dissatisfaction with himself was increased by a dream in which he beheld Jesus regarding him with a stern and wrathful countenance.[5] When he returned to Italy, after nine years spent in studying and lecturing, one of his first acts was to seek out the famous mystic, Angela of Foligno, by whose counsel and influence he became a changed man.[6] He may have

[1] " Ut nunc mihi viderer magdalena peccatrix : nunc quedam ab ipso electa sponsa ; nunc frater et discipulus electus Ioannes ille : nunc pia mater lamentans que ipsum genuit, nunc latro dexter sibi confixus " (Prologue, f. 2 r.b).

[2] " Die dominico cum ad matutinum surgere videbatur mihi quod celum et terra cantaret " (ibid).

[3] " In primis quoque exercitiis sic quasi per XIIII. annos circa forenseca Iesu me suus spiritus occupabat, nondum me introducens ad altas sue mentis perfectionis et inestimabiles cordis sui doloris " (f. 2 v.a).

[4] " Licet autem inter vanos studentum cuneos secundum huius temporis maliciam fueri conversatus : ac sepe philosophicis studiis deditus : spiritus tamen benedicti Iesu super me inpulit ista contemnere " (f. 2 r.a).

[5] F. 3 r.a.

[6] Ibid., f. 3 r.a. The reading of certain manuscripts, amongst others the late fifteenth- or early sixteenth-century German manuscript in Rylands Library (MS. Lat. 200, Philipps MS. 599), is " XXV⁰ anno religionis mee ", not " aetatis mee " as in others and in the incunable, in which case the intercourse between Ubertino and the great mystic would have taken place when he was no longer a very young man. This view is apparently accepted by Ferré in his article on the chief dates in the life of Angela of Foligno in R.H.F. ii. 21-35, for he gives 1298 as the year of their meeting, at which time Ubertino would have already begun his career as a preacher. No confirmation of this opinion can, however, be found in the Arbor, in which the author's intercourse with Angela and John of Parma are described as if they were almost contemporary events in his life. Moreover, Ubertino expressly declares that his visit to Greccio took place four years before John's death, that is, in 1285. Cf. L. V. cap. iii. f. 2 r.a. The same chronological difficulty arises with regard to his sojourn in Paris, for certain scholars, including Father Bihl, date it immediately after his noviciate, while others, and notably Callaey, believe that it took place immediately after his stay in Florence, where, according to the latter, he attended the lectures of Olivi. (Cf. A.F.H. iv. 597 s. and R.H.E. xvii. 538 n., where the question is exhaustively discussed.) I cannot claim to base my opinion on the textual evidence studied with such care by both these eminent authorities, but I incline rather to the view of the former, as I think it is more in accordance with Ubertino's own account given in the Prologue to the Arbor. Although

seen her again the following year, for he was present at the famous indulgence of the Portiuncula, and during the night that he passed there received spiritual understanding of the Rule.[1] Earlier in the year he had gone on a pilgrimage to Rome and visited John of Parma at the little hermitage of Greccio, who comforted him much and instructed him concerning future events.[2] According to Ubertino the old man was still an ardent Joachimite, and believed earnestly in the coming of a new age, when the present Church, which was not Jerusalem the bride of Christ but Babylon the harlot, would be destroyed.[3] This was probably his first initiation into the apocalyptic speculations which were to affect his whole attitude with regard to the ecclesiastical order of his day. Hitherto he had not belonged especially to any party in his Order, but now he was to be a Zealot of the Zealots, and adopt, along with a full measure of their loyalty and faithfulness towards a noble ideal, a narrow and violent fanaticism which embittered his relations with his superiors and made his life a magnificent failure.

Shortly after his return from Paris Ubertino had been sent to Tuscany as a lector or lecturer.[4] Probably he lectured in Florence under Olivi, either upon the Sentences or as a subordinate lecturer on the Bible.[5] His remarkable knowledge of the Scriptures makes the latter supposition the more probable.[6] During his stay in Tuscany he met the three individuals who were to have most influence over his life.[7] His master Olivi introduced him to the sublime heights of mystic devotion which he had striven after during his noviciate, and increased his knowledge of the doctrines of the Abbot Joachim by communicating to him his own beliefs

---

he was recording the events of his life merely with a view to showing their significance in his spiritual development, it is difficult to believe that his intercourse with Olivi was limited to only one year. Moreover, he gives us to understand that his connection with his great master was the turning-point of his life. How then is it possible that immediately afterwards he became so fascinated with his philosophic studies that he lost all interest in his former religious pursuits, to which he had devoted the preceding fifteen years ? Also, Callaey fails to explain why the Franciscan authorities, who would hardly have received Ubertino into the Order at fourteen unless he had possessed remarkable spiritual or intellectual gifts, neglected the cultivation of the latter until he had reached the mature age of twenty-eight.

[1] Prologue, f. 2 *v.a.*

[2] " Sed tunc Romana sanctuaria visitans et ad angelum faciei Iesu vere sanctissimum Ioannem de Parma ad rupem deveniens letus et ab ipso confortatus et instructus " (*ibid.*).

[3] *A.V.* L. V. cap. iii. f. 4 *v.b.*

[4] " Nam ad provinciam Tuscie veniens sub titulo studii " (Prologue, f. 2 *v.*). He was certainly holding a lectorship when he received the news of John of Parma's death in 1289 (L. V. cap. iii. f. 2 *r.a*).

[5] This is the suggestion of Father Martini (*op. cit.* p. 200, and *ibid. n.* 3).

[6] *Ibid.*   [7] Prologue, f. 2 *v.b.*

with regard to the future of the world.[1] In spite, however, of his unbounded affection and reverence for his beloved teacher, Ubertino never lost his independence of outlook. He regarded him as equal in wisdom to the early doctors of the Church, but this did not prevent him from realising that his teaching contained many errors.[2] He also gained much spiritual profit from the society of Peter, the holy comb-seller of Siena, who is mentioned by Dante in the *Purgatorio*,[3] and of a certain devout virgin called Cecilia, who was perhaps a Claress at Cortona.[4] Yet Ubertino's enthusiastic and poetic temperament, which gave him so high a vision of the beauty of holiness, did not suffer him to remain always faithful to his ideal, and the black despair which he felt after his lapses was very bitter to his soul, and possibly led him to exaggerate his sinfulness. After exercising his office as lector for four years he abandoned it for the more congenial duties of preaching, and gained much fame by his sermons, both in Tuscany and Umbria,[5] but especially in the neighbourhood of Perugia. It must have been during one of his visits to this town that he met certain of the followers of Liberato who had lately returned from Greece, for in the *Arbor Vitae* he writes with indignation of the treatment accorded to Liberato and his followers by Boniface VIII., and tells the story of the reading of the Commentary of St. Justin Martyr on the Apocalypse, declaring that he had heard it from the reader himself.[6] His popularity, however, with the crowds who flocked to hear him brought no peace to his soul, for he knew that his life fell far short of the model which he strove to set before them, and so was dismayed at his own hypocrisy.[7] Perhaps he was secretly glad when in 1304 his superiors, disapproving of his violence, inhibited him from preaching, and sent him to the retirement of La Verna.[8] The year which he spent there was probably the happiest period of his life. His imaginative spirit was fired and at the same time soothed by the austerity of the mountain solitudes where St. Francis had received the sacred wounds which set him apart as the chosen herald of a new age. The brethren at the little

---

[1] " Qui me . . . sic introduxit . . . ad intima tertii status mundi" (Prologue, f. 2 *v.b*).

[2] " Non tamen hunc perfectum doctorem quem rationabiliter commendo in aliquibus dictis suis sequor ; quia aliquando bonus dormitat Homerus " (f. 2 *v.b*. Cf. *A.L.K.G.* iii. 88).

[3] F. 2 *v.b*. *Purg*. xiii. 127.

[4] F. 2 *v.b*. This is Father Martini's suggestion (*op. cit.* 256-58). Ubertino was also apparently known to St. Margaret of Cortona (*ibid.*).

[5] Prologue, f. 3 *r.b*.

[6] L. V. cap. viii. f. 4 *r.a*. Cf. *supra*, p. 58.

[7] F. 2 *v.b*. The lax life of which he complains may have been largely due to ill-health.

[8] Prologue, f. 3 *r.b*. Cf. *A.L.K.G.* ii. 132.

hermitage, moreover, observed the Rule of their founder in its original strictness, and the guardian was both friendly and deferential to his famous guest. For the time being all love of self departed from the heart of Ubertino, and his only griefs were the insults to the Crucified, which he saw everywhere in the wickedness and corruption of the Church,[1] and the continual importunity of his friends, who entreated him to employ his enforced leisure in composing some little treatise either on the Scriptures or on the life and passion of Jesus. Others urged him to write an exposition on the Apocalypse,[2] and his most eager petitioner was his brother Joanninus, who both besought him in person and sent frequent letters to the guardian begging him to second his request.[3] The latter was by no means unwilling to do so, and even offered to write at Ubertino's dictation,[4] if only he would yield to the prayers of those who loved him. The result was the famous *Arbor Vitae*, begun in the springtime of the thirty-second year of Ubertino's religious life and finished on the vigil of St. Michael at the hour when the brethren were entering the church for vespers.[5] Possibly, once he had embarked upon his book, Ubertino did not find the labours of composition very difficult, for we cannot accept too literally his statement that he had never before written or dictated anything,[6] and had great difficulty in finding fitting language in which to clothe his thoughts. He would be able to employ much of the material which he had formerly used in his sermons,[7] and his mind and imagination were wrought up to such a pitch that he seemed to himself merely the instrument for recording the thought and will of Christ.[8] During this period he derived much benefit from the friendship of a holy virgin who lived at Città di Castello.[9] Their sympathy was so close that when he had written a third of

---

[1] "Ibi ineffabilibus modis tota simul et vita dei mihi immittitur et inestimabilis fletus super destructione Christi vite et adulterate ecclesie, tota cordis reliquatione, quasi continue immissus est mihi ; et a proprio amore me Iesus exclusit, ut nesciam flere, vel petere, nisi honorem Iesu a reformatione ecclesie et vite sue ; et conversione omnium electorum " (Prologue, f. 3 *r.b*).

[2] *Ibid.* [3] *Ibid.* [4] *Ibid.*

[5] " Et iuxta quod ipsa predixit, dans mihi terminum mensis septembris, illo mense terminavi in virgilia Michaelis Archangeli anni presentis MCCCV a felicissimo ortu veri solis Iesu. A meo vero vili conversione anno XXXII " (f. 3 *v.b*).

[6] F. 3 *r.b*.

[7] " Et populi multitudini Perusina pluries predicando exposui semiplene quam in hoc libro plenius expressi " (f. 3 *r.b*). Father Martini in his analysis of the *Arbor Vitae* has noted many sections which bear unmistakable marks of having originally been intended for sermons (*op. cit.* 212-21).

[8] Prologue, f. 3 *v.a*.

[9] F. 3 *v.b*. Father Martini has identified this holy maiden with a Dominican Tertiary, the blessed Margaret, living at this time in Città di Castello (*op. cit.* 258-63).

his book she was able to tell him the contents of the remainder.[1]
For a long time Ubertino was obliged to suspend his work owing
to a severe fever, from which he suddenly recovered.[2] We know
from another source that he was suffering at this time from an
internal complaint which caused him such pain that he was frequently obliged to cry out even when in public,[3] but it is not certain whether his illness was in any way connected with this.   The
ill-health of its author must have considerably delayed the *Arbor*,
for it was only for little more than three months of the summer
of 1305 that Ubertino was able to devote himself seriously to the
labours of composition—a very short period when we consider the
great length of his book.[4] There are undoubtedly passages which
abundantly justify his proud boast that he himself was merely an
instrument recording the mind of his Saviour, but it does not always rise to such heights.   Ubertino poured the whole of his ardent
temperament, vast creative energy, intellectual powers, and experience of life into the making of it; and we see reflected as in a
mirror his love and devotion to the most pious Jesus and His holy
mother, and his fierce indignation at the indifference, luxury, and
worldliness which he felt were corroding the life not only of his
Order but of the whole Church.   Yet his bitterness was not the
hopelessness of despair, for he dreamed of a time when all the
present evils should be destroyed and the ideals of St. Francis,
whom he regarded with a veneration only second to that which
he felt towards Christ and the Virgin, should reign undisputed in
the hearts of the elect.

Soon after he had finished the *Arbor Vitae* Ubertino left La
Verna as chaplain to the Cardinal Napoleone Orsini, the papal
legate in central Italy.   Probably the two men were already well
known to each other, for the cardinal had certainly been in Perugia
early in 1305, for it was in that year that he gave his protection
to Angelo da Clareno.[5] Moreover, a diploma which he granted
to La Verna in the summer of 1305 is thought by the experts to
bear unmistakable traces of Ubertino's style.[6] It is uncertain how
long he formed part of the cardinal's household.   He was un-

---

[1] Prologue, f. 3 *v.b.*   [2] F. 3 *v.b.*
[3] " Life of St. Clare of Montefalco ", pp. 251-53.   This contemporary
account of the saint by a certain Berengario di Sant' Africano has been edited
by Mgr. Faloci-Pulignani, first in the *Archivio storico per le Marche e per
l' Umbria*, ii., and afterwards as a separate book.
[4] F. 3 *v.a* and *v.b.*   The incunable of 1485 is abridged, but each column
contains roughly 450 words, so that each page contains 900 and each leaf 1800.
The number of leaves in the whole book is 248 (Martini, *op. cit.* p. 213, *n.* 1).
[5] *A.L.K.G.* i. 531.   Cf. *supra*, p. 60.
[6] Martini, *op. cit.* p. 204, *n.* 2.   Cf. Wadding, *Annales*, iv. 1260, p. 156,
§ lvii.

doubtedly with him in 1309 when Orsini, in his character of papal legate, held an inquiry into the life and miracles of St. Clare of Montefalco, a Claress who had died in 1308. In order to convince the multitude of the sanctity of the dead nun, and with no thought for his own profit, Ubertino prayed that by her intercession he might be released from his infirmity. The miracle he desired was performed.[1] We do not know whether it was as the agent and familiar of the cardinal that he carried on a vigorous crusade against the heretics in Umbria, and especially against the apostles, several of whom with " diabolical " cunning had joined the Franciscan Order with a view to spreading their errors among its members.[2] Ubertino's methods won the admiration of his friend Clareno, but appear somewhat unscrupulous to modern ideas, as for instance when with a seeming desire to become initiated into its doctrines he induced the leader of the sect Bentivenga to make a full confession of his errors before prudent and carefully chosen witnesses, and thus was able to secure his detection and arrest.[3] His campaign in Umbria, however, only served further to embitter his relations with his superiors, for Ubertino felt slighted that he received neither recognition nor support from his Order in his work,[4] while they on their side complained that his leniency towards the heretics showed that he was little better than a heretic himself.[5]

Ubertino was summoned from Umbria to take part in the proceedings which Clement V. had initiated at the Curia,[6] hoping

[1] " Life of St. Clare of Montefalco ", *loc. cit.* In the investigation into the miracles of the saint held in 1318 Ubertino is described as " Fratrem Ubertinum di Casali tunc ordinis fratrum Minorum sed nunc Monachum nigrum " (*ibid.* p. 253, *n.*).

[2] " Historia Septem Tribulationum " (*A.L.K.G.* ii. 131).

[3] *A.L.K.G.* ii. 131. According to the contemporary life of St. Clare of Montefalco, Fra Bentivenga was a native of Gubbio, and followed the errors of the sect of the Free Spirit. The saint herself had played an active part in denouncing his errors to the Dominican inquisitors and to the secular authorities, and finally Cardinal Napoleone Orsini, as papal legate, instituted a process against him. It is therefore highly probable that Ubertino was still in the cardinal's service at the time when he procured Bentivenga's detection and arrest (Faloci-Pulignani, *op. cit.* p. 204 *s.* Cf. Fumi, *Eretici e ribelli*, pp. 46 and 47).

[4] " Patet etiam hos per contrarium in illis vilissimis hereticis qui reperti sunt in provincia Sancti Francisci, circa quorum correctionem ministri et prelati alii fuerunt per multa tempora negligentes et ei (Ubertino) qui cum multo labore et periculo prudenter eos deprehendit et punivit, tales referunt grates, ut vos ipsi domini experimini, quia tales sibi persecutiones excitant et ipsum infamari impie non verentur " (*A.L.K.G.* iii. 123).

[5] *Ibid.* p. 124.

[6] *Ibid.* ii. p. 133. His name is also given in the bull " Dudum ad apostolatus nostri " of April 1310, exempting the Spirituals from the jurisdiction of their superiors pending the inquiry (*B.F.* v. 158, p. 65 ; Wadding, *Annales*, vi. p. 168, 1310, § iii.

to put an end to the internecine warfare in the Franciscan Order, and to find some compromise on which both Spirituals and Conventuals could agree. He was the only Italian of his party present, and by far its ablest representative, although many of the others were superior to him in rank and influence.[1]

After the death of Raymund Gaufridi he became the leader of the Zealots, and certainly they could not have had a more vigorous and uncompromising chief.[2] His solution for the questions at issue lay in the separation of the two parties into two distinct orders,[3] and for two years he carried on a campaign of violence and recrimination with Raymund de Fronsac and Bonagratia of Bergamo.[4] At least Ubertino did not sink to the level of his opponents by bringing accusations against their personal integrity and moral character, though he may have damaged his cause by his attacks upon people in high positions, such as John of Murrovalle, a weakness of which his enemies were not slow to avail themselves.[5] Even to the impartial reader his pamphlets have a sincerity of tone which is generally lacking in those of the opposite party, and he certainly flung the whole vigour of his personality into the work before him, whether it was pointing out the many breaches of the Rule so common among the majority of the Order,[6] or defending the memory of his beloved master Olivi, and relating the sufferings of his disciples.[7] It is impossible to read unmoved his passionate appeal to Clement V. that the only hope of settlement lay in separation.[8] The promulgation of the decretal " Exivi de paradiso "[9] during the concluding stages of the Council of Vienne and the deposition of the superiors who had shown themselves most hostile to the Spirituals made it clear that the Pope was still bent on compromise. His own death and that of the peace-loving General Alexander of Alexandria made the success of his policy an impossibility.

We know very little of Ubertino's movements during the

---

[1] *A.L.K.G.* ii. 133.

[2] Certain of Ubertino's treatises have been printed in *A.L.K.G.* ii. 374-416 ; *ibid.* iii. 48-89, 93-137, 160-95 ; and *A.F.H.* x. 116-74. His intense literary activity can be judged by the fact that during the later stages of the controversy he composed no less than nine pamphlets. Cf. Gratien, *op. cit.* p. 465 ; and *A.L.K.G.* iii. 21-23. [3] *Ibid.* p. 87.

[4] For pamphlets composed by Raymund and Bonagratia cf. *A.L.K.G.* ii. 363-74 ; iii. 93-159 ; *A.F.H.* vii. 654-75 ; viii. 56-80.

[5] Now Cardinal Protector. *A.L.K.G.* iii. 128-30.

[6] *Ibid.* pp. 48-137 and 160-95. [7] *Ibid.* ii. 374-416.

[8] *Ibid.* iii. 87. Clareno tells us that when the decretal " Exivi de paradiso " was promulgated, and the Zealots were ordered to live peaceably under the authority of their former superiors, Ubertino on behalf of his party made a passionate protest to the Pope (*ibid.* ii. 141).

[9] *B.F.* v. *n.* 195, p. 80. Cf. *supra*, p. 14.

troubled period which lasted till the election of John XXII. in 1316. He was certainly present at the Conclave, perhaps in attendance on his old patron Cardinal Napoleone Orsini, for Angelo da Clareno wrote that he had consulted him and other members of his party upon the advisability of showing certain letters from his followers in Italy to the cardinals.[1] A fighter like Ubertino must have followed with burning eagerness the different stages in the warfare between the Conventuals and Zealots of Provence, and he probably did his best to secure for the latter the sympathy and support of the Italian cardinals. After the election of the new Pope his enemies lost no time in bringing their accusations against him,[2] but John was disarmed by his boldness and sense of humour. When he was asked whether he had adhered to the rebellious friars of Narbonne and Béziers, or wished to defend the doctrines of Olivi, Ubertino replied that he was prepared to obey the Pope in all things, and therefore at his command would undertake the defence of his master and of his friends. John hastily replied, " We do not wish that you concern yourself with such matters ".[3] Yet although all danger of his sharing the fate of the deputation from Narbonne and Béziers was over, Ubertino's position was by no means assured. As in the case of Angelo, the Pope tried to induce him to return to the Franciscan Order, or at least, for the sake of avoiding a scandal, to spend a few nights at the convent of the Friars Minor at Avignon, promising afterwards to provide for him in some other way. Ubertino answered with biting irony, " If I stayed with them for one day only I should need neither yours nor anyone else's provision in this life ".[4] John yielded for the time being, but finally persuaded him to join some other religious order, perhaps hoping to restore peace to the Franciscans by ridding them of such a firebrand. It is uncertain whether Ubertino's choice of the Benedictines was dictated by necessity or by his own free will. The papal bull consigning him to the abbey of Gemblach, near Liège, speaks of his feeble health.[5] Probably, however, the abbot was never troubled by his presence, for he certainly remained for some time at Avignon. Angelo da Clareno, with his usual unswerving loyalty, describes the annoyance of his enemies at finding that Ubertino was as much respected by the Pope and cardinals in his Benedictine habit as ever he had been as a Franciscan.[6] This, however, was not the opinion commonly

---

[1] *A.L.K.G.* i. 548.   [2] *Ibid.* ii. 142 ; iii. 27.   [3] *Ibid.* ii. 143.

[4] " Post moram meam unius diei cum ipsis non indigebo, nec vestra, nec cuiusquam alterius provisione in hac vita " (*ibid.* p. 151).

[5] *Ibid.* p. 151 ; *B.F.* v. 287, p. 127.

[6] *A.L.K.G.* ii. 152. Father Oliger has lately suggested that the Franciscan Order took advantage of the unfavourable verdict of the theologians upon

K

held at the Curia, for a certain Johannes Burgundi, writing from
Avignon in February 1318 to Bernard of Aversone, notary to the
King of Aragon, expressed a very natural surprise that one who had
attacked so bitterly the laxity of the Friars Minor should become
a member of a far less austere Order.[1] Ubertino was at the papal
court during the early stages of the quarrel between John XXII.
and the Friars Minor, for the Pope, through the medium of Cardinal Orsini, requested his opinion on the subject of the poverty of
Christ and His apostles. The answer he received showed both
moderation and good sense,[2] and might easily have served as a
settlement of the whole question, if the Pope had not already determined to undermine the basis upon which the Franciscan
conception of poverty rested. By civil law the apostles had no
possessions, for their master had expressly commanded them not
to contend before judicial tribunals when their goods were taken
away from them. On the other hand they had a natural right to

---

Olivi's " Postilla in Apocalypsim " (cf. *supra*, p. 113) to institute proceedings
against Ubertino for the part he had played at the time of the Council of Vienne.
He believes that Bonagratia of Bergamo was formally appointed proctor in
1319 in order that he might conduct the case, and that the extracts from his
accusations in *Misc.* ii. 276-79 belong to this process and not to one instituted
in 1325, as was formerly supposed (cf. *infra*, p. 131). His theory is based
on Angelo da Clareno's description of the fury of the Conventuals at the favour
enjoyed by Ubertino at the papal court, and on the fact that by 1325 Bonagratia
was an ardent supporter of the very doctrine of poverty which he had denounced
as heretical when held by Ubertino (cf. *A.F.H.* xxii. pp. 306-307). The trial
took place before Guillaume Peyre Godin, Cardinal of Sta. Sabina, formerly one of the Commissioners to whom Clement V. had committed the
examination of Olivi's doctrines, at the time of the Council of Vienne (cf.
Gratien, *op. cit.* p. 455), and eventually the accused appears to have confessed
his errors (*Misc.* ii. 279). Unfortunately the document is undated, but there
seems to be a reference on p. 276 to the final condemnation of Olivi's commentary by John XXII., which did not take place till February 1326
(cf. *B.F.* v. 601, p. 297 ; and *A.L.K.G.* iii. 455-56), by which time Ubertino
was already a hunted fugitive (*B.F.* v. *n.* 587, p. 292 (September 1325)). Cf.
infra, p. 231. My own feeling is that it is wiser to suspend judgment until
by some happy chance the whole of the accusations brought by Bonagratia
against Ubertino are discovered. I do not think, however, that the fact
that in 1325 he held the views previously maintained by Ubertino on the
question of poverty would have necessarily caused him to refrain from
attacking the latter, for he was not particularly scrupulous, and may even have
pursued this policy as a means of diverting the Pope's attention from himself
and his Order.
    [1] *A.F.H.* ii. 160. Quoted from Finke, *Acta Aragonensia*, p. 672.
    [2] *Misc.* ii. 279-80 ; *B.F.* v. 233 *n.* Mlle. d'Alverny (*op. cit.* p. 7) has proved
that only a part of Ubertino's answer was printed by Baluze, the full version
existing only in MS. Lat. 809 of the Vienna Library. A résumé to which his
name is not attached is contained in MS. Bibl. Nat. (Paris), fonds Lat. 3740,
among the replies of the cardinals and theologians consulted by John XXII.
on the subject of evangelical poverty.

the things which they owned, and could act as stewards and dispensers of the riches presented to the Church.[1] It is probable that both the Dominicans and Franciscans, who had been the original parties in the dispute, would have been prepared to accept this solution, but John's legal and practical mind saw all too clearly the weakness of the legal fiction by which the latter Order was able to boast of its utter lack of possessions, either severally or as a community. By a strange irony the arguments of the Pope had been forestalled by Ubertino in his pamphlets written during the period of the Council of Vienne, and it is tempting to believe that these may have had some influence over the mind of John. If so, Ubertino was amply revenged on his old enemies, for Bonagratia of Bergamo, now proctor of the Order, suffered a year's imprisonment because of the vigour of the official protest [2] which he lodged against the bull " Ad conditorem canonum ",[3] by which the Pope renounced the ownership of the goods which had been left to the use of the Friars Minor. The remarkable resemblance between the Declaration of Sachsenhausen of the 22nd of April 1324 and Olivi's eighth question on poverty [4] gave rise to the supposition that Ubertino was present at the Court of Louis of Bavaria at the time of its composition. This, however, has now been proved an impossibility, for in the July of 1324 he was at Avignon in his old position in the household of Napoleone Orsini, and obviously on good terms with the Pope, for the cardinal employed him as a messenger to John in connection with some very delicate business entrusted to him by the King of Aragon.[5] He had apparently a very high opinion of Ubertino's sagacity, for he made use of his services in the negotiations between Pisa and Aragon.[6] The following year he was brought to trial on a charge of heresy, but apparently fled from Avignon without awaiting the verdict of his judges.[7] The papal bulls of September 1325 describe him as wandering like a vagabond through the world, and order his detention and arrest.[8] The remaining years of his life are wrapped in mystery. Alberto de Mussato, a contemporary and fellow-citizen of the famous Marsiglio of Padua, relates in his chronicle that he was at Rome for the coronation of Louis of Bavaria, and played an active part in

---

[1] *Misc.* ii. 279-80 ; *B.F.* v. p. 233 *n.*

[2] Baluze-Mansi, *Misc.* iii. 213-21 ; *B.F.* v. pp. 237-46 *n.*

[3] *B.F.* v. 486, p. 233.

[4] Cf. *A.L.K.G.* iii. 540-52, where the relevant passages in the two documents are quoted side by side.

[5] *A.F.H.* ii. 161. Quoted from *Acta Aragonensia*, p. 674.

[6] *A.F.H.* ii. 162. Quoted from *Acta Aragonensia*, p. 617.

[7] *B.F.* v. 587, p. 292.

[8] " Per mundum discurrit vagabundus " (*ibid.*), "vagabundus per mundum " (*ibid.* p. 292).

stirring up the people against John XXII.[1]   This is perhaps the saddest part of Ubertino's history, for he can hardly have been so blinded by his hatred of the Pope as to see in the Emperor's puppet, Peter of Corbara, " the angelic pastor " of his dreams.   The politicians of the imperial court, and even speculative thinkers like Marsiglio of Padua and John of Jandun, must secretly have mocked at this wild enthusiast even while they made use of his eloquence to bend the fickle Roman mob to their will.   Romantic devotion and unswerving fidelity to the bride of St. Francis were not common guests in Louis's camp, where lip-service to the cause of evangelical poverty, and a ready pen in its defence, was all that was asked for. We hope that he was not still with the Emperor on his return to Pisa,[2] and thus was spared the pain of meeting Michael of Cesena and his hated enemy Bonagratia.   A document in the archives of Como tells us that he preached in that town against John XXII. in 1329.[3]   A letter of Benedict XII. to the same city, dated 1341, describes him as " quondam Ubertinus de Elia de Casale ".[4]   We know nothing of the way in which he met his end, but a later tradition ascribes his death to violence.[5]   Perhaps his most fitting epitaph is to be found in certain lines from the beautiful Latin hymn which he inserted in his famous book : [6]

> Mors est quies viatoris,
> Finis est omnis laboris,

for the fiery and tortured soul which had found no peace on earth must have passed with deep thankfulness into the eternal quiet.

The Writings of Ubertino da Casale

1. The " Arbor Vitae Crucifixae "

" I was importuned by many that I should expound certain passages of Scripture : others sought that I should compose sermons :

---

[1] *Fontes Rerum Germanicarum*, i. 175.

[2] September 1329.

[3] Cf. H. Otto, " Zur italienischen Politik Johanns XXII." in *Q. and F.* xiv. p. 248.   Absolution given by the Bishop of Como to certain Augustinians.

[4] *Ibid.* p. 117.

[5] " De suoi (Olivi's) discepoli fu quel santo d' alto et di levatissimo spirito fratre Ubertino de Chasale . . . del qual si dice per alchuno che per essa verita (evangelic poverty) fu amazato" (*S.F.*, p. 515).   Taken from a treatise of the Fraticelli written in the second half of the fourteenth century.

[6] *A.V.* L. IV. cap. 25.

others that I should make a commentary upon the Apocalypse, and others more instantly prayed that I should describe the life and heartfelt passion of Christ Jesus." [1]

The manifold desires of Ubertino's friends have left their mark upon his book, for it is very hard to place the *Arbor Vitae* in any known literary category. Perhaps it can best be termed a prose epic of the life and passion of Christ, to which has been added a Commentary on the Apocalypse,[2] bearing unmistakable traces of Joachimite influence. Yet such a description leaves out of account the valuable autobiographical details afforded by the first prologue, as well as Ubertino's characteristic but terrible denunciations of the worldliness, luxury, and indolence of the higher clergy of his day, and his stern contempt for the lives led by the majority of his Order. Nor does it tell us that the sweetest parts of the *Arbor* are the lyrical praises of Poverty and of her lover Francis, which show that its author, despite his austerity, was yet no stranger to the gentler emotions of tenderness and love.[3] In short, Ubertino brought all the force of his intense religious feeling, powerful intellect, and volcanic energy to the making of his famous book. Because of our knowledge of his temperament we are not surprised that at times he rises to heights of poetry and mystic devotion which have seldom been surpassed, and which justify his proud claim that Christ was the beginning, end, and centre of all his labour.[4] At others he sinks to depths of savagery and barbarity which make his boast that he was merely an instrument recording the mind of his Saviour sound almost like blasphemy.[5] The same unevenness of workmanship is displayed in the arrangement of the book. Each chapter is carefully mapped out under a metrical heading, while the scrupulous enumeration of the subsections remind us that its author was an adept in the art of sermon-making. Yet Ubertino is led away into continual digressions which are often longer than his original argument, and these, in spite of the rigid formality of the framework, leave the reader conscious of a total lack of order and symmetry of design. Such matters, however, hardly affect the tremendous impression produced on the mind by the *Arbor*, for it is a prose-poem enshrining the spirit of one who was a mystic and poet of no mean order. Its very imperfections merely serve to reveal more fully the immense force of Ubertino's

[1] " Multotiens molestatus a diversis quod aliqua scripturarum exponerem, aliis petentibus quod predicabilia componerem, aliis quod apocalipsim exponerem ; aliis devotius flagitantibus quod Christi Iesu vitam et cordiales eius passiones describerem " (Prologue, f. 3 *r.b*).

[2] L. V.   [3] L. V. cap. iii.-v.

[4] " Ipse principium medium et finis nostri salutis similiter ipse se fecit principium medium et finem libri sequentis " (Prologue, f. 2 *r.a*).

[5] F. 3 *v.a.*

fiery personality and the depth of his devotion for Jesus and His most holy mother. Such intensity of feeling and passion had to find its own mode of expression, and could not be confined within the limits of any superimposed form.

Like most medieval writers, Ubertino had no scruples about borrowing from other authors. The whole conception and framework of his book is taken from the " Lignum Vitae "[1] of St. Bonaventura, and he must have seen the picture of the tree of life with its twelve branches, each signifying some incident in the life of Christ which serves as a frontispiece to the treatise of the " seraphic doctor ". Both writers tenderly refer to their work as a " bundle of myrrh ",[2] to be offered to their divine Master. Most of Ubertino's metrical chapter headings come from the same source, and he has borrowed others from a rimed liturgy of St. Bonaventura's which may often have been sung in the Franciscan churches. The only alteration which he makes in his scheme is that his tree has a root symbolising the history of the world from the Creation to the birth of its Redeemer, while its fruits are the workings of the Holy Spirit as seen in the lives of the elect.[3] Here, however, the resemblance ceases, for the " Lignum Vitae " is by no means the greatest of St. Bonaventura's works, and its commonplace and somewhat conventional nature is unjustly emphasised when it is contrasted with Ubertino's masterpiece, in which the rhythm of every line seems to pulsate in unison with the throbbings of his heart. It is characteristic of the undying hatred which the Zealots felt towards the successor and persecutor of John of Parma that he never acknowledges his debt to the " seraphic doctor ",[4] although he also borrowed freely from his sermons [5] and his more famous " Apologia Pauperum ",[6] and, like every good Franciscan, was well acquainted with the life of the founder of his Order.[7] Ubertino certainly was familiar with the works of the Abbot Joachim, for they form the basis of his apocalyptic speculations, whilst a comparison of the *Arbor* with Döllinger's version of Olivi's Postilla in Apocalypsim supplies abundant evidence of the disciple's debt to his master.[8] He had obviously been nurtured in the literature and oral traditions so

---

[1] *Opera Omnia*, viii. Cf. Callaey, *R.H.E.* xi. 496-99.

[2] *Lignum Vitae*, Prologue. Cf. *A.V.* f. 2 *r.a-r.b.*

[3] Prologue, f. 4 *r.b.*

[4] Generally Ubertino is very scrupulous about citing his authorities. One of Gerson's accusations against him in later years was his refusal to acknowledge his debt to Bonaventura. Cf. Gerson, *Opera*, i. p. 573.

[5] Cf. Martini, *op. cit.* 221 s.   Callaey, *op. cit.* 499.

[6] *A.V.* L. III. cap. xiii. f. 1 *r. s.*   [7] Cf. Callaey, *op. cit.* 495.

[8] For example, the identification of the locusts in *Apoc.* ix. with the worldly ecclesiastics of the 6th age (*A.V.* L. V. cap. vii. f. 7 *r.a* ; *infra*, p. 139) and the denunciation of the followers of Aristotle (*A.V.* L. V. cap. vii. f. 5 *v.a* ; *infra*,

current among the Spirituals, for he quotes freely both from the older " Speculum " and the writings of Brother Leo, and unjustly charges the Conventuals with the destruction of the famous rolls which had been placed for safety in the great convent of Assisi.[1] Long extracts are given from the popular " de Finibus Paupertatis "[2] of the great Zealot, Hugues de Digne, and also many passages from the *Commercium Sancti Patris Francisci cum Domina Paupertate*,[3] which inspired the glorious description of the close union between Christ and Poverty, which is perhaps the gem of the whole book. The tender prayer of St. Francis to the Christ pleading for tidings of his bride is taken verbatim from the same source.[4] Ubertino especially deserves our gratitude by preserving for us the fine *Lament of the Virgin to the Cross*, which begins " O crux dura quid fecisti ".[5] Unfortunately its author is unknown. He also quotes certain stanzas from the lovely " Jesus decus angelicum ", long attributed to St. Bernard,[6] which he puts into the mouth of the Virgin. The third hymn which he gives is a sequence of great dramatic power, describing the ascension of Christ into heaven and His reception by the angels. As in the case of the *Lament of the Virgin to the Cross*, he throws no light

---

p. 137) are taken almost verbatim from Olivi's Postilla. Cf. *Beiträge*, ii. pp. 554 and 555.

[1] " Cum multo dolore audivi illos rotulos fuisse distractos et forsitan perditos " (*A.V.* L. V. cap. v. f. 2 *r.a.* Cf. *A.L.K.G.* iii. 76). Ubertino's source of information concerning Brother Leo was probably Conrad of Offida (cf. L. V. cap. iv. f. 4 *v.b*). He had certainly met some of the surviving companions of St. Francis, and may have been on intimate terms with the little group which had collected round Brother Giles at Perugia. The Brother Masseo mentioned in L. V. cap. iii. f. 7 *r.b* was not the reputed author of the " Legend of the Three Companions ", but a namesake who had been a knight of Perugia. Cf. Callaey, *op. cit.* p. 704.

[2] Published by Mlle. Florowsky in *A.F.H.* v. 277-90. Cf. *A.V.* L. V. cap. v. f. 2 *r.b*, and *supra*, p. 7, *n.* 4.

[3] The authorship of this beautiful work has been attributed on the authority of the *Chronicle of the 24 Generals* (*A.F.* iii. p. 283) to John of Parma. The recent editors regard this opinion as unsound, since many of the earlier codices give 1227 as the date of its composition, and it is noteworthy that Ubertino describes its author only in very general terms, and not as if he were a contemporary (*A.V.* L. V. cap. iii. f. 4 *r.a*). It has been suggested that the attribution to John of Parma was due to a confusion between him and Johannes Parenti, Minister-General (1226–1232) (" Prolegomena to Commercium ", pp. 30-2). The Bodleian Library possesses two codices containing the *Commercium* (C. Can. Misc. 263 and 525), in the former of which it is followed by a poem of Jacopone da Todi, written in praise of Holy Poverty, the bride of St. Francis.

[4] *A.V.* L. V. cap. iii. f. 3 *v.a*, and *Commercium*, pp. 44-6.

[5] *A.V.* L. IV. cap. xxv. A Flemish translation made at the end of the thirteenth century is still extant. Cf. Callaey, *op. cit.* p. 502.

[6] *A.V.* L. IV. cap. xxxiii. Cf. Callaey, *op. cit.* p. 503.

upon its authorship,[1] and this mystery has never been solved.   His
own vivid imagination is shown by his preference for the dialogue
form even in sacred poems.   It is difficult to understand his statement concerning the shortage of books at La Verna when we consider the extent of his debt to other writers.[2]   Perhaps he drew
largely upon material already contained in his sermons.[3]   Yet,
although his subject-matter and much of his thought was borrowed
from others, Ubertino has so transfused it by the light and splendour of his fervid imagination that it has become utterly and
completely his own.

   The *Arbor Vitae* is not the kind of book which should be read
consecutively, for then it reveals Ubertino's many defects in technique and his total lack of balance and proportion.   Its real glory
is to be found in certain passages, often consisting only of one sentence, which haunt the mind like the memory of some wonderful
sunset, or the majestic harmony of a Beethoven sonata.   No one
who has read the marvellous description of the presence of Poverty
at the Crucifixion can ever forget it.   Even in the *Commercium* it
is a fine piece of imaginative prose,[4] but it pales before the splendour
of Ubertino's imagery and the grave music of his language.   "Thou
wast ever his faithful comrade, and in the conflict of his passion
his sole squire.   When his disciples forsook him and denied his
name thou wast his only companion.   Even his mother because of
the height of the cross could not reach him, but thou wast there
to share in all thy penury with watchful love his bitter suffering,
and embraced him yet more closely."   It was Poverty who fashioned
the three nails which fastened the Saviour to the Cross.   Dante's
three lines in the *Paradiso* :

> Nè valse esser costante nè feroce,
>   Sicchè dove Maria rimase giuso,
>   Ella salse con Cristo sulla croce [5]

in spite of their exquisite melody and polish perhaps lack some of
the haunting beauty of the ruder and less finished imagery which

---

[1] *A.V.* L. IV. cap. xxv.   Cf. Callaey, *op. cit.* p. 503.
[2] Cf. Prologue, f. 3 *v.a.*   [3] Cf. *supra*, p. 125.
[4] Cf. Callaey, *op. cit.* p. 695, where the passages are given side by side.
"Sed et fidelissima consortia dum ad bellum nostre redemptionis accederes:
te est comitata fideliter et in ipso passionis conflictu individuus armiger astitit
et discipulis recedentibus et negantibus nomen tuum, ipsa non discessit sed
te tunc cum toto comitatu suorum principum fidelibus sociavit : immo ipsa
matre propter altitudine crucis ; que tamen te sola tunc fideliter coluit ; et
affectu anxio tuis passionibus iuncta fuit : ipsa inquam tali matre te non valente
contingere, domina paupertas cum omnibus suis penuriis tamquam tibi gratis-
simus domicellus, te plusquam unquam fuit strictius amplexata et tuo cruciatu
precordialius iuncta" (*A.V.* L. V. cap. iii. f. 3 *v.a,* and *Commercium*, pp. 44-6).
[5] *Paradiso*, xi. 70-2.

inspired them. For Ubertino the sacredness of Poverty was due to her connection with Christ and His blessed mother, and the question as to whether the Son of Man and His apostles had observed the " usus pauper ", and the reasons for which they had possessed a purse, had for him more than a mere academic significance.[1] Moreover, it was only by such means that man could attain the close union with his Redeemer for which he himself so ceaselessly strove, and his most bitter complaint against his Order was its neglect of the privileges of its high vocation. His description of the stable at Bethlehem gives rise to a fierce invective against the sumptuous convents which were springing up in so many of the Italian towns, rivalling in their architecture the palaces of princes and great nobles.[2] The reception of alms for the erection of such luxurious buildings was merely a robbery of the poor, on whom the money would have been far more fitly bestowed. Although for him the Rule and Testament of St. Francis were sacred, he was not so bigoted as to believe that those who kept faithfully to the mitigations allowed by the papal declarations were in danger of eternal damnation.[3] Yet he certainly felt for them the bitter contempt so common among enthusiasts for those who strive to serve both God and mammon. The worldly and luxurious prelates of his day, with their intense desire for temporal power and indifference to their spiritual office, also came in for their share of a hatred which was too deep for satire.[4] He attributed the great prevalence of heresy to the riches of the Church [5] and to the love of " pagan learning ", which was at its best a mere waste of precious time.[6] In spite of his vehement protests against the pursuit of secular knowledge he still shows a close familiarity with the questions which were being discussed in the universities.[7] Perhaps he even had attended Olivi's lectures on the subject of the eternity of the world.[8] Although Ubertino's picture of the Church at the end of the thirteenth century is both exaggerated and unjust he was yet capable of deep tenderness and real devotional feeling. It is to be hoped that no scholar will be so unfortunate as to discover that his Commentary on the Lord's Prayer was borrowed from the works of some other writer.[9]

---

[1] Discussed *A.V.* L. III. cap. xiii. f. 1 *v.a.*   [2] L. I. cap. xi. f. 6 *r.b.*
[3] L. V. cap. iii. f. 6 *v.a.*   [4] L. II. cap. iii. f. 2 *v.a.* Cf. cap. viii. f. 3 *v.a.*
[5] L. V. cap. vii. f. 3 *v.b* 3 and cap. viii. f. 2 *v.a s.*
[6] L. V. cap. vii. f. 5 *r.b.* Cf. L. III. cap. xiii. f. 4 *v.b.* The fall of the stars into the abyss signified the destruction of the devotees of pagan learning (L. V. cap. vii. f. 5 *v.a* ; *Beiträge*, ii. p. 555).
[7] L. I. cap. v. ; L. V. cap. v., vi., and vii.
[8] L. I. cap. v. f. 1. " Per hoc enim quod dicitur ex tempore excluditur error ponentium mundum eternum." Cf. *supra*, p. 109.
[9] L. III. cap. xiii. f. 3 *v.b et seq.*

The fifth book of the *Arbor* was probably the one which most fascinated its author's contemporaries, but to us it is perhaps the least interesting, for it contains his apocalyptic speculations. It is difficult to understand the preoccupation of the men of the thirteenth and fourteenth centuries with the advent of Antichrist and their elaborate calculations as to the probable year of his coming. Moreover Ubertino's theories are not particularly original, being founded on those of Joachim, and possibly having as their superstructure the opinions of his master, Olivi. His exegesis is often not at all clear, for he was quite capable of giving three or even four interpretations to one passage in the *Apocalypse*. It is painful also to see a writer of his merit sinking to such depths of scurrility as he does when he uses the beasts of the Book of *Revelation* to symbolise the leading personalities of his age. Like the Abbot of Flora he divides the Christian era into seven periods, the sixth of which was heralded by the appearance of Dominic and Francis, the new Enoch and Elias,[1] and would be marked by the tribulation of the elect under the rule of both the mystic and open Antichrists.[2] Their destruction would initiate a state of tranquillity and peace which would endure until the final resurrection.[3] We do not know how long this blissful age was to last, or whether a period of yet more bitter suffering was to precede the destruction of things temporal.[4] To Ubertino, St. Francis was rather the forerunner and type of the new contemplative order, to whom would be given the spiritual understanding of the Scriptures, than an historical figure.[5] His portrait is more attractive than that given by Clareno, and there is a touch of real imaginative understanding in his description of the " poverello's " command over dumb animals and his love for inanimate nature.[6] Perhaps as a poet he could enter into the mind of one whose very life was a poem. By the stigmata— " the five pearls " imprinted upon the body of Francis—Christ had

---

[1] *A.V.* L. V. cap. i. f. 6 *r.a.* " Sic in sexto statu apparuit novus homo Franciscus cum evangelico statu, quinque plagis a Christo Iesu crucifixus et configuratus in carne." Cf. cap. iii. f. 1 *r.a.*

[2] " Vel si sextam dividas in duas : quarum prima est antichristi mistici, secunda vero antichristi proprii " (cap. i. f. 1 *v.b*).

[3] " Septimus autem uno modo inchoat ab interfectione illius Antichristi " (*ibid.* f. 1 *v.a*).

[4] He writes of the new Gog who was to come at the end of the seventh age (*ibid.* f. 6 *r.b*).

[5] St. Francis is described in the *Arbor* as the Angel having the seal of the living God, who proclaimed the fall of Babylon (*ibid.* cap. iii. f. 1 *v.a*). He was also Benjamin the true brother of Joseph, who symbolised Christ (f. 3 *r.a*). His faithful sons were to be the apostles of the new Church (f. 2 *v.b*). The details, however, which he gives concerning the life of the saint are graphically and accurately described. Cf. *A.V.* L. V. cap. iii. f. 2 *r.a-r.b*, and *supra*, p. 2 and p. 71.   [6] F. 2 *r.b.*

set him apart from all other men. His faithful sons were to be the elect, who, after passing through bitter suffering and persecution, would at last find rest in the new age of righteousness and peace. We cannot tell whether he believed that the saint would again return to the earth in bodily form before the final overthrow of Antichrist,[1] or whether his spirit would be reborn in the hearts of his followers. The " papa angelicus ", however, would certainly represent all that was fairest in the Franciscan ideal.

The popes of his own age were the objects of Ubertino's most bitter hatred. Like many of his party he regarded the abdication of Celestine V. as invalid,[2] although he seems to have taken no part in the Colonna insurrection against Boniface VIII. He identified both the mystic and the open Antichrist with two false pontiffs, whose deeds could fitly be compared with those of Annas and Caiaphas.[3] Boniface to him was not only the mystic Antichrist but the beast arising out of the sea, whose seven heads represented the seven deadly sins, while his ten horns were his infringements of the Ten Commandments.[4] The greedy and self-seeking ecclesiastics who surrounded him were the locusts, whose king was Appolyon.[5] Ubertino relates with solemn earnestness the story of the discovery that the number of the beast spelt in Greek letters " Benedicti ", a fact which Angelo da Clareno, or the disciple of Fra Liberato, to whom he owed his knowledge of the incident, apparently regarded as a good joke.[6] Dante, hater of Boniface though he was, has left us a vivid impression of the horror which the crime of Nogaret and Sciarra Colonna aroused throughout Christendom in the majestic lines :

> Veggio in Alagna entrar lo fiordaliso,
> E nel vicario suo Cristo esser catto. . . .
> Veggio rinnovellar l' aceto e il fele
> E tra vivi ladroni esser anciso,[7]

but it awoke only fierce exultation in Ubertino's breast. Even if to him Boniface was no true representative of Christ on earth, but a usurper who had obtained his position through fraud, we are shocked at the barbarity which could regard a brutal attack on an aged and defenceless man as an act of divine justice. He was so besotted in his blindness that he could regard the gentle and holy Benedict XI. as the open Antichrist.[8] His virtues and learning

---

[1] Perhaps as the holy man like to Enoch or Elias (*A.V.* L. V. cap. ix. f. 1 *r.a*).

[2] *Ibid.* cap. vii. f. 2 *v.b* ; viii. f. 2 *r.b.* Cf. 6 *v.a.*

[3] *Ibid.* cap. i. f. 3 *r.a.*   [4] *Ibid.* cap. viii. f. 2 *v.b.*

[5] *Ibid.* cap. vii. f. 7 *r.a.* Cf. *Beiträge*, ii. p. 554.

[6] *Ibid.* cap. viii. f. 4 *r.a.* Cf. *supra*, pp. 40 and 58.

[7] *Purgatorio*, xx. 86-8. Cf. *A.V.* L. V. cap. viii. f. 4 *v.b.*

[8] " Ille (mystic antichrist) est precursor et preparator vie illius magni et aperti " (L. V. cap. vii. f. 5 *r.b*).

were only a mask, and hypocrisy was a far greater sin than open vice.[1] His election was as illegal as that of his predecessor, for the Colonna cardinals were still unreconciled to the Church, and a certain devout man who had been very much troubled about the matter had heard in a dream the voice of Christ proclaiming " that all the sheep had not been present at the sheepfold ".[2] Benedict, when he jestingly told the Perugian deputation who petitioned him for the restoration of their favourite preacher that they obviously preferred Ubertino to himself, can hardly have been aware of the bitter hatred which he had kindled in the heart of the exile at La Verna.[3] God had permitted such a monster of vice and iniquity to rule over His Church in order that the virtue of his successor might shine with the greater glory.[4] It is to be feared that Ubertino did not find his dream fulfilled in Clement V.

Ubertino's apocalyptic speculations give rise to the interesting question as to how far he was loyal to the Church of his day. He certainly regarded it in its present corrupt state as the harlot of Babylon[5] who had committed adultery with Celestine V.'s successors, but he had no quarrel with the ecclesiastical system of the period. Even the new Jerusalem, whose squares were paved with poverty, and which represented the spiritual church of his dreams, was to be governed by a " papa angelicus ".[6] Dante has shown us that many earnest Catholics held very similar views, and there is no real reason to doubt the sincerity of Ubertino's submission of his book to the judgment of the Holy See, especially as he repeats it, both in his Prologue and in his Conclusion.[7] He certainly regarded himself as a faithful son of the Church, and there is very little trace of hypocrisy in his attitude to Clement V. during the negotiations at the Curia. Although deferential he was always outspoken and independent, as in his protest against " Exivi de paradiso ".[8] Perhaps all the cardinals were present at the conclave of 1307, although logically even this fact would

---

[1] Benedict was the beast ascending out of the earth, whose two horns were " fama veritatis scientie et sanctitatis vite " (L. V. cap. viii. f. 4 v.b).

[2] Ibid. f. 5 r.b.

[3] A.L.K.G. ii. 132-33.

[4] A.V. L. V. cap. viii. f. 5 r.b. This expectation of the immediate coming of a righteous pope was probably the result of Ubertino's intercourse with the followers of Liberato. Cf. Grundmann, " Liber de Flore ", H.J. 49, p. 68. Supra, p. 40.

[5] " Dicitur autem carnalis ecclesia nova Babylon, quia ecclesia vocatur meretrix magna ; tum quia ordo virtutum est in ipsa per deordinationem vitiorum enormiter confusus, et verus cultus et amor sponsi Iesu turpiter adulteratus " (A.V. L. V. cap. x. f. 2 v.a).

[6] Ibid. cap. xi. f. 1.   [7] Prologue, f. 4 r.b ; L. V. cap. xviii.

[8] B.F. v. 195, p. 80. Cf. A.L.K.G. ii. p. 141.

not have made Clement V.'s position legal, as certain of his electors had been created by his predecessors. Ubertino's good sense must have made him realise that it was wisest in the interests of his party to accept the present state of things, though he comforted himself by dreaming of a future Church into which nothing that was evil or defiling might enter. His only mistake lay in his anticipation that it would be but a short space of time before his ideal became a reality.

A very interesting problem arises in regard to the readers of the *Arbor*. Was it intended only for Ubertino's immediate circle, or for all the faithful?[1] Angelo da Clareno, in his description of Ubertino's sojourn at La Verna, calls it a " brief and devout treatise ",[2] so that obviously it was known to many of the Zealots. Scholars have conjectured that he may be referring only to the fourth book, which was finished before Ubertino started upon the others,[3] and is found alone in certain manuscripts.[4] Certainly, no one with any personal knowledge of the *Arbor* in its complete form could declare that shortness was one of its chief characteristics. Perhaps the book was read in secret among the Spirituals, for Bonagratia of Bergamo made no allusion to it in his accusations against Ubertino, either at the time of the Council of Vienne or later in 1325.[5] On the other hand, Occam and Michael of Cesena quoted from it in their manifestos against John XXII.,[6] but it must be remembered that by then both they and its author were fighting on the same side. A just estimate of its effects on the thought and imagination of the period can, however, be gained only by considering its influence over the work of the greatest poet of the Middle Ages.[7] Dante and Ubertino were men of the same austere stamp, yet keenly sensitive to every sort of beauty, although their stern morality condemned much which appealed to their softer feelings. Both felt the same bitter indignation against the evils of their age, so that it is not surprising that the Florentine citizen brooded over the writings of the recluse of La Verna until he had made their imagery his own. His description of Francis and Dominic as :

---

[1] " Universis Christi Iesu vere fidelibus et Sancte paupertatis amicis maxime gementibus et dolentibus super malis inundatibus ecclesie deformate et benedicti Iesu vite impietate sacrilega mortue et sepulte " (Prologue, f. 2 *r.a*).
This introduction might apply to either class of readers.

[2] *A.L.K.G.* ii. 130.

[3] Cf. Martini, *op. cit.* 217, *n.* 1.

[4] The Italian version, now in the Library at Aberdeen University, contains only the fourth book. This was formerly in the Observantine Convent in the same town. Cf. Callaey, *op. cit.* p. 534.

[5] *Misc.* ii. 276. Cf. *supra*, p. 130.

[6] Cf. Callaey, *op. cit.* 726, *n.* 1.   [7] Cf. *supra*, p. 48.

L' un fu tutto serafico in ardore,
L' Altro per sapienza in terra fue
Di Cherubica luce uno splendore [1]

is a paraphrase of Ubertino's,

Among whom like to Elias and Enoch, Francis and Dominic pre-eminently shone, for the former, purified by the seraphic fire and consumed with the divine heat, inflamed the whole world. The other, a mighty cherub, full of the clear light of wisdom and eloquent in speech, illumined the darkness of the earth.[2]

We have already discussed the great picture of poverty at the Crucifixion, which is one of the beauties alike of the *Arbor Vitae* and of the *Divine Comedy*.[3] The elaborate allegories of the triumphal car and the tree of life which are found in the concluding cantos of the *Purgatorio* [4] possibly draw their inspiration straight from the Bible, and not, as certain critics have supposed, from Ubertino's somewhat slight allusions [5] to these two excellent subjects for the imagination of the medieval lover of symbolism. Döllinger was perhaps the first to believe that Dante's Veltro, with his rude clothing, was no great earthly monarch, but typified the great Order of Contemplatives which was to destroy all that was base and corrupt and usher in a new age of peace and righteousness.[6] His view has been upheld by certain modern scholars,[7] but the older theory is perhaps still the more popular. It is sad that Ubertino's work is practically unknown except to the historian and the student of Dante, for parts of the *Arbor* almost surpass the writings of Thomas à Kempis and other great medieval mystics. Michelet, although an enemy to all obscurantism, was unable to contain his admiration both of the book and of its author.[8] Such a treasure should not be buried in the depositories of great libraries,[9] but should be the property of all who have tested by bitter experience the terrible struggle between the forces of good and evil which is being waged continuously both in the world and in the individual soul.

[1] *Paradiso*, xi. 37-9.
[2] " Inter quos in typo Helie et Enoch, Franciscus et Dominicus singulariter claruerunt, quorum primus seraphico calculo purgatus et ardore celico inflammatus totum mundum incendere videbatur. Secundus vero et cherubinus extentus et pretegens lumine sapientie . . . et verbo predicationis fecundus super mundi tenebras clarius radiavit " (L. V. cap. iii. f. 1 r.).
[3] *A.V.* L. V. cap. iii. f. 3 *v.a* ; *Paradiso*, xi. 70-2. Cf. *supra*, 136.
[4] *Purg.* xxix., xxx., and xxxii.
[5] *A.V.* L. IV. cap. xxxix. f. 1; L. V. cap. xii. f. 1 *v.a.*
[6] Gardner, " Joachim of Flora ", p. 69.
[7] For example, Kraus, *op. cit.* p. 476.
[8] Michelet, *Histoire de France*, iv. 80-2.
[9] The only printed edition of the *Arbor* is the incunable of 1485. This is somewhat difficult to read, as the manuscript abbreviations are still retained, but perhaps this only serves to enhance the marvellous beauty of the imagery.

2. *Pamphlets written in connection with the Inquiry upon the state of the Franciscan Order held at the Curia* (1309–12) [1]

Ubertino's admirers have differed profoundly in their estimate of his treatises written at the time of the Council of Vienne, for certain admirers have been deeply shocked that writings of such venom and bitterness should come from the pen of the author of the *Arbor*.[2] Others, including the great scholar Cardinal Ehrle, have regarded them as a remarkable testimony of their author's sincerity, ability, and sterling common sense, and have rejoiced at their freedom from the exaggerations and complicated symbolism of his great book.[3] To my mind, however, all comparison between the two is a mistake, for they appeal to different faculties of the human mind. The *Arbor* is a prose epic of a devotional nature, while Ubertino's controversial treatises can be fitly compared to articles in some daily or weekly paper, written by a brilliant and clever journalist, combining a profound knowledge of his subject with a firm belief in the truth of his own convictions. After reading one of them it is possible to understand why a worldling and politician like Napoleone Orsini placed so high a value on Ubertino's society, for his somewhat ironical humour and power of graphic description must have made him an entertaining companion. After the lapse of so many centuries his descriptions of the many subterfuges resorted to by the Franciscans in order to obtain a settled income while keeping to the letter of their vow of complete poverty are racy reading.[4] Charity was not one of Ubertino's virtues, and he seems almost to gloat over the many breaches of the Rule which the gentler Gaufridi would willingly have concealed for the sake of the honour of the Order.[5] Yet the Pope had wanted information as to the real state of affairs and Ubertino certainly wrote what he believed to be the truth. It may even be accounted to him for righteousness that his attacks on the luxurious buildings, and the pride and arrogance and injustice of the rulers of the Order are somewhat more restrained than in the *Arbor*. Unfortunately, moreover, the statutes of the different Chapters of the Order held during this period [6] show that on the whole the

---

[1] Cf. *supra*, p. 13 *s*. and 128.

[2] Cf. E. Gurney-Salter's " Ubertino da Casale ", in *Franciscan Essays*, p. 122.

[3] *A.L.K.G.* iii. p. 48.   [4] *Ibid.* pp. iii. 66-71, 105 *s*.

[5] Gaufridi's own little pamphlet is contained in the treatise beginning " Infrascripta ", written by Raymund de Fronsac and Bonagratia of Bergamo, probably in June 1311 (*ibid.* pp. 142-44). It must have been written early in 1310, as its author's death took place during the summer of that year. Cf. *supra*, p. 13.

[6] For the statutes promulgated at the different Chapters cf. *A.L.K.G.* vi. 1-138 ; *A.F.H.* iv. 269-302, 508-36. Perhaps the most interesting are the

picture is not too deeply coloured, for they are full of regulations against the acquirement of vineyards and granaries,[1] and a fixed form of income, as well as against minor abuses such as luxury and excess in clothing and food.[2] If these proceedings shocked men like John of Murrovalle,[3] who must have been fully alive to the difficulties of carrying on the work of a great Order with no settled resources upon which to depend, it is not surprising that they aroused fierce and uncontrolled indignation in the heart of a stern enthusiast such as Ubertino. Nor did his enemies express themselves more temperately, for whereas the treatises defending the cause of the Zealots bear all the marks of a passionate, if misguided, sincerity, the Conventuals tried to support a bad cause by making personal aspersions upon the character of their formidable adversary.

Of the four questions upon which the Pope, through the commission of cardinals which he had appointed, was seeking for information, Ubertino, in the writings which have come down to us, has dealt thoroughly with three—to wit, the many infringements of the Rule, the defamation of the memory of Olivi, and the fierce persecutions endured by the Zealots. He was content to answer the question as to the connection of his party with the sect of the Free Spirit with an indignant denial.[4] To his mind the present decayed state of the Order was entirely due to the secret relaxations of the vow of poverty, which were so much the more dangerous because many who availed themselves of them acted in perfect good faith. In defence of his position he quoted, as in the *Arbor*, from the writings of Hugues de Digne, Pecham, and St.

Constitutions of a provincial Chapter held at Nîmes, in Provence, just after the publication of " Exivi de paradiso ", when Alexander of Alexandria was making his well-intentioned efforts to restore peace to the Order. This has been published by Father Delorme in *A.F.H.* xiv. p. 419 *s.* Cf. *supra*, p. 15.

[1] Constitutions of Narbonne, 1260; S. Bonaventura, *Opera Omnia*, viii. p. 464 ; Chapter-General of Assisi, 1269, *A.F.H.* vii. 688 ; Constitutions of Assisi, 1316, *A.F.H.* iv. 281.

[2] Constitutions of Narbonne, *op. cit.* 451, 453 ; Chapter-General of Padua, 1310, *A.L.K.G.* vi. 70 ; Statutes drawn up at Provincial Chapter of Nîmes (1313), *A.F.H.* xiv. 426.

[3] Soon after his election he wrote a letter to the Chapter-General at Genoa forbidding the friars to receive the annual sums of money often left to them by will. Cf. Wadding, *Annales*, vi. 1302, p. 7 *s.*, §§ i. and ii.

[4] He deals with all four questions in " Sanctitas vestra iniunxit " in *A.L.K.G.* iii. 51-89, but dwells most on the second. " Rotulus iste " (*ibid.* pp. 93-137) and the " Declaratio fratris Ubertini " (*ibid.* pp.162-95) are concerned mainly with the second, while his defence of Olivi is found in " Sanctitati Apostolicae " (*ibid.* ii. 377-416). According to Gratien (*op. cit.* p. 444) the former two were composed during the early stages of the controversy, while the others must have been written in the summer of 1311.

Bonaventura.[1] To Ubertino the mere renunciation of possessions
without moderation in their actual use was a mockery of Christ
and of his utter poverty ;[2] and he made his position still clearer in
a little treatise which he wrote in 1310 to confute the arguments
of his adversaries that the " usus pauper " was not included in the
vow.[3] This has a characteristic *incipit*, " Super tribus sceleribus ",
and contains the little pamphlet by Alexander of Alexandria, to
which it is an answer. This is the only writing at present in print
produced by the opposite party which wins our respect. Unfortunately, the future Minister-General was perhaps too honest a man
to make a very good champion of a bad case, and his " usus moder-
atus " is really only the " usus pauper " under a different name,
while Ubertino was able to meet his contention that the indeterminate character of the latter made it impossible for it to be included under the vow of poverty,[4] by re-echoing the argument of
Olivi that cases of extreme necessity must be left to the discretion
of the individual.[5] Every departure from the rule of the strictest
moderation in the use of temporal goods was not mortal sin, but
only luxury and excess. He seems to have had a very poor opinion
of the intelligence of his opponent, for he points out that, although
Christ had given His disciples no instructions with regard to tem-
perance in food, it could never have been His intention that, if
twenty dishes of food were placed before them, they should devour
greedily from them all after the manner of dogs and wolves.[6]

Perhaps Ubertino's acrimonious accounts of the state of the
Order are more interesting than his more theoretical opinions.
He had obviously studied his subject very thoroughly, and his
account of the friars who wandered about accompanied by small
boys bearing wallets for alms, of which their masters had the keys,
is a delightful example of medieval satire.[7] It is impossible not
to accept his conclusion that an Order which appointed its own
proctors to represent it in the law courts, and even allowed its
members to attend these assemblies, to prompt its official agents,
could hardly boast of its complete alienation from worldly affairs.[8]

[1] *A.L.K.G.* iii. 58-61. It is interesting that Olivi also cites these three
authorities in his letter to his judges when defending his teaching with regard
to Poverty (*Quod.* 46 *r.b*-47 *r.b*).
[2] " Certe credo, quod determinare paupertatem evangelicam nullum
moderamen in usu rerum includere, est Christum deridere et suam penuriosam
paupertatem, quam usu servavit" (*A.L.K.G.* iii. 85).
[3] Published in *A.F.H.* x. 116-74, and probably composed before July 1311.
Cf. *ibid.* p. 122. Ubertino's longer answer which began, " Nova bella elegit
dominus ", has not yet been found (*ibid.* p. 174).
[4] *A.F.H.* x. 116 and 117.   [5] *Ibid.* 157-62. Cf. *supra*, p. 97.
[6] " Numquid fuit intentio sua (Christ) quod si XX. fercula apponantur quod
possint se de omnibus ingurgitare, sicut lupi et canes " (*ibid.* p. 158).
[7] *A.L.K.G.* iii. 104.   [8] *Ibid.* 54 and 113.

His complaints against the spacious buildings are the same as in the *Arbor*.[1] Possibly the artist in Ubertino loved the sheen of the rich vestments and the beauty of the finely wrought chalices which his Puritanism led him to denounce so bitterly.[2]   Certainly the Franciscans had to resort to many curious and ingenious devices to raise the money necessary for such embellishments to their services, but probably, as the Conventuals stated in answer to their opponents, it was all done for the honour and glory of God.[3] To Ubertino's austere mind the sale of candles in the church was just as much a profanation of the sanctuary as the presence of the money changers and of those who sold doves in the temple at Jerusalem.[4]   The alms boxes, the masses for which payment was offered, and the absolution of usurers without forcing them to restore their ill-gotten gains were old abuses.[5]   The medieval traveller in Italy must have been as much pestered by the small boys sent by the friars to solicit alms, as his modern representative is annoyed by their descendants.[6]   It is not surprising that the Franciscans were so unpopular both with the secular clergy and with the other religious orders.   According to Ubertino, however, such excessive mendicancy was being abandoned, for many of the Italian convents received a fixed income paid to them yearly by the executors of the rich whom the friars had shriven on their death-beds.[7]   In fact, the only part of the vow of complete poverty which was literally obeyed was the regulation forbidding the actual handling of money.[8]

Like many of the Zealots, Ubertino was bitterly opposed to all merely secular learning.   In his own case he had found that the charms of the scholastic philosophy had diverted his mind from higher things.   It is possible that he would have admitted the value of such studies, if they were kept in due subjection to the more important duties of prayer and meditation, but he deeply regretted the dedication of the time of many of the younger members of his Order to "profitless and arid speculations".[9]

---

[1] *A.L.K.G.* iii. 116. Cf. *A.B.* L. I. c. xi. f. 6 *r.b.* *Supra*, p. 137.

[2] *A.L.K.G.* iii. 70 and 117.

[3] *A.F.H.* viii. 70-71.

[4] "Item in aliquibus locis sacriste ipsimet candelas de sacrista acceptas faciunt super discum poni in ecclesia, ut intrantes viri et mulieres candelas emant, accipiant et offerant et loco earum super discum vel capsulam pecuniam deponant ; et famulus fratrum discum custodit et pecuniam recipit, ita quod eadem candela decies revendetur. Et hec fallacia videtur illi communicare, quam dominus Yhesus de templo eiecisse " (*A.L.K.G.* iii. 105).

[5] *Ibid.* 68 and 105 *s.* Cf. *A.L.K.G.* vi. 48 and 64.

[6] *Ibid.* iii. 105.

[7] *Ibid.* 106 and 115.   [8] *Ibid.* 106.

[9] "Et quia huiusmodi fratres ut plurimum statim post novitiatum mittuntur ad studia philosophie et postmodum in questionibus curiosis et studiis aridis

Moreover, in many cases it was no disinterested love of learning which made the young Franciscans such zealous frequenters of the schools, for the readiest path to promotion in the Order lay through the universities.[1] The lecturers possessed many privileges, and were the most flagrant violators of the Rule, many of them even daring to assert that the " usus pauper " was not included in the vow of poverty.[2] The same self-seeking had dried up the original source of Franciscan eloquence, for in their sermons the preachers no longer sought to draw their listeners to Christ, but to win fame for themselves by the seductive fascinations of oratory and rhetoric.[3] Ubertino's verdict is obviously unjust when applied to the bulk of the Order, and not to a small group within its ranks, but it showed that any attempt to produce a lasting reconciliation between his party and its opponents was unlikely to succeed. It is true that he did not deny the pious intentions which had led to the papal expositions of the Rule,[4] but what he sought for himself and his followers was permission to obey the Rule and Testament of St. Francis in their original strictness.[5] The policy of separation which he advocated so persistently was in reality far more statesmanlike than the path of compromise pursued by Clement V., for the gulf between the two branches of the Order had become too wide to be bridged.

As we have already seen, the task of defending the Conventual position from the attacks of Ubertino fell mainly to the lot of Raymund de Fronsac and Bonagratia of Bergamo,[6] for even the pamphlet which bears the names of the Minister-General and the fourteen Provincials present at the Curia bears almost unmistakable marks of their authorship.[7] It is perhaps unfortunate that

---

occupantur et ab infantia in studiis generalibus a divinis officiis et humilitatis obsequiis eximuntur " (*A.L.K.G.* iii. 118).

Ubertino's accusations are endorsed by Alvaro Paez (*De Planctu Ecclesie*, L. II., Articuli XXXIII. and XXXIV.).

[1] " Quasi ubique per ordinem soli magistri et lectores Parisini dominantur " (*A.L.K.G.* iii. 118).

[2] *Ibid.* Cf. *A.V.* L. I. cap. xi. f. 7 *r.b* ; L. V. cap. vii. f. 5 *v.a.*

[3] " Et sepe nugas et truffas et verba inutilia sermonibus inmiscentes, ut merito eorum predicatio condempnatur, sed nituntur plures singulariter appetere et se predicare non Christum " (*A.L.K.G.* iii. 122; cf. 178 and *A.V.* L. V. cap. v. f. 3 *r.a*).

[4] *A.L.K.G.* iii. 182.   [5] *Ibid.* 87.   [6] Cf. *supra*, p. 14.

[7] *A.F.H.* vii. 654-75 ; viii. 56-80. " Religiosi viri." This treatise was probably composed during the October of 1311, and " Sapientia edificavit " (*A.L.K.G.* iii. 93-137) in the spring of the following year. Cf. *A.F.H.* vii. p. 657. Both pamphlets were written in answer to Ubertino's " Rotulus iste ", which has been edited by Ehrle in such a way that each reply of Raymund and Bonagratia directly follows the accusation made by their opponent (*A.L.K.G.* iii. 93-137).

Gonsalvo de Valboà and his associates trusted so implicitly to the skill of their official representatives at the Curia, for Raymund and Bonagratia lacked the fiery genius of their formidable adversary, nor had they perhaps a very good case to defend. They were probably right in maintaining that Ubertino had magnified a few isolated instances into a general indictment of his Order,[1] though their scornful denial of his contention that certain reforms had resulted from his criticisms is more questionable.[2] Their vehement attacks upon his reputation and good faith were perhaps the most cunning part of their defence. They charged Ubertino with having brought his accusations through anger and malice, because he had not been elected diffinitor at the last general chapter.[3] Moreover, he was notorious as a stirrer up of discord in the provinces of Genoa, Tuscany, and Umbria, and indeed throughout the length and breadth of Italy.[4] There is certainly much truth in this second accusation, for Ubertino could hardly have been a peaceful inmate of any convent not entirely composed of Zealots. The charge that he had been guilty of a moral offence during the generalship of Raymund Gaufridi[5] is substantiated by his own bitter lamentations over his sinfulness in the Prologue of the *Arbor*.[6] Moreover, he certainly was not impervious to the charms of feminine beauty, for in the same book he quaintly declares that Adam was doubly tempted, for if he had refused to eat the apple he would have lost not only the knowledge of good and evil but the charms of Eve's sweet companionship.[7] Yet, it is significant that no accusation was brought until after Gaufridi's death. Perhaps the most delightful picture in all this welter of virulent querulousness is that of Ubertino riding triumphantly into Vienne, in flagrant violation of the Rule, and thus imperilling the life of no less a person than the Provincial of England, Master Richard of Conyngton, who was striding ostentatiously along the miry road.[8] The pious horror of his opponents could hardly have been greater if his victim had been the Minister-General himself.

[1] *A.F.H.* vii. 662.

[2] Cf. "Sapientia Edificavit", Bibl. Nat. MS., Lat. 4350, f. 31 *r*. Cited by Gratien, *op. cit.* p. 461.

[3] " Quia enim ambiebat, ut esset diffinitor, et fratres noluerunt eum in diffinitorem eligere, ideo recessit a consortio fratrum illius provincie et fecit se caput alibi ut alius Machometus " (*A.L.K.G.* iii. 119).

[4] *A.F.H.* viii. 72.

[5] *A.F.H.* viii. 76 and 78. Cf. *A.L.K.G.* iii. 124.

[6] F. 2 *v.b.*   [7] L. I. cap. iv. f. 1 *v.a.*

[8] " Respondetur pro parte ordinis, quod si opponens ivisset nuper in Vienna peditando, non posuisset cum pedibus equi, cui insidebat, magistrum theologie peditantem per lutum, fratrem Rycardum ministrum Anglie in tanto periculo, sicut fecit " (*A.L.K.G.* iii. 104).

Richard of Conyngton's exemplary observance of the Rule was not, however, the only weapon which he employed in the defence of his party. During the latter stages of the controversy he composed a long treatise, justifying the Franciscan conception of poverty.[1] He must have been a man of great conscientiousness, for the whole of the earlier part of his work is devoted to an elaborate discussion of the exact nature of the poverty of Christ and His apostles, one of the few questions upon which the two parties in the Order were in complete agreement.[2] Like many of his colleagues, the English Provincial adhered to the interpretation of the Franciscan Rule embodied in " Exiit qui seminat ";[3] but, in spite of his obvious sincerity and the clearness of his arguments, his pamphlet is somewhat tedious and completely lacking in any originality of outlook or warmth of expression. It has far more resemblance to a comprehensive survey of the Minorite position, delivered in the friaries of Oxford or Cambridge,[4] than to a writing composed in the midst of a controversy affecting the destiny of the Order of St. Francis. Possibly, its best claim to attention lies in the fact that, like the short treatise of Alexander of Alexandria,[5] it reflects the views of the moderate party who were honestly desirous of furthering the Pope's efforts towards a peaceful settlement. The " Abbreviatura " following Conyngton's pamphlet is possibly a summary of his conclusions made for the benefit of the papal commissioners.[6] This concise and admirable little document deals briefly with the nature of the Franciscan vows. The true basis of the Rule lay in the three great virtues of poverty, chastity, and obedience,[7] and its other provisions were merely elaborations and definitions of these fundamental principles.[8] Not even the Pope had the power of dispensing any friar from the observance of the threefold vow he made at his profession,[9] although he could modify and temporally suspend certain minor regulations affecting the Franciscan manner of life.[10] Because of its indeterminate nature the " usus pauper " formed no part of the vow of poverty, but this in no way implied that the Order was not bound to a moderate and restricted use of temporal goods.[11] Even in this short statement of their position the Conventuals were unable to

---

[1] " Beatus qui intelligit super egenum et pauperem." Edited in *A.F.H.* xxiii. pp. 57-105, 340-60. Cf. Catalogue of Raymund de Fronsac (*A.L.K.G.* iii. 23, § xxxvi.). [2] *A.F.H.* xxiii. pp. 70-105.

[3] *B.F.* iii. pp. 404-16. Cf. *A.F.H.* xxiii. p. 73.

[4] Before he became Provincial in 1310, Conyngton had been lector both at Oxford and Cambridge (*Eccleston*, p. 73). Cf. *Grey Friars at Oxford*, p. 164.

[5] " Circa materiam de usu paupere " (*A.F.H.* x. 116-22). Cf. *supra*, p. 145.

[6] *A.F.H.* xxiii. pp. 66-9. Cf. *ibid.* p. 61, and *A.L.K.G.* iii. pp. 24 and 44.

[7] *A.F.H.* xxiii. p. 67, §§ v. and vii. [8] *Ibid.* §§ v.-viii.

[9] *Ibid.* p. 68, § ix. [10] *Ibid.* §§ x. and xi. [11] *Ibid.* p. 69, § xiii.

refrain entirely from attacking their opponents;[1] nor was this to be expected, since the majority of the Zealots, and especially Ubertino, were also strangers to the virtues of charity and tolerance. The latter's reply to Conyngton is unfortunately still unprinted, for it would be interesting to know with what feelings the fiery Italian regarded the prosaic and sober-minded Englishman.[2] It may be that he preferred the malicious violence of Bonagratia of Bergamo to the careful and somewhat tedious reasoning of his English adversary, for, like many enthusiasts, he regarded moderation and restraint as akin to lukewarmness and indifference. Perhaps the high reputation of the English province for sound learning and the strict observance of the Rule, is the best proof of its provincial's loyal adherence to the Franciscan ideal.[3]

Ubertino's pamphlet in defence of Olivi was written in answer to a protest made by his enemies against the Exemption Bull of April 1310,[4] on the ground that the Spirituals, as disciples of a man guilty of so many errors, were heretics and therefore not entitled to the papal protection.[5]   Most of the chief points in his answer [6] have been dealt with in the account given of his master in the preceding chapter, and in spite of his devotion to Olivi's memory he does not on the whole reach his general level of passion and eloquence except when describing the persecution of the followers of the great Spiritual.   In this treatise he displays an unexpected power of logical reasoning and methodical arrangement.   He was obviously well acquainted with the writings of his great teacher and thus was able to prove that his adversaries had often wilfully distorted his meaning, giving, as his fixed convictions, views which he had expressed only tentatively, or had quoted because of their historical bearing upon the subject in question.   He brings forward his authorities in support of Olivi's arguments with all the care and meticulousness of a modern scholar, and it is sad that the ancient codex of St. Matthew's gospel, the text of which would support Olivi's view that Christ was pierced with the lance before He " gave up the ghost ", has never been traced.[7]   Ubertino's refer-

---

[1] " Isti turbatores Ordinis ", p. 66, § iii.

[2] Something of the nature of Ubertino's reply is revealed by its incipit. " Beatus vir qui non habiit in consilio impiorum " (*A.L.K.G.* iii. 45).   It is not included in Raymund de Fronsac's catalogue.

[3] Cf. *A.F.H.* vii. p. 662.

[4] *B.F.* v. *n.* 158, p. 165; Wadding, *Annales,* vi. 1310, p. 168, § iii.

[5] *A.L.K.G.* ii. 365-74.   Ehrle suggests March 1311 as the probable date.

[6] *A.L.K.G.* ii. 377-416. Cf. *supra,* p. 92.

[7] In Ubertino's Codex the reading would be as follows : " Et continuo currens unus, accepta spongea, implevit aceto et imponit arundini et dabat ei bibere.   (Alius autem accepta lancea pupugit latus eius et exivit sanguis et aqua.)   Ihesus autem clamans voce magna emisit spiritum " (*A.L.K.G.* ii. 404).

ence is so exact that he was certainly telling the truth when he declared that he himself had seen the manuscript, probably in his student days at Paris. His chief weapon of defence was that Olivi had been persecuted because of his strict adherence to the " usus pauper ", and that his memory was now being blackened in order to divert the Pope's attention from the many abuses existing in the Franciscan Order.[1] Moreover, his superiors, by appointing him to the position of lector both at Sta Croce and later at Montpellier, were by their own confession guilty of heresy.[2] He himself, although he had both revered and loved his master, was prepared to admit that in certain matters he had been mistaken,[3] but would have men remember that few such prolific writers had been so singularly free from error.[4] Besides, Olivi had submitted his works unreservedly to the censure of the Holy See,[5] and his disciples were ready to accept its verdict.[6] If Ubertino was unable to secure the complete acquittal of his master he was at least able to prove his good intentions, and the loyalty and devotion of his followers towards the Church.

Ubertino's personality and achievements are too complex and varied in their nature to be easily assessed. It is perhaps no exaggeration to call him a man of genius, possessing all the sensitiveness of the artistic temperament, and a deep and genuine love of all that was noble and beautiful. He was less interested in philosophical and intellectual problems than Olivi, but his reasoning power was equally acute. Although by no means deficient in good sense, he lacked the moderation and sense of proportion possessed so abundantly by the former, but this perhaps made him a more courageous thinker. Like many men of strong and vivid imagination and deep emotions he was dominated rather by his heart than by his head, and this perhaps explains the many inconsistencies of his career. He possessed in full measure the gift vouchsafed to certain great poets and mystics of piercing far into the unknown, and of reaching heights of spiritual understanding which have been revealed to few, but the vision soon faded, leaving behind it weariness and desolation in proportion to his former ecstasy. It was probably during these periods of spiritual dryness and depression that Ubertino made his gravest mistakes. Angelo da Clareno was able to pass unscathed through the horrors of a

---

The passage is from Matt. xxvii. 49-50. Cf. F. C. Burkitt, " Ubertino da Casale and a variant Reading ", *Journal of Theological Studies*, xxiii. pp. 186-88 (January 1922).

[1] *A.L.K.G.* ii. 380, 384.   [2] *Ibid.* 382.

[3] *Ibid.* 406. Cf. Prologue to *A.V.* f. 2 *v.b.*

[4] *Ibid.* 406. Olivi's books were almost seventeen times as bulky as the Sentences.

[5] *Ibid.* 384, 409, 411.   [6] *Ibid.* 413.

medieval prison and the subtler and more dangerous atmosphere of the papal court, for he possessed all the calm serenity of one whose life was passed habitually in the presence of God.   Such security was denied to Ubertino, for to his passionate, restless nature even religion could bring no lasting peace.   Yet, we are the gainers by his loss, for during that year at La Verna, an oasis in a troubled and stormy life, he penetrated very far into the heart of the mystery of the love that won its triumph through rejection and suffering.   It is to the lonely musings of a tortured soul, haunted by the splendour of a noble but unattainable ideal that we owe the *Arbor Vitae.*

PART I: THE CONTROVERSY BETWEEN JOHN XXII.
AND THE FRANCISCAN ORDER UPON THE
QUESTION OF THE POVERTY OF CHRIST
AND HIS APOSTLES

"SOL ortus est et humiles exaltati sunt. . . . Hic sol in altissimis oriens . . . est beatissimus pater et dominus Iohannes." [1]

In the year 1321, when Raymund de Fronsac made his collection of the documents relating to the struggle between the Spirituals and the Conventuals, the Franciscan Order was enjoying an unwonted measure of tranquillity. Under the firm rule of Michael of Cesena, supported as he had been by the Pope, the opposition of the Zealots had been crushed, and although certain of them had succeeded in escaping from the clutches of the Inquisition and had swelled the growing number of the Fraticelli, such obscure heretics probably caused the Order no very serious disquietude.[2] As for the Béguins, with their crude and mistaken loyalty to the memory of Olivi,[3] they could be left to the care of the Holy Office. No one could have guessed that from the trial of one of these simple enthusiasts a spark was to be kindled which was to divide the Christian world into two opposing camps,[4] and endanger the good relations which had existed for over a hundred years between the followers of St. Francis and the Papacy. Nor was the tumult to die down until after a schism had been created within the ranks of the Friars Minor, which deprived the Order of her ablest and most loyal sons, and turned the most ardent and devoted supporters of John XXII. into his bitterest opponents. The " Martyrs of Marseilles " [5] were amply avenged when the Minister-General, who had condemned them, fled from Avignon a fugitive, and passed the remaining years of his life excommunicate and degraded from his high office, carrying on a fierce and unremitting warfare with Christ's representative on earth.

The matter which gave rise to the great dispute between John XXII. and the Minorites seemed at first hardly more than an incident in the long rivalry between the two great mendicant

---

[1] *A.L.K.G.* iii. p. 7.

[2] A band of Spirituals succeeded in escaping from Provence, and took refuge in Naples under the protection of Philip of Maiorca. Cf. Tocco, *S.F.* p. 520. Cf. *infra*, p. 215.

[3] Cf. *infra*, p. 252 s.

[4] Even the Florentine banker, Villani, describes the papal decretal, " Ad Conditorem Canonum ", as " grande novità nella chiesa di Roma " (*Istorie Fiorentine*, L. IX. p. 156).

[5] Cf. *supra*, p. 19 s.; *Misc.* ii. 247-51, 270-71.

Orders.[1]   At the end of the year 1321 a certain Béguin was brought before the Inquisition at Narbonne and charged with spreading publicly the doubtful doctrine that Christ and His apostles had owned nothing, either severally or in common.   One of his judges, Béréngar Talon, lector at the Franciscan convent of Narbonne, declared that this belief far from being heretical, was one of the dogmas of the Church, and when called upon to recant by his Dominican colleague, appealed to the Pope.   The subject was brought up at a Consistory, held on the 6th of March, and the Franciscan cardinals present, Vidal du Four [2] and Bertrand de Tour,[3] as well as the Archbishop of Salerno [4] and the Bishop of Kaffa,[5] who had also formerly been members of the same Order,

[1] Our chief source for the history of the whole struggle is the contemporary chronicle of " Nicholas the Minorite ", which contains transcripts of most of the original documents.   Extracts from this are printed in *Misc.* iii. pp. 206-358.   Following the error found in the fifteenth-century manuscript (Cod. Vat. Lat. 7316), where the copyist had transcribed " J " instead of " N ", Baluze gives the name of the author as " John ".

Cf. Eubel, " Zu Nicolaus Minorita ", *H.J.* xviii. 373-86.

The original documents themselves are found in MS. Vat. 4009.   A specimen of the handwriting of Michael of Cesena is to be found in his corrections of the rough draft of his appeal from Avignon (f. 16-19), while his actual signature appears at the end of the final version.   Cf. *ibid.* p. 377.

[2] Vidal du Four (cardinal, 1312–1337).   As lector of Toulouse he had played an important part in the persecution of the Zealots in Provence at the beginning of the fourteenth century (*A.L.K.G.* iii. 157).

Provincial of Aquitaine at the time of the Council of Vienne, in which capacity his name appears in the reply of the Superiors of the Order to the accusations of the Spirituals (*ibid.* ii. 356, *n.* 1).   Cf. *supra*, p. 12, *n.* 5.

He also sat on the Commission appointed by Clement V. to examine the writings of Olivi.   Like his colleague, Richard de Conyngton, Vidal apparently kept ostentatiously to the letter of the Rule, only wearing shoes at the express command of the Pope.   Cf. *A.F.H.* vii. 674.   For further connection with Spirituals, cf. *supra*, p. 20.

[3] Bertrand de Tour, Archbishop of Salerno, 1319 ; Cardinal of San Vitale, 1320–1332.   Cf. *supra*, pp. 17 and 113.

[4] Arnald Roiard, Bertrand de Tour's successor as Archbishop of Salerno in 1321, and formerly lector of Toulouse.   Cf. *supra*, p. 113.

[5] Jerome of Catalonia, formerly Provincial of Romania (cf. *supra*, p. 58, *n.* 8) and afterwards suffragan to the Archbishop of Pekin, 1311–1316 (?) (*B.F.* v. 176, p. 74), Bishop of Kaffa, 1316 (?)–1324.   At Avignon in the beginning of 1318, where his elevation to the See of Kaffa was confirmed by John XXII. (*ibid.* 303, p. 142).   On a subsequent visit to the Curia he spoke in the Consistory of March 6, 1322, declaring that even among the schismatic Greeks the doctrine of the complete poverty of Christ and His apostles was so hotly defended, that anyone publicly preaching the contrary would have been stoned.   Extracts from his speech are given in the Italian version of the chronicle of Nicholas the Minorite, printed in *Scelta di curiosità letterarie*, li. 64-73.   Shortly after this he returned to the East, but was again in Avignon in 1324.   He died either at the end of 1325 or at the beginning of 1326, perhaps at Constantinople (Golubovich, *op. cit.* iii. 38-57).   Other references are found (*ibid.* ii. 192 ; iii. 178 and 210).

hotly defended the opinion of their representative, the same view being maintained by the celebrated canonist, Béréngar Frédol.[1] The question was further complicated by the fact that Nicholas III. at the end of his decretal, " Exiit qui seminat ",[2] after he had declared that the Friars Minor by their complete renunciation of all possessions were following the example of Christ and his apostles, had forbidden, under pain of anathema, that his statute should be commented upon in the Schools.[3] In order to promote the free discussion of the subject, John XXII. by his bull, " Quia nonnunquam ", of March 26,[4] suspended temporally this part of the provisions of his predecessor. At the same time, he requested Cardinal Napoleone Orsini to obtain a statement in writing of the views of Ubertino da Casale upon the matter.[5] His answer might have afforded the basis for a compromise, but the Pope had probably already determined to settle the question upon his own lines. His solution would naturally deal rather with the legal and practical than with the theoretic and religious aspect of the problem.

Meanwhile the Franciscan cardinals had taken the momentous step of requesting an expression of the united opinion of the leading men of their Order assembled at the Chapter-General of Perugia. Since the complete possessionlessness of Christ formed the basis of the Minorite ideal of perfection it is not surprising that they gave their decision in no measured terms. Two letters were directed to all the faithful in the name of the Minister-General and four Provincials and three doctors of theology, and of all the representatives from the different provinces present at the Chapter, in which it was stated, emphatically and uncompromisingly, that the utter poverty of the Redeemer of the human race during His earthly life had already been for many years a dogma of the Church.[6] The second of these [7] was approved not only by the Chapter but by all the forty-one bachelors of theology, both of Paris and of Oxford, who were members of the Franciscan Order. The name of the English provincial, William of Nottingham, is found in both encyclicals.[8] At the same time the Chapter sent a deferential

---

[1] *Hist. Litt.* xxxiv. 443. In this volume John XXII.'s biographer, M. Valois, gives a very fine exposition of the whole question from the papal standpoint. Cf. pp. 442-72.   [2] *B.F.* iii. 404-16.   [3] *B.F.* iii. 415 *s.*

[4] *Ibid.* v. 464, p. 224 ; *Misc.* iii. 207.

[5] *B.F.* v. p. 233 *n.*; *Misc.* ii. 279-80. Cf. *supra*, p. 130.

[6] *B.F.* v. p. 234 *n.* ; *Misc.* iii. 208.

[7] *B.F.* v. p. 234 *n.* ; *Misc.* iii. 208. Over 100 copies of the two letters were made and dispatched before December 1322 (*A.F.H.* xxiii. p. 123).

[8] In both documents his name follows that of Michael of Cesena. The names of the two English doctors of theology, Hugh of Newcastle and William of Alnwick, also appear at the beginning of both letters . The Nicolaus, Provincial of France, whose name follows that of the latter, was probably Nicholas de Lyra. Cf. *Hist. Litt.* xxxvi. p. 358.

letter to John XXII., begging him as one to whose protection they had formerly been indebted, to stop the mouths of their rivals and detractors by replacing the anathema of Nicholas III. upon all those who discussed the meaning of his decretal.[1]   In the light of future events, the frequent and carefully organised intercessions by which they strove to prolong the life of the already aged pontiff sound almost ironical.[2]

Besides the letters from Perugia, the Franciscan Order, through Bonagratia of Bergamo, now its official representative at the Curia,[3] made a formal protest [4] against the suspension of the clause at the end of " Exiit qui seminat", forbidding on pain of excommunication the discussion of the questions dealt with in that decretal.[5]   Even the lively proctor must have been aware of the delicacy of the situation, for his pamphlet is not spoiled by his usual insolence, but is a clear, reasoned and, on the whole, temperate statement of the position of the Friars Minor.   It may perhaps be regarded as an explanation of the theological and legal meaning of Nicholas III.'s pronouncement, especial care being taken to clear away various difficulties which had been raised by its interpretation of certain matters.   Bonagratia begins by defining very exactly the limits of the question of the poverty of Christ and his apostles. From its very nature it could only concern itself with the earthly life of the former, and with the latter after their assumption to the apostleship.[6]   Moreover, it only affected them in their character as preachers of the gospel and not as prelates and dispensers of the property of the Church.[7]   After this he distinguishes between the various senses of the verb "to have", namely, legal ownership, simple use as in the case of the slave, the monk, or the friar, and the power of administering the wealth of the Church, which had been committed to her ministers, who held it in trust for the poor.[8] Like Nicholas III. in " Exiit qui seminat " he is at pains to prove that the apostles and the Minorites in their abdication of all legal

---

[1] Z.K.G. vi. pp. 106-108.

[2] " Demum ut ille pater celestis, a quo omne datum optimum et omne donum perfectum venit, cujusque vices geritis et locum tenetis in terris, ad sui honorem et ecclesie cui presidetis gubernacionem pacificam et salubrem in longeva prosperitate utriusque hominis vos conservet, spiritualia orationum suffragia—a quolibet videlicet sacerdote nostri ordinis X. missas, et a quolibet fratre clerico non sacerdote X. psalmos penitentiales cum letania, a quolibet vero layco III. pater noster cum ave Marias X. devota mente et humili statuimus offerenda, nos ipsos et ordinem nostrum totum brachiis vestre caritatis humiliter commendantes " (ibid. p. 108).   [3] Cf. supra, p. 129, n. 6.

[4] The " Tractatus de Christi et Apostolorum Paupertate ", edited by Father Oliger in A.F.H. xxii. pp. 292-335, and 487-511.   Practically the whole of this treatise is found in the De Planctu Ecclesie of Alvarus Pelagius (L. II. Articulus LX.).   [5] B.F. iii. p. 415 s.

[6] A.F.H. xxii. p. 323.   [7] Ibid.   [8] Ibid. 324-25.

title to the things which they used were not exposing themselves
to starvation, since they retained a natural right to the necessities
of life even though this claim was not supported by the civil law.[1]
He realised fully that John XXII.'s intention was to undermine
the foundation upon which the Minorite ideal rested, and therefore the object of his treatise was to prove that by her official
recognition of the Franciscan mode of life the Church had asserted
that the doctrine that Christ and his apostles had possessed nothing,
either severally or in common, was not heretical, but Catholic
and orthodox.[2] This view had been definitely put forward in the
decretals, " Exiit qui seminat " and " Exivi de paradiso ", which the
present Pope in his bull, " Quorundam exigit ", had commended
as mature and well-judged pronouncements.[3] Moreover, by his
recent canonization of St. Louis of Toulouse, who had abandoned
an earthly kingdom to assume the habit of the Friars Minor,
John XXII. had recognised the especial sanctity of the life he had
chosen, by adding another to the number of the Franciscan saints.[4]
Christ was the mirror and standard of perfection, and if St. Francis
had endeavoured to adopt a higher degree of poverty than He had
observed during His earthly life, his Rule would have been a mere
travesty of the Gospel, and ought never to have received the papal
approbation.[5] True to the spirit of his age, Bonagratia considered
that a solemn and binding promise to observe a certain manner of
life had an especial merit of its own, and therefore declared that
the apostles had not merely observed the strictest poverty, but had
been bound by vow to do so.[6] Further, if they had owned property
in common, their position would have differed in no way from
that of the early converts, whose example had been followed by the
members of religious Orders holding property in common.[7] In
fact, according to Bonagratia and other Franciscan writers, the
apostles might be taken as typical members of the Order of St.
Francis. Like St. Bonaventura and his School he found that the
chief argument against the Minorite conception of poverty lay in

[1] *A.F.H.* xxii. 326. Cf. *B.F.* iii. 408.

[2] *A.F.H.* xxii. pp. 326-27.

[3] *Ibid.* p. 330. Cf. *B.F.* iii. p. 404 *s.*; *ibid.* v. 195, p. 80, and 289, p. 128.
Supra, pp. 9 *s.*, 14, and 19.

[4] *A.F.H.* xxii. p. 329.

[5] " Et Christus in Evangeliis docuerit paupertatem, ut regulam et mensuram,
et regula et mensura non possit excedi ab aliquo, cuius ipse Christus seu doctrina
eius sit regula. Quia si excederit regulam evangelii, sive Christi, potius esset
regula ipsius quam econtrario. Sequitur quod, si beatus Franciscus vovit et
promisit evangelium, vivendo sine proprio in speciali et in communi, quod
talis fuit doctrina et regula evangelii, et per consequens quod Christus non
habuit in speciali nec in communi. Quia quod docuit Christus prius fecit "
(*A.F.H.* xxii. p. 330).

[6] *Ibid.* pp. 333-35.   [7] *Ibid.* p. 494.

the fact that Christ had possessed a purse,[1] and resolutely sets himself to surmount this difficulty. Not only does he meet it by the usual answers, that the bag carried by Judas had been mainly for the offerings held in trust for the poor, that the Redeemer of mankind out of charity had sometimes condescended to the way of the imperfect, who were not called to the surrender of their temporal possessions, and that at the time of the passion much was temporally permitted which was foreign to the general manner of life of the apostles, but he adds that Christ's return each evening to Bethany was a proof that he had no money to pay for a lodging in the holy city.[2] Finally, from the supposed letter of St. Clement to the Church at Jerusalem, which was afterwards incorporated in the canon law,[3] he draws the conclusion that the life of the early Christians was a return to the state of innocence in which there had been no private or legal ownership, but all men had possessed the natural right of availing themselves of the fruits of the earth according to their necessities.[4] Moreover, Christ's temporal life[5] had been a renewal of the conditions which had existed before the Fall, and his complete poverty was a doctrine held by the early fathers. From these he gives many citations as a confirmation of his own convictions with regard to this matter.[6]

In the second part of his treatise Bonagratia deals with the legal position of his Order,[7] a subject upon which his opinion is valuable, since he was first and foremost a lawyer and only secondly a theologian. He realised that its great weakness lay in the fact that most of the necessities of life were consumed by use, and therefore could not be reclaimed from the Franciscans by their legal owner, the Holy See, which thus got no benefit from such goods.[8] In this case it appeared a contradiction in terms to speak of use without ownership, an argument later to be adopted by John XXII. as a complete refutation of the Minorite claim to utter possessionlessness.[9] Bonagratia, however, justified their

---

[1] Cf. "Apologia pauperum", *Opera Omnia*, viii. p. 285; "Exiit qui seminat", *B.F.* iii. p. 408.

[2] *A.F.H.* xxii. pp. 332 and 496-99.

[3] Corpus Iuris Canonici, Causa xii. 91, c. 2.

[4] "Quia cum de iure naturali et divino omnium rerum spectantium ad vitam humanam 'communis usus debeat esse omnibus hominibus, et per iniquitatem factum sit, ut dicatur hoc meum, hoc tuum', ut habetur XII. 9. I. c 'dilectissimis' et VIII. dist. in principio c (i) 'quo iure'" (*A.F.H.* xxii. p. 489).

[5] "Et ipse Christus venerit ad docendum perfectissime omnium terrenorum contemptum, et vitam quietissimam et ad omnem materiam sollicitudinis temporalium perfecte eum sequi volentibus amputandam et ad statum innocentie renovandum" (*ibid.*)

[6] *A.F.H.* xxii. p. 495, etc.

[7] *Ibid.* pp. 502-11.   [8] *Ibid.* p. 502.

[9] Cf. "Ad conditorem canonum", *B.F.* v. 486, p. 237 s. and *infra*, p. 160.

position by comparing it to that of a slave or a son who had no legal right to his father's or his master's property, or even to the goods acquired through his own labour, but received from the latter a pittance which sufficed for his daily needs, and to enable him to perform the services required of him. The same comparison also could be applied to the monk, who had only the use of the possessions belonging to his monastery, even if with the consent of the community he were entrusted with their management.[1] Thus, even the renunciation of property in common, and a simple use of fact without any legal rights, was possible by civil law; nor did it involve suicide or starvation, since by natural law every man could avail himself of the means of preserving life.[2] God and the faithful were the real owners of the goods used by Christ and the apostles,[3] and if, as in the case of food and other consumable objects, it were impossible to separate possession and use it would not follow that they possessed such things in common, but as individuals, which was contrary to all Christian truth.[4] Moreover, by this argument, each of them would have been the individual possessor of money,[5] an idea utterly abhorrent to the feelings of all good Franciscans, who were taught by their Rule to despise the precious metals as dross. The Roman law of usufruct, by which the user was allowed to keep for himself the profit which accrued from the property committed to his charge, provided that he preserved its substance intact for the original owner, did not apply to goods consumed by use.[6] For these a principle of " quasi usufruct " had been evolved, by which not the actual objects themselves but their equivalent were returned at the end of the appointed term.[7] Yet, neither of these two conceptions affected the simple use of fact, the essence of which was its divorce from any form of dominion or ownership, or from any right of using which could be upheld by a court of law.[8] Thus, the position laid down in the decretal, " Exiit qui seminat ", was valid, and a horse could as truly be said to possess the oats provided for it by its master as the Friars Minor the goods which the Holy See graciously permitted them to use.[9] The treatise ends with a " Deo Gratias ",[10] perhaps as a sign that Bonagratia felt that he had not only established his own case but had demolished the arguments of his adversaries; but in reality it

---

[1] *A.F.H.* xxii. p. 502. Cf. *B.F.* v. 239, and *Misc.* iii. 215.
[2] *A.F.H.* xxii. pp. 503 and 505.
[3] *Ibid.* p. 506. Cf. *B.F.* v. p. 238, and *Misc.* iii. 214.
[4] *A.F.H.* xxii. p. 507. Cf. *B.F.* v. p. 243, and *Misc.* iii. 218.
[5] *A.F.H.* xxii. p. 508. Cf. *B.F.* v. p. 243, and *Misc.* iii. 218.
[6] *A.F.H.* xxii. pp. 508-509. Cf. *B.F.* v. 243, and *Misc.* iii. 218.
[7] *A.F.H.* xxii. pp. 509-10.
[8] *Ibid.* p. 510.
[9] *Ibid.* pp. 510-11.   [10] *Ibid.* p. 511.

marked the beginning and not the end of a long and stormy conflict.

When we consider the courageous, not to say rash and obstinate, character of John XXII. it is not surprising that he went his way undeterred by the protests of the Franciscan Order. In the December of 1322, he promulgated the famous bull, " Ad conditorem canonum ",[1] which completely overthrew the legal position of the Friars Minor. Following the arguments of Aquinas, the Pope declared that the complete renunciation of possessions did not necessarily involve perfection, since charity, not poverty, was the basis of a perfect life.[2] Moreover, experience had proved that, in comparison with the other Orders owning property in common, the Minorites were more rather than less solicitous with regard to temporal goods.[3] The dominion of the Holy See over the movables and immovables left to their use was burdensome rather than profitable, and derogated from the honour of the Roman Church, since in defence of these she was involved in constant lawsuits both with the secular and regular clergy.[4] The whole argument of the " usus facti " rested on very flimsy foundations, since no one could lawfully make use of anything if they did not possess the right to do so.[5] Unlike Bonagratia of Bergamo he could see no real distinction between use and ownership in the case of goods consumed by use, and he justified this contention by an appeal to the Roman law of usufruct.[6] Both the Pope and the Franciscan friar were expert lawyers, so that it is somewhat difficult to know which had legally the better case. Yet, when we remember the many subterfuges to which the Minorites had recourse in order to maintain the fiction of their complete poverty, it is impossible not to feel that John XXII.'s attitude was to some extent right. During the period of the Council of Vienne, Ubertino da Casale had protested fiercely against the insincerity of his Order, who, while boasting of their complete alienation from the world, were yet able to make free use of its delights, and enjoyed all the benefits of ownership without any of its disadvantages.[7] It is not surprising under these

[1] B.F. v. 233-36 n. ;   Misc. iii. 211-13.

[2] " Cum perfectio vitae christianae principaliter et etiam essentialiter in charitate consistat " (ibid. 235). It is interesting in this connection to notice that the arguments of Aquinas concerning the sanctity of individual ownership were made use of by Leo XIII. in his encyclical " Rerum Novarum " of May 1891. Cf. Schnürer, Kirche und Kultur im Mittelalter, iii. p. 39.

[3] B.F. v. 235 n.

[4] Ibid. and p. 243 s.

[5] " Praeterea si simplex usus absque iure utendi haberi posset ab aliquo, constat quod non iustus esset actus utendi huiusmodi reputandus, cum ille usus fuerit cui non competebat ius utendi " (ibid. p. 242 s.).

[6] B.F. v. 237 s.   [7] A.L.K.G. iii. 54-5, 86-7. Cf. supra, p. 145.

conditions that the other Orders were inclined to regard the Franciscans as a band of sanctimonious hypocrites.[1] Finally the Pope, on behalf of the Apostolic See, renounced all dominion over the goods left to the use of the Friars Minor and repealed the decretal of Martin IV. allowing them to appoint proctors, whose function it was to take legal action in the name of the Church if the Order was in any way molested in the free use of these.[2] Such representatives might indeed be nominated in future, but they would rank as the agents of the friars and not of the Curia.[3]

Although no dogmatic question was affected by the new papal pronouncement, it naturally caused great anxiety among the Franciscans, who saw only too clearly that it was merely a prelude to an attack upon the theoretic basis of their position. At a public consistory held on the 14th of January Bonagratia of Bergamo made a new protest in the name of the whole Order.[4] In this he practically repeats the arguments used in his former pamphlet, though the theological basis of the Franciscan position —namely, their conception of the poverty of Christ—is less extensively dealt with, perhaps because for the present at least it remained unaffected by the new decretal. The comparison between the position of the Minorites and that of a slave or monk is again found,[5] and it is moreover asserted that the Holy See benefited from her dominion over the goods of which she permitted the friars to make use, nor since she held these in trust for the poor could she renounce her rights over them. Such a surrender was possible only in the case of an individual or of a religious body.[6] Bonagratia repeats almost verbatim his former opinions with regard to the inapplicability of the Roman law of usufruct

---

[1] The Pope had the hearty support of all the religious Orders as well as of the secular clergy in his struggle with the Franciscans. A late thirteenth-century treatise of a Benedictine, Richard of Bury, existing only in manuscript, but which, through the kindness of Mr. Pantin, lecturer in Medieval History at Manchester University, I was permitted to see, not only devotes itself to proving that the life of the religious Orders holding property in common was the highest in itself, but sharply attacks the mendicancy of the friars. It is interesting that the writer uses to support his conclusions the very citations from the Scriptures and the Fathers often quoted by the friars as arguments in favour of their own cause. It is significant also that the generals of the Dominican and Augustinian friars, as well as the Carmelite Gui Terré, afterwards Bishop of Elne in Majorca, later wrote pamphlets upholding the opinions of John XXII. (*Hist. Litt.* xxxiv. p. 453). For summary of Gui's treatise, De Perfectione Vitae Evangelicae, cf. *ibid.* xxxvi., pp. 456-58.

[2] " Exultante in domino " (*B.F.* iii. 40, p. 501).

[3] *B.F.* v. p. 246.

[4] *B.F.* v. pp. 237-46 *n.* ; *Misc.* iii. 213-21.

[5] *B.F.* v. 239 and 242 ; *Misc.* iii. 215.

[6] *B.F.* v. 238 ; *Misc.* iii. 214.

M

to objects consumable by use,[1] and again declares that private ownership was a result of the fall and existed only by civil and not by natural law.[2]   The chief difference between his two treatises lies in the change of tone, for there is a mocking insolence about the second which is completely at variance with his former sober, logical, and reasoned exposition of the Franciscan position.   This is clearly seen in his conclusion, where he declares that the mind of the Holy Father had been poisoned by the wicked lies of the enemies of his Order, and appeals from the Pope who had acted in ignorance to the Pope now that he was fully informed of the truth.[3]   It is not very surprising that as a result of his protest he was arrested, and for a year was an inmate of the papal prison.[4]   Yet his appeal did not remain altogether fruitless, for a revised version of " Ad conditorem canonum " was published, by which the Holy See retained the ownership of the churches, oratories, convents, books, and vestments used by the friars, and renounced in their favour all rights over certain goods of very little real value.[5] Even in this form, however, the bull marked one stage in the Pope's attempt to undermine the basis of the Franciscan conception of poverty.

Even before the promulgation of "Ad conditorem" John had been cautious enough to obtain a statement of the views of the leading theologians at the Curia upon the question of the poverty of Christ.   The cardinals were also asked to give their opinions in writing upon the subject, and the compiler of the manuscript[6] which contains these obviously attached great importance to those of Vidal du Four and the other Franciscans who had spoken at the Consistory where the matter was first brought up for discussion   Not only are their answers given in full, but also in a summarised form,[7] and their refutations of the arguments of their opponents are also carefully cited.   On the whole the replies of the cardinals are not very impressive, the most interesting being that of Béréngar Frédol.[8]   According to him the draft of John's new decretal, "Cum inter nonnullos", was in no way a contra-

---

[1] *B.F.* v. 243 *n.*; *Misc.* iii. 218.

[2] *B.F.* v. 240 *s.*; *Misc.* iii. 216 and 217.   [3] *B.F.* v. 246; *Misc.* iii. 221.

[4] *Ibid.* Cf. Appeal of Michael of Cesena from Pisa, *B.F.* v. 270.

[5] *Ibid.* 486 ; pp. 233-46.

[6] MS. Vaticanus Lat. 3740. Mlle. d'Alverny has examined this MS. with great care in her thesis. Cf. *op. cit.* p. 7 *s.* In his *Quistione della povertà nel secolo XIV.* Tocco gives many long extracts from the copy of this codex which exists in the Marciana at Venice.

[7] Perhaps these were the speeches originally made in the Consistory. I have, unfortunately, seen only the extracts published by Tocco, which give only their summarised form.

[8] Codex Marciana, f. 135 *v.*-138 *v.*; Tocco, *op. cit.* 143-52.

diction of " Exiit qui seminat ",[1] and yet he was not prepared to admit that Christ and His apostles had held property in common except in a very broad and general sense, or that they had possessed the right of selling, transferring, and of alienating the goods of which they had the use, save with the permission of their original owners.[2] Two of the cardinals even were honest enough to confess that they had not studied the question at issue and so were quite prepared to abide by the decision of the Pope, whatever that might be.[3] Perhaps this might almost be termed the view of the sacred college if taken as a whole, for John had made it perfectly clear where his sympathies lay.   In a public consistory he furiously interrupted Vidal du Four, telling him that he was speaking heresy,[4] and his canonization of St. Thomas Aquinas, during the summer of 1323, was a further attack upon the Franciscan position.[5] The University of Paris and the Dominican theologians were moreover warm supporters of the Pope, and the latter carried on a fierce contest against Bonagratia and Michael of Cesena.[6] The chief secular defender of the Franciscan position was Robert of Naples, who during the spring of 1323 composed a pamphlet in favour of the opinion that Christ and His apostles had owned nothing either severally or in common, at the same time declaring his willingness to accept the decision of the Holy See with regard

---

[1] " Nec etiam, ut mihi videtur, in aliquo obviat, quantum apparet prima facie, primus articulus scriptus in cedula noviter lecta et mihi missa quae incipit ' Cum inter nonnullos ' " (p. 144). Béréngar's reply and that of Guillaume Testa, Cardinal of St. Cyriacus in Thermis, were not delivered at the same time as those of the other members of the sacred college. Cf. d'Alverny, op. cit. p. 7.

[2] Tocco, op. cit. pp. 145 and 151. " Sed in contrarium est quod ius vendendi et donandi in venditore et donatore supponunt proprietatem rei, quae venditur et donatur, alias cum per venditionem et donationem transferatur dominium in emptorem et donatorem, transferret quis in alium rem non suam, quod omnino videtur iniustum, ac de Christo et apostolis nullatenus esse dicendum " (p. 151).

He was relying also on John's own argument in " Ad conditorem " that use and ownership could not be separated in the case of goods consumable by use " (p. 145).

[3] Arnald de Pelagru and Gian-Gaetano Orsini.

[4] Misc. iii. 270.

[5] The first name put forward by the Dominicans for canonization was that of Raymund of Pennáfort.

[6] The reply of the university doctors was as follows : " Exiit qui seminat " had practically been revoked by " Quia nonnunquam " and Christ's teaching about poverty might be interpreted allegorically. For the unofficial controversy between the Dominican and Franciscan theologians cf. d'Alverny, op. cit. p. 8. The Franciscan, François de Meyronnes, afterwards Provincial of Provence, composed two questions on the subject of evangelical poverty, the second of which is found in MSS. Dd. iii. 47 and Ff. iii. 23 of the university library at Cambridge. Cf. ibid. and Hist. Litt. xxxvi. pp. 335-36.

to this matter. From the final chapter of his treatise it seems that the king would have preferred the Pope to leave the whole question undetermined, since it was concerned with no issue directly affecting the creed of the Church.[1] In spite of this advice, however, John promulgated the decretal "Cum inter nonnullos" in the November of 1323.[2] This, although couched in cautious terms, was in reality a complete overthrow of the foundation upon which the Franciscan ideal of poverty rested, for it made it heretical to assert that Christ and His apostles were not the owners of the property which the Scriptures expressly declared that they possessed. A like penalty was attached to the statement that they had not the right of freely using such goods. Like its predecessor, the bull was affixed to the door of the Church of Notre Dame at Avignon and copies were sent to the universities.

At first it seemed that the Pope's bold pronouncement had had the effect of crushing all opposition. Vidal du Four and the former champions of the contrary doctrine at the Curia hastened to record their submission.[3] Still more significant was an attempt made to reconcile the doctrine put forward in "Cum inter nonnullos" with that maintained by Nicholas III. in "Exiit qui seminat" and by St. Bonaventura and other Franciscan theologians by distinguishing between the different meanings of ownership and the right of using. It was even possible to assert that the teaching of the lately canonized Aquinas upon the subject of the highest form of poverty did not differ materially from that of the Franciscan thinkers, especially if his final decision was interpreted in the light of his earlier declarations concerning the matter in question.[4] The Franciscans themselves moreover made no public or united protest against the papal declaration. Still, there can be no doubt that William of Alnwick in his sermon

---

[1] An extract from the concluding chapter is given by Tocco, *op. cit.* p. 294, *n.* 1, and Father Sigismund Brettle hopes shortly to publish a complete edition of the treatise in *Miscellanea Franciscana*. In his article "Ein Tracktat des Königs Robert von Neapel De Evangelica Paupertate" in *Festgabe zum 70sten Geburtstag H. Finke* he comes to a completely different conclusion from Professor Tocco—namely, that Robert of Naples would have welcomed a pronouncement of the Holy See as a means of putting an end to the controversy. To my mind the carefully weighed arguments of the final chapter seem to point in a contrary direction, but it is of course difficult to judge from such a fragment. The treatise is mentioned in Michael of Cesena's appeal from Pisa, where he certainly quotes the king as a champion of his own cause (*Misc.* iii. 270).

[2] *B.F.* v. 518, p. 256.   [3] *Misc.* iii. 270.

[4] This treatise was found in the Vatican Archives (Arch. Vat. xxx. 42, f. 89-93) and is printed in *B.F.* v. pp. 256-58 (notes). It is also found in the *De Planctu Ecclesie*, Liber II. Articulus LIX., which has led certain Franciscan scholars to attribute its authorship to Alvaro Paez. The sole difficulty in the way of this supposition is his habit of transcribing the works of other writers into his own book. Cf. *supra*, p. 156, *n.* 4.

at Bologna, where he openly maintained the contrary opinion,[1] was voicing the views of the majority of his Order. A new defender of the doctrine of evangelical poverty, however, arose in the person of the king of the Romans, Louis of Bavaria, who was already opposed to the secular policy of the Papacy. His friendship with the Franciscans was very sudden, for in the Declaration of Nürnberg issued at the end of 1323 he had complained bitterly of their frequent violations of the secrets of the confessional.[2] Five months later in the Declaration of Sachsenhausen he declared the new decretals to be an insult to the poverty of Christ and His blessed mother, whose utter lack of worldly goods had been for many years part of the faith of the Church.[3] The Rule of St. Francis had long been regarded as being in complete harmony with the example set by the Saviour and His Apostles, and this had been recognised by the official pronouncements of many earlier popes, and especially by Nicholas III.[4] What had once been solemnly defined by Christ's Vicar on earth was unalterable, for the gift of the keys to St. Peter had symbolised the power to discern truth from falsehood.[5] John was therefore not merely a heretic but a heresiarch, for he strove by his errors to pervert the whole of Christendom. The latter part of the Declaration is certainly of Franciscan authorship, but the actual writer is unknown. One long passage is taken practically verbatim from Olivi's eighth question—namely, the one dealing with evangelical poverty,[6] and certain parts are moreover reminiscent of Bonagratia of Bergamo's protest.[7] The author therefore cannot be identified as a member of either the Spiritual or the Conventual party. Attempts have been made to prove the presence of Ubertino da Casale or the later leaders of the opposition to John XXII. at the Bavarian Court, but the evidence is unfortunately all in a contrary direction. A widespread tradition would make Franz of Lautzen, an apostate from the Order about whose career very little is known, responsible for the latter part of the Declaration, but recent historians have come

---

[1] *B.F.* v. 520, p. 259. Avignon, December 1, 1323. Cf. *ibid. n.* 4, for probable identification of preacher with William of Alnwick. For a long time the William " de Anglia " mentioned was supposed to be Occam.

[2] *B.F.* v. p. 271, *n.* 3.   [3] *Misc.* iii. 224-32.

[4] " Et ut apparet evidenter presentibus et futuris regulam a beato Francisco editam et ab Ecclesia confirmatam esse vere illam, quam Christus apostolos docuit et in se ipso firmavit " (*ibid.* p. 229). In " Ad conditorem canonum " John XXII. " haeretica contradicat constitutioni catholice felicis recordationis domini Nicolai III." (*ibid.* p. 230).

[5] " Quod enim per clavem scientie per Romanos pontifices semel determinatum est in fide et moribus rectae vitae est immutabile, eoque Ecclesia Romana est inerrabilis in fide et veritate " (*ibid.*).

[6] *Ibid.* p. 231 *s.* A comparison of both documents is given by Ehrle in *A.L.K.G.* iii. 540-52 ; cf. *supra*, p. 131.   [7] Cf. *B.F.* v. p. 280 *n.*

to the conclusion that the imperial notary, Ulrich Wild, found and made use of an anonymous treatise of Franciscan origin, probably written in Lombardy between the years 1322 and 1324 for the purposes of antipapal propaganda.[1] Whatever may have been its origin, it marks the beginning of the Emperor's career as champion of the cause of evangelical poverty and as protector of its most zealous upholders.

The Pope did not allow a long interval to elapse before taking up his adversary's challenge, for his next bull, " Quia quorundam mentes ",[2] was published on November 10. In it he merely reaffirms his former position with definite reference to the arguments used in the Declaration, and attempts to reconcile his own decisions with the decretals of his predecessors, and especially with " Exiit qui seminat ". The ordinances of the Chapter-General of Lyons held the following year reveal the general indignation felt by the Franciscan Order at his proceedings, for Michael or Cesena was obliged to issue stringent instructions to the provincials, threatening with imprisonment any friar who should dare to speak disrespectfully either of the person of the Pope or of his enactments.[3] The movements of the Minister-General after the conclusion of the Chapter are somewhat uncertain. In 1326 he was in Paris,[4] and during the summer of 1327 in Italy, where he received an urgent letter from the Pope summoning him to Avignon.[5] He alleged sickness as an excuse for not obeying the command, and it is probable that his illness was quite genuine, for he was visited at Tivolì by the physician of Robert of Naples, who testified to his unfitness for the journey. Whatever may have been his suspicions, John was obliged to accept the excuse, and received Michael's messengers with marked kindness.[6] Two months later he received letters from the captains of the Guelph party at Perugia, apologising humbly for having made use of these men as a means of communicating with the Curia, since the Minister-

---

[1] *A.F.H.* xiv. p. 361. In his later negotiations with Benedict XII. the Emperor declared that the latter part of the Declaration had been written without his knowledge (Riezler, *Die literarischen Widersacher der Papste zur Zeit Ludwigs des Bayers*, pp. 25 and 92).

[2] *B.F.* v. 554, pp. 271-80 ; *Misc.* iii. 233-37.

[3] " Monet insuper generalis minister cum generali capitulo universo omnes fratres et singulos, ac per obedientiam salutarem eis mandat, quatenus de sancta Romana ecclesia et sanctissimi domini nostri papae persona ac de constitutionibus eius cum debitis sobrietate et reverentia loquantur. . . ." (*A.F.* ii. 135).

[4] *Ibid.* 136.   [5] *B.F.* v. 667, p. 325 (June 8, 1327).

[6] *Ibid.* 687, p. 334. The messengers are described as " dilectos filios Johannem Fidansolae et Humilem Beneauditi tui ordinis". The date is probably September 8, as suggested by Father Bihl (*A.F.H.* ii. 161), and not November 8, 1327.

General was known to be intriguing with Louis of Bavaria, now in Italy, and had expectations of becoming antipope.[1] When Michael finally arrived at Avignon in December, the Pope, dissembling his feelings, received him with his accustomed cordiality, and informed him that he wished to confer with him upon certain matters touching the discipline of the Franciscan Order.[2] As the result of this, certain provincials were deposed from their offices, but the Minister-General was not allowed to leave the papal court. For four months all was outward smoothness while the two men took stock of their respective positions. Michael was possibly ignorant that his secret negotiations with Louis of Bavaria were known at Avignon. Probably he was anxious to avoid an open breach with the Papacy, for, although tenacious and keenly sensitive in matters affecting the honour of his Order, he was by temperament conservative rather than revolutionary. Moreover, he may still have been actuated by a sense of personal loyalty towards the man whose firm support had enabled him to crush the Zealots, and still have hoped to bring about a compromise. The Pope, on his side, was making every effort to undermine the General's influence in his Order and to keep him from openly joining the king of the Romans and becoming antipope.[3] In the last he was completely successful, for Louis, after his triumphal entry into the Eternal City amid the acclamations of the Roman mob, declared "James of Cahors" to be deposed from his high office, and the election of his successor to belong by right to the Senate and people of Rome.[4] A few days later an obscure Franciscan, Peter of Corbara, was chosen as pope, and amid general rejoicing set the imperial crown upon the head of his benefactor.[5] In the first part of his policy John was not so successful. He refused to allow

---

[1] "Qui ex unione quam habet cum Bavaro expectans, ut dicitur, fieri papa per eum, conatur ad sanctitatis vestre non modicum detrimentum et scandalum, necnon ad dicti ac universalis ecclesie divisionem et scisma et quantum in eis est subversionem totalem fidei orthodoxe." This letter was written from Perugia on August 28, so probably did not reach Avignon until after the dispatch of the Pope's letter to Michael (*A.F.H.* ii. 161). Taken from Finke, *Acta Aragonensia*, ii. pp. 675-76.

[2] Wadding, *Annales*, vii. 1327, p. 69, § viii.

[3] There is a contemporary tradition that when Michael of Cesena applied to the Pope for permission to attend the Chapter-General of his Order held at Bologna in the Pentecost of 1328, John XXII. refused with the significant words, "We know well that thou wouldst be pope in Lombardy". To this the Minister-General replied, "I am only a poor master of theology and believe firmly that you alone are the minister of God on earth" (Langlois, "Formulaires de lettres du XIIe, du XIIIe, et du XIVe siècles" in *Notices et Extraits*, xxxiv. p. 321. Given in *Hist. Litt.* xxxiv. p. 463, *n.* 2).

[4] The Deposition decree is found in *Misc.* iii. 240.

[5] Chronicle of Alberto de Mussato, *Fontes Rerum Germanicarum*, i. p. 175. Peter of Corbara was elected pope on Ascension Day (May 12).

Michael to attend the Chapter-General of Bologna, and gave his legate, the Cardinal of Ostia,[1] instructions to do all in his power to bring about his deposition and the election of a new General.[2] The friars, however, were loyal to their old leader, and sent him a letter confirming him in his former rank and begging him as a favour to accede to the earnest prayer of the French queen and hold the next Chapter-General at Paris.[3] Before their messengers reached Avignon the long-suppressed indignation of the Pope had broken forth with all the additional fury and passion caused by an unaccustomed dissimulation of his real feelings.[4] At a Consistory held on April 9 he declared openly and with considerable violence that the decision of the Chapter-General of Perugia concerning the poverty of Christ was false and heretical.[5] Michael, who had been responsible for the declaration of the Chapter, according to his own account, resisted him to his face as St. Paul had done to St. Peter,[6] whereupon John, losing all self-control, denounced him openly as a heretic, an adherent of heretics, and a serpent nourished in the bosom of the Church.[7] Finally, he ordered him, under pain of deprivation and excommunication, not to leave the papal court without his express permission.[8] When he returned to the Franciscan convent where he was lodging Michael was fully alive to the danger of his position. He drew up a secret protest against the proceedings of the Pope, giving his own version of what had taken place and the names of eye-witnesses, amongst others the Franciscan cardinal, Bertrand de Tour.[9] This was signed by his friend, Francesco d'Ascoli, and by Bonagratia of Bergamo, still proctor at the Curia, as well as by an English bachelor of theology, William of Occam,[10] who had already spent four years at Avignon pending an inquiry into certain speculative errors found in his commentaries on the Sentences, and who previously had taken little interest in the

[1] Bertrand du Pouget.

[2] John's letter to the friars assembled at the Chapter-General refers to Michael in very flattering terms. Cf. *B.F.* v. 706, p. 341.

[3] Mariano da Firenze, *op. cit. A.F.H.* ii. p. 639.

[4] Wadding's phrase, "in quo putridum livoris vulnus erupit" (*Annales*, vii. 1327, p. 70, § viii.), is very striking.

[5] *Misc.* iii. 237. "Quam litteram dixit et asseruit fuisse haereticam pluries et frequenter."

[6] "In facie sibi restiti ad instar Pauli" (Manifesto of Michael to Chapter-General of Perpignan, 1331 ; *B.F.* v. p. 498 ; Goldast, *Monarchia*, ii. p. 1235).

[7] "Inter multa alia increpando, quod erat stultus, temerarius, capitosus, tyrannus, fautor haereticorum, et quod erat sicut serpens nutritus in sinu ab ipsa ecclesia" (Appeal of Michael written at Avignon, *Misc.* iii. 237).

[8] *Ibid.*

[9] *Ibid;* *B.F.* v. p. 341.

[10] *Misc.* iii. 239 ; *B.F.* v. p. 341.

question at issue between his Order and the Pope.[1] Six weeks later the four friars fled from Avignon.[2] Outside the walls of the city they were met by a band of soldiers sent by the Emperor, and made their way to Aigues Mortes, where a ship was in readiness to take them to Italy. John in alarm dispatched the Cardinal of Porto to induce the fugitives to return, but his efforts were unsuccessful.[3] Early in June they reached Pisa,[4] where they were welcomed with every semblance of respect by the Emperor's representatives. Even before he arrived in the city Michael and his accomplices had been excommunicated and degraded from their offices.[5] This action, however, did not pass uncriticised, and the Pope was forced to write many letters to the different princes of Western Europe in order to justify himself in their eyes. Not only Michael's old supporters the kings of France and Naples interceded for him, but also Edward and Isabella of England.[6] The religious Orders and the secular clergy however remained staunch in their support of the Pope. After the flight of Michael and his companions, Gui Terré, Bishop of Elne in Majorca, and formerly general of the Carmelites, who had already taken part in the early stages of the controversy, wrote a new pamphlet defending his former opinions against Bonagratia of Bergamo and

[1] In his letter to the Chapter-General at Assisi (1334) Occam declared that he had spent four years at the Curia before realising the heresy of the Pope, and had purposely avoided reading his decretals, not wishing to be convinced of his guilt. It was only at the command of his Superior that he had studied them. This is very possible when we consider that a man awaiting his trial hardly would endanger his position still further by delving into such perilous matter. Michael of Cesena while resident at the convent at Avignon would naturally do his utmost to win the brilliant young bachelor for his party. This view was held by Father Hofer (*A.F.H.* vi. 440), and has been confirmed by the discovery of the manuscript containing the verdict of the doctors commissioned to examine Occam's writings, in which there is no mention of the subject of evangelical poverty. Cf. Pelzer, "Les 51 Articles de Guillaume Occam censurés en Avignon", 1326; *R.H.E.* xviii. pp. 240-70. It was probably the knowledge of their unfavourable verdict which caused Occam's flight from Avignon. The tendency of former scholars to place his active participation in the controversy at a much earlier date was due to a confusion between him and his namesakes, William of Nottingham and William of Alnwick, who both generally are called William of England in documents.

[2] May 26. Michael had not yet dared to publish the appeal he had composed after the events which took place at the Consistory of April 9 (*Misc.* iii. 239). The date of the bull ordering the capture of the fugitives is May 28 (*B.F.* v. 711, p. 345).

[3] *B.F.* v. 714, p. 348.

[4] June 9. It was probably here that Michael published his appeal written at Avignon (*Misc.* iii. 237-40; *B.F.* v. pp. 341-43).

[5] *Ibid.* 714, p. 346.

[6] Wadding, *Annales*, vii. 1328, p. 86, § xxi. Sancia of Naples actually sent John XXII. a justification of the declaration of the Chapter-General of Perugia. Cf *Hist. Litt.* xxxiv. p. 464.

all "the manifest heretics and schismatics belonging to the Franciscan Order ".[1]   Men who had taken part in the famous conflict between the French clergy and the Franciscan Order were still alive and saw the opportunity for revenge.   One of these, Jean d'Anneux, a Parisian doctor of theology, who had been silenced by the decretal "Exiit qui seminat", was actually in Avignon as chaplain to the Cardinal of San Lorenzo,[2] and was not slow in relieving his pent-up feelings.   In the December of 1328 he produced a treatise, which went even further than John XXII. in its condemnation of the opinions and behaviour of the Friars Minor.[3]   Its author regarded the fact that Christ had been born King of the Jews as a complete proof that He had possessed temporal wealth,[4] and declared that the Franciscan Rule was based on a complete misunderstanding of the Gospels.[5]   Moreover its precepts were entirely contrary to every kind of law, whether civil, natural, or divine[6]; nor was this surprising, for St. Francis, although a saint, was both foolish and unlettered,[7] and had been guilty of the sin of presumption in following a rule of life which was harder than that observed by St. Gregory or St. Augustine or other holy fathers of the Church.[8]   The utter

[1] Before his flight from Avignon Bonagratia had written a gloss to Gui's previous treatise, the " De Perfectione Vitae Evangelicae ", citing and confuting the opinions of the learned Carmelite.   Cf. *A.F.H.* xxii. p. 308.   The new pamphlet, the " Defensorium tractatus de Perfectione Evangelicae ", was written in answer to this, and to a defence of the Minorite conception of poverty composed by James of Aragon, Archbishop of Tarragona.   It was written before Gui's appointment to the bishopric of Elne in 1332, but after the flight of his adversary from Avignon, since he always refers to him contemptuously as " Schismaticus ".   Cf. *Hist. Litt.* xxxvi. pp. 458-61.   Of about the same date is the pamphlet De Paupertate Christi et Apostolorum contra Michaelem de Cesena of the Dominican, Pierre de la Palu.   Cf. d'Alverny, *op. cit.* p. 8.

[2] Annibaldus de Ceccano, afterwards Cardinal Bishop of Tusculum.

[3] This treatise, which begins "Filios enutrivi et exaltavi, ipsi autem spernerunt me ", is found in MS. Bodleian 52 f. 179 *r.*-202 *r.*, formerly in Merton College Library.   The manuscript, which contains certain other writings of different periods directed against the Franciscans, was presented to his old college in 1425 by a former fellow, John Maynsforth, and was given to the Bodleian by Cotton in 1605.   The collection of documents as well as the marginal comments to Jean d'Anneux's pamphlet show that the controversy between John XXII. and the Friars Minor still aroused a certain amount of interest in the beginning of the following century, and that the bitterness felt by the university doctors and the secular clergy towards their rivals had by no means died away.   A short account of Jean d'Anneux and a summary of his treatise is found in the *Hist. Litt.* xxxv. p. 455 *s.*   For date of treatise cf. MS. Bodl. 52, f. 202 *r.*

[4] F. 180 *r.*

[5] F. 185 *r.*   [6] Ibid.

[7] " Simplicis ydiote licet sancti " (f. 186 v. ; cf. f. 184 *v.* and f. 185 *r.*).

[8] " Iste Franciscus insipiens licet adinvenit novum modum vivendi quem nescierunt tanti doctores ipsum precedentes, Augustinus, Gregorius et alii doctores et sancti Spiritu Sancto inspirati, et quod ecclesia que duravit ante

impossibility of his ideal was shown by the numerous papal decretals needed to defend it from attack, whereas the regulations of the other founders of religious Orders had required no such sanction, since their merits were apparent to all men.[1] "Exiit qui seminat" had been the result of an unscrupulous attempt on the part of the friars to impose silence upon their critics, and Nicholas III. had been deceived by false information.[2] Moreover the "usus facti" was productive of hypocrisy and entirely contrary to any right interpretation of the laws of property.[3] John XXII., like a second Baptist,[4] had been sent from heaven to remedy the mistaken policy of his predecessors towards the Franciscan Order, and to put an end to the danger and injustice to which this had led.[5] Instead of accepting his correction in a spirit of meekness and submission, the Minorites had dared to advance the audacious and unheard-of opinion that no pope could repeal the enactments of his predecessors, a theory quite contrary to the civil law [6] and which the Holy Father in his recent bull, "Quia quorundam", had rightly condemned as false and erroneous.[7]

The bitterness felt by the secular clergy with regard to the encroachments of the friars is especially apparent in the passages describing their vices. Jean d'Anneux accuses them of hypocrisy and presumption, for while boasting of the especial sanctity of their Rule and manner of life they neglected many of its precepts.[8] In spite of the legal fiction of their utter poverty, their convents, churches, and books were as magnificent as those of other Orders, and were acquired by the alms wrung from the poor, in direct violation of the wishes of St. Francis.[9] Moreover, in his Testament he had bidden them submit themselves meekly to all bishops

---

ipsum per mille annos non habuit hoc, et tunc erat perfectior et homines perfectiores in centuplo quam sunt modo, nec modus ipsius Francisci potest observari nisi ab heremitis in deserto" (MS. Bodl. 52, f. 185 r.).

[1] F. 186 v.

[2] F. 187 r.   [3] F. 188 r.

[4] "Ideo merito vocatur Johannes ut de ipso sicut de alio Johanne dicitur 'Fuit homo missus a deo'. Hic venit in testimonium ut testimonium perhiberet veritati" (f. 187 v.).

[5] F. 187 r.

[6] "Et sedes apostolica quandoque revocat facta priora quia quod inconsulte factum est a predecessore revocari debet a successore." (Extra : de regis iure, cap. i.) (f. 185 v. Cf. f. 197 v.).

[7] "3ᵃ ratio est quia sedes apostolica sepe facit et exponit contra statuta predecessorum suorum, ut bene declaratum est in illa constitutione *quia quorundam*" (f. 186 v.).

[8] "Prima presumptio istorum fratrum est regulam suam rudiorem aliis nimis sustinendo sine mitigando . . . 3ᵃ est se esse perfectiores omnibus religiosis dicendo" (f. 191 v. Cf. f. 186 r.).

[9] F. 182 r. ; f. 186 r., and f. 196 r.

and curates,[1] and ask for no privileges from the Holy See, which instructions they completely disregarded.[2]   Their present attitude to the Vicar of Christ was a complete contradiction of the oath of obedience taken by their founder to Honorius III. and his successors.[3] This hypocrisy was the more dangerous because their seeming sanctity [4] and exaggerated accounts of the virtues of the Franciscan saints gave them undisputed sway over the hearts of the laity.[5]   Besides, their annexation of many of the rights of the secular clergy had deprived the latter of much of their former influence with their flocks.[6]   Like the majority of his Order, Jean is especially indignant that the faithful should be allowed to use the Franciscan churches as burial places, and to choose confessors from among the friars, declaring that the princes who had had Franciscan confessors had been remarkable for their tyranny and evil lives.[7] The bishops and clergy were the true heirs of the Apostles and the disciples, whereas the friars owed their existence entirely to the Holy See,[8] who had treated them as a tender foster-mother,[9] and whose kindness they had repaid by rebellion and schism, actually lending their support to the cause of Louis of Bavaria and his antipope.[10]   The fault of the Emperor might be forgiven him provided he sought reconciliation with the Church, since he was a layman and, as was clearly manifested by the Declaration of Sachsenhausen, had been led astray by their evil counsels; [11] but for the Franciscans there could be

---

[1] " Modo vero curatos cecant, tuebant et obfuscant, quia ipsos dampnificant, parrochianos subtrahendo, iura sua minuendo et in predicationibus suis eos pungendo, quod est contra dictum testamentum in quo dicitur sic de ipsis ' domini mei sunt omnes, et nolo considerare in eis peccatum ' " (MS. Bodl. 52, f. 190 *r*.).

[2] " Ubi dicitur quod sint omnibus subiecti, nec impetrent privilegia in curia romana et quod habeant pauperculas domos et habitaciones.   Nunc vero sunt sic exaltati quod nec regulam nec testamentum sancti Francisci quantum ad predicta servent " (f. 189 *v*.   Cf. f. 199 *r*.).

[3] F. 192 *v*.

[4] F. 189 *v*. and f. 192 *v*.

[5] " Videtur eis quod nihil sit in tota ecclesia nisi de ipsis, nec de aliis sanctis nisi de suis, et plus faciunt de sancto uno pro uno sompnio quam alii de uno martiro " (f. 195 *v*.).   [6] F. 188 *v*.-189 *r*.

[7] " Modo videmus quod principes et divites quorum fratres sunt confessores sunt peiores et magis tiranni quam solebant esse " (f. 189 *r*.   Cf. 188 *r*.-189 *r*.).

[8] F. 188 *r*.

[9] " Et sic dicta sedes dicere potest illud *I. Thess*. 2 ca° ' Tanquam ' (v. 7) ' si nutrix foveat filios suos '.   Sed e contrario illi fratres, id est illi filii sic nutriti, similes sunt cocatrillo de quo dicitur quod postquam mater sua nutriverit eum occidit matrem suam " (f. 190 *r*.).

[10] " Ideo etiam Bavaro adheserunt et pseudo papa de ordine suo approbaverunt " (f. 190 *r*.).

[11] " Sed Bavaro, si veniam petat, est compatiendum quia credo quod nunquam fecisset ea que fecit nisi auxilio, consilio, favore et confidencia aliquorum fratrum,

no pardon, for they could not have been ignorant of the legitimacy of the election of John XXII.,[1] and opposition to Christ's lawful Vicar was blasphemy against Himself.[2] Such men might well be regarded as the false prophets whose coming had been foretold by the apostle Paul,[3] or as the third horseman seen by the writer of the *Apocalypse*, who was thought to represent the third great tribulation which should befall the Church.[4]

Jean's thirst for vengeance was not abated until he had discussed the question of the punishment of his adversaries, the danger of whose attack on the Holy See was greatly increased by their popularity both with common people and with the nobility.[5] Possibly he would have liked John XXII. to have followed the example of his predecessor with regard to the Templars, but he realised that such a step would have caused widespread discontent.[6] It was impossible to take adequate police measures in connection with an Order whose members did not live in settled communities but wandered from place to place,[7] nor had they, like the secular clergy, any temporalities which could be confiscated.[8] The only means of coercion at the Pope's disposal was the curtailment of their privileges, and especially of those which, like the right of hearing confessions, lessened the authority of the parish priests.[9] A restoration of the authority of the bishops over the friars in each diocese also would tend to the restoration of order and discipline, since the spirit of criticism and revolt had been greatly fostered by the fact that the Superiors of the Order were responsible only to the Pope.[10] John XXII., however, was not so carried away by the insults offered to his office to take the advice given him by his zealous defender. He was content with the measures already taken against Michael of Cesena and the other leaders of the revolt, and perhaps realised the folly of proceeding to further extremities. He appointed the Franciscan cardinal, Bertrand de Tour, as his vicar to manage the affairs of the Order until arrangements could be made for the election of a new general.[11]

Soon after his arrival at Pisa Michael had sent a circular letter

---

quod protunc ex hoc quia non est verisimile quod in appellatione sua sciret loqui de perfectione evangelica et de ordine fratrum minorum nisi eum docuisset, cum esset laicus, vel illiteratus " (MS. Bodl. 52, f. 191 *r*.).

[1] F. 192 *r*.
[2] " Nam qui spernit papam spernit Christum " (f. 193 *r*.).
[3] F. 183 *v*. and 192 *v*. [4] *Ibid*.
[5] F. 189 *v*. and f. 196 *r*. [6] *Ibid*. and f. 195 *v*.
[7] F. 189 *v*. [8] *Ibid*.
[9] F. 197 *r*. [10] *Ibid*. and 190 *r*.
[11] *B.F.* v. 716, p. 349. On the 18th of June the new vicar wrote to the different Franciscan convents in Italy ordering the seizure of the rebels (*A.F.H.* viii. 672-75). The processes against Michael seem to have been very generally published among the friars (*B.F.* v. p. 351).

to the Superiors of his Order giving an account of the events which had taken place at the Curia.[1]   According to him John's wrath had been so terrible that even the cardinals, who had always favoured the Friars Minor and were on terms of personal friendship with himself, had not dared to intercede for him.[2]   By both divine and human law the Pope's will should be obeyed in all things not contrary to the Word of God or to the decrees of his predecessors.[3] By his bull, "Quorundam exigit",[4] John XXII. had expressed his agreement with that doctrine of the poverty of Christ which had been sanctioned both by "Exiit qui seminat"[5] and by "Exivi de paradiso".[6]   Michael also sent an exposition of his views to the University of Paris, and this was affixed on the principal door of Notre Dame by Gerard Rostagni, one of the companions of his flight from the Curia.[7]   Later it was taken down and publicly burned in the presence of the Bishop and the Chancellor of the University.[8]

Michael's more formal appeals from Pisa were written at the convent of the Friars Minor and directed to all the faithful.[9]   The matter contained in them is the same, although possibly the shorter one was the best known.[10]   They give a careful statement of the position of himself and his followers, together with a detailed confutation of the numerous errors found in the three papal decretals. Perhaps in view of the imperial deposition John is alluded to as "dominus Joannes qui se papam XXII. appellat".   Nine errors were discovered in "Ad conditorem canonum", two in "Cum inter nonnullos", and seven in "Quia quorundam mentes". The use without ownership of consumable goods, which John had declared to be contrary to law and reason, existed in Holy Writ, for the Levites had subsisted upon the tithes which had been offered to God.[11]   Such legal conceptions as usufruct, and indeed all ownership and dominion, existed only by civil law, and were the result of sin.[12]   In a state of nature such distinctions had had no meaning, though all men had had the right of using the fruits of the earth at their pleasure.   The life of the Apostles and of the early Christians had been a return to the state of innocence, and this was

[1] *Misc.* iii. 244 ; *B.F.* v. p. 347.
[2] *Ibid.*   [3] *Ibid.*
[4] *B.F.* v. 289, p. 128. Cf. *supra*, p. 19.
[5] *B.F.* iii. pp. 404-16.   [6] *B.F.* v. 195, p. 80.
[7] Denifle, *Cart. Univ. Paris*, ii. 330.
[8] *A.F.H.* ii. 163, from *Acta Aragonensia*, 298, pp. 446-48.
[9] *Misc.* iii. 246-310 ; *B.F.* v. pp. 408-25 *n*.
[10] It was the one answered by the Pope in his bull, " Quia vir reprobus " (*B.F.* v. 820, p. 408).
[11] *Misc.* iii. 247-53 ; *B.F.* v. pp. 412-13 ; authority, *Numbers* xviii. 23 *s.*
[12] *Misc.* iii. 249 *s.* ; *B.F.* v. 413 ; authority, *Luke* xix. 11 ; *Matt.* xxv. 14.

confirmed by the letter of St. Clement, the successor of St. Peter, to the Church at Jerusalem.[1] Nor was it possible to declare that to use without a definite legal claim was to abuse, for the word "use" was often found in the Scriptures,[2] and it was generally agreed that Christ had forbidden those who wished to be perfect to contend in the law courts, since they had renounced all civil rights to the goods of which they retained the use.[3] The position of the friars with regard to the Church resembled that of a son who during his father's lifetime was permitted by his bounty to make use of his possessions, but had no legal or formal right to do so.[4] This view was upheld by many papal interpretations of the Franciscan Rule, and indeed "Exiit qui seminat"[5] was merely a confirmation of these.[6] It derived additional authority from its inclusion in the Sext. and from the bull, "Exivi de paradiso", promulgated by Clement V. at the Council of Vienne.[7] John himself in earlier days had commended the decisions of his predecessors as solid, clear, and well judged, though he now strove to destroy their validity by every means in his power.[8] "Cum inter nonnullos" was a flagrant violation of the former teaching of the Church upon the subject of evangelical poverty, for it admitted of no interpretation which did not make Christ and His apostles the actual owners of property in common.[9] The former could have possessed no legal rights, since He was in no way subject to the civil law.[10] If it were once allowed that the Pope had the power of altering the enactments of his predecessors the whole faith of the Church would be shaken and its foundations would become unstable.[11] In making use of his position to undermine the whole teaching of the Church upon so vital a matter as the complete renunciation of temporal goods being the only road to perfection, John was clearly a heretic. Moreover, he had persisted in his errors in spite of repeated warnings both from Robert of Naples and from the Emperor,[12] whose public reproof merely had caused

---

[1] *Misc.* iii. 249 *s.* Corpus Iuris Canonici, Causa XII. Q. i., c. 2. Cf. Bonagratia of Bergamo, "Tractatus de Paupertate Christi et Apostolorum" (*A.F.H.* xxii. p. 489; *supra*, p 158).

[2] "Occasio tribuitur dogmatizandi et credendi quod quotiescunque Christus et apostoli et alii sancti viri comederunt et biberunt, aut induerunt, toties huiusmodi rebus usu consumptibilus sunt abusi, quod abhorrent piae aures fidelium audire" (*Misc.* iii. 255).

[3] *B.F.* v. p. 414.

[4] *Misc.* iii. 260. Cf. Bonagratia de Bergamo, "Tractatus de Paupertate Christi et Apostolorum" (*A.F.H.* xxii. p. 502; *supra*, p. 159).

[5] *B.F.* iii. 404-16.   [6] *Misc.* iii. pp. 260-69.

[7] *Ibid.* pp. 267 and 268; *B.F.* v. 195, p. 80.

[8] *Misc.* iii. p. 269.

[9] *Ibid.* p. 272.   [10] *Ibid.* p. 298.   [11] *Ibid.* p. 309.

[12] *Ibid.* pp. 270 *s.* and 299. Cf. *supra,* 163 and 165.

him to defend more vehemently his former heresies, and even to add to their number. For the benefit of the faithful, Michael gives a highly coloured account of the events which had taken place at the Curia since the opening of the controversy, and stresses his adversary's violence and impatience of contradiction.[1] The protection afforded by John to the famous Dominican mystic, "Master Eckhart",[2] and the English necromancer and alchemist, Thomas "de Branucerton",[3] was a further proof of his guilt. It was unnecessary to await the judgment of a General Council upon the question of his heresies, since a notoriously heretical pope was "ipso facto" deposed, and became of less account than the humblest Catholic.[4] According to canon law he could be corrected even by a harlot. Michael ends his treatise by appealing in the name of his Order and of all the faithful to the holy Catholic and Apostolic Church.[5] The scant significance which he attaches to the functions of a General Council is all the more remarkable when we remember its theoretic importance in the manifestos of Louis and his advisers, and is a proof of his essential conservatism. Occam might support the original and daring political theories of Marsiglio of Padua with speculations even more radical and brilliant, but his Superior clung tenaciously to the old paths. The defence of the honour of his Order and the strength of his own convictions had driven him into the imperial camp, but he had by temperament too much respect for law and tradition to be at all a typical rebel.

The appeal from Pisa both in its longer and in its shorter form was affixed upon the door of the Duomo, together with a new version of the imperial decree deposing John XXII.[6] This bears distinct traces of the influence of the Franciscan manifestos; especially in its enumeration of the errors found in the three

---

[1] *Misc.* iii. pp. 270-73.

[2] *Ibid.* p. 302. At the trial in 1330 of Franciscus Bartoli of Assisi, one of Michael's followers, the accused declared that he had seen an anonymous letter sent to the General at Pisa, the writer of which was reputed to be Albert of Bassiano, lector at Cologne (*A.F.H.* xx. 303). This Albert was probably one of Eckhart's judges. Cf. *A.L.K.G.* ii. 627 *s.*

[3] *Misc.* iii. p. 302.

[4] "Ex quo textu habetur, quod quilibet haereticus . . . etiam si dicitur Papa, minor est quolibet Catholico, et quilibet Catholicus est illo superior (*Dist.* lxxxix. c. 9). Item, licitum est Clericis et etiam laicis talem sicut Sedis Apostolicae invasorem et occupatorem illicitum anathematizare et humano auxilio a Sede Apostolica pellere. Et procedi potest ad alterius pontificis Catholici electionem" (*Misc.* iii. p. 299).

[5] "Ego ad sanctam Romanam Ecclesiam Catholicam et apostolicam provoco et appello" (*ibid.* p. 303).

[6] *Ibid.* p. 310. The appeals themselves are dated from the Convent of the Friars Minor at Pisa, September 18, 1328 (*B.F.* v. p. 425 *n.*).

decretals, and its adhesion to the theory that an heretical pope immediately lost his authority.[1] In March, Louis, who must have realised that his Italian expedition had proved a failure, left the city, probably accompanied by Michael and his companions, although the antipope remained behind. Louis lingered for some months in northern Italy, and the ex-Minister-General was certainly in his train when he visited Parma, for on the Feast of St. Nicholas [2] he preached in the cathedral against John XXII., accusing him of heresy and simony.[3] In spite of his quarrel with the Pope it is possible that he was not on very friendly terms with his rival. In a letter to his former secretary, Andreas de Galiano, now chaplain to the Queen of Naples, he declared that he had written from Avignon to try to induce the Emperor to refrain from the election.[4] His objections may have been due either to a dislike of the long discredited policy of setting up an antipope, or to a personal knowledge of the character of Peter of Corbara.[5] From the same source we learn that he refused all the tempting offers of the so-called Nicholas V., who was anxious to raise him to the rank of cardinal.[6] Certainly his name has not been found in any of the registers of the antipope, and the early tradition that he was created Cardinal of Ostia has very little foundation.[7] On the other hand, he does not seem to have prevented his followers from accepting promotion, and Berengar de Mari, one of the actual signatories of the Pisan manifestos, had already been consecrated Archbishop of Genoa.[8] The court of Avignon was apparently ignorant of his movements, for besides letters addressed to the Archbishop of Cologne and his suffragans, and to the Markgraf of Baden and other noblemen, ordering the capture and arrest of the fugitives,[9] there is one to the English bishops giving similar instructions, for a rumour had reached the Curia that Occam and

---

[1] This version is in *Misc.* iii. 310-14, and is dated December 12.

[2] December 6, 1329.

[3] *Chronicon Parmense* in *Rerum Italicarum Scriptores* (Ed. Fiorini), ix. 203.

[4] *B.F.* vi. Appendix I. p. 601.

[5] It must be remembered that Michael, who had been General of the Franciscan Order for twelve years, was probably already acquainted with the character of Peter of Corbara. The general scorn felt for the antipope can be seen in Angelo da Clareno's letter to Philip of Majorca (*A.L.K.G.* i. 567). Cf. *supra*, p. 65. John XXII. would probably have explained his attempts to prevent the election as being due to his own desire for the position of antipope.

[6] *B.F.* vi. Appendix I. p. 601.

[7] On May 28, 1328, the antipope created James of Prato, Bishop of Castello, Cardinal of Ostia and Velletri. Cf. Otto, " Zur italienischen Politik Johanns XXII.", *Q. & F.* xiv. p. 171.

[8] *B.F.* v. p. 721 *n.*

[9] *B.F.* v. 773 and 783, pp. 376 and 379. The dates are March 7 and April 2, 1329.

certain of his companions had escaped to England.[1]   After the flight of the Emperor his puppet pope fell easily into the hands of John.   Even when he had first entered Pisa, in the heyday of his prosperity, the citizens, in spite of their Ghibelline sympathies, had given him a forced welcome,[2] so that his rival was able to bribe a neighbouring noble to deliver him into his hands.   He was induced to make a public confession of his errors, and passed the rest of his days in Avignon in a kind of honourable captivity.

Meanwhile the papal court had not allowed the protests of Michael to pass unchallenged.   There is a very able unofficial answer which points out that the appeal from the Pope to the whole Church was tantamount to an acknowledgment of his authority.[3]   Moreover, if John XXII. was a heretic, the Minister-General had formerly been a supporter of his errors, since at the Chapter-General of Lyons he had forbidden the friars to speak disparagingly either of his person or of his decretals.[4]   Michael's reply is interesting as showing a marked change in his attitude towards the temporal power, for he now puts forward the right of the Emperor to depose a notoriously heretical pope, especially if the prelates of the Church refused to take any action against him.[5]   John's own answer has the characteristic incipit "Quia vir reprobus"[6] and is perhaps the most interesting of all his bulls. M. Valois has well said that it is more like the reasoned defence by a university professor of some cherished theme than an authoritative pronouncement of the head of Christendom.[7]   The basis of the Pope's arguments is that the renunciation of property had little to do with perfection.   Christ's instructions to His disciples to take nothing with them on the way referred only to the time when He sent them out by twos to preach to the people.[8]   On their return they had possessed temporal goods, in common, if not individually.[9]   The early Church had actually owned the goods which were distributed among the faithful according to their

[1] *B.F.* v. 784, p. 380. (April 5.) By May 5 the Pope had more information of the movements of the fugitives, for in a letter to the Queen of France he describes them as being in the train of the Bavarian when he left Pisa, and as having separated from him at Cremona (*ibid.* 788, p. 384).

[2] Villani, L. X. p. 163.

[3] Extracts given in *B.F.* v. p. 425, and taken from the Chronicle of Nicholas the Minorite. Codex Vaticanus, 4009, f. 29, contains the answer of the Franciscans to this treatise. It must be a weighty piece of work, for they allege twenty-five different reasons for disproving the arguments of their adversaries. Cf. *H.J.* xviii. p. 376.   [4] *B.F.* v. p. 425.

[5] " Ad imperatorem pertineat amovere et deponere papam, cum agit contra fidem, maxime quando prelati in ecclesia negligunt remedium adhibere " (*Z.K.G.* vi. p. 83).

[6] *B.F.* v. 820, p. 408. (Avignon, November 16, 1329.)

[7] *Hist. Litt.* xxxiv. p. 465.   [8] *B.F.* v. p. 444.   [9] *Ibid.*

needs, and had only not encumbered herself with landed property because she had realised that her mission was to convert the Gentiles.[1] After the distribution each Christian was the sole and undisputed possessor of the share allotted to him.[2] Moreover, it was erroneous to suppose that ownership did not exist in the state of innocence, for God had given Adam lordship over the whole earth. If this had been bestowed before the creation of Eve he alone benefited by the gift, but if it was conferred later he and his wife as representatives of the human race possessed dominion in common. St. Clement's letter to the Christians at Jerusalem referred to this rather than to any natural right of using the fruits of the earth.[3] Nicholas III. in his decretal, when discussing the different kinds of ownership, was clearly thinking only of goods not consumable by use,[4] and in the Scriptures the latter word was often used for consume,[5] as for example in St. Paul's advice to Timothy to use a little wine. Property was indeed of divine origin, for Christ had been hailed as a king by the prophets. He had preferred to make no use of His royal rights, but had not abdicated them, just as any earthly sovereign upon returning from a long journey might choose to remain for some time unknown to his subjects.[6] Far from putting an end to the discussion of evangelical poverty, the Pope's decretal merely served to whet the ingenuity of his opponents, who found it an even more fruitful field for the discovery of heresies than his earlier ones. At the same time it supplied many of his supporters with good arguments against the Franciscan position, as can be seen in the case of Richard Fitz Ralf, Archbishop of Armagh.

Probably the real triumph of the Papacy is to be found in the practical rather than in the theoretic sphere—namely, in the alienation of the loyalty of the Franciscans from their former leader. This is best seen in the election of his successor, the Pope's fellow-citizen, Guiral Ot, at the Chapter-General of Paris in 1329.[7]

---

[1] *B.F.* v. p. 412.

[2] *Ibid.* p. 415. In *Acts* xii. 8, the angel when rescuing St. Peter from prison commanded him to cast his garment about him.

[3] John XXII. interpreted St. Clement's letter " Dilectissimis ", as meaning the " common ownership " of, and not merely the use of, the goods divided among the early Christians. On the whole, he inclined to the view that " dominion " over the earth had been granted to Adam before the creation of Eve (*ibid.* p. 422).   [4] *Ibid.* p. 424.

[5] *Ibid.* pp. 427-30.   [6] *Ibid.* p. 443.

[7] *Misc.* iii. p. 314 ; *B.F.* v. p. 388. Villani's statement (*Istorie Fiorentine*, L. X. p. 313) that Guiral came from the same region as John XXII. has now been verified, and the names of his brother and nephews figure conspicuously in the papal registers. It is possible also that he was a kinsman of Bertrand de Tour. Although a master of theology, he does not seem to have held any important office in the Order prior to his election (*Hist. Litt.* xxxvi. pp. 203-206).

It is probable that this was the result of careful preparations on the part of John and his vicar, for Bertrand had obtained the Pope's consent to the deposition of certain of the provincials of the Order, in whose power the election lay.[1]   Perhaps also Michael's chief supporters—Henry of Kelheim, Francis of Ascoli, Bonagratia, and Occam—were right when they publicly protested that barely half the electors had been present.[2]   Yet the ex-General could hardly congratulate himself that his letter forbidding the Chapter to be held had borne much fruit.[3]   In this he refers to the Pope as " Jacobus de Caturco " and as " ille qui de facto praesidet in Avinione." [4]   His general desertion by his Order was probably the result of his open adhesion to the Emperor. His successor was not popular with the better elements among the Franciscans, who disapproved strongly of the papal decisions, though not prepared for open rebellion.[5]   One of the proudest traditions of the Friars Minor was their loyal devotion to the Papacy, and the memory of Elias of Cortona was still execrated because of his friendship with Frederick II.   Thus, in spite of the efforts of Michael's numerous agents, he met with little real support except in Italy, and even there his partisans quickly reconciled themselves with the Church as soon as he and Louis had departed.   In France there were isolated manifestations in his favour, as when a certain Brother " Veranus ", lector of Montpellier, told John XXII. to his face that he was a heretic,[6] but less than a fortnight later he had confessed his error and sought absolution.   A more serious case was that of another lector, Conrad of Weilheim, who in the early part of 1330 was arrested for preach-

---

[1] *B.F.* v. 791, p. 387. (May 15, 1329.)

[2] " Allegationes religiosorum virorum Henrici de Talheim, Francisci de Appiniano dicti de Esculo, Guilhelmi de Occam in sacra pagina magistrorum et fratris Bonagratiae de Pergamo " (*Misc.* iii. 315-23 ; *B.F.* v. 388-96). According to the authors, twenty of the provincials were absent, and four of the remaining fourteen had previously been deposed by Michael of Cesena (*ibid.* p. 393). Henry of Kelheim had formerly been Provincial of Germany, but resigned his position in 1326 (*A.F.* ii. 135).

[3] *B.F.* v. p. 387 *n.* ; *Misc.* iii. 314. (Pisa, November 26, 1328.)

[4] *Ibid.*

[5] Already at the Chapter-General of Lyons in 1325 Guiral had tried to get the stringent regulations contained in the Franciscan Rule with regard to money changed. At the Chapter-General of Perpignan he again brought the matter forward and extorted the consent of certain of the Superiors of the Order. John XXII., however, refused to alter the Rule (*B.F.* v. 921, p. 503). Cf. Letter of Michael to Guiral in *A.F.H.* ix. 154, and Alvaro Paez, *De Planctu Ecclesiae*, L. II. f. 269 *v.* The Minister-General's enthusiastic support of the Pope over the matter of the Beatific Vision did not add greatly to his reputation for sincerity (*Hist. Litt.* xxxiv. 609 *s.*).

[6] " Continuateur de la Chronique de Guillaume de Nangis " (*Spicilegium*, iii. p. 92 ; *B.F.* v. p. 406 *n.*). (October 21, 1329.)

ing openly in Paris in defence of the Franciscan doctrine of the poverty of Christ.[1] His boldness in the support of this conception won for him powerful protectors, and in the November of the same year the Pope wrote to Queen Jeanne of France promising to set him free if he showed signs of repentance.[2] Possibly he had received information that Conrad had shown signs of regretting his previous obstinacy, since at the same time he gave instructions to the Bishop of Paris for his release and restoration to his Order on condition of his recantation of his former errors.[3] Probably the German friar, like so many of his companions, realised the hopelessness of continuing the conflict. Two years later a riot occurred at Dijon, when the confession of the antipope was read.[4] The case of " Bartholomaeus " de Bruguière, who declared that he did not know which pope to pray for in the Mass, is more interesting, for, judging by their anxiety to prevent his being examined by the Dominican inquisitors, the custodian and the other friars at Carcassonne seem to have shared in his errors, but even they speedily, made a somewhat ignominious submission.[5] Poor " Bartholomaeus " himself was expelled from the Order and was not reinstated till 1335.[6] During the pontificates of the successors of John XXII. there are isolated instances of friars who were burned for preaching openly in complete contradiction to the decretal " Cum inter nonnullos " that Christ and His apostles had possessed nothing either severally or in common,[7] but their connection either with the followers of Michael of Cesena or with the old Spiritual party has never been definitely proved.

During Michael's stay in Italy he aroused a certain amount of enthusiasm, especially among the friars living in regions actually occupied by the imperial forces. He probably had many agents working for him in different parts of the country, amongst others his nephew Azzo, whom he appointed as his vicar in Lombardy.[8]

---

[1] *B.F.* v. 842, p. 460. *Iohannis Vitodurani Chronica* (ed. Baethgen), p. 97. The Swiss chronicler calls Conrad " Master Wilnheim ", a fact which led earlier historians to confound him with Occam.

[2] *B.F.* v. 885, p. 484. Jeanne was perhaps the rich patroness mentioned by John of Winterthur (*op. cit.* p. 98) who sent Conrad seventy florins during his imprisonment.

[3] *B.F.* v. 884, p. 483. (November 23.) John of Winterthur (p. 98) declares that he was set free after spending seventeen weeks in captivity, and that his release was due to the fact that his enemies were unable either to meet his arguments or to shake his constancy. Conrad died in 1349 (*B.F.* v. p. 483 *n.*).

[4] *Ibid.* 893, p. 489. (January 22, 1331.)

[5] *B.F.* v. *n.* 785, p. 381. (April 5, 1329.)

[6] *Ibid.* 874, p. 479 ; vi. 7, p. 7.

[7] Baluze, *Vitae Paparum*, pp. 202, 311, and 389 ; *B.F.* vi. *n.* 665, p. 287. Cf. *supra*, p. 20.

[8] Wadding, *Annales*, 1328, p. 85, § xx.

The nature of the support which he received can best be seen by tracing the career of Francesco Bartoli of Assisi, the writer of the well-known treatise on the Indulgence of the Portiuncula.[1]   He was at this time lector of Borgo San Sepolcro, and was in constant correspondence with the General, both during his enforced stay at Avignon and later, when he was at Pisa.   Bartoli was a convinced Michaelist, always referring to the Pope as " James of Cahors ",[2] and even made the delivery of an affectionate message to a friend conditional upon his believing that John XXII. was a heretic.[3]   He wrote to Michael in the September after his arrival at Pisa, declaring his willingness to enter fire for the sake of the truth, but at the same time asking to be removed from his lectorship, where he dared not freely express his opinions.   If he were sent to Monte Alverna, or to some convent in the territory controlled by the Emperor, he would be able to perform even greater services than a certain Isaac of Arezzo.[4]   Later he visited Pisa, where his request was granted,[5] since he wrote from Monte Alverna to certain friends trying to arrange a secret meeting at " Rasinopolis ", whither they were to come on the pretext of having business with a neighbouring feudatory.[6]   He was probably employed as an agent for the spread of propagandist literature, for at the time of his capture two bulls of the antipope,[7] as well as a treatise, probably by Bonagratia, were found in his possession.[8]   An elaborate system for the transmission of letters seems to have been arranged by himself and his confederates, and he often gives them tidings of movements of the Emperor, asking in his turn for information as to the proceedings of the Chapter-General at Paris,[9] and the contents of the latest papal letters to Florence and Siena.[10]

[1] Cf. *supra*, p. 118. The documents showing Bartoli's connection with Michael have been printed in *A.F.H.* xx. 260-304.

[2] " Ille dampnatus hereticus de Caturcho " (*ibid*. p. 292. Cf. p. 270).

[3] *Ibid*. p. 276.

[4] *Ibid*. p. 277. Dated from Borgo San Sepolcro, September 1, 1328.

[5] " Cum quo (Bonagratia of Bergamo) et etiam cum generale a tempore carnis privii (Lent) usque ad eorum recessum mansi cum eis Pisis, et post octavam pasce recessi " (*ibid*. p. 270).

[6] *Ibid*. p. 279.

[7] XII. and XIII. (*ibid*. p. 295 s.). The first is directed to all Christian princes, and the second to the clergy. They make known the deposition of John XXII., and grant a year's indulgence to all who should take part in the General Council summoned by the Emperor.

[8] *Ibid*. pp. 286-8. Dated Perugia, January 1329 : " Tempore domini Ludovici imperatoris."   In another treatise the author with his accustomed ingenuity defends Michael's attitude at the Chapter-General of Lyons by declaring that the prohibition to speak lightly of the Pope and his decretals implied that the friars were to consider the question seriously and then speak according to their convictions (p. 274).

[9] *Ibid*. p. 275.   [10] *Ibid*. p. 276.

Sometimes he discusses the characters of various friars and the likelihood of their adhesion to the Michaelist party. It is amusing that he evidently regarded his future captor, Peter of Prato, as a broken reed.[1] He must have been arrested almost before Michael's departure from Italy, for the date of his reply to the charges brought against him was the 23rd of January 1330.[2] Besides preaching publicly the pernicious doctrines that the most holy father was a heretic and that the Emperor had the power of deposing him, he had written two treatises upon the iniquities of John XXII., basing his arguments upon St. Francis's prophecies concerning the decline of the Order and the uncanonically elected pastor.[3] He was obviously well steeped in the literature current among the Spirituals, and made great use of Olivi's commentary on the Apocalypse,[4] though he informed his judges that he had read it only at the ex-General's express command.[5] As might be expected from the general prudence of his character, Francesco Bartoli's repentance was not long deferred.[6] He probably spent the rest of his life at the Portiuncula writing the book which is his chief title to fame. His example was followed by most of Michael's former supporters, for even the rebellious friars of Todi, who had received the Emperor and his antipope in procession with the cross borne before them, sought a speedy reconciliation with the Church.[7] Perhaps the most famous of the Michaelists was Alvaro Paez, the correspondent of Angelo da Clareno,[8] who later became papal penitentiary.[9] He fell into the hands of the rector of Spoleto,[10] but he had already won the favour of John XXII. by his ability. The Pope took up the matter himself, writing personally to the prisoner, and promising him forgiveness and promotion if he submitted.[11] Two years later Alvaro was made bishop of Coron in Greece,[12] but he never quite forgot his early sympathies. In his book, *De Planctu Ecclesie*, he writes with considerable vigour against the bull " Ad conditorem canonum ",[13] and was bitterly prejudiced against Michael's

---

[1] *A.F.H.* xx. p. 275.

[2] *Ibid.* p. 300 s. Cf. *B.F.* v. 847, p. 464. (March 15, 1330.)

[3] *A.F.H.* xx. pp. 280-85. Cf. vi. and vii.

[4] *Ibid.* pp. 280-82.   [5] *Ibid.* p. 301.

[6] *Ibid.* pp. 300-303. Cf. *B.F.* v. 942, p. 511. (November 2, 1331.) By this bull, John XXII. gives the Bishop of Florence and the Inquisitor, Peter of Prato, the power of absolving Francesco as penitent.

[7] *A.L.K.G.* i. 158-64.   [8] Cf. *supra*, p. 66.

[9] In 1330. *Hist. Litt.* xxxiv. p. 480, *n.* 3. He wrote his famous book, *De Planctu Ecclesie*, between 1330 and 1332, at the request of the Pope (*ibid.*).

[10] Letter of Pope to rector of Duchy of Spoleto, March 23, 1329 (*B.F.* v. 778, p. 378).

[11] *B.F.* v. 779, p. 378.

[12] *Ibid.* 985, p. 529. He was translated to Silves in 1333 (*ibid.* 1023, p. 549).

[13] L. II., Articuli LV. and LVI.

successor.[1]   In fact his outlook was that of all the better elements in the Order, with certain affinities towards the Spirituals.[2]   There is nothing in his after-career which would lead to the supposition that his conversion had been dictated merely by motives of self-interest.   The Pope and his vicars in Italy were wise enough to make the path of submission very easy.   All that was required was a public confession of guilt and an acknowledgment of John as the true Vicar of Christ, with the result that it was soon necessary to grant to the Superiors of the Order the power of absolving the penitent.[3]   Even in Germany Michael was probably not obeyed outside the dominions of Louis of Bavaria, although the Franciscan chronicler, John of Winterthur, writes warmly in his favour.[4] Another partisan was Nicholas the Minorite, extracts from whose account have been edited by Baluze, and are perhaps our best source for the whole controversy.[5]   He may perhaps be identified with a certain Nicholas of Friesingen, an inmate of the convent at Munich, who was one of the witnesses who signed an appeal by Michael against " Quia vir reprobus " in 1330.[6]   His great value as an historian is due to his careful collection and transcription of the greater part of the original documents used in the controversy.

The seeds of revolt lingered longest at the court of Naples. Robert and his queen had been in close personal relations with Michael of Cesena, and for a long time the former refused to allow the papal bulls relating to the struggle to be published in his dominions.[7]   The two Franciscan chaplains [8] attached to the royal household made their influence felt in a similar direction, nor did

---

[1] L. II., Articulus LXVII.

[2] *De Planctu Ecclesie*, Articulus LXVII. f. 168 *r*.

[3] *B.F.* v. 877, p. 480 (1330). The Provincial of Germany was allowed to give licence to the custodians to absolve those who had formerly adhered to Michael. Cf. *ibid.* 967, p. 522. At the end of 1331, however, certain friars in the diocese of Prague were still preaching against the papal decretals (*ibid.* 955, p. 517). In 1337 the Minister-General and diffinitors were allowed to receive the submission of all the rebels with the exception of Michael of Cesena, Francis of Ascoli, Bonagratia, Occam, and all who had received offices from the antipope (*B.F.* vi. 62, p. 47).

[4] *Iohannis Vitodurani Chronica*, pp. 92-99. This chronicle was probably composed between 1340 and 1348 (*A.F.H.* xxii. 567).

[5] Cf. *supra*, p. 154.

[6] *Z.K.G.* vi. p. 87. Cf. *B.F.* v. p. 427. An Italian version of his chronicle was printed by Zambrini, *Scelta di curiosità litterarie*, li. pp. 61-117, from C. Magliabecchiana, xxxiv. *n.* 76. This must have been copied after 1377, since it carefully mentions that the Curia was at Avignon during the struggle.

[7] *B.F.* v. 916, p. 502. Letter to Robert of Naples. (July 8, 1331.)

[8] Andreas de Galiano and Petrus de Cadeneto. The former had been at one time the " socius " of Michael of Cesena (*B.F.* vi. p. 601) and was one of the provincials deposed by Bertrand de Tour (Otto, *op. cit.* p. 182). Cf. *supra*, p. 177.

the visit of the new General to the kingdom in the autumn of 1331 bring about any change of policy.[1] Early in 1332 John XXII. wrote to Guiral Ot telling him that he had interceded for him with the king, and ordering him to do all in his power to fulfil the wishes of Robert and his consort.[2] The General's stay in Naples did little to increase his popularity with the friars of the province, where his usual nickname was " the malignant dragon ".[3] He apparently held an inquiry into the correspondence still carried on between his predecessor and Andreas de Galiano and his fellow-chaplain, Petrus de Cadeneto.[4] The matter was so serious that he brought it to the notice of the Pope, who cited the two friars to Avignon.[5] The queen, however, intervened in their favour, and John, who was anxious to propitiate her husband, finally allowed the Archbishops of Naples and Benevento and the Abbot of Sta Sophia to decide the case.[6] The two friars were absolved from the sentences of excommunication which they had incurred through contumacy, promising for their part to refrain in future from preaching against the papal decretals and from helping Michael and his adherents.[7] After John's death, however, his successor, Benedict XII., again took up the case. Petrus de Cadeneto was now dead, but Andreas was cited to Avignon,[8] where a long and careful inquiry was held in order to establish the charges brought against him, many of the leading persons at the Neapolitan Court bearing witness in his favour.[9] The evidence on both sides is very contradictory, but it was never denied that the chaplain had formerly been an adherent of the ex-Minister-General, and had carried on a correspondence with him since his exile in Munich.[10] It is also quite probable that he had read and distributed many of his pamphlets,[11] and that Michael had sounded him as to whether he could find shelter in the kingdom of Naples in the event of a reconciliation

[1] Letter of John XXII. to Robert of Naples, August 1331 (Otto, *op. cit.* p. 183 ; and p. 244, § xxii.).
[2] March 13, 1332. *Ibid.* p. 249, § xxvi.
[3] Letters of Matthew of Piedmont, guardian of Manfredonia to Andreas de Galiano and the lector at Sta Chiara at Naples (*ibid.* p. 263 *s.* xxxvi. and xxxvii.).   [4] In October 1331 (*ibid.* p. 183).
[5] Letter of John XXII. to Guiral Ot, November 13, 1331 (*B.F.* v. 945, p. 513. Cf. *B.F.* v. 1001, p. 537).
[6] *Ibid.* 1016 and 1017, pp. 544-47. (April 18 and 19, 1333.)
[7] *Ibid.*   [8] *B.F.* vi. 27, p. 17. (June 12, 1336.)
[9] The whole inquiry is printed in *B.F.* vi. Appendix I. pp. 597-627. Among the witnesses were the Countess of San Severeno, and Roger, Count of Mileto. Cf. *supra*, p. 66, *n.* 7. Andreas was not formally acquitted till May 1338.
[10] *B.F.* vi. p. 601.
[11] *Ibid.* Articles XLIV.-XLVII. Cf. also p. 610. He also was accused of reading a certain commentary written by Olivi, probably his Postilla in Apocalypsim, and of making its contents known to many other friars (Articles XXI.-XL.).

taking place between Louis of Bavaria and the new pope. Andreas confessed freely that he desired to use the influence of King Robert as a means for facilitating his old leader's return to the Church.[1]   His visit to Philip of Majorca on the eve of the latter's famous sermon against John XXII. was also well attested,[2] but in the end he was acquitted, by purging himself canonically of the charges brought against him.   It is doubtful, however, if he would have escaped so lightly but for the protection afforded to him by his royal master.   When the queen, upon the death of her husband, was received into the Order of St. Clare, she took with her a collection of the documents relating to the controversy, and on her death-bed confided these to the charge of the nuns. Clement VI., in 1346, ordered the Bishop of Monte Cassino to remove these dangerous writings with as much secrecy as possible and to send them straight to Avignon.[3]

Perhaps the most interesting manifestation of the feeling of the Franciscans towards their former General occurred at Tabriz in Persia during the years 1332 and 1333.[4]   Even after the fall of Acre the colonies of Italian merchants still maintained their position in the East and the missionaries belonging to the two great mendicant Orders continued their heroic labours, penetrating even as far as India[5] and China,[6] and ministering to the needs of the Christian traders who had settled in certain of the more important towns.   Unfortunately, even on the mission field their old rivalry persisted, nor did the action of John XXII. in organising Persia and the adjacent territories into a separate province under the control of a Dominican archbishop, with suffragans chosen from the same Order,[7] tend to establish a more friendly spirit between them.   The result was that when tidings of the great controversy concerning evangelical poverty reached the East, the Friars Minors of Tabriz, then a town of

---

[1] Answer of Andreas to Article VIII. p. 600.

[2] Article XVI.   B.F. vi. p. 598.   Cf. supra, p. 65.

[3] B.F. vi. 384, p. 187.   (August 9, 1346.)

[4] The documents concerning the question of evangelical poverty in the East were discovered in the Vatican Archives (Regest Aven 54 Benedicti XII.) by a Barnabite, Father Giuseppe Boffito, and have been edited by Golubovich (op. cit. iii. p. 436 s.) and by Tocco in S.F. i. pp. 311-38.

[5] Thomas of Tolentino, Angelo da Clareno's fellow-sufferer in his imprisonment and afterwards his companion in Armenia, was martyred at Tana (Asow) in India in 1321 (A.L.K.G. ii. 303, and supra, p. 52).

[6] In 1307.   Clement V. created the metropolitan province of Cambaliensem (Pekin), appointing the Franciscan Giovanni da Montecorvino as its first archbishop, with suffragans belonging to the same Order (B.F. v. 85, p. 37).

[7] Sultanieh.   As Persia had before formed part of the province of Pekin, this arrangement caused great annoyance to the Friars Minor, who had looked upon it as their special preserve.   Cf. B.F. v. 318 a, p. 148 (1318).

some importance, the seat of one of the lately constituted bishoprics and of a flourishing Italian colony, made it the excuse for openly flouting the commands of their bishop,[1] declaring him to be nominee of a heretic, and refusing to celebrate Mass at an altar which he had consecrated.[2] He in his turn retaliated by holding a secret inquiry into their orthodoxy, the results of which were communicated to the Curia in the spring of 1334 by his assistant, Fra Raniero da Vercelli, who delivered his testimony and that of his superior to a commission of two cardinals, both belonging to the Franciscan Order.[3] It is probable that much of the evidence brought was greatly exaggerated, for the wildest rumours seem to have been flying round the little European community. Yet if even a portion of it were true the Dominicans were perhaps justified in their assertion that they were acting from the purest and most disinterested motives, their sole desire being to put an end to further scandal in the Church in the East.[4] The fact, however, that the sowers of error and discord were members of the rival Order possibly increased their zeal for a full and complete revelation of the state of things existing in Tabriz.

The incidents described are certainly racy, and their equivalents are sometimes found in the modern press. A certain friar, George of Adria, preaching in the Franciscan Church on the subject of the coming of Antichrist, made a covert reference to John XXII. by naming a certain beast and declaring that his hearers would know to whom he alluded.[5] A member of the congregation rebuked him, and bade him speak of other matters,[6] whereupon the preacher replied defiantly, " I declare to you the words of Holy Scripture and of the saints ; he who wishes to hear, let him hear, and he who does not, let him leave the church ".[7] The celebrant, Fra Fredo of Gubbio, now entered the fray, asking the assembly if they refused to believe the plain meaning of Holy Writ as interpreted by his colleague.[8] When Mass was

---

[1] Guglielmo de Cigiis, appointed in 1329 (Golubovich, *op. cit.* 444).

[2] *Ibid.*

[3] "Anno domini Millesimo Trecentesimo XXXIII. die XX. mensis Marcii. Hoc est testimonium quod ego Raynerius de Vercellis, requisitus sub iuramento per Reverendos patres et dominos, dominum Raymundum Sancti Eusebii, dominum Petrum Sancti Stephani in Celio monte, presbiteros Cardinales " (*ibid.* p. 442).

[4] " Timeo eciam valde, quod nisi de proximo salubre remedium apponatur scisma periculosissimum in illis partibus nutrietur " (*ibid.* p. 445).

[5] *Ibid.* p. 442.

[6] " Melius esset loqui de alia materia " (*ibid.*).

[7] " Ego predico vobis dicta sacre scripture et sanctorum, qui vult ea audire audiat, qui non, vadat extra ecclesiam " (*ibid.*).

[8] " Ipse predicat vobis de divina scriptura, numquid vultis credere sacre scripture ? " (*ibid.*).

ended certain of the merchants who had been present visited the Franciscan convent and reproved Friar George.[1]   Five of them even went so far as no longer to attend the church of the Friars Minor, and in order to make their protest more effective remained on the terrace outside while Mass was being celebrated within.[2] It is easy to realise what a stir these proceedings must have caused in the little European community, and the secret inquiry must have added greatly to the excitement, justifying the circulation of the wildest reports under the cloak of zeal for the faith.   Nor were the Franciscans guarded in their utterances.   A certain Fra Ubertino of Gubbio confessed frankly to Raniero da Vercelli, not only that John XXII. was a heretic and tolerated by the cardinals only through fear, but that Thomas Aquinas was wrongly canonized, for by his teaching on the question of poverty he had been guilty of the same crime as the Pope, and God would never permit any miracle to be worked through his intercession.[3]   On being asked by the Dominican, with whom he was apparently on friendly terms,[4] to whom he supposed the coat woven without a seam belonged, if Christ had only the use of it, the simple friar replied, " To Him to whom the air belongs ".[5]   George of Adria went even further in the expression of similar views, for when rumours of the Pope's pronouncements on the Beatific Vision reached Tabriz he replied to a certain merchant who doubted their authenticity that John XXII. had made an even more fatal declaration on the subject of the poverty of Christ, for he had controverted the teaching of all his predecessors from the time of St. Clement onwards,[6] and therefore could be regarded no longer as the lawful Pope.[7]   Rather than retract this opinion he was prepared to be burnt,[8] since for anyone to admit that Christ had possessed anything of His own was the same as declaring that the Scriptures were false and God was not God.[9]   " Frater Fredo " even went so far as to maintain in a public sermon preached before the bishop that St. John the Baptist and Christ had been Friars Minor in all except the habit.[10]

---

[1] " Dure reprehenderunt dictum fratrem de illa predicatione " (Golubovich, *op. cit.* p. 442).   [2] *Ibid.*   [3] *Ibid.* p. 444.
[4] " In presentia mea familiariter dicendo " (*ibid.*).
[5] " Cuius est aer " (*ibid.*).   [6] *Ibid.*
[7] " Ex quibus concludebat quod dominus papa ceciderat a potestate sua et erat hereticus " (*ibid.*).   [8] *Ibid.* p. 445.
[9] " Quicunque dicit quod Christus habuerit dominium rerum quibus utebatur, falsat scripturam sacram, et dicit quod Deus non est Deus " (*ibid.* p. 446).
[10] *Ibid.* p. 444.   The witness adds that he was not sure if " Frater Fredo " was referring to property held in severalty or in common, as typified in the case of Christ and St. John the Baptist.

An active correspondence was carried on between the Minorites of Tabriz and certain members of their Order who were attached
to the household of the Armenian Archbishop of Maku to instruct
him and his followers in the Catholic faith. These men, who had
been sent out by the new Minister-General, Guiral Ot, were not,
like their brethren in Persia, supporters of Michael of Cesena.[1]
Their leader, Guillaume Saurati of Aquitaine, was a diligent
student of the writings of Olivi, and made great use of his commentary on the Apocalypse in his lectures to the Armenian
monks.[2] His correspondents, to whom the works of the great
Spiritual were forbidden fare, pestered him with questions about
the expected coming of Antichrist.[3] To the Franciscans in the
East it was of vital importance to know in what region he would
appear, and if when he came he would be a pagan or a Christian,
a pope or a temporal ruler.[4] One of them even went so far as
to inquire whether he might not have already appeared in the
person of Louis of Bavaria, in which case the antipope could
perhaps be regarded as the dragon.[5] The writer concludes with
reflections on the uselessness of converting the heathen, since
they would certainly fall away in the evil days which were approaching.[6] Sometimes also details of European news were
given, and there is a long letter from George of Adria, who apparently hoped that Friar William, from his study of the writings
of Olivi, would be able to throw some light on the present un-
precedented state of affairs in the Franciscan Order. In spite of
his respect for the opinion of the Aquitanian friar, he found it
difficult to accept his statement that the deposition of Michael
of Cesena was valid since it had been brought about with the
consent of the universal Church,[7] for although perplexed and
somewhat bewildered, he still felt that John XXII. was a heretic
and that the Minister-General had stood firmly for the truth.[8]
In the light of modern Catholic dogma it is interesting to learn
from another letter that an Armenian monk named Vertebet,
who had openly proclaimed the doctrine of papal infallibility,

---

[1] The three missionaries sent to the archbishop in 1332 were Guillaume
Saurati, Lorenzo da Bobbio, and Raniero da Firenze (Golubovich, *op. cit.* 407,
439, and 447). It was probably as the result of their correspondence with
their brethren in Persia that they came to be suspected of heresy.

[2] *Ibid.* pp. 447 and 449.

[3] Cf. letters addressed to Guillaume Saurati in 1333 by George of Adria
and others (*ibid.* pp. 447 and 449-50).

[4] *Ibid.* p. 450.   [5] *Ibid.*

[6] " Item si Antichristus istis temporibus obtenturus est orbem, quid est
quod gentes nunc convertantur ? Iterum in brevi erroribus involvendi " (*ibid.*).

[7] *Ibid.* p. 447.

[8] " Frater Michael a magno tempore steterit pro veritate contra illum
pessimum draconem (presumably John XXII.) et eius sequaces " (*ibid.*).

was forced publicly to retract his opinion in the presence of the archbishop.[1]

It is sad that no record of the fate of the friars of Tabriz has survived, with the possible exception of a story told in the *Chronicle of the Twenty-four Generals* of twelve friars in Persian Armenia who were expelled from their convent on account of their zeal for the observance of the Rule.[2]   This is immediately preceded by a very laudatory account of Fra Guillaume Saurati, from whom as a compatriot the author may have obtained his information,[3] and the number of the accused friars in the evidence furnished by the Bishop of Tabriz was eleven.   Yet the details given by the chronicler are too vague to be applied with any certainty to George of Adria and his companions.[4]   We cannot even speculate as to whether the powerful and comparatively numerous settlements of Fraticelli, whose presence in Greece in the fifteenth century is attested both by a bull of Nicholas V. and by the records of the Italian Inquisition,[5] owe their origin to them or to some more Western source.

From Munich Michael and his followers carried on an active campaign of propaganda.   The former was not slow in discovering no less than twelve errors in " Quia vir reprobus ", and communicated the result of his researches to the Chapter-General of Perpignan, together with a protest against the validity of the election of his successor,[6] with the result that he was involved in an acrimonious correspondence with Guiral Ot.[7]   The most telling weapon employed by both writers was personal abuse, the latter accusing the former of presumption in likening himself to Paul the humble,[8] a more apt comparison being that afforded by their common predecessor, Elias.[9]   It was not John XXII. who resembled the heretical pope, Anastasius, but Michael, who frequented the society of Marsiglio of Padua and John of Jandun.[10] Although his opponent declared that his former letter had been dictated both by fraternal charity and a desire for peace, little trace

---

[1] Letter from Lorenzo da Bobbio to Raniero da Firenze (Golubovich, *op. cit.* p. 448).

[2] *A.F.* iii. p. 507.   [3] *Ibid.* 506.

[4] The whole question is discussed by Golubovich, *op. cit.* iii. p. 451.

[5] Cf. *A.F.H.* vi. pp. 429-30 ; *A.L.K.G.* iv. p. 113.   Cf. *infra*, p. 143.

[6] *B.F.* v. pp. 497-500. (Munich, March 25, 1331.) Cf. also protest of January 24, 1331 (*ibid.* pp. 427-38, and *Misc.* iii. 356-58). Extracts from the manifesto of March 26, which was directed to all the faithful, are given in *B.F.* v. pp. 426-27.

[7] Printed in *A.F.H.* ix. 134-83.   [8] *Ibid.* p. 140.

[9] " Nonne cogitas, fili incredulitatis, exemplum quod frater Elias meus et tuus in officio, sed tuus in scismatico scandalo praedecessor, apostata fuit schismaticus et hereticus ? " (*A.F.H.* ix. p. 142).

[10] *Ibid.* p. 144.

of these lingers in his reply,[1] and each section ends with the triumphant refrain, " Therefore thy ways and not mine are manifestly
heretical ".[2] He had not compared himself to Paul, but had
followed his example in reproving John XXII., whereas his adversary was likening himself to God by beginning his letter with
the text " Quid niteris ".[3] Finally, he took exception to a quotation from Aristotle used by Guiral, for such a recourse to a pagan
writer was a further proof of his departure from the true faith, and
of his attempts to seduce others from its teaching.[4] In spite of the
small measure of success which attended his efforts, Michael persisted in his endeavours to point out to his Order the errors of the
Pope, besides issuing a more general manifesto to the Emperor
and other secular princes.[5] In this he declared that the spiritual
power was at present eclipsed, so that the only hope of the Church
lay with the secular authority.[6] He finally appealed to the judgment of a General Council of the Church, since it alone was superior
to the Pope.[7] He was ably seconded by Francis of Ascoli and
Bonagratia of Bergamo, who also wrote pamphlets in support of
the imperial policy as well as more definitely theological treatises
directed generally to the Chapters-General of the Franciscan
Order.[8] It is noteworthy that all the arguments against " Quia
vir reprobus " found in the later treatises of the Fraticelli[9] are
merely developments of the original list of its many errors drawn
up by Michael.

[1] " Quam pacifice et caritative, zelo fidei et boni communis evangelica lege
servata tibi scripserim " (*A.F.H.* ix. p. 153).
[2] *Ibid.*
[3] *Ibid.* p. 163. " Quid niteris bonam ostendere viam tuam " (*Jer.* ii. 33).
[4] *Ibid.* p. 183.
[5] Goldast, *Monarchia*, ii. (Frankfurt, 1614) 1344–1360. Probably directed
either to the Diet of Nuremberg (1330) or Frankfurt (1333). The latter is
the more likely, as in the manifesto he mentions a sermon of John XXII.
beginning " Gaudete in domino semper ", preached on the 14th December
1331.   [6] P. 1355.
[7] P. 1360.
[8] A pamphlet composed by the former against " Quia vir reprobus " is
contained in C. Laur. S. Crucis Plut. 31 Sin Cod. 3, f. 23-85. It has the incipit
" De patre impio queruntur filii ", and in it John XXII. is described as
" a perverse and insane heretic, fulminating with mad rage against the apostles
and a perverter and subverter of divine and human law ". Cf. *A.F.H.* xi.
254-55, and *B.F.* v. p. 438. Can this treatise be an answer to that of Jean
d'Anneux ? Cf. *supra*, p. 170 s.
[9] Cf. the famous and often-printed treatise formerly ascribed by Baluze
to Michael (*Misc.* iii. 341-55), and by Brown, who printed it in *Fasciculus
Rerum Expetendarum*, ii. 436-65; and by later scholars, with the notable
exception of Müller (*Z.K.G.* vi. p. 82), to Occam. It has now been proved by
internal evidence to have been written in Italy not earlier than the second half
of the fourteenth century, but before 1378. Cf. Father Oliger's " De Dialogo
contra Fraticellos S. Jacobi de Marchia " (*A.F.H.* iv. 19-23). *Infra*, p. 231, *n.* 1.

The chief answer of the Michaelists to the papal decretal was, however, Occam's famous " Opus Nonaginta Dierum ", afterwards incorporated in his famous *Dialogus*.[1] This was probably composed between 1331 and 1333, for it contains a reference to the heresy of John XXII. regarding the Beatific Vision, but makes no allusion to the errors found in certain of his sermons preached about the same time.[2] It owes its title to the number of days Occam is supposed to have spent over the labours of writing. Certainly he must have studied " Quia vir reprobus " with great meticulousness, since there is not a sentence which he does not controvert, and he even points out minute errors in grammar and in the quotations from the Scriptures.[3] In spite of its great length the work is interesting reading, and possesses a liveliness and vigour lacking in the writings of Michael of Cesena, for Occam was gifted with the mental agility of the modern journalist. Some of his arguments are ingenious rather than profound, but traces of his later political speculations are apparent, especially when he discusses the vexed question of the temporal power of the Pope. In spiritual matters the Emperor and all other princes were subject to his authority, but any influence which he possessed in secular concerns was conferred upon him by the faithful and revocable at their pleasure.[4] The lands of the Church had been bestowed by one emperor, and his successors could therefore resume his gift.[5] In fact, these and all her other possessions belonged to the whole Christian commonwealth, which embraced both clergy and laity.[6] Bishops would be well advised to follow the example of the Apostles and hand over the temporalities of their sees to lay administrators, who would hold them in trust for the poor while they devoted themselves to the spiritual functions of their office.[7] Like all orthodox Franciscans, Occam believed that Christ had owned nothing, not even His clothes.[8] The strait gate in the parable

---

[1] *Monarchia*, ii. 993 - 1236. The Opus was probably intended to be included in the third part of the *Dialogus* under the title of " De Gestis fratris Michaelis de Cesena ". Cf. *ibid*. p. 771, and Little, *Grey Friars in Oxford*, p. 229. From an examination of the existing manuscripts, however, scholars have come to the conclusion that Occam never completed his great work (*ibid*. p. 231, and Scholz, *Unbekannte Kirchenpolitische Streitschriften aus der Zeit Ludwigs des Bayern*, i. p. 148).

[2] *Monarchia*, ii. p. 1233.

[3] " Qui aedificat domum suum sed textus est aedificavit " (*ibid*. p. 1206).

[4] *Ibid*. p. 1158.

[5] *Ibid*. p. 1162.   [6] *Ibid*. p. 1128.

[7] *Ibid*. pp. 1128-29. It would be interesting in connection with this idea to know if Occam had studied the writings of Olivi. Cf. *supra*, p. 98.

[8] *Monarchia*, ii. pp. 1167 and 1169. Like St. Bonaventura he believed that the latchet of Christ's shoe might be understood mystically. Cf. " Apologia Pauperum ", *Opera Omnia*, viii. p. 306.

symbolised the renunciation of all worldly things,[1] while he solved
the problem of the ownership of the goods used by the early Christians by declaring that, like the vessels employed in the temple
services, they belonged to God alone.[2] He attacked John XXII.
violently for his reluctance to submit to the verdict of a General
Council,[3] but did not dwell much on the part to be played by
such an assembly. His " Compendium Errorum Iohannis Papae "[4]
is concerned with much the same questions, but lays more stress
on the errors found in the Pope's sermons. In fact, the somewhat
rash pronouncements of John XXII. during the last years of his
life, and especially the scandal occasioned by his speculations on the
Beatific Vision,[5] gave a fresh impetus to the attacks of the exiles
at Munich, whose former arguments had now become somewhat
stale. Their hopes for a change in their own fortunes [6] and for
the success of the Bavarian party were likewise greatly raised, for
certain of the cardinals had grown impatient with the Pope's in-
creasing obstinacy and were anxious to bring about his deposition.[7]
As can be seen from a letter sent by Michael of Cesena to the

[1] *Monarchia*, ii. p. 1150.   [2] *Ibid*. p. 1195.
[3] *Ibid*. p. 1233.   [4] *Ibid*. 957-77.
[5] The first sermon of John XXII. on the subject was that preached on All
Saints' Day, 1331. Occam's " De Dogmatibus Iohannis XXII." (*ibid*. 740-70)
is concerned almost entirely with the Beatific Vision and the kindred heresies
of the Pope. In his " Contra Iohannem XXII." (Scholz, *op. cit*. ii. pp. 396-403),
composed after the death of John XXII., he deals both with his errors concerning the Beatific Vision and those found in his four decretals on the subject of
evangelical poverty (pp. 399-402). His treatise has the significant beginning,
" Non invenit locum penitencie Iohannis XXII.", and in it he advances the
opinion that the Pope's death-bed recantation was a forgery (p. 399). Two
unedited pamphlets of Bonagratia of Bergamo, both entitled Appellatio contra
Iohannis XXII. errores de Visione beatifica, and composed at Munich, the
first in 1332 and the second in 1334, still exist in manuscript. Cf. *A.F.H.* xxii.
309-12.
[6] Since his return from Italy the Emperor had endeavoured to enter into
negotiations with the Pope, a fact which rendered the position of the fugitives
at Munich very insecure. At the end of 1331 Louis had gone so far as to offer
to do all in his power to bring about their submission, and, if his efforts were
unsuccessful, to withdraw his protection from them (Riezler, *op. cit*. p. 84).
According to Preger, however, the secret instructions given by Louis to his
ambassadors at Avignon, which are still preserved in the Munich archives, show
that the Emperor had very little intention of ever fulfilling the conditions to
which he declared he was prepared to agree, in the hope of continuing the
negotiations. His promise to deny further protection to the rebellious Minorites was couched in such terms as to afford many very excellent pretexts for its
non-performance. Such being his attitude, it is not surprising that during the
later discussions Benedict XIII. showed so little anxiety to reach a final agreement. Cf. " Der kirchenpolitische Kampf unter Ludwig dem Baier und sein
Einfluss auf die öffentliche Meinung ", in *Abhandlungen der Bayerische Akademie der Wissenschaft*, xiv. pp. 10-13.
[7] *Hist. Litt.* xxiv. p. 620.

imperial vicar at Mantua, Luigi di Gonzaga, upon the subject of the return of the emperor to Italy, the Franciscans were useful not only as pamphleteers but as negotiators and politicians.[1] A widespread conspiracy against the old Pope was now formed, the chief confederates being Cardinal Napoleone Orsini, the Archbishop of Trèves, and Michael. Their aim was to summon a General Council at Bologna, and the agent employed by them was a friar named Walter.[2] The death of the old Pope, however, defeated their schemes. This event greatly increased the dangers of the fugitives' already critical position, since their protector had resumed his negotiations with John's successor, Bendict XII., apparently with every hope of bringing them to a prosperous issue. His ambassadors at Avignon stated, probably with perfect truth, that their master as a soldier had never entered into the theoretic aspects of the question at issue between the Franciscan Order and John XXII., but believing the Minister-General and his followers to be learned and pious men, had made use of their services in his struggle with the papacy.[3] Luckily, the French influence at Avignon and the vacillating character of Louis, torn between the injured national pride of the German princes, who would brook no further humiliation at the hands of an alien Church, and his own strong desire for peace, prevented the negotiations from bearing any fruit. At the times when the emperor was forced to yield to the patriotic sentiments expressed by the Diets of Rense and Frankfurt, he made use of the pens of the Franciscans, and especially of Occam, for the defence of his claims.[4] Moreover, they still

---

[1] *A.F.H.* iv. 417. The date is April 25, 1330 or 1331. A list of the political pamphlets of Bonagratia is found in Father Oliger's introduction to his edition of the " Tractatus de Christi et Apostolorum paupertate " (*A.F.H.* xxii. 312-313). R. Scholz (*op. cit.* ii. pp. 392-466, 349-63) has printed a short continuation of the Dialogue and six hitherto unedited political and religious treatises of Occam, composed between 1335 and 1347. One of these, written between 1338 and 1340, the time of the alliance between Edward III. and Louis of Bavaria, is concerned with the question, " An Rex Anglie pro succursu guerrae possit recipere bona ecclesiarum " (*ibid.* pp. 432-53).

[2] Perhaps the notary, " Frater Gualterius filius Bontii de Arimino de Justipolim " (Capo d' Istria), who drew up and witnessed Michael of Cesena's protest against " Quia vir reprobus ", which was directed to all Christian kings and princes (*Monarchia*, ii. p. 1360 ; cf. Eubel, *H.J.* xviii. pp. 378 and 384). In the same article extracts are printed from a document giving the details of certain arrangements made between the conspirators. Cf. also Carlini, *Fra Michelino e la sua eresia*, pp. 182-83, and Riezler, *op. cit.* p. 84 s.

[3] *Ibid.* pp. 92-39. The Franciscans did all they could to prevent any reconciliation from taking place between Emperor and Pope, even going so far as to ask for a safe conduct to Avignon so that they could defend themselves in person (Carlini, *op. cit.* p. 188).

[4] Riezler, *op. cit.* p. 254. Scholz regards Occam's " Allegationes de Potestate Imperiali", which he has himself edited (*op. cit.* ii. pp. 417-31), as a defence

continued the struggle on their own behalf. Occam's letter to the Chapter-General of Assisi in 1334, defending his attitude with regard to John XXII. and attacking his numerous errors,[1] was followed by many others, perhaps the best known being that written by Michael of Cesena in 1338, in which he declared that Benedict XII. was an even greater heretic than his predecessor, for he had defended and had done his best to further the spread of his pestilential doctrines.[2] In the eyes of his adversaries at Munich, John's final recantation of his views concerning the Beatific Vision in no way diminished his guilt.[3] Death and defection, however, were thinning their ranks. In 1341 Francis of Ascoli fell into the hands of the Inquisition in Italy, confessed his errors, and was reconciled with the Church.[4] Later writers belonging to the orthodox party lay much stress on this conversion, and his confession became the general formula subscribed to by all the returning Michaelists.[5] Of the little band left in Munich, Bonagratia probably died in 1340, and the old Minister-General soon followed

---

of the Declaration of Frankfurt. For the part played by Bonagratia of Bergamo at the Diet, cf. John of Winterthur, *op. cit.* pp. 156 and 157. I do not discuss here any pamphlets not connected with the theological aspect of the struggle, that is, with the question of evangelical poverty, to which everything else was subsidiary.

[1] Baudry, " La Lettre de Guillaume d'Occam au Chapitre d'Assise " (*R.H.F.* iii. pp. 185-215 ; Brampton, *Gulielmi de Ockham Epistola ad Fratres Minores*). The former suggests that the letter was written as an answer to the Franciscan masters of theology who, before 1331, had besought Michael of Cesena to return to the unity of the Order and the Church. Cf. *B.F.* v. pp. 497-500.

[2] Carlini, *op. cit.* pp. 289-308. Cf. especially 300-305. At the end Michael solemnly appeals to a General Council (p. 306). He mentions a larger treatise composed by himself on the subject of the Beatific Vision, " et nominatim contra prefatum Benedictum tanquam manifestum hereticum " (p. 305). Occam also wrote a " Tractatus contra Benedictum XII." about a year earlier (cf. Scholz, *op. cit.* ii. 403-407). In this, besides his defence of the errors of his predecessor and his political crimes, his revision of the Statutes of the Franciscan Order (*B.F.* vi. 51, pp. 25-42) and his protection of Eckhard (cf. Michael of Cesena's " Appellatio Maior " from Pisa, p. 302 ; *supra*, p. 176) are also alleged as accusations against him. Occam also declares emphatically that in matters of faith the sole authority lay in the decision of a committee of theologians, and discusses exhaustively the measures to be taken against a pope who had fallen into heresy.

[3] " Reprobatio revocationis quam fecit dominus Iohannis in morte quodam non valuit." This pamphlet is described in *Z.K.G.* vi. 98-99. Cf. Occam's " Contra Iohannem XII.", where the death-bed repentance of the Pope is regarded as fictitious (Scholz, *op. cit.* ii. 399, and *supra*, p. 193, *n.* 5).

[4] A fragment of his examination before the Cardinal of San Sabina is found in *Misc.* ii. 281-83. The date given is February 6, 1341. He had been active both in France and Italy, so that his defection must have been a serious blow to his party. Cf. *B.F.* v. 765, p. 373 (February 6, 1329) and Guiral Ot's letter to Michael of Cesena, *A.F.H.* ix. p. 151.

[5] *B.F.* vi. 275, p. 149. (June 17, 1344.)

him to the grave.[1] During his last years he must have been rather a lonely figure, for proud, tenacious, and aloof, he probably viewed with growing disfavour the revolutionary speculations of Occam and Marsiglio of Padua, which were entirely foreign to his somewhat conventional theory of the relations between Church and State, nor is there any proof that his alliance with Bonagratia was founded on any real compatibility of temperament. The probable year of his death is 1342. On his death-bed he gave the seal of his Order to Occam, whom he appointed as his vicar.[2] There is very little foundation for Wadding's assertion that he died repentant,[3] and his so-called confession is certainly a seventeenth-century forgery.[4] Michael had always been a man of iron determination and of a rigid and somewhat narrow outlook, and his was essentially too strong and too unimaginative a nature to be deflected from the beliefs and convictions of a lifetime, even when he lay face to face with the unknown. After the death of his companions, Occam was left alone to justify by his political writings the well-known story of his first greeting to Louis of Bavaria : " Hail, Caesar! I will defend thee with my pen if thou wilt shield me with thy sword".[5] Every step taken by the Emperor, even in the matter of the irregular marriage of his son to the heiress of the Tyrol, Margaret Maulasch, found in him a warm and enthusiastic advocate.[6] Nor did he entirely neglect the old subjects of controversy, for the second part of his " De Imperatorum et Pontificum Potestate ", probably composed in 1347, after the coronation of Charles IV., is devoted to the errors of John XXII. on the subject of evangelical poverty. The arguments used are the same as in his earlier writings, but there is a lack of freshness and spontaneity about his whole treatment of the matter, just as if he were wearied with going over an old and familiar theme. This is in striking contrast to the first

---

[1] Michael of Cesena, Bonagratia, and Occam were buried in the Franciscan church at Munich, but their graves have been destroyed. Copies of the inscriptions on these, however, are still preserved, and give the year 1347 as the date of the death of all three of them. This is completely incorrect, as Occam was certainly alive in 1349, while in Louis of Bavaria's act of submission, drawn up in 1343, Bonagratia is described as " quondam ". Most modern scholars, relying mainly on the fifteenth-century necrology still kept at the Convent of the Friars Minor at Munich, and on certain marginal notes found in a South German manuscript of the same date, accept the years 1340 and 1342 as the dates of the deaths of Bonagratia and Michael of Cesena. Cf. *A.F.H.* xxii. 302-303. John of Winterthur (*op. cit.* p. 192) also gives 1342 as the year of the death of the Minister-General.

[2] Wadding, vii. *Annales*, 1344, p. 313, § vii. Cf. Preger, *op. cit.* p. 36, *n.* 1.

[3] *Annales*, vii. 1344, p. 313, § vii. It amounts to little more than a pious hope.

[4] In Muratori, *Rerum Italicarum Scriptores*, iii. pt. ii. 513-27. The question of its authenticity is dealt with more fully in the last chapter. Cf. *infra*, p. 267.

[5] Trithemius, *Liber de Scriptoribus Ecclesiasticis*, f. 82 ; Riezler, *op. cit.* p. 71.

[6] *Ibid.*

section of the pamphlet, where he displays all his usual animation and subtlety in dealing with the question of the limits to the papal authority.[1] In his last days he also seems to have sought reconciliation with the Church, for in June 1349, a bull of Clement VI. gave licence to the Minister-General to absolve certain Michaelists, and especially William of England, since he had returned to him the ancient seal of the Order which he had retained for so long.[2] If the date on Occam's tomb at Munich is correct he had already been dead two months.[3] The Black Death was raging in the city, and he was perhaps one of its many victims. Since no reference to his submission to the Church is found in any contemporary writers he probably died unabsolved.[4]

The deaths of the principal actors in the struggle did not, however, put an end to the controversy, for it was carried on with much more vigour than intelligence by the Michaelists in Italy, or, as they had now come to be called, the " Fraticelli di opinione ". They were generally men of little education, and merely made use of the old weapons to defend their position, their best arguments being in many cases the blamelessness of their lives and their fierce devotion to the cause of evangelical poverty. On the literary side at least the papal party had the advantage. Alvaro Paez was perhaps the first writer to attempt to reconcile the decretals of John XXII. with " Exiit qui seminat ",[5] and this policy was pursued by the Florentine inquisitor, Andreas Ricchi, who wrote in the year 1381, during a recrudescence of opinion in favour of the Michaelists.[6] The author had an unrivalled knowledge of his

---

[1] The first part of the " De Imperatorum et pontificum Potestate " was published by Scholz (op. cit. ii. 453-80). The portion of the treatise dealing with the errors of John XXII. is edited in A.F.H. xvi. 469-92, and xvii. 72-97, by the Jesuit Father Mulder, who discovered the complete version in a manuscript belonging to the Atheneum Library at Deventer when engaged in examining the incunables possessed by the same institution.

[2] B.F. vi. 508 A, p. 230. (June 8, 1349.)

[3] April 10. This date is taken from the inscription upon Occam's tomb. It is possible that the day and month given may be correct, though the year is certainly wrong. Cf. A.F.H. vi. p. 662, n. 2, and supra, p. 196.

[4] The whole question is discussed by Hofer (A.F.H. vi. 661 s.). The papal writers who laid so much stress on the submission of Francis of Ascoli all seem to assume that Occam died unrepentant. Cf. Andreas Ricchi, A.F.H. iii. 277 s. ; 524 ; and Jacopo da Marchia, " Dialogus contra Fraticellos ", Misc. ii. 600.

[5] De Planctu Ecclesie, L. II. Art. LIX. For the question of the authorship of this chapter, cf. supra, p. 156.

[6] Edited by Father Oliger in " Documenta inedita ad historiam Fraticellorum spectantia " (A.F.H. iii. pp. 267-79 ; 505-29 ; 680-99). This treatise, together with the other documents on the same subject, which were originally printed in the A.F.H. iii.-vi., have now been published as a separate book. For the question of the date, cf. A.F.H. iii. 260, where an extract from the pamphlet is compared with the new laws against heresy promulgated by the Commune of Florence in 1381.

subject, for in his youth he had been a disciple of the Franciscan lecturer at Oxford, Ludovico de Castilione of Arezzo, who had given him an autograph copy of a discourse delivered at the university in favour of John XXII.[1] The date of this lecture must have been after the reconciliation of Francis of Ascolì with the Church, for in it Ludovico declared that he had been present at the Consistory, where he had confessed his errors.[2] Ricchi himself had been at Montpellier at the time of the death of the Antipope,[3] and in middle life had gained much experience of the errors of the Michaelists as Inquisitor in Tuscany.[4] He seems, moreover, to have written several pamphlets against them, and now as an old man girded himself again for the fray,[5] at the request of Giacomo di Tolomei, Bishop of Narni and papal commissioner against heretics in Tuscany and in other provinces.[6] The end of the treatise is missing, and it breaks off abruptly at a point where the author seems about to give an account of the later stages of the controversy, a subject upon which his evidence would be of paramount value.[7] Its whole tone is moderate and persuasive, and Ricchi obviously aimed at convincing his opponents rather by the weight of his arguments than by the fury of his denunciations. In his opinion the Church was infallible, even though an individual Pope might err, therefore the fact that the decretals of John XXII. had been accepted by his successors and the whole body of the faithful was a striking proof of their orthodoxy.[8] The popularity of his work is shown by the use made of it by St. James of the March in his dialogue against the Fraticelli,[9] and the translation of certain parts of it into the vulgar tongue.[10]

The most remarkable book produced by the controversy was possibly the *De Pauperie Salvatoris* of Richard Fitz-Ralf, Arch-

[1] " In singulari adduco venerabilem magistrum meum Magistrum Ludovicum de Castilione aretino, qui regens Oxonie, ibidem hanc questionem determinavit concordiam astruens cum magna laude et totius universitatis illius complacentia, quam determinationem de propria manu illius scriptam habeo " (p. 277). Extracts perhaps from this lecture are found in the *Nitela Franciscanae Religionis* of Wadding's friend, Hicquey, printed at Lyons in 1627. Ludovico shows warm admiration for the many virtues of Michael of Cesena, and bitterly deplores his errors, declaring that even after his separation from the Church he had lived the life rather of an angel than of a man. Cf. *ibid*. ii. 637. Quoted by Carlini, *op. cit.* p. xxvi. Cf. *infra*, p. 208.   [2] *A.F.H.* iii. pp. 277-78.
[3] *Ibid.*   [4] He was inquisitor from 1370 to 1373 (*ibid.* p. 261).
[5] " Veteranus igitur miles veterana nunc bella resumo, et contra iam turpiter victos noviter dimico, non dubitans iterum turpius devincendos " (*ibid.* 267).
[6] *Ibid.*   [7] *Ibid.* p. 699.
[8] *Ibid.* iii. pp. 519-22.   [9] Cf. *infra*, p. 241.
[10] Extracts in Italian, probably taken from the beginning and end of the treatise, are to be found in Codex Magliabecchiana, xxxi. 65, f. 2 r.-6 v., and have been printed in *S.F.* 496-99, and in *Memorie della Reale Accademia dei Lincei.* Cf. *infra*, p. 236.

bishop of Armagh, which was composed between 1350 and 1356 at the request of Clement VI.[1] The author first discusses the divine origin of property, for according to him " dominion " over the earth and its fruits had been given to Adam as the representative of the human race, and this had been restored to him after the Fall, since he had repented of his sin.[2] Fitz-Ralf's conception of ownership, however, did not really differ greatly from that of the " usus facti ", so popular among the Franciscans, for man held his property only through the sufferance of his Creator.[3] Individual property was not the result of sin, for if the human race had persisted in the state of innocence every one would have had the right of appropriating such of the fruits of earth as he required for his own sustenance, as long as what remained over sufficed for the needs of his fellows.[4] Fundamentally, perhaps, the Franciscans and their opponent had in their minds much the same picture of the morning of the world when all things existed under the sway of natural law, but they described it in different terms. Fitz-Ralf, after investigating the origin of property, goes on to discuss the position of Christ, who, as the descendant of Adam, possessed a natural right to that dominion over all created things which was the heritage of every member of the human race, and which he could not abdicate without exposing himself to the danger of death through starvation.[5] This, too, in different words, was also a commonplace of Franciscan thinkers, who had always held that no man could surrender the right of making use of the fruits of the world to satisfy his immediate needs, though they were opposed to any selfish appropriation of these which would deprive others of a similar power.[6] In the last book he reconciles, perhaps with some

[1] The first four books are edited by Dr. R. L. Poole as an appendix to Wyclif's *De Dominio Divino*, publications of the Wyclif Society, London, 1890, pp. 257-476. For circumstances under which the book was written, cf. Prologue, p. 273.

[2] "Videtur ita posse describi, quod Ade dominium fuit racionalis creature mortale ius sive auctoritas originalis possidendi naturaliter res sibi subiectas conformiter racioni " (*De Pauperie Salvatoris*, ii. cap. 2, p. 336. Cf. cap. xiii. p. 355 ; and cap. xvii. p. 358).

[3] " Sic quod humanum dominium nequaquam verum aut vere dominium dici potest ; set quilibet dominus temporalis istarum rerum comparatus Deo et eius dominio usuarius et magis proprie commoditarius. . . ." (L. II. cap. i. p. 335).

[4] L. III. cap. xiii. p. 400 ; cap. xiv. p. 403. Fitx Ralf interprets the often quoted *Dilectissimis* (Corpus Iuris Canonici, cap. 12, q. 12) to mean that private property existed " de facto " under natural law but not " de iure ".

[5] *De Pauperie Salvatoris*, L. II. cap. x. pp. 350-52 ; *ibid*. xx. p. 362 ; xxiii. p. 367.

[6] Cf. " Exiit qui seminat ", B.F. iii. 404-16 ; and St. Bonaventura, " Apologia Pauperum ", *Opera Omnia*, viii. p. 309, for a summary of the Franciscan position.

ingenuity, the decretals of John XXII. with the famous determination of Nicholas III., the source of the whole controversy.[1] Whatever, however, may have been the fallacies lurking in Fitz-Ralf's arguments, his treatise will always rank as the only original contribution to medieval thought among the innumerable pamphlets written by both parties during the long and momentous struggle. It appears to have been widely read in England at least among the religious orders, who were delighted at being provided with such a weapon against their hated rivals. A contemporary encyclopaedia of medieval knowledge, compiled by a Cistercian monk called James,[2] is full of long extracts both from the " De Pauperie Salvatoris " and from Fitz-Ralf's sermons against the mendicants.[3] At least they are less scurrilous than the author's own reflections on the subject of the friars and their methods, which are found under a section significantly entitled " Adulatores ".[4] It would be interesting to know more of this obscure monk, who had obviously followed with palpitating eagerness every stage in the quarrel between the Archbishop and the Minorites. A last echo of the long controversy can perhaps be heard in Cardinal Bellarmine's contention that it was only in " Cum inter nonnullos " that John XXII. made a pronouncement on a matter of faith which affected the whole Church.[5]

Such was the story of the breach between the Franciscan Order and the Papacy. In spite of the magnitude of the issues involved it does not arouse the same enthusiasm and sympathy as the record of the sufferings of the Zealots. With the exception of Occam, the brilliant and daring thinker, who strove to conceal his profound scepticism under a cloak of rigid orthodoxy, the actors in the struggle were not men of remarkable personality, and win our respect rather than our affection. The headstrong and fiery old Pope, with his violent temper and dangerous but naïve delight in theological controversy, is a far more attractive and lovable figure than the stern and unfaltering disciplinarian in whose hands lay the destinies of the Franciscan Order. The real reason, however, for our indifference is perhaps that the

[1] *B.F.* iii. 404-16.

[2] British Museum, Roy. MSS. 6, E. VI. and E. VII. For author, cf. E. VI. f. 18 *v.*

[3] The subject matter under " Fratres ", E. VI. f. 154 *r.a*-162 *v.b*, is taken mostly from William of St. Amour's "De Periculis Novissimorum Temporum" and from Fitz-Ralf's sermons against the mendicants.

6 E. VII., f. 234 *r.*-236 *v.* and f. 390 *v.* are also extracts from Fitz-Ralf. Cf. also f. 526 *v.*-530 *r.a* (" Christus "). [4] MS. Roy. 6, E. VI., f. 50 *v.*

[5] *De Romanis Pontificibus*, L. IV. c. 14.

The Observantines, until reunited to the main body of the Franciscans in 1897, always lived under the regime set up by " Exiit qui seminat ". " Ad conditorem canonum " was practically annulled by the Constitution " Amabiles fructus " of 1428.

question which was the cause of the controversy had long ceased to have any practical bearing and had become purely theoretical. Michael and his companions were indeed sincerely convinced that Christ and His apostles had owned nothing, and that the only perfect life was to be found in a complete renunciation of all temporal wealth, but they lacked that joyous spirit of adventure which had led St. Francis to strip himself even of his very garments, and wander singing through the streets of Assisi, begging his bread from house to house. Certainly the Minister-General surrendered much for the sake of his convictions, crushing for ever his dreams of a great career in the Church,[1] and it cannot have been easy for a man grown old in obedience to oppose Christ's Vicar upon earth, yet somehow his sacrifice is destitute of the salt of poetry and romance which hallowed the utter self-immolation of the "poverello". Often perhaps it is those who do not rise to great heights, and yet follow in the main firmly and unflinchingly what they believe to be the truth, who meet with the hardest verdict at the hands of posterity, that of indifference or detraction. Wadding, who combined a loyal affection for his Church with a heartfelt admiration for all true service in the cause of a fine ideal, has, perhaps from his long study of the subject and his imaginative understanding of the minds of those concerned, the best right to deliver the final verdict. "They did not follow their own desires, nor were they driven by the evil lure of the world or the flesh, but by overmuch zeal for their Order and by an unreasoning love of that poverty which they had professed."[2] This devotion was not as intense or as all-pervading as that of the Spirituals, but none the less it was a very real factor in their lives.

[1] Many of Michael's predecessors had been elevated to the cardinalate after a successful period of office. Without any undue conceit he might have expected such a reward since he had brought the Order safely through a crisis in its history, especially as Vidal du Four and Berengar de Tour had been only provincials before being created cardinals. The doubtful testimony of the letter of the leaders of the Parte Guelfa at Perugia is our only evidence for believing that he ever plotted to become Antipope, and it is far more likely that he joined the Emperor's party only in desperation, and from no interested motives. A man of his experience and sagacity must have realised the futility of any attempt to set up a rival to John XXII. As for Occam and Bonagratia, they were probably too hopelessly disgraced to hope for any great promotion in the Church.

[2] "Non abierunt post suas concupiscentias, nec mundi aut carnis agitabantur illecebris, sed nimio zelo sui instituti et insipienti affectu paupertatis, quam profitebantur. Eam in sacris scripturis indicari, in Pontificiis decretis aperte doceri, et a sanctis patribus manifeste praedicari iudicarunt, in eo maxime errantes, quod suum iudicium praetulerint interpretioni et definitioni Pontificis, ad quem uti spectat Canones condere, ita et interpretari. Bonam rem haud bono modo aemulati sunt " (*Annales*, vii. p. 85, 1328, § xix.).

Part II: THE ATTITUDE OF THE ENGLISH FRANCISCANS TO JOHN XXII. DURING THE CONTROVERSY CONCERNING EVANGELICAL POVERTY

NO general statement can be made with regard to the attitude of the English Franciscans to John XXII. Their provincial, William of Nottingham, and his namesake, William of Alnwick, certainly played an important part in the opposition to the Pope during the early stages of the controversy.[1] They appear, however, to have had little share in its later developments, for the former was not among the Superiors deposed by Bertrand de Tour,[2] while the latter was elected Bishop of Giovanezzo in 1329, and the following year presented letters from John XXII. to Robert of Naples.[3] Moreover, it must be remembered that they were both living in the very centre of events, and therefore their reactions to the papal policy cannot be taken as typical of those of the majority of their compatriots. Nor, on the other hand, does Occam's confession of his former lack of interest in the matters at issue between the Pope and his Order furnish us with any evidence in a contrary direction, for, as we have seen, his mind was preoccupied with his impending trial, and it would have been folly for a man in his precarious position to take any part in the quarrel.[4] Thus, when trying to determine the feelings of the English Franciscans during this critical period, we are faced on one side with a cautious and self-interested indifference, and on the other with a determined and energetic opposition.

Fortunately, a small manuscript in Bishop Cosin's library at Durham [5] contains material which throws a valuable light on the attitude of the English province at least during the earlier stages of the controversy. It contains three treatises on evangelical poverty —the first written by the ex-provincial, Richard of Conyngton,[6]

---

[1] *Misc.* iii. p. 208 ; *B.F.* v. p. 234, and *n.* 520, p. 259. Cf. *supra*, pp. 155 and 165.

[2] *Supra*, p. 180.   [3] *B.F.* v. 1001, p. 537, *n.* 6.

[4] Letter to Chapter-General of Assisi (*R.H.F.* iii. 202. Cf. *supra*, p. 169, *n.* 1.).

[5] MS. V. iii. 18, described in the appendix to *Catalogi Veteres Librorum Ecclesiae Cathedralis Dunelm.* p. 170, the account probably being taken from a catalogue made about 1727 by the Rev. Thomas Rud, librarian of the Cathedral Library at Durham (*ibid.* Preface, p. xix.). It came into the library through the gift of Bishop Cosin's chaplain, George Davenport, whose name appears on the binding, but its previous history is unknown. I am publishing the text of this manuscript in *A.F.H.* xxiv.

[6] MS. V. iii. 18, f. 1 *r.*-4 *v.* Cf. f. 4 *v.* " Expliciunt Responsiones fratris Ricardi de Conyngton ad rationes papales que ponuntur in illo statuto ' ad

who was now living in retirement at Cambridge, and the second by a young friar, Walter of Chatton,[1] who had not yet made a reputation for himself. The third is much mutilated,[2] and the name of the author is missing, but his treatment of the subject and his references to two sermons by Grossetête in praise of the Franciscan manner of life naturally leads to the supposition that he was a member of that Order.[3] Conyngton's pamphlet is in the form of a dialogue between the Pope and a friar, and must have been composed soon after the promulgation of " Ad conditorem canonum ", for all the papal arguments are drawn from that decretal.[4] Like the majority of his Order, he regarded the ideal of poverty as embodied in the Rule and in " Exiit qui seminat " as the highest form of perfection to be attained on earth.[5] The time-worn theories of the distinction between civil and natural law,[6] and of the goods of the Church being the patrimony of the poor,[7] as well as the examples of the slave, son, and monk,[8] given as a defence of the claim of the Franciscans to complete possessionlessness, show his usual lack of originality. There is, however, a ring of genuine pride in his allusion to the signal services rendered by his Order to the Church [9] and a certain ingenuity in his contention that, if its original derivation were considered, " abuse " in no way implied an illegal use of goods, but might be taken as a special term for denoting the right of using such things as were consumed by being used.[10] There is perhaps more solidity in his argument that one man might allow another to use certain of his possessions without giving him any legal claim over these, since the donor was able at any moment to revoke his grant.[11] Conyngton devotes the last part of his treatise to a confutation of the views of the Dominican

---

Conditorem Canonum '." Another copy of this treatise is contained in MS. Brussels Bibl. Royale, 1613 (ii. 1159), f. 60-64 r.

[1] " Tractatus de Paupertate Evangelica editus a fratre Waltero de Chatton Oxon " (f. 5 r.-18 v.). Chatton was already a member of the Franciscan Order when he was ordained a sub-deacon by John de Halton, Bishop of Carlisle, in 1307 — Registrum Ioannis de Halton (Publications of the Canterbury and York Society, London, 1906–13, i. p. 279)—but was probably not a regent master at Oxford till 1330. Cf. Little, Grey Friars at Oxford, p. 170. This treatise is also contained in C. Laurentianae Florentinae S. Crucis, 31 Sin Cod. 3, f. 185 v.a-190 r.a, but the end is missing.

[2] F. 20 r.-f. 23 v. The missing leaves are 19 and 24-26.

[3] " Pauper et ignobilis " (Ps. lxxiii. 21), f. 21 v.; " Beati pauperes " (Matt. v. 2), f. 20 v. Extracts from this second sermon, which was actually preached at a Chapter of the English Minorites, are printed in Eccleston, Appendix vii. p. 178-87.

[4] B.F. v. 486, p. 236 s. Cf. supra, p. 160 s.

[5] F. 1 r., f. 1 v., and f. 4 r.

[6] F. 2 v. and f. 3 v.

[7] F. 1 r. Cf. supra, 161.

[8] F. 1 v. Cf. supra, 159.

[9] F. 1 v.

[10] MS. Durham, V. iii. 18, f. 3 r.

[11] F. 2 v.

chronicler, Nicholas Trivet, with whom he may have been acquainted in his Oxford days.[1] As might have been expected from a man of his temperament, he was no rebel, and the first words of his pamphlet reveal his utter submission to the Pope ; [2] and he ends on a note of dismayed resignation, though he still appears to have nourished a faint hope that John XXII. might yet reverse his new policy.[3] According to Bale, he even subsequently wrote a defence of the opinions of John XXII. against the attacks of Occam.[4] If this is so, it must have been composed during the last months of his life, for he died at Cambridge in 1330.[5]

Walter of Chatton's treatise is a far more interesting piece of work than that of the ex-provincial. He must have composed it soon after the promulgation of the revised version of " Ad conditorem ", and at the same time as he was engaged upon his commentary upon the fourth book of the Sentences, for in both writings he expresses much the same opinions, and refers to the papal pronouncement as " illam constitutionem novam ".[6] Unlike Conyngton he does not confine himself only to the legal side of the Franciscan position, but devotes the earlier part of his

[1] Trivet resumed his lectures at Oxford in 1314, and was probably lecturing there also at an earlier period (Ehrle, " Nikolaus Trivet, sein Leben, seine Quodlibet und Quaestiones Ordinarie ", in *Beiträge zur Geschichte Philosophie des Mittelalters*, Suppl. Bd. ii. p. 3).

The treatise controverted by Conyngton and Chatton is perhaps the Scutum Veritatis, mentioned in the Catalogue of Urban V.'s Library, for a later Dominican writer, " Antonius Senensis ", gives as its full title, " Scutum Veritatis contra Impugnantes Statum Perfectionis " (*ibid.* p. 18). In 1317 or 1318 John XXII. wrote to the papal collector in England, ordering him to give Trivet the money necessary for carrying on a certain work upon which he was engaged (*ibid.* p. 4).

[2] " Flecto genua mea ad dominum patrem meum, pontificem summum et vicarium domini nostri Iesu Christi " (MS. Durham, V. iii. 18, f. 1 *r.*).

[3] F. 4 *v.*

[4] *Scriptorum Brytanniae*, p. 404, xxxii. Cf. Wadding, *Scriptores Ordinis Fratrum Minorum*, p. 203.

[5] *Scriptorum Brytanniae*, p. 404, xxxii., and *Index Britanniae scriptorum*, p. 343. This is repeated by Pits, *De illustribus Angliae scriptoribus*, p. 424. Cf. MS. f. 4 *v.*, but is not found in Leland, *Comentarii de scriptoribus Britannicis*, C. cccxli. p. 331, referred to by Bale as his source. Conyngton, however, was certainly buried in the church of his Order at Cambridge (Brewer, *Monumenta Franciscana*, pp. 538 and 553).

[6] " Solvam obiectiones quae sunt in contrarium in quadam nova constitutione quae incipit ' ad Conditorem Canonum ' " (MS. Bibl. Nat. Flor. Conv. Sopp. c. 5, 367, f. 209 *v.b.* Cf. *Tractatus de Paupertate*, MS. Durham, V. iii. 18, f. 8 *r.*, f. 17 *v.*, and f. 18 *r.*). For citations from the revised version of " Ad conditorem " cf. f. 12 *r.*, f. 13 *v.*, f. 15 *v.*, and f. 16 *r.* For the description of Chatton's Commentary on the Sentences, as well as for much of my information concerning him, I am indebted to Father Longpré for his article in *Studi Francescani*, ix., and to Dr. A. G. Little for the loan of his own invaluable notes.

treatise to the question of the poverty of Christ and his apostles, proving both from the Scriptures and the Fathers that they had owned nothing either severally or in common.[1] Thus the Minorites, by following closely in the footsteps of the Son of Man, had achieved the highest form of perfection attainable on earth, and their manner of life was further approved by the dictates of human reason and by the decrees of former Popes. He argued that the renunciation of all property, both individually and in common, betokened a greater love towards God and confidence in His mercy than the mere surrender of personal possessions, and that ownership in common was a mere fiction, since each individual had a partial claim to the goods of the community. Chatton goes on to define " dominium ", not in its legal sense but in the way in which it was understood by those who took the vow of poverty. According to him it consisted in a free and lavish use of possessions, and the right of legal redress if they were taken away, or wrongly withheld. It was clear from the Scriptures that Christ and His apostles had never held property in this way, but had been content with the little that had sufficed for their daily needs. In the middle of his treatise he discussed the position of his Order as affected by the new decretal. He gave it as his opinion that the Pope's definition of "dominium" need not be taken either in the usual or in the strictly technical sense of the term, but might be used to denote the right of using certain classes of goods, in which case " Ad conditorem " would make very little difference to the existing state of things. Moreover, the legal ownership of the Holy See over the goods belonging to the Franciscans had been a mere matter of convenience, and John XXII.'s action in renouncing it in no way altered the complete possessionlessness of the friars. It is impossible not to admire the way in which Chatton deals with " Ad conditorem ", interpreting it in such a way as to deprive it of all real significance and yet avoiding the least suspicion of irreverence and unorthodoxy. His frequent declarations that the authoritative definition of the new decretal belonged alone to the Holy See and must be accepted with due humility, show that he fully realised that his interpretation was not the same as that of its promulgator. Finally, he controverts in detail the opinions contained in the lost treatise of Nicholas Trivet, following his arguments so closely that it is almost possible to reconstruct the main outlines of the pamphlet of the Dominican chronicler.[2] Trivet's position was

[1] For authority for most of the statements in this and the succeeding paragraph, see Durham MS., f. 5 r.-18 v.

[2] MS. Durham, V. iii. 18, f. 16 r.-18 v. Cf. Commentary on the Sentences, MS. Bibl. Nat. Flor. Conv. Sopp, c. 5, 367, f. 210 v.b.

that Christ and His apostles had held property in common, since its renunciation was repugnant to the principles of natural law. As far as we can judge from a perusal of Chatton's own composition, he was completely successful in his attack upon the conclusions of his opponent. We do not know what part he played in the later stages of the controversy, but in 1333 he was in Avignon, where, like the Minister-General and certain other members of his Order, he supported the views of John XXII. on the subject of the Beatific Vision.[1] After the Pope's death he was a member of the commission appointed to examine Benedict XII.'s treatise on the same question, written at the request of his predecessor but containing opinions entirely opposed to his.[2] The bull, "Benedictus dei", of 1336, which finally condemned John XXII.'s theories by proclaiming the opposite doctrine as the one officially held by the Church, was perhaps the result of the labours of Chatton and his colleagues.[3] The same year he was also consulted by the Pope over his revision of the statutes of the Franciscan Order, which were being remodelled on the lines of the Benedictines.[4] Chatton's share in this work shows that he was in sympathy with the views of the Minister-General rather than with those of the bulk of the Order who wished, at least formally, to retain their original manner of life. Clement VI. continued the favours of his predecessors, making him one of his penitentiaries,[5] and later creating him Bishop of St. Asaph.[6] Chatton, however, did not live to enjoy his new honours, for he died at Avignon very shortly after the appointment was made. His European reputation is shown by the fact that he is one of the few English Franciscans of the period mentioned by Bartholomew of Pisa.[7]

The greater part of the third treatise which remains to us consists of a long discussion of the meaning of the terms " heretic "

[1] *Hist. Litt.* xxxiv. p. 587, *n.* 3 ; *ibid.* p. 591, and *Cart. Univ. Paris,* ii. p. 517, *n.* 975. Cf. *supra,* p. 193.

[2] *Cart. Univ. Paris,* ii. pp. 453 and 454, *n.* 995.

[3] It must be remembered that John XXII. had never maintained that he was speaking " ex cathedra " on the subject of the Beatific Vision, but declared expressly that he was giving his opinions as those of a simple doctor of the Church (*Dict. de Theol. Cath.,* ii. pp. 670-71).

[4] " Redemptor noster ", *B.F.* vi. 51, pp. 25-42 (Avignon, November 28, 1336). Cf. *Cart. Univ. Paris,* ii. p. 471, *n.* 1001. Shortly after Benedict's death his statutes were repealed at the urgent petition of the Franciscan Order.

[5] In a bull of March 1343 he and certain other Minorites are described as " Domini papae poenitentiariorum " (*B.F.* vi. 185, p. 106).

[6] *B.F.* vi. Appendix iii. 657. According to Bale (*op. cit.* p. 420, *n.* lvii), Chatton died at Avignon in 1343, but the date of his appointment to the See of St. Asaph is 1344 (*Cart. Univ. Paris,* ii. p. 424, *n.* 7).

[7] *Liber de Conformitate; A.F.* iv. 339.

and " heresy ".[1] Its author obviously regarded the great controversy concerning the poverty of Christ as one of the temptations sent periodically to the Church to prove her steadiness in
the paths of sound doctrine,[2] but it breaks off shortly after he begins
expressing his own views on the question. Enough is left, however, to show that he regarded the subject from a definitely Franciscan standpoint. In some ways he displays greater learning and
erudition than either Conyngton or Chatton, and his citations
from the Fathers and from both canon and civil law are very
numerous.

Except for the Durham manuscript our only evidence concerning the attitude of the English Franciscans to John XXII. are
certain papal letters of the years 1329 and 1330. In August
1329, the nuncio, Itherio de Concoreto, was commended for the
zeal he had displayed over the capture of certain friars who had
been preaching openly against the Pope's enactments, and was
instructed to send his prisoners to Avignon.[3] A letter of the same
day directed to Edward III. gives the names of Peter of Saxlingham
and John of Hacklington, mentioning that they were now in the
custody of the guardian of the Franciscan convent at Cambridge,
and begging the king to do all in his power to further the efforts
of his representative in particular with regard to the dispatch of
the captives to the Curia.[4] Early in September, John XXII. wrote
again to Itherio de Concoreto, giving the names of two other
friars, Henry of Costeseye and Thomas of Helmdon, who had
previously been cited to appear at Avignon. Rumours had apparently reached him that their offences were not so great as had
previously been supposed, and he therefore instructed his agent
in England to hold an inquiry over the nature and extent of these.
If the former charges were substantiated, the two friars were to be
sent to the papal court to stand their trial, together with Peter of
Saxlingham and John of Hacklington, in accordance with the
Pope's previous instructions.[5] Presumably, the case went against
them, for in March 1330, William of Nottingham was directed

---

[1] MS. Durham, V. iii. 18, f. 20 *v*.-22 *r*.

[2] F. 20 *v*.

[3] *B.F.* v. 806, p. 401 (August 24, 1329). Cf. *Calendar of Papal Letters*
(1305–1342), p. 492.

[4] *B.F.* v. 807, p. 401. The tone of the letter implies that he was somewhat
nervous lest the king should refuse to allow the prisoners to leave England.

[5] *Ibid.* v. 809, p. 402 (September 5). Henry of Costeseye, or Cossey, was the
author of certain Biblical commentaries, of which only those on the Psalms of
the Apocalypse survive. According to Bale (*Index Britanniæ Scriptorium*,
p. 160) he died at the Franciscan convent of Babwell, near Bury St. Edmunds,
in 1336. Cf. Little, *Grey Friars at Oxford*, p. 234. Nothing is known about
his companions except the fact of their arrest.

to send the four prisoners to the papal court.[1]   What fate befell them at Avignon is still unknown.

As far as we can tell from the evidence at our disposal the excitement of the English Minorites appears to have been quieted by the strong measures taken by John XXII.   Even the lectures of Ludovico de Castiglione at Oxford on the bull, " Quia vir reprobus ",[2] may have been undertaken as part of his duties as a regent master, and have nothing to do with his position as lector at the Franciscan convent, for it was customary for the popes to send copies of their pronouncements to be commented on in the schools.[3]   Unfortunately, " Frater Andreas Ricchi ", while dwelling upon the satisfaction given to all the university authorities by his master's discourses,[4] omits to record the feelings of his own Order, which was far more deeply concerned in the matter.   Yet Ludovico's warm and generous testimony to the many virtues of Michael of Cesena, shows that he was not a very ardent champion of the Pope.[5]   It is probable that, like the majority of their Order, the bulk of the English Franciscans still retained a certain respect for their former General, while strongly disapproving of his open alliance with the enemies of the Church.   At any rate, considering the high reputation of their province for sound learning and strictness of life, it is unlikely that they were warm supporters of the policy of his successor.[6]

[1] *Ibid.* 849, p. 464 (March 22, 1330).   A letter was also sent to the guardian of the friary at Cambridge, ordering the surrender of the prisoners to the provincial.

[2] Cf. *supra*, p. 198.

[3] John's decretals were certainly sent to Paris to be commented upon, and in 1330 he ordered his agent in England to distribute copies of " Quia vir reprobus " to the bishops and to the universities (*Calendar of Papal Letters*, p. 496).

[4] *A.F.H.* iii. 277.   Cf. *supra*, 198.

[5] Cf. *supra*, p. 198, *n.* 4.

[6] Cf. *supra*, p. 150.

Part I: THE FRATICELLI

THE early biographers of the " poverello " relate the beautiful story of how once on his way to Siena the saint was met by three poor women who greeted him with the words " Bene veniat domina paupertas ".   Afterwards the friars who accompanied him interpreted this vision as signifying the three great Franciscan virtues of Poverty, Obedience, and Chastity,[1] and thus the legend may well be taken as an allegory of the whole spirit of the new movement.   Its originality lay not so much in the glorification of the first of these lofty ideals as in the combination of an intense devotion to poverty with an equally ardent loyalty towards the Church.   Only a few years before the birth of St. Francis a prosperous merchant of Lyons, Peter Waldo, had divested himself of his riches, and had wandered through the country preaching the gospel to the poor, only to find his work hindered, and himself and his followers finally condemned by the ecclesiastical authorities.[2]   It is one of the commonplaces of history that most medieval heresies originated as a fierce protest against the wealth and luxury of the clergy, and one of their most cherished dogmas was that the only way to perfection lay in the renunciation of worldly possessions, since by no other means could men follow the example of Christ and His apostles.   Like all great religious adventurers St. Francis was too much occupied in making his dream a reality for himself and his followers to trouble himself greatly over the theoretical aspects of the question of poverty, nor did he ever seek to enforce his ideal upon the majority of mankind.[3] We have seen how in the century which followed his death certain of his most devoted followers found it increasingly difficult to reconcile the manner of life enjoined by their master with the obedience which they owed both to their Superiors and the Church, and thus were led unwillingly and almost imperceptibly into the paths of schism and revolt.[4]   The theological side of the problem was reflected in the breach between Michael of Cesena and the Papacy, and it is from these sources that the great bulk of the

[1] Thomas of Celano, *Vita Secunda*, cap. lx.   *A.F.* x. p. 185.   Cf. S. Bonaventura, " Legenda Maiora ", *Opera Omnia*, viii. cap. vii. § 6.
[2] Waldo's exact dates are not certain, but his followers, the " poor men of Lyons ", were finally condemned at the Council of Verona in 1184 (Mansi, *Concilia*, xxii. p. 493).
[3] His instructions to his friars to refrain from judging those whom they saw clad in soft raiment and enjoying all the good things of the world, but to attend to their own souls, show that he was at least aware of the existence of this problem. Cf. Reg. ii. cl. 2, *Opuscula*, p. 65.
[4] Angelo da Clareno and Olivi can be taken as examples of unwilling " rebels ", the latter doing all in his power to avert a schism in the Order.

Fraticelli, or more correctly Fraterculi,[1] drew their origin. The name is often used in papal and other official documents to denote heretics who had no connection with the Franciscan Order, but with such we are in no way concerned in this chapter. Here we deal only with the history of the descendants of the old Spiritual party, or " Fraticelli de paupere vita " as they came to be called, and with the Michaelists, or " Fraticelli de opinione." [2]

It has already been seen that the first band of Zealots to separate themselves from the Order were the followers of Liberato and Angelo da Clareno.[3] During the last years of the life of the latter he was the leader of a flourishing community, with settlements in Rome and the March of Ancona, as well as in the kingdom of Naples.[4] The brothers won the admiration of the populace by the simplicity and holiness of their lives,[5] and were a cause of endless preoccupation to the Holy Office, since they were often protected by the nobility,[6] and in some cases even by the bishops and clergy.[7] Yet even before Angelo's death it is possible to notice a deterioration in their character, or perhaps it would be more just to say that they never attained to the high spiritual and intellectual level of their leader.[8] When he died there seems to have been no one of sufficiently commanding personality to take his place, for no

---

[1] This would be the correct Latin form of the name, but is very seldom found, Fratricelli or Fraticelli being far more usual. Cf. *A.L.K.G.* iv. 139.

[2] The confusion is further increased by the fact that the name Fraticelli was often bestowed on individuals or on small groups of hermits living under the jurisdiction of the bishops but belonging to none of the recognised Orders. The close resemblance between their manner of life and that of the " heretics " subjected them to frequent persecutions on the part of the Inquisition. In 1417 the papal vicar at Rome, Cardinal James Isolani, was forced to take certain small communities of this type living in the neighbourhood of the city under his especial protection in order to save them from such attacks (*A.L.K.G.* iv. p. 170). For further accounts of these hermits, cf. *ibid.* 168-72 and *A.F.H.* vi. 727-33. Perhaps the careful division of the offshoots from the Spiritual party and the Michaelists into Fraticelli " de paupere vita " and " de opinione " found in the Inquisition records sprang from an attempt to safeguard the reputation of the orthodox.

[3] Cf. *supra*, p. 64.   [4] *Ibid.*

[5] Cf. letters written in February 1334 by John XXII. to Angelo, Bishop of Viterbo and papal vicar at Rome (*A.L.K.G.* iv. pp. 17-20).

[6] In 1337 the rector of the March of Ancona was ordered to cite before the Curia a nobleman called Gentile da Camerino for giving assistance to the " Fraticelli de paupere vita " (*B.F.* vi. 69, p. 50).

[7] In 1336 Benedict XII. ordered the Bishops of Camerino and Fermo to be summoned to Avignon for giving protection to the Fraticelli and bestowing upon them a special habit and rule (*A.L.K.G.* iv. p. 73). Three years later the two bishops were finally absolved by the rector of Spoleto on condition that they swore to refrain from similar practices in the future (*B.F.* vi. 106, p. 67). In 1360 the Bishops of Fermo, Città di Castello, and Perugia conferred on the Fraticelli the habit of St. Augustine (*A.F.H.* vi. p. 269). See note, p. 65, *infra*.

[8] Cf. *supra*, 64.

record of the name of his successor has survived. We do not even know whether the " fratres fratris Philippi de Maioricis " [1] who were found in Naples in the second half of the century were a separate body, or merely the followers of Angelo under a new name. Certainly Philip, from his close intimacy with the great Zealot and his connection with the royal house of Naples, was well fitted to succeed to the vacant office.[2] His renewed attempt to secure the consent of the Papacy to his foundation of a reformed branch of the Franciscan Order may even have arisen from a desire to legalise the position of the former disciples of Liberato and Angelo.[3] His sojourn at his brother-in-law's court attracted thither the survivors of the Spiritual party in Provence who had succeeded in escaping from the clutches of the Inquisition.[4] Their number was further swelled by fugitives from Sicily,[5] and there was even a band of Michaelists settled within the boundaries of the kingdom who subsisted on the bounty of the queen.[6] In short, Naples appears to have been a refuge for all the Franciscan malcontents, and there they were comparatively free from molestation and persecution, since the whole success of the papal policy in Italy depended upon the support of Robert the Wise. Unfortunately, this has led to a confusion between the different sects which it is practically impossible to dissolve, owing to the almost complete absence of any official documents.[7]

During the second half of the fourteenth century the darkness which surrounds the later history of the Fraticelli in Naples is broken by one gleam of light, for in 1362 a process was instituted by Cardinal Albornez against their patron and supporter, Louis of Durazzo, the cousin of Giovanna I.[8] The inquiry was probably rendered fruitless by the death of the accused,[9] but this does not in

---

[1] *A.L.K.G.* iv. 100.

[2] A brother Philip was certainly living in the neighbourhood of Aspromonte when the record about Angelo's miracles was drawn up, and was visited there by certain people of high position who had known him before he withdrew from the world. Cf. Codex Magliabecchiana, xxxix. *n.* 75, f. 219 *v.*

[3] *B.F.* vi. 123, p. 77. Letter of Benedict XII. to Robert of Naples refusing Philip's request (August 8, 1340). Cf. *supra,* p. 65.

[4] *S.F.* i. 520 ; *infra,* p. 215.

[5] Letter of John XXII. to Provincial of Calabria, Avignon, March 1327 (*A.L.K.G.* iv. 65 ; *B.F.* v. 650, p. 320).

[6] Article XXII. in process against Andreas de Galiano (*B.F.* vi. p. 605). Cf. *supra,* p. 177.

[7] My researches into the *Saggio di codice diplomatico* of Signor C. M. Riccio (Naples, 1878–83) and the *Inventario cronologico-sistematico dei Registri Angioini conservati nell' Archivio di Stato in Napoli* of Signor Capasso (Naples, 1876) have been fruitless. There is also very little in the *Archivio Storico per le provincie Napoletane* (Naples, 1876). [8] *A.L.K.G.* iv. 95–104.

[9] June 1362. *S.F.* i. 341. The process cannot have been intended to be a very serious one, for the Archbishop of Naples was endeavouring at the same

the least impair the value of the evidence collected by the inquisitors, most of which was furnished by prisoners belonging to the sect.   According to one of these, a certain " Frater Novellus de Roccabantre ", the Fraticelli had already split up into three different bodies.[1] He could say little about one of these, the disciples of brother Angelo, except that they held somewhat different opinions from the rest.[2] The band under the leadership " of the minister " was perhaps an offshoot from the community founded by Clareno,[3] or had been formed from the survivors of the Tuscan or the Provençal Zealots who had eventually taken refuge in Naples.[4] The witness himself belonged to the group headed by Thomas of Boiano, a man with a singularly romantic history.   He had originally been a member of the Franciscan Order and had been created bishop of Aquino in 1349.[5] Five years later he disappeared, to reappear as the leader of an heretical sect called by some the " brethren of the poor life ", and by others the " followers of brother Philip of Majorca ".   Sometimes they were even given the name of " the true friars minor ".[6] The bishop and his community were under the special protection of Louis of Durazzo,

time to mediate between the queen and her cousin, who had fallen into her hands earlier in the same year (*S.F.* i. 340).   Cardinal Ehrle regards the Fraticelli as too insignificant for it to be possible to attribute Louis's support to political motives (*A.L.K.G.* iv. 103).   [1] *Ibid.* p. 97.

[2] " Dixit, quod imo sunt tres septe dictorum fratricellorum, videlicet dicti fratris Thome et sequacium eius, quam vocant de paupere vita, qui tenent supradictam septam.   Alii vocantur de ministro, et minister . . . est frater Berardus de Sicilia, et isti non concordant, sicut dixit, in omnibus cum dicta septa, sed in aliquibus.   Alii vocantur de fratre Angelo, de quibus non scit septam vel opiniones eorum, set non concordant cum aliis " (*ibid.* p. 97). Angelo da Monticelli or de Monte Vulcani, the leader of the hermits of Monte Maiella, with whom Rienzi lived after his exile from Rome in 1347, can perhaps be identified with this " frater Angelus " (Puir Burdach, *op. cit.* ii. (5), p. 301, and Chiappini, *Profilo di storia Francescana in Abruzzo dal secolo XIV al XVI* (Aquila, 1927), p. 10).   The name of the General of the second sect is uncertain, as there is a lacuna in the manuscript.   From *A.L.K.G.* iv. p. 101 we would gather that he may have been a certain " Frater Petrus de Novaria " who played a prominent part in the negotiations between the two sects.   Cf. *ibid.* p. 103.

[3] This is the view of Cardinal Ehrle, which appears to be based on the deposition of another witness, " Jacobus de Scalis ", who declared that there were only two branches of Fraticelli—namely, the adherents of the " minister " and those who recognised Thomas da Boiano as their head.   Cf. *ibid.* 100 and 103.

[4] " Petrus de Novaria " had certainly some connection with the Provençal Spirituals, but it is difficult to be clear as to how far these had amalgamated with the other groups.   Cf. *S.F.* i. p. 521, and *infra*, p. 215.

[5] *B.F.* vi. 496, p. 226.

[6] " Qui (the followers of the bishop) aliquando vocantur fratres de paupere vita, aliquando fratres evangelici, aliquando fratres veritatis, aliquando fratres fratris Philippi de Maioricis, et aliquando veri fratres minores " (*A.L.K.G.* iv. 100).

who permitted them to preach and to celebrate Mass before him.[1]
This sect was more extreme than the other Fraticelli, for not only
did it hold that John XXII. had been a heretic, and that therefore
all the bishops and clergy who adhered to him necessarily shared
his guilt and thus lost their judicial authority, but it even denied to
them the power of administering the Sacraments. While the other
leaders sought to get their disciples ordained by some neighbouring
bishop, Thomas always reordained those of his followers who were
already in holy orders.[2] Louis of Durazzo and the Bishop of
Trivento,[3] a prelate who seems to have been very favourably disposed towards the Fraticelli, attempted to mediate between the
different branches of the sect, and a meeting between the leaders
was arranged at Monte San Angelo, a castle belonging to the
former. All efforts, however, to bring about a reconciliation resulted in failure, and the bishop's parting words concerning his
opponents were, "Let them withdraw with the devil".[4] After
the stormy ending of this conference little more is known about
the history of the Fraticelli in Naples.

Further light is thrown on the fortunes of the descendants of
the old Spiritual party by two treatises now printed in *Studii
Francescani*.[5] These are written in the vulgar tongue for the
benefit of the simple, and the second, which is the longer of the two,
is perhaps the more interesting.[6] The writer was obviously steeped
in the traditions of the Zealots. According to him the three great
champions of the faith had been Jacopone da Todi, Conrad of
Offida, and Olivi, the memory of the last of these being evidently
still held in as great veneration as it had been among his personal
followers.[7] He mentions also Arnold of Villanova and Ubertino

---

[1] *A.L.K.G.* iv. p. 99.
[2] The witness Jacobus de Scalis, who had formerly been a priest, together
with his companion, a certain Raynerius, was forced by the bishop to renounce
his former orders. After they had been absolved from the excommunication
which they had incurred by their previous adherence to the Pope they were
solemnly reordained (*ibid.*). By a strange irony of fate Jacobus, after con-
fessing his errors and being absolved by the Archbishop of Naples, was in
1372 again permitted by Gregory XI. to perform his priestly functions. Cf.
ibid. p. 97, *n.* 4. The subject of the validity of orders when conferred by a
bishop under the obedience of the Pope was one of the main questions at issue
between the two sects of Fraticelli (*ibid.* 100).
[3] Franciscus Marchisius, Bishop of Trivento, 1361–79. At the time of the
conference he was still archdeacon of Salerno (*ibid.*).
[4] *Ibid.*   [5] *S.F.* i. 502-24.   [6] *Ibid.* 512-24.
[7] *Ibid.* p. 515. "Ma il vero chanpione potentissimo padrone a chavare i
perigliosi di questo tenpestoso mare, la chui doctrina è una navicella che chi vi
navicha perviene sichuro a porto di salute, fu quel veramente figliuolo et seghui-
tatore del beato Francescho fra Pier Giovanni da Nerbona, cholui il quale
profeto labate Joachim."

da Casale as disciples of the great Spiritual,[1] and was acquainted with both the "leggenda vecchia" and the "leggenda nuova", as well as with the "Fioretti", the Laudi of Jacopone da Todi, and the "Chronicle of the Seven Tribulations".[2] It is noteworthy that he refers to Angelo da Clareno without any special mark of esteem. Besides these he cites the manifestos of Michael of Cesena, Occam, and Francis of Ascoli as the sources of his knowledge of the errors of John XXII.,[3] who was no true vicar of Christ but rather the mystic Antichrist.[4] Before his elevation to the Papacy the latter had been an apostate from the Dominican Order, and had dwelt among the infidels, where he had renounced his faith. Later, when he had become the chancellor of the king of Naples, he had excited the enmity of Arnold of Villanova because of his iniquity.[5] His successor Benedict XII. had not dared to condemn his decretals for fear of jeopardising his own position.[6] In spite of his interest in the struggle there was obviously little connection between the writer and the Michaelists, for he mentions the latter as a separate body.[7] For the Osservanti he had all the contempt of the extremist for the moderate reformer,[8] but he reserves the full blast of his fury for the survivors of the old Conventual party and for their General, Guiral Ot, the destroyer of the Rule of St Francis.[9] It was these who were accused by their rivals the Dominicans of having their armories filled with the heresies of Brother Gerard, to whom they retorted, "Yours are full of those of Brother Thomas".[10] The part which is concerned with

---

[1] *S.F.* i. 516. The story of the violent death of the latter comes from this treatise. Cf. *supra*, p. 132.

[2] *Ibid.* 515. There is still a considerable amount of discussion as to what writings concerning the life of St. Francis are denoted by the terms "Leggenda Antiqua" and "Leggenda Nuova". The question is discussed by M. Masseron in his "Sources de la Vie de Saint François" in *Saint François d'Assise : son œuvre—son influence* (Paris, 1927), pp. 9-57. Can the work alluded to here be by any chance the vernacular version of the first two parts of the "Chronicle of the Seven Tribulations", with additions from the "Speculum" and the "Legend of the Three Companions", about the authorship of which there has been so much dispute ? Cf. *infra*, p. 260.

[3] *S.F.* i. 513.

[4] "Per la qual chosa (the Conventuals) meritorono di perire nel grande diluvio delle heresie del misticho antichristo papa Giovanni XXII" (*ibid.* 514).

[5] *Ibid.*

[6] *Ibid.* 516. Benedict XII. is also charged with avarice, drunkenness, and cruelty (*ibid.* 517). [7] *Ibid.* 518.

[8] "Onde i sopradicti frati non vogliendo usare la decta soperchianza de' frati della chomunità, nè etiandio la realità et purità de' detti veri frati spirituali, presono la decta mezanità" (*ibid.*). From time to time certain of them had been led by the divine mercy to join the true followers of St. Francis—namely, the survivors of the Spirituals (*ibid.* 519). [9] *Ibid.*

[10] "I frati corbi (Dominicans) quando vogliono dire un gran male de' frati nibbi (Franciscans), dichono voi avete pieni gli armari delle heresie di frate

the later history of the Spirituals is of especial interest. During the persecutions in Provence they took refuge in various parts of Italy, and even in Greece and Crete, though the majority had been attracted to " Apulia " by the presence of Philip of Majorca, and there they united themselves with others of their party.[1] After the death of Philip and of a certain Bernard of Azona who had been one of the refugees from Provence, Brother Vitale of France seems to have succeeded to their position as head of the sect.[2] At the time of writing they still had settlements in Naples and Calabria, but were also to be found in the March of Ancona and in other regions of Italy, and especially in the neighbourhood of Rome.[3] Probably their diffusion was due largely to the disturbances caused by the Great Schism, which rendered the Papacy almost powerless to combat their growing influence.

The other letter attacks with an even greater vigour the heresies of John XXII.,[4] and denounces in no measured language the luxury and wickedness of the clergy, whose vast wealth was spent on the enrichment of their own families and on the building of spacious palaces, or on preparations for battle.[5] They were guilty of the twofold sin of heresy and simony, and though they still retained the power of administering the Sacraments they did so to their own damnation.[6] Their Church was rather the synagogue of the devil than the community of the faithful,[7] for the true Church, whose message was to be spread by twelve evangelic men,[8] would be righteous and holy in all her works.[9] The writer was evidently an ardent Joachimite, for he quotes from the "Concordia", and his treatise has a certain kinship with the apocalyptic works of the Spirituals.[10] It is interesting that instead of dividing the period following the death of Christ into seven smaller ages he dates his seven epochs from the creation of the world.[11] Now the sixth age had begun, in which the flood of iniquity would be loosed

---

Girardo et i nibbi respondono loro : ' Et voi gli avete pieni di quelli di frate Tomaso ' " (Aquinas), p. 518.

[1] *S.F.* i. 518 and 521.

[2] *Ibid.* It is interesting that among the leaders of the sect a certain priest called Peter of Novara is mentioned. Cf. *supra*, 212, *n.* 2 and 3.

[3] *Ibid.* Cf. *infra*, p. 220.   [4] *Ibid.* 502-12.

[5] " O Singnore, cierto non fu questa la intentione di coloro che llasciarono i beni loro alle chiese, che fussero nutricate le fancielle et parenti de' cherici, et che faciessono guerre et palazzi et fortezze et che ingrassassino chavagli et altri mali che fanno ; ma ffu, che nutricassono et sovenissono alli poveri " (*ibid.* p. 511). Almost identical words are used in the letter of a Perugian fratecello (*A.F.H.* iv. 698 *s.*). Cf. *infra*, p. 218 *s.*

[6] *S.F.* i. 511.

[7] " Non e chiesa di Christo, ma sinagoga del diavolo " (*ibid.* p. 508). Cf. *A.F.H.* iv. 707. *Infra*, p. 219.   [8] *S.F.* i. 510.

[9] *Ibid.* p. 508.   [10] *Ibid.* p. 502.   [11] *Ibid.* p. 509.

against the Rule of St. Francis, which had been symbolised by the Ark.[1] It is sad that we have no knowledge concerning the authorship of these two documents, or even of the region in which they were composed.

The last purely Joachimite treatise produced by the successors of the old Spiritual party was the " Revelationes Joachim ", which appeared at Florence shortly after the return of the Papacy to Italy.[2] At that time the Fraticelli were particularly active in the city, for as the centre of the resistance to Gregory XI. it afforded a safe refuge to the enemies of the Church, and the sentiments of many patriotic and influential citizens were fiercely anti-clerical.[3] This new series of prophecies also begins with Nicholas III., and adheres rigidly to the model laid down by the " Vaticinia Anselmi ", with the difference that the Popes are not featureless abstractions but historical personages whose portraits are drawn with firm and vigorous lines, the religious prejudices of the author giving colour to the whole composition. His earlier sketches are probably taken from the " Liber de Flore",[4] but the later ones are presumably original, and the opprobrious epithets applied to Clement V., the deserter of his lawful spouse,[5] and John XXII., the destroyer of the true ideal of St. Francis,[6] are certainly an expression of the author's own political and religious convictions. In his passionate prayer to Urban V. to return and guide the destinies of the dove he was only giving voice to the ardent longings of all patriotic Italians, and indeed of all faithful Catholics.[7] Yet the fulfilment of these hopes brought only bitter disillusionment, for the return of Gregory XI. did not give peace to a distracted Italy, and all feeling of love and

---

[1] " Ma più principalmente in questo stato sesto d' ora, però che tutto il suo furore a voltato inverso dell' archa cioè della reghola evangielicha di santo Franciescho " (S.F. i. p. 509). In true Franciscan style the saint was represented by the angel having the seal of the living God (Apoc. vii. 2) and the strong angel descending from the sky (Apoc. x. 1). Ibid. i. p. 503.

[2] A.K. xix. p. 117. Grundmann believes that the treatise appeared about 1378.

[3] Ibid. p. 120. Florence being at that time under an interdict as a punishment for her opposition to the Pope would afford a very good field for the spread of heresy.

[4] Cf. Nicholas IV., " primam sponsam viduatam relinquens " (ibid. p. 112). As in the "Vaticinia Anselmi" and the "Liber de Flore", Martin IV. is described as a man of blood (ibid.).

[5] Ibid. p. 113.

[6] " Contra columbam hec imago turpissima clericorum pugnabit." Title to picture representing John XXII. (ibid. p. 113). As in the "Liber de Flore" and similar works, the dove is the symbol of the Franciscan Order.

[7] " Dirige columbam " (ibid. p. 118). Urban V. did actually endeavour to put an end to the Babylonish captivity by returning to Italy in 1367. Three years later, appalled by the ruined state of Rome, he went back to Avignon, where he died in 1370.

reverence vanished when the Pope employed Breton mercenaries to reduce his revolted dominions.[1] The red flowers which distilled a pleasant odour, described in the fourteenth prophecy, may well be a reference to the part played by Florence in the conflict, for the arms of the commune were red fleurs-de-lys.[2] The last illustration, which shows a many-headed beast, each head being surmounted by a royal crown, is clearly meant to be a representation of Antichrist ; nor is it surprising that in a period of disappointment and uncertainty even sober-minded and devout Catholics like the Vallombrosian hermit, Giovanni dalle Celle, were disposed to believe that there might be some element of truth in this prediction.[3] Curiously enough, the only codices in which the treatise is still found separate from the " Vaticinia Anselmi " are of French origin, and in these the last prophecy is usually applied to Urban VI.[4] Generally the treatise is anonymous, and it is only in a Tours manuscript that it is attributed either to Johannes de Rupescissa or Joachim.[5] Possibly the desire to combine in one volume the two most typical features of the eschatological speculations of the Fraticelli—their belief in the coming of Antichrist and the advent of a line of angel Popes—was responsible for its union with the " Vaticinia Anselmi ".[6] The later history of the double series of prophecies has been dealt with elsewhere.[7]

One of the cities in Italy where the Fraticelli appear to have been especially powerful was Perugia. As early as 1334 John XXII. gave instructions to the Inquisition to take proceedings against them, but apparently with little result,[8] for in 1360 they are found in possession of the Abbey of Monte Salvi outside the walls of the city.[9] Even earlier they were settled at the Carceri, a hermitage in the neighbourhood of Assisi hallowed by many memories of St. Francis.[10] By 1374 their influence in Perugia was so strong that certain faithful Catholics begged Paoluccio de' Trinci, the founder of the Osservanti, to settle in the city in order that he might prevent the further diffusion of their errors.[11] In this he was completely

---

[1] Gregory XI. returned to Italy in 1376. The following year a troop of Breton mercenaries, under the leadership of the cardinal Robert of Geneva, later the antipope Clement VII., crossed the Alps. They were responsible for the bloody suppression of the revolts at Cesena (February 3, 1377) which further alienated Italian feeling from the Pope (*A.K.* xix. 119).

[2] " Flores rubei aquam odoriferam distillabunt " (*ibid.* p. 122).

[3] *Ibid.* p. 115 *s.* In a letter to his friend Guido del Palagio, Giovanni cites the whole of the fourteenth prophecy.

[4] *Ibid.* p. 125.   [5] *Ibid.*   [6] *Ibid.* p. 124.

[7] Cf. *supra*, p. 40 *s.*

[8] *A.L.K.G.* iv. 18. (February 9, 1334.)   [9] *A.F.H.* iv. 691.

[10] Fumi, *Eretici et Ribelli in Umbria*, p. 20.

[11] *A.F.H.* iii. 259 ; iv. 691. (From Ridolfi, *Historiarum Seraphicae Religionis libri tres*, L. II. f. 154 *a*.)

successful, even procuring the banishment of his rivals, who, however, speedily returned during the eight years' struggle between Perugia and the Church, which lasted till 1378.[1] An interesting letter was written by one of their number during the time of the Great Schism [2] as an answer to the slander of their enemies,[3] who declared that they refused to believe in the validity of the Sacraments, or to recognise the orders of the bishops and clergy who had adhered to John XXII. and his successors.[4] The writer rebuts this charge by delivering a fearful tirade against the wealth and other vices of the priests, whom he declares to be guilty not only of heresy but of simony, for they accepted money for the administration of the Sacraments.[5] As heretics they had lost the power to bind and loose,[6] but in spite of their wickedness and other errors the bread which they consecrated in the sacrifice of the Mass was verily and indeed the body of Christ.[7] The Friars Minor were also the subject of his bitter indignation, for their splendid churches and luxurious lives formed an ironical contrast to the strict poverty which they had vowed to observe.[8] In such an atmosphere it had been impossible to observe the manner of life enjoined by the founder of the Order.   For this reason the separation of his party from the friars had been in complete accordance with the instructions of St. Francis contained both in the Rule and in the records of his life which had been preserved.[9] The present schism in the Church was the result of her denial of the poverty of Christ in the days of John XXII., whose decretals his successors had recognised as valid.[10] Finally, the faithful were called upon to judge between the Fraticelli and their enemies, for a Church in which reigned discord and enmity, immorality, treason, avarice, and other forms of sin

---

[1] *A.F.H.* iii. 259 ; iv. 691.   [2] *Ibid.* pp. 697-712.

[3] The treatise begins as follows : " Questo è uno tratatello fatto a Perugia da uno de' frati poveri, che oservano la vera reghola di San Francescho, per levare certe calonie ch' erano loro aposte " (p. 697).

[4] " Questo falsamente ci aponghono perochè nè noi, nè niuno informato da noi, nè di niuno nostro detto si seguita, che lli veschovi non sieno veschovi, posto che 'l papa sia heretico, nè che lli preti non sieno preti, nè che il corpo di Xpo non sia corpo di Xpo, da qualunque iniquo prete cosegrato " (*ibid.* p. 699).

[5] Cf. *ibid.* pp. 697-98, 704, 708-709.

[6] *Ibid.* p. 707.

[7] Cf. *ibid.* p. 699. Yet it was better for the faithful to remain without the visible signs of the Communion and communicate invisibly with God than to receive the host from the hands of an heretical priest (*ibid.* p. 708).

[8] *A.F.H.* iv. 701.   [9] *Ibid.* p. 702.

[10] " E che questo sia oggi in tra lloro, apare per isperienza evidente che papa Iohanni XXII e gli altri successori si partirono, e partono dalla unione e vera chiesa per lo male intendere la Scriptura inverso la povertà di Xpo. Ancora sono in divisione per la discordia che è intra lloro, per volere ciaschuno il papato e possedere la prelazione. Alchuni tenghono per papa quello che fu fatto a Roma (Urban VI.), alchuni quello di Fondi o da Vignone. Quello da

could not be the Church of Christ but "the synagogue of the devil ".[1] The characteristics of the true Church were rather peace, love, and charity coupled with the faithful observance of the commandments of God.[2] Although this treatise was written in the vulgar tongue its writer was obviously a man of culture, for he not only quotes from St. Bernard [3] and St. Augustine,[4] but alludes to the *Paradiso* of Dante.[5] His knowledge of purely Franciscan literature was also profound, for he was acquainted with the works of Pecham and St. Bonaventura as well as with the constitutions of various Chapters-General.[6] His citations from the " Historia Septem Tribulationum " [7] and his allusion to the polemical writings of Occam [8] are not particularly surprising, for his mind would naturally have been nourished upon such controversial literature. Perhaps no other manifesto of the Fraticelli reaches quite such a high intellectual level.

There is a remarkable likeness between the letter of the Perugian Fratecello and another, also written in the vernacular and directed to the whole of Christendom,[9] the object of which was to justify the separation of the author and his co-religionists from the

---

Roma, schomunicha quello da Vignone e quello da Vignone quello da Roma " (*ibid.* p. 706).

A similar schism had taken place in the Franciscan Order since the rival Popes had appointed different Ministers-General, who are described in the treatise as the " master " and the " minister " (*A.F.H.* iv. p. 706). As the former title can apply only to Urban's supporter, Ludovico Donati, who was created a cardinal in 1382, and Clement VII. did not settle at Avignon till the summer of 1379, the pamphlet must have been written some time between these dates. Cf. Oliger, *ibid.* 692.

[1] *Ibid.* p. 707. Cf. *S.F.* i. p. 508. *Supra*, p. 215. According to the writer of the treatise, men expose themselves to the danger of eternal perdition if they shirk their responsibility of judging between good and evil (*A.F.H.* iv. p. 711). To those in authority was especially entrusted the duty of reforming the corruption rampant in the Church (*ibid.* pp. 699-700).

[2] *Ibid.* p. 707. Cf. *S.F.* i. p. 508. *Supra*, p. 215.

[3] *A.F.H.* iv. p. 701. Epistle to Adam the monk. Migne, *P.L.*, 182, 95.

[4] *A.F.H.* iv. p. 697. Father Oliger was unable to trace this quotation.

[5] *Ibid.* p. 699. *Paradiso*, xxix. 108.

[6] *A.F.H.* iv. p. 701. His knowledge of the " De Finibus Paupertatis " and the writings of Olivi on the subject of poverty is more natural, for these were carefully studied by the Zealots.

[7] *Ibid.* There is a remarkable similarity both in tone and in certain of the sources used between this treatise and those published in *S.F.* i. pp. 503-24, but the Perugian manifesto displays greater erudition and power of thought.

[8] *A.F.H.* iv. p. 705.

[9] " Ad tucti li universali fedeli di Cristo ad li quali questa lettera perverrà. Noi poveri servi di Yesu Christo, fedeli et cattolici, perseguitati per la deffenssione de la evangelica verità, offeriamo pace con eterna salute " (p. 7). Published by Vanzolini in *Scelta di curiosità letterarie inedite o rare* (Bologna, 1865), vol. 55.

Church.[1] The reasons given are the same—namely, heresy, simony, and fornication [2]—and many of the same citations from the fathers are found in both treatises.[3] "Cum inter nonnullos" is the only decretal of John XXII. which is mentioned,[4] but it is clearly and emphatically stated that by legislating in direct contradiction of the Scriptures and to the enactments of his predecessors he had been guilty of the sin of heresy.[5] As in the Perugian manifesto, much stress is laid on the iniquity of the clergy, and even the few whom the writer admits to be neither fornicators nor simoniacs had been guilty of the same sin, since they had not denounced the wickedness of their colleagues.[6] The doctrine of the validity of the Sacraments when administered by heretics is almost a repetition of the former work, as are the reasons alleged for not taking part in the sacrifice of the Mass when the celebrant was a member of that church which through its support of John XXII. had lapsed into heresy.[7] Strong in the justice of their cause the writers of the letter challenged their adversaries to convince them of error, for they welcomed controversy as a means of establishing the truth,[8] and like their Perugian brethren were convinced of the responsibility of the individual Christian to decide for himself between truth and error.[9] It is unfortunate that so little is known concerning the date or authorship of this interesting appeal.

During the second half of the fourteenth century the position of the Fraticelli at Rome was secured by the friendship of one of their leaders, a certain Paul of Florence, with some of the Roman barons, and especially with the prefect of the city, Giovanni di Vico,[10] the sturdy opponent of Cardinal Albornez.[11] Only one of their letters has come down to us and this was directed to the rulers of the Eternal City as a protest against a sentence passed against them.[12] Like the Perugian treatise, this was written in Italian, and was

---

[1] " Noi essendo pregati che de le molte rasione che noi assegnamo, per le quali ne siamo separati dal papa et da li altri prelati, ne dobbiamo scrivere aliquante sobbrevità, in commune volgare, ad ciò che si possano intendere da onne persone " (Vanzolini, op. cit. p. 17).

[2] Ibid. pp. 9-15.

[3] For example, the quotation from the seventh book of Occam's Dialogus, p. 20. Cf. A.F.H. iv. p. 263.

[4] " Cum inter nonnullos " was proved by the author to be a direct violation of " Exiit qui seminat " (Vanzolini, op. cit. pp. 9-12).

[5] Ibid. pp. 22-26. Cf. p. 8, where John XXII. is described as " Jacopo chiamato papa Iohanni XXII."

[6] Ibid. p. 15 s.

[7] Ibid. pp. 14-15, 26-27. Cf. A.F.H. iv. 699 and 707-709.

[8] Vanzolini, op. cit., p. 21.

[9] Ibid. pp. 18-19.   [10] S.F. i. 522. Cf. supra, p. 215.

[11] Cf. Mollat, Les Papes d'Avignon, pp. 167-69.

[12] A.F.H. v. pp. 74-84.

probably the joint production of the chief representatives of the sect, for in the beginning the authors describe themselves as " certain friars minor who truly observe the Rule of St. Francis ".[1] They declare themselves to be faithful sons of the Church, following her teaching in all matters of faith and believing devoutly in the seven Sacraments.[2] The Pope " of Rome " was indeed Christ's Vicar on earth, but his power had been given him for edification and not for destruction, and if he should be guilty of heresy he forfeited his position and became of less importance than the humblest Catholic.[3] Indeed according to canon law he could be reproved even by a harlot.[4] Like the other Fraticelli they held that heretical priests and bishops could still administer the Sacraments although they forfeited their power of conferring absolution.[5] Even in the " schismatic " Greek Church the bread in the Mass was converted into the body of Christ.[6] By canon law, however, the faithful had been inhibited from frequenting the services held by simoniacs, for attendance at these was dangerous to the soul.[7] The treatise goes on to declare that in the eyes of the Fraticelli John XXII. was a heretic doomed to eternal perdition,[8] and gives examples of his many errors, six of these being drawn from his sermons and seven from his decretals.[9] This summary corresponds with that given by Michael of Cesena in his manifestos against the Pope, and its incompleteness is probably due to the fact that the end of the letter is unfortunately lost.

An earlier exposition of the doctrines of the Fraticelli is found in a letter written to the leading citizens of the commune of Narni,[10] probably about the year 1354, for the authors expressly declare that thirty years had elapsed since the poverty of Christ and His apostles had been condemned by John XXII.[11] Moreover, they refer to

---

[1] " Seguono i capituli della riposta che feciono certi frati minori dell' osservanza della reghola di Santo Francescho a quelli che regievano Roma, sopra una sentenzia data contro a essi frati " (*A.F.H.* v. p. 74).

[2] *Ibid.* pp. 74-78.

[3] *Ibid.* pp. 78-80. The expression " Papa di Roma " has been taken by Father Oliger to denote that the pamphlet was written at the time of the Great Schism.

[4] *Ibid.* p. 80.

[5] " Noi tegnamo che gli preti e gli altri prelati non possono assolvere de' pecchati, nè benedire nè maladire " (*ibid.* p. 81).

[6] " Appare ancora questo per lo exenpro delli preti greci, li quali sono scismatici e heretici e disobedienti al papa e alla chiesa di Roma, e non di meno danno e recevono l' ordini e consacrano il corpo di Xpo " (*ibid.* p. 77).

[7] *Ibid.* p. 82. The authority cited is *Distinctio*, xxxii. cap. 6.

[8] " Noi tegnamo papa Iohanni XXII heretico e dannato " (*ibid.* p. 84).

[9] *Ibid.*

[10] *Ibid.* vi. 276-90, 515-23.

[11] *Ibid.* p. 288.

Innocent VI. as "papa Hodiernus".[1] After the significant incipit " Ave Maria gracia plena " and a personal greeting to the rulers of the city,[2] they give their reasons for writing. Two of their number, Fra Petrucchio and Fra Stefano, had fallen into the hands of those sons of Belial, the Friars Minor, and had been treated with such cruelty that the former was already dead, and it was feared that a like fate might befall his companion if he were not speedily released.[3] The reputation enjoyed by the sect at Narni was so great that the friends of the victim were amazed that the citizens had not already intervened on his behalf, especially as at Todi, Perugia, and other places the populace had stormed the prisons of the Inquisition to rescue the Fraticelli from its clutches.[4] The letter, which is written in Latin, is even more violent in tone than those from Perugia and Rome, and the bitterest venom of the writers is reserved for the " fratres minores ", if they can rightly be given such a name, since from their pride, cunning, and covetousness they should more justly be termed " Maiores ".[5] In another place they are described as following the ways of Antichrist,[6] among whose principal disciples were John XXII. and his supporters.[7] At the same time the writers protested that they adhered to the principal articles of the faith, but they quoted the reprimand given by Paul to Peter as a proof that even a Pope might err.[8] Since the condemnation of the poverty of Christ the state of abomination and desolation foretold by Daniel had existed in the Church,[9] for all the heresies of the Arians, the Sabellians, the Pelagians, the Nestorians, the Manichaeans, the Valdenses, and the Greeks did not contain such abominable errors as the decretals of John XXII.[10] This Pope of

---

[1] *A.F.H.* vi. p. 519. Innocent VI. (1352–62). He must be the Pope intended, as he was reigning thirty years after the promulgation of " Cum inter nonnullos" in 1323. Cf. *ibid.* p. 521, where Innocent VI. is mentioned by name among the successors of John XXII.

[2] *Ibid.* p. 276. The rulers are addressed by name.   [3] *Ibid.* p. 277.

[4] " Et alique istarum liberaverunt xi pauperculos de manibus et carceribus istorum perversorum cum manu armata et potente " (*ibid.* p. 278). The other cities mentioned are Assisi and Pisa.

[5] " Si minores possent appellari, quia non sunt Minores, scilicet in humilitate et simplicitate, set Maiores in superbia, astucia, ambitione, et abusione, ut est manifestum toti mundo " (*ibid.* p. 277).

[6] *Ibid.* They are also described as " sons of Belial " and followers of " the way of Balaam " (*ibid.*).

[7] " Donec veniat maior Antichristus, quem breviter expectamus, quia dictus Iohannes cum omnibus fautoribus infinitis sunt eius nuncii et discipuli principales " (*ibid.* p. 518).

[8] *Ibid.* pp. 279–80.   [9] *Ibid.* p. 288.

[10] *Ibid.* pp. 289 and 518. This is reminiscent of the manifestos of Michael of Cesena against the bull " Quia vir reprobus ". It is curious that although they give examples of erroneous doctrine from John XXII.'s other decretals they do not refer to this one. Cf. *ibid.* pp. 289–90 and 515–18.

cursed memory, whose coming had been foretold by the Abbot Joachim,[1] had in his lifetime set forth and defended more than two hundred false doctrines.[2] The Fraticelli of Narni and Rome had much the same conception of the position of the priesthood, both confirming their arguments by an appeal to the example of the Greek Church.[3] At the end of the letter the writers stated that it was their duty to denounce the heresies and crimes against Christ and His saints which were so rampant in the world.[4] They had even that very year sent a letter containing the aforesaid truths to the Pope and his cardinals, none of whom had been able to answer them.[5] There is a ring of mockery in their challenge to their adversaries to meet them with solid arguments and not with empty words.[6] Yet such boldness did not avail them much, for some twenty years later a rubric was inserted in the statute book of Narni enacting that the papal constitutions against the heretics should be hereafter faithfully observed.[7]

The presence of the Fraticelli at Narni in 1350 is of especial interest since in the next century two settlements of hermits are found in the commune,[8] and these are described in a papal bull of 1446 as belonging to the congregation of " brother Angelo of Clareno ".[9] The origin of this community is veiled in mystery, but it has been conjectured that it was indeed an offshoot of Angelo's original brotherhood, whose orthodoxy after the lapse of over a century was at last recognised by the Church. The traditional connection between its founder and the Osservanti presumably helped to confirm its reputation for orthodoxy.[10] The Clarenists, as they came to be called, were found in other regions besides Narni, for in 1437 the commune of Treia provided the brothers settled at

---

[1] *A.F.H.* vi. p. 519. The writer is quoting from the commentary on Jeremiah, which he regarded as a genuine work of Joachim.

[2] " Quod plusquam ducentos errores vel hereses predicavit vel instituit, dogmatizavit vel defendit, iste Iohannes maledictus " (*ibid*. p. 289).

[3] *Ibid*. p. 523. The faithful, however, should not receive the Sacrament from the hands of heretics, the only exception being baptism in times of urgent necessity (*ibid*.).

[4] " Et certe si nos taceremus, specialiter nos evangelii, fautores hereticorum valde bene esse possemus, videndo et audiendo tanta scelera, tot errores et hereses contra nostrum salvatorem dominum nostrum Ihum Xpum et eius sanctos et contra Ecclesiam sanctam suam " (*ibid*. p. 522).

[5] " Et sciat indubitanter vestra nobilitas et probitas, Reverendi domini, quod iste veritates et conclusiones et multe alie fuerunt scripte et presentate anno isto coram ipso papa et coram toto suo collegio, quibus nunquam potuerunt nec sciverunt respondere " (*ibid*. p. 523).

[6] " Et si quis est, qui contra hanc confessionem et diffinitionem fidei catholice vellet aliquid dicere vel arguere, non verberet verbis aerem, set ostendat veris rationibus et auctoritatibus rationem seu rationes " (*ibid*.).

[7] *Ibid*. p. 272.   [8] *Ibid*.

[9] *Ibid*. p. 735. See note, p. 280 *infra*.   [10] Cf. *supra*, p. 66.

Valle Cerase with habits, besides giving them alms for the reparation of their monastery.[1] Two years later their benefactors were released from a sentence of excommunication at their intercession.[2] In 1446 Eugenius IV. intervened on behalf of the community at Narni, for by the will of a certain priest called " Paulus Jocii " the hospital of Sta Croce had been left to " their use ", since like the great Franciscan Order from which they were descended they could own no property even as a community. The hospital had been handed over to the administration of the rectors of the hospital of San Jacopo, and they had let it to a certain Minichelus di Giorgio on the understanding that he should pay a yearly rent to the brothers. For three years the Clarenists had received nothing, and so decided to sue for their rights.[3] There is something strangely ironical in the display of such concern for their temporal interests, especially when we consider how repugnant it would have been to the whole spirit of their founder.[4] In 1473, at its own request, the Order was united to the Osservanti though the brethren remained under the Rule of their own vicar, Petrus Hispanus.[5] It is in connection with this event that the Observantine chronicler, Bernardinus Aquilanus, records the injunction of the dying Angelo to his followers that they should return to the Franciscan Order when they found that its members were once more observing its Rule in its original strictness.[6] Their curious habit must have excited great surprise among the friars, for besides being modelled on the short and skimpy pattern supposed to have been worn by the original followers of St. Francis, it possessed a second hood which was presumably used as a protection for the chest.[7] At the same time the sisters belonging to Angelo's foundation were permitted to become part of the Franciscan Order.[8] Certain of the brethren who wished to remain independent continued to live as hermits under the juris-

---

[1] *A.F.H.* vi. p. 733.   [2] *Ibid.* pp. 733-35.

[3] *Ibid.* p. 735. Bull of Eugenius IV. of 1446.

[4] Cf. Oliger, *ibid.* p. 732.

[5] By the bull " Dominus noster Ihesus Christus " of Sixtus IV., March 5, 1473, the text of which is given in De Gubernatis, *Orbis Seraphicus*, i. 607. Cf. *A.F.H.* iii. 254.

[6] B. Bernardini Aquilani *Chronica Fratrum Minorum Observantiae* (ed. Lemmens, Rome, 1902), p. 6. Quoted in *A.F.H.* iii. 254, *n.* 1. Cf. *supra*, p. 68.

[7] " Diverso habitu incedentis, scilicet brevi habitu, capucio ante et retro ad cordam usque, pyramidali forma cui a tergo pannea lingua haerebat." Ridolfi, *Historiarum Seraphicae Religionis libri tres*, Liber II., f. 155 *a*. The coloured illustration in Hélyot's *Histoire des ordres religieux*, vii. p. 61, is perhaps inspired by this account. It is noteworthy that a description of the original Franciscan habit is found as a kind of appendix to the " Historia Septem Tribulationum ". Cf. *A.L.K.G.* ii. p. 153.

[8] Cf. the bull " Pia nos excitat " (October 19, 1473), De Gubernatis, *op. cit.* i. p. 608.

diction of the bishops.[1] During the next century many attempts were made by the Popes to fuse Angelo's foundation entirely with the Osservanti,[2] but its members seem to have desired to maintain their independence. In 1510 certain of the Clarenists and Amadeists had been given the option of joining either the Conventuals or the Osservanti,[3] with the result that the majority of both bodies decided to unite themselves to the stricter branch of the Franciscans. A bull promulgated two years later enacted that all who refused to submit to the papal regulations should be excommunicated.[4] The Order was finally suppressed by Pius V. in 1568, and its convents and other possessions were handed over to the Observants.[5] At the time of their dissolution the Clarenists possessed no less than two settlements in Rome—one at St. Pietro in Monte Aureo and the other at St. Bartholommeo in Insula de Urbe, the second of which had been bestowed on them by Paul III.[6] The value of the historical material surrendered can be judged by the fact that one of the earliest and best manuscripts of Angelo da Clareno's " Expositio " is supposed originally to have belonged to their convent at Stroncone.[7] The majority of the brothers shared the same fate as their property, but certain of their number evidently preferred to cast in their lot with the Conventuals, for a bull of Gregory XIII. absolves them from the ecclesiastical censures which they had incurred for ignoring the enactment of his predecessor.[8] After 1581 the name of the congregation of the Clarenists disappears from the annals of the Franciscan Order.

The second branch of the Fraticelli—namely, the Michaelists, or the " Fraticelli de opinione " [9]—had possibly a greater influence

[1] De Gubernatis, *op. cit.* pp. 607 and 609. Cf. *A.F.H.* vi. 731, *n.* 7.

[2] Cf. the bulls " Cum multae et graves " of Julius II. (1506) and " Ite et vos " of Leo X. (1517) (De Gubernatis, *op. cit.* i. 609-611).

[3] " Licet nuper per quasdam " (*ibid.* p. 609).

[4] " Ad hoc praecipue cordis nostri " (*ibid.*).

[5] By the bull " Beatus Christi Salvatoris ". Cf. the continuation of Wadding's " Annales XX. Registrum Pontificum XLI." The brothers are described as " Clarenorum de la becca ". This step on the part of the Pope was the outcome of the attempts of the Minister-General " Franciscus Zamoriensis " to suppress all separate organisations in his Order, with the exception of the Conventuals and the Observants (*ibid., An.,* 1568).

[6] By the bull " Sacri apostolatus ministerio " (1536) (De Gubernatis, *op. cit.* i. p. 611). Attached to their convent was the old church where Otto III. is supposed to have worshipped.

[7] Now Codex S. Isidori de Urbe 1/92. Cf. Oliger, *Introductio Expositioni Regulae Fratrum Minorum,* p. xii. He makes use of this manuscript and another also dating from the fourteenth century, Codex Vat. Ottobonianus Lat. 522, as the basis for his text (*ibid.* p. xix).

[8] " Sedes apostolica " (1581) (De Gubernatis, *op. cit.* i. p. 613).

[9] The names " Fraticelli de opinione " and " Fraticelli de paupere vita " are very significant, for the former had separated from the Church over the

over the life of the Middle Ages, and especially over that of the common people, than the descendants of the old Spiritual party. Although at first the struggle between Michael of Cesena and John XXII. seemed to have aroused little enthusiasm even among the Franciscans,[1] a revival of interest took place in the latter part of the fourteenth century, possibly as the result of the indignation excited in Italy by the continued absence of the papal court, and the scandal of the Great Schism which followed almost immediately upon its return. The converts to the new movement, however, were men of a very different stamp from its founders, generally belonging to the artisan class, and influenced rather by a general discontent with the conditions existing in the Church and in society than by any intellectual convictions.[2]   Unlike the " Fraticelli de paupere vita " the Michaelists [3] seem to have organised themselves upon the model of the existing Church, the only difference being that their priests, who believed themselves to belong to the true Order of St. Francis, observed at least outwardly the strictest poverty.[4]   Their great centre was the March of Ancona, and from there they sent preachers to the different cities to visit the faithful in secret and to give them the consolation of the Sacraments.[5]   In order to reach their destinations in safety they were often forced to travel disguised as ordinary traders and sometimes even as soldiers.[6] The sect was especially active in Florence during the latter part of the fourteenth century, and its influence was so dreaded by the commune that in 1382 the heresy laws of Frederick II. were solemnly re-enacted.[7]   Seven years later the city was to witness the martyrdom of the itinerant preacher, Michael da Calci, who was burnt outside the city walls.   The story of his sufferings is told in

theoretical question of the poverty of Christ, while the latter had been driven from the Franciscan Order because they had wished to live in strict accord with the Rule and Testament of St. Francis.

[1] Cf. *supra*, p. 179 *s*.

[2] This fact is used by " Frater Andreas Ricchi " in his treatise to prove that the Michaelists were heretics, for every orthodox movement grew rather than declined in numbers and influence, and attracted men of learning, position, and character (*A.F.H.* iii. 524 and 526).

[3] This name is very common in the second half of the fourteenth century. Cf. *ibid.* p. 268. The nickname " Nicholaite " is also found, perhaps because of their reverence for the decretal " Exiit qui seminat " of Nicholas III., which had been one of the original causes of the controversy. Cf. *ibid.* 269.

[4] Cf. " Dialogus contra Fraticellos " of S. James of the March (*Misc.* ii. 597 ; *ibid.* i. 482 and 484).

[5] *Misc.* i. 482, and Zambrini, Intro. to " Storia di Fra Michele minorità, come fu arso in Firenze nel 1389," pp. 1-3.

[6] *Misc.* ii. 597. " *Catholicus.* ' Aliqui vadunt sicut saeculares cum birectis et caligis, et giorneriis cum lancia, aliqui portant claves ad vendendum ' . . . *Haereticus.* ' Nos imus hoc modo ex timore.' "

[7] *S.F.* i. pp. 414 and 495.

the rude vernacular of the people by the companion of his imprisonment, whose very bitterness against the ecclesiastical authorities, if not perhaps truly Christian, increases the dramatic force of his narrative.[1] It is impossible to over-estimate the heroism of the victim, who was a young man still in his noviciate and with the whole of his life before him.[2] At the end of three months' sojourn at Florence Michael was betrayed by certain women who had enticed him into their house on the plea of wishing to confess to him.[3] When he reached the prison all his papers and even his breviary were taken from him,[4] and he and his companion were thrust into the common room along with the other prisoners ; yet even here he was able to rejoice that he had been deemed worthy to suffer for his faith.[5] The two questions at issue during the trial were the poverty of Christ and His apostles and the errors of John XXII., whom Michael persistently asserted to have been " not a Catholic but a heretic ".[6] He admitted that even the Fraticelli might be mistaken on certain matters, but this did not affect their orthodoxy since they submitted themselves unreservedly to the holy Church and to the holy Pope, whose coming they expected.[7] Even in the short space of time that elapsed between his final condemnation and the day appointed for the execution he was not left in peace, but was pestered by the visits of certain friars and doctors of theology, whose motive appears to have been curiosity rather than any desire for the conversion of the prisoner.[8] The latter

---

[1] Printed by Zambrini, *op. cit.* pp. 1-57, from Codex Magliabecchiana, xxxi. 65. It has recently been translated by Dr. Coulton in his *Life in the Middle Ages*, iv. pp. 284-98. An example of the bitterness of the writer is his description of the Bishop of Florence as " el principe de' farisei " (Zambrini, *op. cit.* p. 9).

[2] " E noi, novizii di due dì . . . ci vuole Iddio d' un poco di fatica tanto rimunerare " (*ibid.* p. 7).

[3] *Ibid.* p. 3. They are described as " certe figliuole di Giuda ".

[4] *Ibid.* p. 7. A priest who was also in prison allowed him to use his breviary (p. 18).

[5] He and his companion had only a corner of the common room of the prison in which to sleep, the walls of which were so damp that the water flowed down from them (*ibid.* p. 32). Besides praying to God, Michael recommended himself to " his father ", St. Francis, and to certain members of his sect who had perished at the stake (*ibid.* p. 17).

[6] " Et quando dicea ' il venerabilissimo et sanctissimo papa Giovanni XXII ', rispondea ' ma eretico ' " (*ibid.* p. 29). For his examination, cf. *ibid.* p. 12 *s.*

[7] " Errare possiamo, ma eretici non possiamo essere, imperò che sottomettiamo noi e ogni nostro detto alla correzione della santa chiesa, e dal papa santo da venire " (*ibid.* p. 22).

[8] *Ibid.* pp. 24-25. Many of the common people also visited him, " il quale, sotto atto di grandissima compassione, tormentava l' anima del santo il dì e la notte " (*ibid.* p. 33). One of these with a truer pity than the rest gave him a crucifix (*ibid.*).

were impressed by his arguments, but the former withdrew in indignation, declaring that he had " the devil on his back ".[1] The most vivid part of the whole story is perhaps the account of his journey to the stake, for the reader seems actually to see the terrible procession winding in the spring sunshine [2] through the narrow streets of the city, which were thronged with the riff-raff of Florence, some of them mocking the sufferer and others with noisy sympathy pestering him to recant.[3] When he was urged to listen to the voice of the people, since it was the voice of God, Michael answered with contemptuous indignation that the Jewish mob had crucified Christ.[4] Among the crowd was a member of his own sect who bade him remember the passion of the Saviour, and turning to him with a joyous countenance he murmured, " O faithful Christian, pray to God that He grant me strength ".[5] At last the procession reached Santa Croce, where the friars had assembled to jeer at the prisoner, but he paid no heed to them, even when they pointed scornfully to a picture of their founder painted over the gateway and called to him to avail himself of the intercession of the Saint.[6] Michael, however, stood in need of no such counsel, for he raised his eyes to heaven and cried, " Francis, my father, plead with Christ for me ".[7] Even when they reached the place of execution his resolution was unshaken, though the young noble who commanded the soldiery of the commune had had instructions to bring him safely back if at the last he recanted.[8] As they lighted the faggots which were heaped round him he began to intone the " Te Deum ", and his last prayer was " In manus Tuas, Domine, commendo Spiritum meum ".[9] When all was over many even of his adversaries were convinced that they had burned a saint,[10] while among the Fraticelli his memory was revered as if he had been one of the early martyrs of the Church.[11]

[1] Zambrini, *op. cit.* p. 25.
[2] The actual day of execution was April 30, 1389 (*A.L.K.G.* iv. 105). May Day was the great Florentine holiday, so the condition of the populace on the previous day can well be imagined.
[3] " E a tutti increscendone, diceano ' deh non voler morire ' " (Zambrini, *op. cit.* p. 44).
" Quando giunse a santo Giovanni essendogli detto ' pentiti, pentiti, non voler morire ' " (*ibid.* p. 45).
[4] " E colui comincio a dire : ' Voce di popolo, voce di Dio '. Ed e' disse : ' la voce del popolo fece crucifiggere Christo, fe morire San Piero ' " (*ibid.* p. 48).
[5] *Ibid.*   [6] *Ibid.* pp. 49 and 52.   [7] *Ibid.* p. 49.
[8] *Ibid.* p. 55.   [9] *Ibid.*
[10] " E morto molti diceano : ' e pare un Santo ' : eziandio delli avversari ' (*ibid.* p. 56).
[11] The other martyrs belonging to the sect to whom Michael had commended himself were Bartolomeo Greco, Bartolomeo da Buggiano, and Antonio de Aqua Canina. Cf. *ibid.* p. 17. Olivi was apparently regarded as one of their Saints (*ibid.* p. 22).

After the heroism displayed by Michael da Calci and the tragedy of his death the record of the trial of certain Fraticelli at Lucca which took place in the year 1411 comes somewhat as an anticlimax.[1] In this case the victims were men of humble origin, the most important among them being a wineseller named Bartolomeo Lemmi.[2] The chief charge against him and his companions was that they had received preachers belonging to the sect at their houses,[3] and had not fulfilled the religious duties enjoined on them by the Church.[4] Yet Bartolomeo had not dared to attract suspicion by absenting himself from the Easter Communion, but before visiting the church of St. Michael he had feasted openly at a wine shop, and although he had received the blessed Sacrament from the hands of the priest he had not actually partaken of it.[5] Neither he nor his companions were desirous of paying the penalty of their errors, and were easily induced to recant. The inquisitors, who seem to have been gifted with a considerable amount of humour, were not disposed to deal harshly with them. Even Bartolomeo was only sentenced to hear Mass daily, and to kneel devoutly with uncovered head during the consecration of the host, and to visit Rome within a year, in order to receive a blessing from the Pope, whose authority he had previously denied.[6] It is to be hoped that these penances were duly performed, but the very suddenness of the repentance of Bartolomeo and his companions casts grave suspicion upon their sincerity. Moreover, a feigned submission was apparently a recognised method among the Fraticelli of extricating themselves from perilous situations,[7] though the bolder spirits naturally shunned such an expedient and preferred to die for the defence of their beliefs. Apart from the comedy of the whole of the proceedings the most interesting fact revealed by the evidence is the name of the patriarch of the Fraticelli, Brother Francis of Terni, whose position seems to have been similar to that of the Pope.[8] His authority, however, was probably not so unquestioned, for, like many other heretical sects, his followers displayed a tendency to break up into little independent groups [9]—a fact which adds greatly to the difficulties of the would-be student of their history.

---

[1] *Misc.* i. pp. 481-85.   [2] *Ibid.* p. 482.

[3] *Ibid.* One of these preachers who celebrated Mass for the members of the sect was a certain Laurence of Perugia. Another was Paul of Florence. Cf. *supra*, p. 220.

[4] Bartolomeo had not gone to confession for two years (*ibid.*).

[5] *Ibid.* He had spat the host secretly into his sleeve.

[6] *Ibid.* p. 483. Like all the Fraticelli he had held that there had been no true Pope over the Church since the days of John XXII. (*ibid.* p. 482).

[7] Cf. the process of 1466 against the Fraticelli of Poli and Maiorlati (*infra*, p. 245, and *A.L.K.G.* iv. pp. 127 and 132).

[8] He ordained all the bishops of the sect (*Misc.* i. p. 482).

[9] Cf. *infra*, p. 243, and *A.L.K.G.* iv. 114.

Like the " Fraticelli de paupere vita " the Michaelists composed many pamphlets defending their position, and one written at the close of the fourteenth century can probably be taken as typical of the rest.[1] It is in the form of a letter directed to all the faithful,[2] and deals exhaustively with the accusation so commonly brought against the members of the sect—namely, that they denied the validity of the sacrifice of the Mass.[3] In the eyes of the Fraticelli all the priests who remained under the obedience of John XXII. and his successors were necessarily heretics, but, as we have seen, this did not in any way injure their sacramental powers, though they exercised these to their own damnation.[4] Many of the arguments used are clearly derived from the writings produced during the early stages of the struggle, the most important of these being that Christ and His apostles had possessed no legal claim to the goods which they used, but had been content with a mere " usus facti ".[5] The passage at the end of the treatise might appear strange if it were not remembered that the Michaelists regarded themselves as members of the true Church and their opponents as heretics.[6] Their offer of submission if convinced by logical arguments of the

---

[1] *A.F.H.* iii. 263-66. In one respect it differs from the others which have come down to us, for it is written in Latin instead of in the vernacular. Father Oliger believes that this treatise was composed to meet some definite attack of the Catholic party, and points out how exactly it answers the charges brought against the Fraticelli by the blessed Giovanni dalle Celle in his first letter to them (cf. Wesselofsky, *Scelta di curiosità letterarie inedite o rare*, 86 (1), p. 338). He therefore considers that it was probably written sometime between 1375 and 1389, during which period the controversy took place between the Camaldolite hermit and the leaders of the sect. This is all the more interesting since only a fragment of one of the letters of the Fraticelli to Giovanni has survived. Cf. *A.F.H.* iii. 258-9, and *infra*, p. 232.

[2] " Universis Christi fidelibus utramque partem questionis audire volentibus et optantibus iuxta commune proverbium ' audi aliam partem ', et omnibus, quibus hec lictera pervenerit. Nos de pluribus suspecti et infamati, presertim de illa falsa et herronea consequentia et conclusione, que dicit, quod papa non est papa et cetera " (*A.F.H.* iii. 263). [3] *Ibid.* pp. 263 *et seq.*

[4] " Dum intendit facere illud, quod ecclesia facit, et formam ecclesie tenet et observat, semper episcopus ordinat, et vere presbiteros consecrat et presbyter semper corpus Xpi conficit, set in preiudicium et dampnationem suarum animarum " (*ibid.* p. 265).

[5] " Item dicimus, tenemus et confitemur, quod Xs, in quantum homo viator, et apostoli eius viam perfectionis tenentes et ostendentes, iure proprietatis et dominii civiliter vel mundane non habuerunt aliqua in speciali vel in communi, preter simplicem usum facti, sine quo nemo preterire potest, ut patet extra ' De Verborum significatione c°. Exiit qui Seminat ' " (Sext. v. 12, c. 3) (*ibid.*).

[6] " Cuius (sacra mater ecclesia) correctioni et cuilibet catholico fideli nos metipsos et hec dicta nostra et omnia alia, tamquam veri eius obedientes filii, subicimus et quicumque iuridice nobis oppositum demonstrabit, parati sumus plenam scientiam sumere de predictis, domino concedente. Amen " (*ibid.* p. 266).

falsehood of their opinions was probably purely formal. The conditions, however, which they laid down were unlikely to be fulfilled, since the questions at issue between the two parties had now become matters of prejudice rather than of intellectual conviction.

The best known treatise of the Fraticelli is the famous " Appellatio ", formerly ascribed to Occam.[1] Modern criticism, however, has proved that it was written in Italy probably about the year 1378. Like most of the writings of the Michaelists it is directed to all the faithful, but differs from them both by its great length and its exhaustive summary of the errors of John XXII., taken largely from the works of Occam and his companions at Munich. Its most salient characteristic is its complete lack of originality, all the chief arguments, and even most of the numerous citations from the Fathers, being derived from earlier sources.[2] It is strange that scholars should ever have credited Occam with its authorship, for though many of his ideas are repeated parrot fashion, the tone of the treatise is apocalyptic, and its appeal is to the feelings rather than to the reason, great stress being laid on St. Francis's prophecy concerning " the pastor uncanonically elected ".[3] Its importance is due to its popularity among the Fraticelli, for many have identified it with the " Liber Veritatis " which figures in the Inquisition records.[4] Moreover, there was no other of their writings which provoked so many refutations from the orthodox party, perhaps the most famous of these being the " Dialogus contra Fraticellos " of the blessed James of the March.[5]

The Catholic writers of the fourteenth and fifteenth centuries were not slow in taking up the challenge which had been dropped by the Fraticelli. As in the case of the latter, their writings do not reach a very high intellectual level, and they are generally content to re-echo the old arguments which had been used in the earlier

[1] Although this treatise is not found in the collection of Nicholas the Minorite (cf. *Z.K.G.* vi. p. 78), Baluze printed it with the other documents connected with the early stages of the controversy in *Misc.* iii. pp. 341-55. Father Oliger discusses the question of its date and authorship at length in *A.F.H.* iv. 19-23, and has come to the conclusion that it was written in Italy before 1378. The allusion to the three Popes in *Misc.* iii. 352 is not found in the versions printed in *Fasc. Rerum Expetend.* ii. and in the *Firmamentum,* and in only one other codex besides the one used by Baluze, so that it was probably a later addition. If it had formed part of the original the date of composition must have been shortly before the Council of Constance (1418). For the older theories concerning its authorship, cf. *supra,* p. 19.

[2] Most of the authorities cited are also to be found in the manifestos of Michael and his followers. [3] *Misc.* iii. p. 341.

[4] Cf. *A.L.K.G.* iv. 114 and 137 ; and *A.F.H.* vi. 745, where this question is discussed.

[5] *Misc.* ii. 595-610. Cf. *A.F.H.* iv. 16-19.

stages of the controversy. Perhaps the most zealous champion of the orthodox views was the Camaldolite hermit, Giovanni dalle Celle, a scion of a noble Tuscan family, who in 1351 had held the office of Abbot of Sta Trinità at Florence, but had afterwards withdrawn to a cell above Vallombrosa to lead a life of prayer and penance.[1] He did not entirely lose touch with the world, and his early intimacy with Angelo da Clareno's friend and disciple, Simon of Cassia,[2] and his later correspondence with St. Catherine of Siena brought him into contact with many of the finest spirits of the age.[3] So highly was he esteemed among them that in 1378 he was summoned to Rome by Urban VI. to help him in his schemes for the reform of the Church.[4] It was about this time that he began to realise the danger caused to his native city by the spread of the doctrines of the Fraticelli, whom at first he had regarded with favour since their lives seemed, outwardly at least, to be an expression of the highest Christian ideal.[5] His eyes were opened by the conversion of one of his penitents, a Florentine carpenter called Maso, and his endeavours to win him back resulted in an active interchange of letters between himself and the leaders of the sect.[6] The correspondence was carried on in the vernacular, and it is unfortunate that only a fragment of the first letter of the Fraticelli has survived.[7]

[1] The first letter of Giovanni dalle Celle to the Fraticelli and a fragment of their answer is edited by Wesselofsky in *op. cit.* lxxxvi. pp. 335-67, and the second by Tocco in *S.F.* i. pp. 431-94. Signorina Pia Cividali, a pupil of the latter, published two more, together with certain other letters of the Vallombrosian hermit, as part of a critical study of his life and works written as a thesis for the doctor's degree at the University of Florence. This is now printed in the *Memorie della Reale Accademia dei Lincei* (1907), xii. pp. 354-477.

[2] Simon was in Florence between 1346 and 1347, so that this was probably the period of Giovanni's connection with him. It cannot have been later, since the Augustinian hermit died in 1348 (Pia Cividali, *op. cit.* p. 361).

[3] *Ibid.* p. 367. Two letters of St. Catherine to Giovanni are still in existence. Signorina Cividali has edited two of his letters to Brother William of England, one of the saints' most faithful companions, as well as certain others written in her defence, amongst them one to Simon of Cassia's former secretary, John of Salerno, to whom we probably owe the collection and transcription of the letters of Angelo da Clareno (*ibid.* pp. 432-47). Cf. *supra*, p. 69.

[4] Pia Cividali, *op. cit.* p. 370. St. Catherine wrote personally to Giovanni, urging him to obey the summons.

[5] " Dixistis quod ad manus vestras pervenerunt due littere mee, quarum una dirigebatur quibusdam pauperibus, sic vocatis, ecclesie suspectis et scomunicatis. Ego, pater mi, talibus non credidi scripsisse, sed christianis ferventer portantibus crucem Christi et maxime paupertatis " (Letter to John of Salerno, Pia Cividali, *op. cit.* p. 432. Cf. p. 399 and *S.F.* i. p. 465).

[6] *S.F.* i. p. 431.

[7] Wesselofsky, *op. cit.* pp. 365-67. Unfortunately there is not sufficient of the letter remaining to know how the Fraticelli met Giovanni's main accusation, namely, that by denying the authority of the Pope and the Catholic clergy they destroyed the validity of the Sacrament (*ibid.* p. 338). This charge, which

They answer the taunts of their adversary who had mocked at the smallness of their number by a quotation from St. Anselm concerning the fewness of the elect.[1] This, and the arguments concerning the wickedness of the clergy,[2] and the position of an heretical Pope[3] are commonplaces of this sort of propaganda. More interesting is the account of a disputation arranged by the Signory of Florence between the leaders of the Fraticelli and the most learned of the Florentine clergy which was to take place at the church of San Piero Scheraggio, but failed through the action of the bishop in forbidding his supporters to take part.[4] It is significant also that at the beginning of their letter they describe themselves as the "poor friars minor", for it shows that they still regarded themselves as the only true followers of St. Francis.[5]

The four remaining letters of Giovanni dalle Celle are our chief source for the different stages of the conflict. Few antagonists could have entered the fray with less knowledge of the position of their opponents, for even at an advanced stage in the controversy he frankly confesses that he had never studied the decretals of John XXII.[6] He certainly very much under-estimated the intelligence of his adversaries,[7] for their own manifestos prove that they were not ignorant and unlettered fanatics,[8] and there is little to justify the somewhat superior attitude which he adopted towards them. Yet his genuine piety and evident desire to bring about the conversion of the Fraticelli are apparent in every line of his letters, though his utter inability to appreciate their standpoint makes it unlikely that his laudable endeavours met with any result. Still, his simple

---

was also brought forward at the trial of Michele da Calci (cf. *supra*, p. 226 *s.*), is answered in the Latin letter of the Fraticelli to all the faithful which Father Oliger edited in *A.F.H.* iii. 163-68, and which he believes to have been written at much the same time as their correspondence with Giovanni dalle Celle, that is, between 1375 and 1389. Cf. *ibid.* pp. 258-60, and *supra*, p. 230, *n.* 1.

[1] Wesselofsky, *op. cit.* pp. 356-57. The same quotation is found in the letter of the Perugian Fratecello. Cf. *A.F.H.* iv. 697. For Giovanni's answer to this argument cf. *S.F.* i. p. 432.

[2] Wesselofsky, *op. cit.* pp. 357-58.

[3] *Ibid.* pp. 361-62.

[4] *Ibid.* p. 359.

[5] "In nomine Iesu Cristo povere crocifisso Amen. A don Giovanni dalle Celle i povere frati minori, perseguitati per la verita del vangelio . . ." (*ibid.* p. 356).

[6] "Dico adunque in prima che io non so se quelle cose (errors attributed to John XXII. by the Fraticelli) disse il papa Giovanni, o se queste cose mise nelle decretali che fece, impero che mai io le vidi perchè sono estravagante" (Pia Cividali, *op. cit.* p. 458).

[7] In every letter there are scathing allusions to their ignorance and presumption.

[8] Cf. especially the letter published by Father Oliger (*A.F.H.* iii. 263-68; *supra*, p. 230).

directness and shrewd common sense, together with an apt if somewhat homely gift of expression and illustration, give a piquant charm
to his letters which is not always to be found in more scholarly and
profound controversial writings.[1]

John's first letter is a striking testimony to the lightness with
which he entered into the struggle, for he makes no serious effort
to meet the arguments of his opponents. He does not deign to
discuss the errors of John XXII., but merely rebukes the Fraticelli
for presuming to declare that since his fall into heresy there had
been no legitimate Pope,[2] and that therefore there could be no
true bishops and priests, and the bread and wine consecrated in the
Mass was not the body and blood of Christ.[3] The question as
to whether Christ was rich or poor was no concern of poor and
ignorant men, since for such it was sufficient for them to realise
that He was their Redeemer and reward.[4] For his own part he was
willing to go to the stake before he would deny His poverty during
His earthly life, but since this formed no part of the creed of the
Church he was ready to allow others to think as they pleased about
the matter.[5] He sharply criticises the arrogance of his opponents in
concerning themselves with subjects which should be left to the
decision of the learned and in setting themselves up as judges of
the character of the clergy,[6] and reproaches them for their hypocrisy
in making a parade of their poverty.[7] Even if John XXII.
had fallen into heresy it did not follow that the Fraticelli were the
sole remaining representatives of the true Church, since their priests
had never received consecration from any metropolitan or bishop,[8]
nor had the sect any authority to choose a Pope.[9] Such arguments
show that Giovanni's good sense had made him realise the illogic-
ality of the position of his opponents, who justified their separation
from the Church by quoting certain parts of the canon law while

---

[1] The delightful passage where he compares the Fraticelli, who outwardly
appeared to be true Franciscans, to the bushes growing outside taverns, which
could not always be taken as a sure sign that wine was sold within (*S.F.* i. p. 475),
is an example of his vivid, if somewhat unpolished, style of writing.

[2] Wesselofsky, *op. cit.* pp. 337 and 355.   [3] *Ibid.* p. 338.

[4] " Che ai tu a pensare se Cristo fu povero o ricco, dapoi che tu credi che sia
il tuo salvatore, tuo redentore, tuo cibo, tuo prezzo, tuo premio. Questo ti
basta a salute " (*ibid.* p. 354).

[5] " Io certamente credo che Christo fosse povero, e per questo n' andrei
per lo fuoco, s' altro non mi nocesse, salva sempre ogni cosa che ne tenesse la
santa madre e chiesa cattolica e apostolica. Ma perchè uno altro mi diciesse :
' Io credo che Cristo avesse proprio. . . .' Io direi ' E tu ti credi ' " (*ibid.* p. 354).
As might be expected, the Fraticelli in their answer were very indignant
at this indifference to the fundamental article of their creed (*ibid.* pp. 366-67).

[6] " Avegna che sieno peccatori (the clergy) non di meno anno i sagramenti
divini, e non gli debbono diguidicare i fraticiegli, ma Iddio o i loro prelati "
(*ibid.* p. 344).   [7] *Ibid.* p. 338.   [8] *Ibid.* p. 339.   [9] *Ibid.* p. 341.

ignoring others.[1] With similar adroitness he twisted the apocalyptic speculations of the Fraticelli against themselves by declaring that they were the wolves in sheep's clothing, whose appearance was to herald the coming of Antichrist.[2]

The second letter is really a variant on the same themes.[3] The errors of John XXII. are still not dealt with in any detail, for since his decretals had been accepted by the universities, to dispute them was a proof of ignorance and vanity.[4] Moreover, his subsequent recantation was a proof of his orthodoxy.[5] He is probably right in maintaining that the Fraticelli charged the bulk of the clergy with offences which were in reality committed by only a small minority.[6] At the same time he admits that there were some whose lives were a grave scandal to their Order ; [7] but since men generally were given the rulers they deserved,[8] to draw attention to their vices was to repeat the sin of the sons of Noah, who had mocked at the drunkenness of their father,[9] especially as their moral character did not affect the validity of the Sacraments.[10] St. Peter Damien had declared that in the Eucharist the priest acted as the ambassador of the faithful, and just as an earthly emperor would not concern himself greatly with the iniquities of an envoy sent by the Florentines, so the King of Kings looked rather on the faith and devotion of the laity who partook of the sacred elements than on the misdeeds of the consecrating priest.[11] The abuse poured by the Fraticelli on the Friars Minor and their obstinate refusal to receive enlightenment were a proof that they themselves were no true sons of the humble Francis.[12] Giovanni also shows himself well acquainted

---

[1] " Se tengono il dicreto et dicretali, tengano in tutto et non in parte " (Wesselofsky, *op. cit.* p. 340).

[2] *Ibid.* p. 338. Cf. *S.F.* i. p. 453, and Pia Cividali, *op. cit.* p. 459, for other passages which show Giovanni's intimate knowledge of the apocalyptical theories of the Fraticelli. He had certainly read the " Revelationes Joachim ". Cf. *supra*, p. 217.

[3] *S.F.* i. pp. 431-94.   [4] *Ibid.* p. 439.

[5] *Ibid.* Giovanni denies in connection with the recantation of John XXII. the truth of the tradition current among the Fraticelli that the cardinals had wished to burn his body because of his heresies (*ibid.*).

[6] " Ma perchè tu vegia una semoniaco o fornicatore, non dei però giudicare che tutta la Chiesa sia così fatta " (*ibid.* p. 446).

[7] *Ibid.* p. 465.   [8] *Ibid.* p. 480.

[9] *Ibid.* p. 481. In another passage he compares the critics of the higher clergy to the deacon who was smitten with death for venturing to touch the Ark of the Covenant. This is a reference to the story of Uzzah the son of Abinadab in 2 *Samuel* vi. 7.

[10] *S.F.* i. p. 455. The Fraticelli had never contended that it did. Cf. *supra*, p. 218 *s*.

[11] *S.F.* i. p. 455.

[12] " Et dite che siete frati di San Franciescho, e non è il vero ; inpero che fu humilissimo et voi siete superbissimi " (*ibid.* p. 475. Cf. pp. 442 and 474).

with the apocalyptic doctrines of his adversaries, and especially with their belief in the coming of a line of angel Popes.[1] The fact that in one of their letters to him they had quoted from a treatise attributed to Rabanus may perhaps be taken as a proof that the " papal prophecies " were still read in their circle.[2] His allusions to the organisation of the Fraticelli are both instructive and amusing, especially his pious horror at their employment of women preachers.[3] He is probably justified in his criticism that they attached far too much importance to poverty,[4] but it was certainly going too far to suggest, as he did, that the right use of riches was a higher test of sainthood than their renunciation because of the manifold temptations which they entailed,[5] though he supports his contention by the example of Zacchaeus and other righteous rich.[6] According to him Christ had chosen to lead a life of poverty as an example to the multitude of believers for whom wealth and luxury might prove too great a snare.[7] In spite of such arguments there is no doubt that Giovanni himself would have followed the path of poverty and self-surrender, for a wonderful passage describing the true meaning of the cross shows how near he was in spirit to the ideal of the Franciscan Spirituals.[8] In the two following letters Giovanni at last makes a real attempt to answer the objections of his opponents with regard to John XXII.[9] He had obviously been reading an Italian version of the treatise of Fra Andreas Ricchi,[10] for like the earlier writers he reconciles John's decretals with " Exiit qui seminat " by differentiating between the natural and legal significance of the

---

[1] *S.F.* i. pp. 453 and 457-60.

[2] "Alegate ancora Rabano el quale figurò ancora questo papa santo incoronato dagli angioli " (*ibid.* p. 454). Cf. *supra*, p. 40.

[3] " Anchora che voi fate predichare le femmine per Firenze e amaestrare della fede cosa chosì pericholosa " (*ibid.* p. 490).

[4] " Voi fate uno vostro idolo di questa povertà " (*ibid.* p. 460).

[5] *Ibid.* p. 460.   [6] *Ibid.*

[7] " Et perciò Christo prese forma di povertà, non perchè egli non avesse saputo bene dispensare le richeze, ma astenettesene per nostro amore ; perchè vedeva ch' elle pericolovano la gente, et che pochi erano buoni chavalchatori di così malagevole chavallo " (*ibid.* p. 462).

[8] " Che è crocie ? È una mortifichazione della propria volontà e di tutti i sensi. Et questa è lla vera obedienzia, la quale chonficcha i piedi al suddito che non può andare dove vorrebbe ; conficchagli le mani, acciò che non posse aoperare quello che vuole " (*ibid.* p. 473).

[9] Pia Cividali, *op. cit.*, Letters IX. and XI., pp. 452-55 and 458-77.

[10] The Italian version of this treatise is very much abbreviated, whole sections being omitted. Although it is found in the same manuscript as Giovanni's letters (Codex Magliabecchiana, xxxi. 65, f. 2 *r.*-6 *v.*), Signorina Cividali, who published it along with these (*op. cit.* 447-52) does not believe that Giovanni was the translator, or the author of the " Pistola della povertà e difensione del papa " (*op. cit.* 455-58), written for the benefit of a certain beloved spiritual son to enable him to avoid the delusions of the Fraticelli, which is also found among his correspondence.

" ius utendi " ;[1] and his accounts of the recantations of Francis of Ascoli,[2] and of the antipope, Peter of Corbara,[3] as well as of Ubertino da Casale's celebrated reply concerning the poverty of Christ and His apostles,[4] are almost exact reproductions of those given by the Franciscan apologist. These instances make it certain that Giovanni's opponents were Michaelists and not the survivors of the old Spiritual party, though, like the latter, they regarded themselves as the only true sons of St. Francis.[5] Even their opponent realised that a certain measure of truth was mingled with their errors, and quaintly compares heretics to mules, since their teaching was a mixture of truth and falsehood—a fact which greatly increased their power of deceiving the simple.[6] We realise from this letter how great the danger was at this time in Florence, when men's consciences were disturbed by the Great Schism and the city was a prey to a strong current of anticlerical feeling. The enigmatical answer, " Yes, if he is a Catholic ", given by the Fraticelli when challenged to declare whether they regarded Urban VI. as the lawful Pope, must have sown the seeds of doubt and uncertainty in the minds of many.[7] Their concealment of the existence of their own patriarch [8] is certainly understandable, since they could only

---

[1] Pia Cividali, *op. cit.* p. 452. The Fraticelli had sent him a list of thirteen errors taken from the decretals of John XXII., and Giovanni was endeavouring to prove that they had interpreted these documents in a totally different sense from the Pope who promulgated them.

[2] *Ibid.* p. 454. Cf. *A.F.H.* iii. 277-78 and 524. *Supra,* p. 198.

[3] Pia Cividali, *op. cit.* p. 454. Cf. *A.F.H.* iii. 278. *Supra,* p. 198.

[4] Pia Cividali, *op. cit.* p. 454. Giovanni calls Ubertino " uomo santo e di levatissimo ispirito ", a description found both in the translation and in the original Latin version of the treatise of Fra Andreas Ricchi (cf. *ibid.* p. 449, and *A.F.H.* iii. 274). The " Pistola della Povertà " (Pia Cividali, *op. cit.* p. 455) in quoting the same opinion calls him " il santo e beato uomo ". All these works make the mistake of believing that his answer was made at the request of Benedict XII. instead of at that of John XXII. Cf. *ibid.*

[5] *Ibid.* p. 454. By the time that Giovanni was writing it is possible that the original distinction between the two branches of Fraticelli was growing somewhat hazy, for in his second and fourth letters he describes them as the " Fraticelli della povera vita " (*S.F.* i. p. 431, and Pia Cividali, *op. cit.* p. 458). From his third letter, however, it is clear that they regarded themselves as " Michaelists ". Since the descendants of the Spiritual party also were active in Florence the two bodies may at this time have become one in fact, or it may be that the difference between them was not realised by their adversaries.

[6] " Non dico che voi non diciate di molte veritadi, ma dico che altrimenti non potresti ingannare la gente se no mescolasti, ne' laggiuoli della resia alcuna verità, onde gli eretici sono assomigliati al mulo ch' è mescolato di due nature, d' asino e di cavallo " (*ibid.* p. 453).

[7] *Ibid.* This reference to Urban VI., 1379-1385, furnishes us with a valuable indication of the date of the correspondence between Giovanni and the Fraticelli.

[8] *Ibid.* A favourite reproach of the Camaldolensian hermit to his adversaries was the doubtful position of their Pope and bishops. Cf. Wesselofsky, *op. cit.* 339-41.

extend their influence by avoiding any cause for scandal which might upset the wavering and force the Signory to take active measures against them. Perhaps also they dreaded lest too certain a knowledge of their organisation might lead to the detection and arrest of their leaders. Apart from the light it throws on the position of the Fraticelli in Florence, the letter is interesting as showing its author's conception of the papal authority. According to Giovanni the question as to whether a Pope had fallen into heresy was the concern of a general council, or of the cardinals' college, or of the Emperor and his advisers, and not of a small and ignorant body like the Fraticelli.[1] As in his other letters, he rebukes them for bringing unproved accusations against the Catholic clergy instead of lamenting over their own sins.[2]

In his last letter Giovanni endeavours to answer in detail the list of errors from " Quia vir reprobus " which had been sent him by his opponents. He seems to have studied the decretal in question with some care, for his answer, although couched in more homely language, is written in the spirit of John XXII.[3] Like him he distinguishes between the different meanings of the verb " to possess ", and declares the impossibility of separating " use " from " ownership ".[4] It was not the renunciation of property but lack of covetousness which made men holy, and this was the spirit which had characterised the early Church.[5] The apostles and the Virgin had a house in Jerusalem to which they returned after the Ascension,[6] and though the first converts laid their goods at the feet of the twelve, at the redistribution each of the faithful had an undisputed right over the portion allotted to him, for the garments of Mary Magdalene belonged to her and not to St. Peter.[7] He tells a delightful story of a Franciscan friar who was much troubled in his mind about the ultimate salvation of John XXII. Finally he exposed his doubts to St. Bridget of Sweden, to whom, as she was praying in the church of Santa Maria Rotunda at Rome, the Mother of God appeared in a vision and told her to tell her faithful servant that although it was not lawful for him to know the fate of the

---

[1] Pia Cividali, op. cit. p. 452.   [2] Ibid.

[3] It is very extraordinary that this is the very letter in which Giovanni confesses that he had never read the decretals of John XXII., for many of his arguments seem to have been taken straight from the bull in question. The list of errors from " Quia vir reprobus " must have been practically the same as that originally drawn up by Michael of Cesena. Cf. supra, p. 191.

[4] Pia Cividali, op. cit. pp. 457-58 and 461-62.

[5] Ibid. pp. 459, 460-61, and 464, where he declares that the division of property was by divine law and that in " Dilectissimis " (Causa xii. Q. 1, c. 2) St. Clement had been thinking of the spirit which had animated the first Christians. Cf. supra, p. 158, for the part played by this epistle in the controversy.

[6] Pia Cividali, op. cit. p. 465.   [7] Ibid. p. 461.

Pope yet he might rest assured that his decretals contained no error against the Catholic faith. In proof of this she declared that the coat without seam which she had herself woven for her blessed Son was indeed His own.[1] Her condemnation of all those who followed the doctrines of the Fraticelli is perhaps Giovanni's own addition.[2] To his mind Christ was the example and pattern for all to follow ; but had not always kept to the same manner of life, for sometimes, like the Dominicans and Franciscans, He and His disciples had taken no thought for the morrow, while at others they had had a common purse in which was kept the means for providing for their necessities, and in this they were followed by St. Benedict and other saints.[3] Neither way could be declared more perfect than the other, though perhaps the complete renunciation of possessions even in common was the easier path for poor human fragility to pursue, since to have riches in common and yet live poorly was a far more difficult task.[4] In this letter also Giovanni ridicules the contention of his opponents that they and not the friars at St. Croce were the true sons of St. Francis, though he admits that the latter did not observe the Rule in its original sense.[5] Yet it was impossible for any religious Order to retain its original fervour, and the attempts of many good and devout men to stem the tide of development were foredoomed to failure.[6] This had been the mistake of Liberato and Angelo, whom he describes as just men, who through an error of judgment had separated themselves from their Order. He fully believed the story of the latter's miraculous acquisition of the Greek tongue, since he had acquired favour with God for his good intentions, though by his works he had led others into disobedience and schism.[7] In the latter part of

[1] Pia Cividali, *op. cit.* p. 468. The vision took place in the year 1371, according to Giovanni, whose connection with St. Bridget and her circle makes the whole story more probable than it at first appears.

[2] " Sappi ancora che tutti coloro che dicono ch' el papa non è vero papa, nè i preti sono veri preti, nè direttamente ordinati, nè non è vero corpo del benedetto figliuolo meo, il quale nella celebrazione della messa è consegrato per prete, essi e tutti coloro che tali errori affirmano sono enfiati di spirito diabolico et infernale " (*ibid.*).

[3] *Ibid.* p. 466.

[4] " Impero che più perfetta cosa mi pare vivere nelle ricchezze in commune poverissimo e tenelle sotto i piedi, che gittarle per non avere questa virtù " (*ibid.*).

[5] *Ibid.* p. 468.

[6] " Nondimeno niuna religione mai si pote mantenere in quella santità e fervore ch' ella si cominciò impero che quanto più ci dilunghiamo dal capo nostro per anni e tempi, tanto più pare che intepidiamo " (*ibid.*).

[7] *Ibid.* p. 469. His account of Liberato and Angelo begins as follows : " Cosi vollono fare i fra' minori che furono chiamati i fraticelli della povera vita." In the margin of the original MS., a little lower down, is inscribed in a different hand the note " frati di Chiarino ". In this and in his earlier letter

the letter Giovanni again attempts to justify the arguments used by John XXII. in "Quia vir reprobus".[1] His real difficulty in understanding the position of the Fraticelli lay in his impatience at the smallness of the differences which separated them from the orthodox party. To his mind the question as to whether or not Christ had actually owned the coat without seam, or had a legal claim to the things He used, was completely unimportant in comparison with the fact of His poverty—a doctrine accepted by both parties.[2] If John XXII. had been rash enough to affirm the contrary to be the official teaching of the Church, separation might have been justified ; but the trivial reasons alleged by the Fraticelli for taking so serious a step were a sign of shallowness, presumption, and conceit.[3] As a controversialist Giovanni is often lacking in depth and persuasiveness, but none the less his genuine piety, complete sincerity, sturdy good sense, and a certain generosity of outlook make him a very lovable and human personality.

In the earlier years of the fifteenth century the Fraticelli were forced to meet the attacks of a new and formidable enemy, for the Observantines had now established their position in the Franciscan Order, and were not merely tolerated but favoured by the Papacy. The strictness of their lives won for them the respect of the common people, and thus they were able to undermine the popularity of the Michaelists, many of whose settlements fell into their hands.[4] Like many new religious foundations they had all the fiery zeal of

---

(*S.F.* i. p. 440) Giovanni shows that he had read the " Epistola Excusatoria ", but here he is far more generous in his estimate of its author and does not dismiss him merely as a rebel and schismatic. His description is the more interesting because of his intimacy with Simone de Cassia and John of Salerno. It is also noteworthy that in his reply to a certain Fra Ruffino, who had ventured to criticise St. Catherine of Siena, he quotes from an Italian version of Angelo's translation of Climacus (Pia Cividali, *op. cit.* p. 447).

[1] *Ibid.* p. 469 *s.* On p. 476 Giovanni uses the comparison between Christ and a king of France returning in disguise to his kingdom, which is found originally in " Quia vir reprobus " (*B.F.* v. p. 443). Cf. *supra*, p. 179.

[2] " Or vegnamo alla gonnella che Cristo portò per istrema necessitade. S' ella fu propria sua, sì come disse il papa Giovanni, in che è pero menevata la povertà di Cristo " (Pia Cividali, *op. cit.* p. 459).
" Voi dite che Cristo Iesu fu povero e questo medesimo disse il papa Giovanni e tutti la chiesa il dice " (*ibid.*).

[3] " Ora udite voi, popoli che credete loro, come per sì piccola differenza voi n' andate allo inferno ; udite come per frivola questione voi abbandonate la Santa madre chiesa " (*ibid.*).

[4] As early as 1350 they had superseded the Fraticelli at the Carceri (*A.L.K.G.* iv. 183), and the invitation of the Perugians to Paoluccio de' Trinci is also significant. Cf. *supra*, p. 217. In 1418, Martin V. gave instructions that the hermitages in Western Tuscany and the Romagna from which the Fraticelli had been expelled were to be given to the Observantines (*B.F.* vii. 1393, p. 511. Cf. *A.F.H.* iv. p. 3).

crusaders for the extermination of heresy, and Martin V. found them his most active allies in his efforts to destroy this growing cancer in the life of the Church. The appointment of St. John of Capistrano and the blessed James of the March, the friends and fellow-workers of St. Bernardino of Siena, as inquisitors of heretical depravity,[1] marks an important step in a vigorous campaign, which did not end with the sack of the villages in the district round Maiorlati, the chief centre of the sect in the March of Ancona.[2] Nicolaus de Fara, the contemporary biographer of St. John of Capistrano, writes with fervent approval of the numerous victims whom he sent to the stake, and the terror which he inspired was such that many fled over the seas to Greece.[3] In their turn the Fraticelli made violent reprisals, seeking by every means in their power to destroy their formidable adversaries. Both inquisitors had many narrow escapes, James once being saved by his confessor, to whom his would-be murderer had revealed his intentions.[4]

James of the March did not trust solely to the sword as a method of conversion, for he is the author of a dialogue against the Fraticelli, composed in its first form between probably 1450 and 1452.[5] Certain of his arguments, and much of his historical knowledge concerning the controversy, are derived from Andreas Ricchi,[6] but James possessed none of the moderation of the good Franciscan, which is perhaps not surprising when it is remembered that he stood in hourly danger of assassination. To the modern mind, moreover, the arguments of the heretic with regard to evangelical poverty [7] and the evils due to the wealth of the Church are often

---

[1] *B.F.* vii. 1710, p. 653.

[2] In 1429. Cf. " Dialogus contra Fraticellos ", *Misc.* ii. 609. The villages destroyed were Massaccia, Poggio Cupo, and Mergo, as well as Maiorlati itself. Cf. *A.L.K.G.* iv. 109.

[3] *Ibid.* p. 135, *n.* 3. According to the saint's biographer no less than thirty-six villages were burnt in his crusade against the Fraticelli.

[4] *Misc.* ii. p. 610. In 1458 the Fraticelli did actually succeed in killing one of their opponents, a Camaldolite hermit called Angelo, who has since been beatified (*ibid.*).

[5] *Ibid.* pp. 595-610. Cf. *A.F.H.* iii. 259. The passage accusing the Fraticelli of the murder of the blessed Angelo is possibly a later addition. Perhaps an Italian version was composed at the same time as the Latin one (*ibid.* iv. p. 10). The dialogue was probably written as an answer to the arguments set forth by the Fraticelli in the " Liber Veritatis ". Cf. *supra*, p. 231 ; *A.F.H.* iv. 16-19 ; and *Z.K.G.* xlv. pp. 224-30.

[6] Cf. *ibid.* pp. 12-16. *Supra*, p. 198. It is interesting that James' use of Andreas's argument, that the Church was infallible though individual Popes might err, was one of the difficulties which had to be dealt with at the time of his canonization in 1726 (*A.F.H.* iv. p. 5). He also was well acquainted with the bulls of John XXII. (cf. *Misc.* ii. pp. 601, 602, and 604) and with certain of the writings of Michael of Cesena (*ibid.* p. 597).

[7] *Ibid.* pp. 601 and 605.

R

more convincing than those of his opponent.[1] It is surprising to
find a Franciscan writer using the example of the Dominicans as
a defence of the position that the ownership of temporal goods was
by no means incompatible with perfection.[2] Like John XXII. in
"Quia vir reprobus", James interprets Christ's prohibition to His
disciples with regard to the matter of litigation as applying only to
property held *in proprio*.[3] His disapproval of the disguises adopted
by the Fraticelli to carry on their work of propaganda is hardly
reasonable,[4] but the historical details which he gives are full of
interest. It is from him that we learn of the patriarch, Gabriel " of
Philadelphia ", whose letters, directed to all the faithful, were discovered at the sack of Maiorlati,[5] and of the Bishop Matthew who
lived in captivity at the court of Nicholas V.[6] His frequent complaints of the efforts of his enemies to deceive the simple show that,
even in the middle of the fifteenth century, they retained a certain
hold over the lower classes,[7] and his comparison of their work to
that of the Hussites in Bohemia is also significant.[8] On the other
hand, the fury of the Fraticelli at the growing popularity of the
Osservanti is attested by their identification of St. Bernardino of
Siena with Antichrist.[9] In spite of the testimony of his eighteenth-
century biographer, a perusal of his pamphlet leads to the belief
that the numerous conversions ascribed to James and his fellow-
inquisitor were the result of fear rather than of persuasion.[10] An
attractive treatise had been written nearly seventy-five years earlier
by another James, who rebuked in friendly language the tendency
of the Fraticelli to live upon the alms of the faithful.[11] Perhaps the

----

[1] " Et ideo ostensa sunt, quia infinita scandala in mundo guerrarum dissen-
sionum et huiusmodi, quia Praelati ecclesiarum miscuerunt secum aliis terrenis "
(*Misc.* ii. p. 604). "Mirabile quidem est vos omnino vultis cum armis pro
defensione rerum temporalium occidere homines, pro quibus in cruce Christus
mortuus est " (*ibid.*).

[2] *Ibid.* p. 596.

[3] *Ibid.* p. 607.

[4] *Ibid.* p. 597. Cf. *supra*, p. 226.

[5] P. 609. Philadelphia is probably a symbolic title. He is presumably
identical with the patriarch, Gabriel of Florence. Cf. *A.L.K.G.* iv. 114.

[6] *Misc.* ii. p. 597. There were also bishops belonging to the sect at Venice
and Florence (*ibid.* p. 610).

[7] *Ibid.* pp. 605 and 609.

[8] *Ibid.* p. 605. [9] *Ibid.* p. 610.

[10] " Plurimos ex dictis haereticis a vera fidei via aberrantes, sua praedicatione,
doctrina, prudentia, et constantia ad ecclesiae gremium revocavit." *Compendium
vitae, virtutum et miraculorum necnon actorum in causa canonizationis B. Iacobi
de Marchia Ordinis Minorum S. Francisci de Observantia* (Rome, 1726).
Cited by Fr. Oliger, *A.F.H.* iv. 4.

[11] The Introduction is printed in *A.F.H.* vi. 524-6. The treatise was written
at the request of Alfonso, Bishop of Jaen (1359–1368), the friend of St. Bridget
of Sweden (*ibid.* p. 273).

kindly attitude of its author was due to the fact that his own orthodoxy had been questioned by certain Neapolitan masters of theology.[1]

The last important appearance of the Michaelists in history is perhaps the Inquisition process of 1466 against certain of their number who were captured at Assisi at the time of the indulgence of the Portiuncula.[2] The prisoners were sent to Rome to be tried, and the actual examination began on August 11, 1466.[3] Most of the victims came from the district round Poli and Maiorlati in the March of Ancona,[4] and were lay people of humble origin, though among them was a bishop of the sect named Nicholas of Massaro,[5] and a priest called Bernard of Bergamo.[6] The evidence given by the latter is especially interesting, for he had spent his noviciate at a convent possessed by the Fraticelli in Greece,[7] and gives the names of their other settlements in that country.[8] His testimony is confirmed by the bull of Nicholas V. ordering the arrest of the Fraticelli in the same region, and especially of one who called himself " their pope ".[9] Bernard had received holy orders while still in the East, but, after his arrival at Poli, had been reordained by a bishop called Michael,[10] who after his death had been buried secretly in the church of St. Stephen, outside the town, with the connivance of the parish priest.[11] He throws further light on the history of Gabriel " of Philadelphia ", whose letters had been discovered by James of the March.[12] After holding the generalship of the sect for the allotted period of three years he had refused to resign his

---

[1] *A.F.H.* vi. p. 525.

[2] *A.L.K.G.* iv. 110-38. The Portiuncula seems to have been a great centre of pilgrimage for both branches of the Fraticelli, for shortly before his death Angelo da Clareno's " socius ", Nicholas da Calabria, asked him for permission to visit this centre of Franciscan devotion. Cf. Codex Magliabecchiana, xxxix. 75, f. 215 *v.*

[3] *A.L.K.G.* iv. p. 113. A second investigation took place in October, which gave rise to many pamphlets written from the standpoint of the orthodox party, none of which has been printed. Two of the inquisitors, Nicholas, Bishop of Orti (1455–1467), and Roderick, Bishop of Zamora (1440–1467), were among those who expressed their views in this manner. Cf. *A.F.H.* vi. p. 746.

[4] *A.L.K.G.* iv. p. 122.

[5] " Nicolaum de Massaro pro episcopo fraticellorum de opinione nuncupatorum se gerentum " (*ibid.* p. 121).

[6] *Ibid.* p. 113.

[7] " Idem Bernardus accessit ad monasterium sancte Marie Athenarum ordinis Sancte Francisci ' de observantia ' " (*ibid.* p. 113).

[8] " S. Franciscus in civitate Thebarum ", " S. Georgius in Castrum Succaminis (Surraminis ?) ", " Walta in diocesi Atheniensi " (*ibid.*).

[9] *A.F.H.* vi. pp. 529-30 (February 13, 1451).

[10] *A.L.K.G.* iv. p. 113.

[11] *Ibid.* p. 114. In margin of document, " Cuius corpus fuit exhumatum et concrematum " (*ibid. n.* 1).

[12] Cf. *supra*, p. 242. See also Note on page 242, *infra*.

office, and thus had caused a division among its members.[1] Bernard of Bergamo also furnishes details with regard to his activity as a preacher. His teaching comprised the usual tenets with regard to evangelical poverty and the errors of John XXII., and, like all the Fraticelli, he was very bitter against the orthodox clergy.[2] He apparently derived most of his doctrines from the " Liber veritatis ".[3] The inquiry also throws light on the diffusion of the sect at Poli, where apparently no less than half the inhabitants were Fraticelli.[4] Moreover, the lord of the village, Stefano de Conti, gave them his protection,[5] and Bernard had once been summoned secretly to Palestrina by a great lady belonging to the Colonna family who had desired to confess to him.[6] At Poli itself the sect met by night in the house of a certain Maria Stallionis,[7] where they celebrated Mass. Before dawn all the lights were extinguished and they sang the weird incantation, " Stegui la lucerna, avelamo ad vita eterna, alleluia alleluia; chiunque home se pigli la soa ", after which the men and women present proceeded to know each other carnally.[8] The evidence concerning this horrible rite, which was called the " barilottum ", is exceedingly doubtful, as in many cases it was only given under torture, and certain of the prisoners strenuously denied ever having witnessed it.[9] The same is probably true of an equally disgusting ceremony at which the worshippers partook solemnly of wine which had been mixed with the ashes of an infant whose life had been sacrificed for this purpose,[10] for it must always be remembered how frequently the different heretical sects were charged with

---

[1] " Item dicit, quod a XL. annis citra facta fuit quedam divisio inter eos ex quod generalis vocatus frater Gabriel de Florencia debebat renunciare in fine trium annorum iuxta ritum eorum et id facere recusavit. Qua de causa aliqui secum remanserunt . . . alii vero se subtraxerunt et fecerunt alium generalem vocatum fratrem Paulum de Florencia, que divisio adhuc durat " (*A.L.K.G.* iv. p. 114). Perhaps Paul was one of the itinerant preachers who had visited Lucca. Cf. *Misc.* i. 482, and *supra*, p. 229.

[2] *A.L.K.G.* iv. p. 114. Their tenets with regard to John XXII. and his successors, and the position of the clergy who adhered to them, are found *ibid.* pp. 122 and 123.

[3] *Ibid.* p. 114. Cf. *supra*, p. 231. [4] *Ibid.* p. 114.

[5] *Ibid.* p. 115. He was imprisoned by Paul II. in Castel St. Angelo for the favour he had shown to the Fraticelli (*ibid. n.* 1).

[6] Sueva, mother of Stefano Colonna, Count of Palestrina. A great lady belonging to this family was imprisoned by St. John Capistrano and compelled to renounce her errors. Cf. *ibid.* and *n.* 2.

[7] *Ibid.* p. 113.

[8] *Ibid.* pp. 117 and 127. The younger members left before the "barilottum " took place. At Maiorlati the Fraticelli met for their services in the crypt of a church (*ibid.*).

[9] *Ibid.* pp. 129 and 130. A common insult to the Fraticelli in the district round Maiorlati was " Tu es natus ex barilotto " (*ibid.* p. 128).

[10] *Ibid.* pp. 117 and 127.

similar practices. Yet it cannot be denied that there were some grounds for the accusation of impurity, for the bishop, Nicholas of Massano, shamelessly admitted that he had lived in open sin with another of the prisoners, a certain Katherine of " Palunbaria ".[1] Even if this confession was untrue it shows the degraded character of the members of the sect, especially as it did not even debar him from the exercise of his episcopal functions, while she had continued to preach and hear confessions, as was customary, for certain of the women members of their community.[2] It is extraordinary that the inquisitors should have accepted the recantation of such individuals, since they both cynically avowed that they had often before made a pretended abjuration of their errors, only to return to them again once the danger of persecution had passed.[3] With such leaders it is not surprising that the other prisoners were almost equally submissive, though there is a certain pathos attached to the case of one of their number, Antonius de Sacco. In spite of repeated applications of torture he had adhered firmly to his former beliefs, and perhaps was only induced to surrender in the end through his fears for the fate of his young daughter Francesca, who had been arrested at the same time as himself.[4] It can hardly have been these Fraticelli whose courage won the admiration of the Milanese agent at Rome, Agostino de Rossi.[5] The following year another batch of prisoners from Poli were brought to the Eternal City. With the terrible mockery which forms so marked a feature of the medieval procedure against heretics, these were publicly exhibited in the Campidoglio, wearing the San Benitos and paper mitres of the Inquisition. The papal vicar and five other bishops exhorted them to repent, and in certain cases their efforts met with success. Yet even those who recanted were not allowed to abandon their conspicuous costume, nor is it certain that they were set at liberty.[6]

The doctrine of the complete poverty of Christ and His apostles excited considerable interest even among the envoys of the different Italian States,[7] perhaps because it stood in marked antithesis to the state of things which existed at the court of the luxurious Venetian pontiff, Paul II., whose chief preoccupation

---

[1] *A.L.K.G.* iv. p. 126.   [2] *Ibid.* p. 127.
[3] *Ibid.* pp. 131 and 132.   [4] *Ibid.* pp. 129-31. Cf. p. 134.
[5] Cf. letters sent from Rome to Cecco Simonetta, and especially the one dated November 1466. Fumi, " Eretici in Boemia e Fraticelli nel Roma ", *Archivio della R. Società Romana per la Storia Patria,* xxxiv. pp. 117-30. " Ma ben vi prometto che di loro ancora se ne trova molti constanti ne la opinione sua, taliter che 'l gli n' è de quilli che sustengono ogni martirio et tormento anzi che la vogliano negare. Quin ymo pareno desyderare lo foco et ultimo supplicio per quella fede " (*ibid.* p. 126).
[6] Stephanus Infessura, " Diarum Romanae Urbis ", Muratori, *Scriptores rerum Italicarum,* iii. Pt. II. p. 1141.   [7] Fumi, *op. cit.* p. 125 s.

was rumoured to be his collection of precious stones.[1] At the time when Agostino wrote, the Fraticelli were still probably numerous in Rome, though their ranks were being thinned by the activity of the Inquisition.[2] The end of the century was to witness the final disappearance of the sect, though among the folds of the Umbrian hills a few remnants still maintained a precarious existence.[3]

In conclusion a few remarks should perhaps be made with regard to the diffusion of the Fraticelli outside the boundaries of Italy, for although primarily belonging to that country they exercised a certain influence over other regions. In 1466 certain heretics in Germany are described as " similar to those Fraticelli of the opinion ", but little more is known about them.[4] An interesting revival of the Spiritual movement took place in Spain under the leadership of an Observant friar, Philip Berbegall, whose piety had won for him the friendship of St. John Capistrano.[5] When in 1430 the two branches of the Franciscan Order were united together by the constitutions of Martin V., Berbegall separated himself from the main body and made himself the leader of a community known as the Capucciolae, whose aim was to revive the primitive ideal of St. Francis.[6] A treatise of St. John Capistrano has survived,[7] exhorting his former friend to abstain from taking such a step, and alluding to the example of Michael of Cesena, who had created a schism in the Order by preferring poverty to obedience.[8] In 1434 Eugenius IV. referred the question of the condemnation of the sect to a commission of Cardinals,[9] and we see from the papal letters directed to the Communes of Barcelona and Valencia [10] that active measures were taken against its adherents,

[1] " Dominus vero Bernardus Iustinianus, oratore venetiano, inanti che 'l se partisse de qua, diceva che non se maravigliava zà de questa rixia, ma si bene che 'l non ne fosse ancora più, attenti li modi et la pompa intollerabile de tutta questa corte, et maxime che 'l papa tutto 'l dì sta in numerare et asortire dinare et infilare perle, loco di pater nostri " (Fumi, *op. cit.* p. 126 *s.*).

[2] " Le presone tutte de questa terra ne sono oramay pieni, videlicet de quisti che vanno dreto a la opinione chiamata de li Fraticelli " (*ibid.* p. 125).

[3] Cf. *A.F.H.* vi. p. 747.

[4] See note on page 282.

[5] He begins his letter opposing the errors of Philip " Venerabili religioso fervidoque Praeconi divino fratri Phylippo Berbegallo " (*A.F.H.* vi. 713).

[6] *Ibid.* p. 710 ; Wadding, *Annales*, x. 1433, pp. 213, xi.

[7] Fragments printed in *A.F.H.* vi. 717-19.

[8] *Ibid.* p. 718. A few years later the charge of reviving the heresy of the " Fraticelli di opinione " was brought against the Osservanti themselves by the Conventual Roberto Caracciolo of Lecce, one of the leading popular preachers of the middle of the fifteenth century (letter of Nicholas of Fara to John of Capistrano (June 5, 1455) (*A.F.H.* xv. p. 1399). Cf. Chiappini, *Profilò di storia Francescana in Abruzzo*, p. 34.

[9] *Annales*, x. 1433, pp. 213, xi.

[10] *A.F.H.* vi. 715-16. No date is given.

especially since rumours had reached the Pope that they preached doctrines similar to those of the Hussites and Fraticelli, and subversive of the existing order of society.[1] Both men and women were numbered among Berbegall's followers,[2] and from the descriptions given both by Eugenius and St. John Capistrano he appears to have revived the short and skimpy habit affected by the Spirituals.[3] Nothing further is known of his history, but it is generally believed that success attended the Pope's efforts against the Capucciolae. The " Congregation of the Hood " or of " the Holy Gospel ", which existed in the days of Leo X., was possibly a totally different organisation.[4] Thus the descendants both of the Zealots and the Michaelists pass out of the pages of history, but their memory lingers even to-day in certain remote districts. The little hermitage of San Lorenzo, near Bracciano, is still known by the inhabitants as the " home of the bad friars ".[5] Standing in the woods below the Carceri and looking at the simple building which seems a natural part of the stony hillside and of the austere Umbrian landscape, it is impossible not to believe that what was finest in their spirit will always survive in the Order of St. Francis, and in the hearts of all who strive to discover the true meaning of his message.

[1] " Dicitur quod ipse et sui sequaces miscendo articulos et sectam Bohemorum cum secta fraticellorum qui sunt in Italia, predicant et docent, faciuntque seditiones et scandala non ferenda, et inde populus insurgit contra clerum et nobiles " (*A.F.H.* vi. p. 716). Cf. *Z.K.G.* xlv. pp. 231-33.

[2] *Ibid.* These were called " Veguini " and assumed the habit of the Third Order of St. Francis.

[3] *Ibid.* p. 715. Capistrano cites the papal bulls " Exiit qui seminat ", " Exivi de paradiso ", and " Quorundam exigit " as proofs that the habit should be left to the discretion of the Superiors of the Order (p. 719).

[4] *Ibid.* p. 715.

[5] *Ibid.* p. 268, *n.* 7.

PART II: THE BÉGUINS OF PROVENCE AND SOUTHERN FRANCE

THE visitor to Bruges who has seen the pleasant little Beguinage, with its Renaissance doorway reflected in the waters of the river, and has watched the busy labours of its placid inmates, retains the impression of a peace and tranquillity which have no place in the world outside. No such atmosphere of mellow sunshine can be found in the stormy annals of the Provençal Béguins, whose very name recalls the fierce Albigensians and their terrible struggle against one of the greatest of the medieval Popes.[1] The origin of the sect is somewhat obscure, but it was perhaps the outcome of one of those religious movements so frequent in southern France in the middle of the thirteenth century, many of which centre round the person of the famous Spiritual, Hugues de Digne.[2] It was not, however, till the early years of the fourteenth century that the Béguins began to trouble the peace of the Inquisition, but from that time onwards they were a source of endless anxiety to the Holy Office.[3] The famous Dominican Bernard Gui, afterwards Bishop of Lodève, devotes a whole chapter of his *Practica officii Inquisitionis heretice pravitatis*[4] to a description of their errors. Their chief centres were Narbonne, Toulouse, and Provence, but their influence was very widespread in the south of France, and extended even as far as Catalonia.[5] A very interesting and curious

[1] This view of the origin of the name is taken by Fr. Van Mierlo, S.J., in a memoir presented to the Flemish Royal Academy in 1926. The title of this work is "Lambert li Beges in verband met den oorsprong der Begijnen". Cf. Callaey's article, "Lambert le Bégue et les Béguines" (*R.H.E.* xxiii. p. 254), in which he attacks certain of the views of Van Mierlo.

[2] Cf. *supra*, p. 7. Hugues was the reputed founder of a mendicant Order called the Saccati, suppressed like many of the others at the Council of Lyons (Salimbene, *op. cit.* p. 254). His sister Douceline, who, although she joined no regular Order, was renowned for her holy life, gathered round her a band of women, organised rather on the model of the Franciscan Tertiaries (*ibid.* p. 554).

[3] "Ceperunt autem manifestari et detegi in suis opinionibus erroneis circa annum Domini MᵐCCCᵐXVᵐ, paulo plus minusve, quamvis prius suspecti communiter a pluribus haberentur" (*Practica Inquisitionis*, p. 108).

[4] This has been edited with a French translation by G. Mollat under the title of *Manuel d'Inquisiteur*. For the Béguins cf. i. pp. 108-193.

[5] "Successivis annis in provincia Narbonensi et Tholosana et in Cathalonia plures capti et detenti et deprehensi in erroribus, et plures utriusque sexus inventi sunt et judicati heretici et combusti, ab anno Domini MᵒCCCᵒXVIIᵒ citra, maxime Narbone, Biterris et in dyocesi Agathensi (Agde) et in Lodova (Lodève), et apud Lunellum (Lunel), Magalonensis dyocesis (Maguelonne) et in Carcassona et Tholose tres alienigene" (*ibid.* p. 108). A bull of February 1322 orders certain of the bishops in the south of France to hold an inquiry into the beliefs of the Tertiaries in their diocese, and to admonish and commend the orthodox, while punishing those who were found guilty of heresy (*B.F.* v. 462,

feature of the sect is its close connection with the Spiritual Franciscans, for the Béguins claimed to be members of the Third Order,
often describing themselves as the poor brothers and sisters of
penitence, and calling their houses the Homes of Poverty.[1] Certain
of them lived a community life, supporting themselves either by
manual labour or by mendicancy,[2] while others dwelt in their own
homes, differing from their neighbours only by a greater strictness
of life and a more frequent attendance at church, where their
exaggerated devotion caused them to be looked upon with a certain
amount of suspicion.[3] Like the Franciscan Order, of which they
claimed to be an off-shoot, they believed firmly that Christ and His
apostles had owned nothing either severally or in common.[4] St.
Francis had been the greatest exponent of poverty after Christ and
His mother,[5] and his Rule was a renewal of the evangelic counsels
and was therefore sacrosanct, not even the Pope being able to
grant a dispensation from the threefold vow of poverty, chastity, and
obedience.[6] Perhaps because of their own humble origin they
looked with no very tolerant eye upon the wealth of the clergy,
regarding all those who lived delicately and luxuriously as the
followers of Antichrist.[7] It would seem, therefore, that after the
suppression of the Spiritual movement in Provence many of its

p. 222). As early as 1317, however, the Commune of Massa had written to the
Pope, defending the members of the Third Order in their city from the charge
of Béguinism (*S.F.* i. p. 236).

[1] " Beguinorum secta, qui fratres Pauperes se appellant et dicunt se tenere
et profiteri tertiam regulam sancti Francisci " (Bernard Gui, *op. cit.* pp. 108 and
118).
" Beguini itaque predicti habitantes in villis et castris habent mansiunculas
in quibus aliqui simul cohabitant et eas appellant domos paupertatis " (*ibid.*
p. 114).
[2] " Notandum quoque est quod inter eos sunt aliqui qui publice mendicant
hostiatim. . . . Sunt et alii qui non mendicant publice, set aliqua suis manibus
operantur et lucrantur. . . ." (*ibid.* p. 116).
[3] " Item orantes in ecclesia vel alibi sedent acrupiti, verso vultu seu facie
communiter ad objectum parietem, vel similem locum vel ad terram capuciati ;
et raro videntur stare flexis genibus et complosis manibus, sicut faciunt ceteri
homines " (*ibid.* p. 118).
[4] " Dicunt et asserunt . . . se credere et tenere quod Dominus Jhesus
Christus, in quantum fuit homo, et ejus apostoli nichil habuerunt in proprio
nec etiam in communi " (*ibid.*).
[5] " Item, dicunt quod beatus Franciscus post Christum et ejus matrem, et
aliqui addunt post apostolos, fuit summus et precipuus observator vite et regule
evangelice et renovator ejus in isto sexto statu Ecclesie in quo dicunt jam nos
esse " (*ibid.* p. 120).
[6] *Ibid.* pp. 120 and 122. The same sanctity was attached to the Rule of
the Third Order.
[7] " Item, dicunt quod prelati et religiosi habentes vestes superfluas et pretio-
sas faciunt contra perfectionem Evangelii et contra preceptum Christi et juxta
preceptum Anti-Christi, et tales ac etiam clerici incedentes pompose sunt de
familia Anti-Christi " (*ibid.* p. 134).

ideals and aspirations passed to the Béguins. Yet these had lost much of their old poetic and mystic fragrance, and had become crude, fantastic, and exaggerated.

The close connection between the Zealots and the Béguins is further attested by the similarity of their speculations with regard to the future of the world. Like them they looked earnestly for the coming of the Spirit,[1] which would be marked by the triumph of the faithful and the destruction of the carnal church, in their eyes justly identified with Babylon the harlot who was drunk with the blood of the saints.[2] The world was now in the sixth period of the age of the Son,[3] but a hundred years after the death of St. Francis a new era would begin in which the heathen would be converted by a band of evangelists belonging to the Franciscan Order, and the Holy Spirit would be poured out in full measure on all the faithful.[4] Before these events took place, however, there would be a fierce persecution of the elect on the part of the evil and corrupt church,[5] whose ruler might fitly be compared to Herod, or to Caiaphas the wicked high priest who had derided and finally condemned Christ.[6] Yet the day of her own doom was at hand, and some were even hopeful enough to believe that Frederick of Sicily was the instrument appointed by Providence to bring about the final destruction of the Church.[7] He was to have ten kings as his allies, corresponding to the ten heads of the beast in the Apocalypse,[8] and the plain of Salsès in the Pyrenees was the place where the last scene in the terrible drama would take place.[9] This would be followed by the horrors of a Saracen invasion,[10] and as a result of war and massacre the shortage of men would be so great that the women would embrace the trunks of trees in order to satisfy their lust.[11] After this an era of righteousness and peace would ensue which would endure for a hundred years.[12] During this golden period of peace and righteousness St. Francis would return in bodily form to the earth, and his spirit would reign in the hearts of all men.[13]

[1] Bernard Gui, *op. cit.* p. 146. [2] *Ibid.* pp. 142, 144, and 146.
[3] *Ibid.* pp. 120 and 144. [4] *Ibid.* pp. 146 and 150.
[5] *Ibid.* p. 144. [6] *Ibid.* p. 152.
[7] " Item, dogmatizant quod ecclesia carnalis, videlicet Romana ecclesia, ante predicationem Anti-Christi est destruenda per bella que contra ipsam faciet Fridericus, rex Sicilie, qui nunc regnat" (*ibid.* p. 144).   Until 1337 Frederick was still technically at war with the Church.
[8] *Ibid.* (*Apoc.* xvii. 12.)
[9] Vidal, " Procès d'Inquisition contre Adhémar de Mosset, noble Roussillonnais, inculpé de Béguinisme " (1332–34), *Analecta Gallicana*, i. p. 580.
[10] Bernard Gui, *op. cit.* p. 150.
[11] *Ibid.* Cf. Vidal, *op. cit.* p. 580. [12] Bernard Gui, *op. cit.* pp. 152 and 172.
[13] *Ibid.* p. 172.   Like the Zealots and many other members of the Franciscan Order they identified St. Francis with the Angel having the seal of the living God (*ibid.* p. 148. Cf. *Apoc.* vii. 2).

The attitude of the Béguins towards the Pope was far more violent than that of the Zealots. Even the more moderate among them believed that the Holy Spirit had deserted the Church from the day on which John XXII. had dared to issue regulations concerning the habit of the Friars Minor by promulgating the decretal "Quorundam exigit".[1] From that moment the Pope had lost all authority to bind and loose, and was identified by many with the mystic Antichrist.[2] Certain of the extremists even went so far as to believe that since all the papal interpretations of the Franciscan Rule were equally evil, the promulgation of " Exiit qui seminat " [3] by Nicholas III. had been the signal for the withdrawal of the divine grace,[4] and that he and his successors had become vessels of iniquity and the agents of the devil. Their favourite nickname for the Pope was Caiaphas, or Herod, while certain of the more poetically minded compared him to the boar out of the wood or to a ravening wolf.[5] John XXII. was commonly believed to be the mystic Antichrist who was to prepare the way for one greater and even more wicked than himself.[6] There was considerable dispute amongst them concerning the person of the open Antichrist, some identifying him with a mighty temporal ruler, either Christian or Saracen,[7] while others thought that he would be an apostate from the Franciscan Order, and both Philip of Majorca and Angelo were cast for this rôle.[8] Yet the Church organisation of their age retained a firm hold over their imaginations, and they looked for the coming of a "papa angelicus". Some of them believed him to be even now present in the person of Angelo da Clareno, or Philip of Majorca, or of a certain Friar Minor named Guillaume Guiraud.[9]

---

[1] Bernard Gui, *op. cit.* p. 124. Cf. Vidal, *op. cit.* p. 583, and *B.F.* v. 289 (October 7, 1317), p. 128, and *supra*, p. 19.

[2] " Item, graviter et ignominiose oblo` `cuntur contra dominum papam vicarium Jhesu Christi, quem sicut insani mente et scismatici vocant et dicunt esse misticum Anti-Christum majoris Anti-Christi, precursorem et preparatorem vie ejus " (Bernard Gui, *op. cit.* p. 152).

[3] *B.F.* iii. 404-16.   [4] *A.L.K.G.* ii. pp. 371 and 410.

[5] Bernard Gui, *op. cit.* pp. 152 and 174. Cf. the Confession of Na Prous Boneta, a Béguin who was tried at Carcassonne in August 1325 (*Hist. Litt.* xxxiv. p. 433, *n.* 4).

[6] " Et dicunt esse primum Anti-Christum illum papam sub quo fiet et sub quo jam fit, ut aiunt, persecutio et condempnatio eorundem " (Bernard Gui, *op. cit.* p. 148. Cf. Vidal, *op. cit.* p. 587.

[7] " Septimum vero caput (cf. beast with seven heads, *Apoc.* xvii. 3) exponit magnum Anti-Christum cum rege monarcha sibi coherente " (Bernard Gui, *op. cit.* p. 172 ; cf. pp. 144 and 150).

[8] Cf. Vidal, *op. cit.* p. 587 *s.* Another suggestion was Ubertino da Casale. In a technical sense all three were apostates, for Philip of Majorca had once been a Dominican novice, but had never taken the final vows. Cf. Vidal, " Un Ascète du sang royal : Philippe de Majorque ", *Revue des questions historiques,* lxxxviii. p. 365.   [9] *Hist. Litt.* xxxiv. p. 434, *n.* 4.

Another very striking characteristic of the Béguins was the reverence which they attached to the memory of Olivi. Their veneration for him was so great that they regarded his writings almost as the Scriptures of the coming age,[1] and spoke of him as the holy but uncanonized father.[2] A certain measure of error was contained in the teaching of every doctor of the Church except St. Paul and Brother Peter John, but their words would endure for ever, and not one tittle of their doctrine could be altered.[3] They possessed many of the writings of the latter translated into the vulgar tongue,[4] and set great store by his "Postilla in Apocalypsim", which had not yet been finally condemned by the Church.[5] Possibly most of their apocalyptic speculations were derived from this work, but they had no scruples about making its author the origin of an even wilder and more exaggerated series of prophecies.[6] Among their other writings in the vulgar tongue was a little treatise called the "Transitus Sancti Patris", which was studied frequently in their conventicles.[7] The passage in the Apocalypse describing the angel whose face shone as the sun and who bore in his hand an open book was often interpreted as symbolising the great Spiritual.[8] Olivi was the great light sent by God into the world, for lack of which men had for long been stumbling in the darkness of heresy.[9] If the Pope himself should venture to condemn his doctrines he might justly be regarded as a heretic.[10] They accepted Olivi's opinion that Christ had been pierced by the spear while yet alive, explaining it by the supposition that He was already so pallid and exhausted by His sufferings that the bystanders were convinced that He was already dead, and that this error had survived in the writings of the evangelists.[11] It is not surprising that Olivi was commonly

---

[1] Bernard Gui, op. cit. p. 140.   [2] Ibid. p. 138. Cf. supra, p. 81.

[3] Bernard Gui, op. cit. p. 138.

[4] Amongst these was a certain small treatise on Poverty (ibid. p. 142).

[5] Ibid. p. 112. Its condemnation would possibly have even increased its merits in the eyes of the Béguins.

[6] Ibid. Amongst these was the prophecy regarding the Saracen invasion. Cf. p. 150.

[7] Ibid. p. 190. Cf. Ehrle, A.L.K.G. iii. 411.

[8] "Item, dicunt et exponunt quod dictus frater Petrus Johannis fuit spiritualiter ille angelus de quo scribitur (Apoc. x. 1) quod facies ejus erat sicut sol et habebat librum apertum in manu sua" (p. 138. Cf. Vidal, op. cit. p. 585).

[9] Bernard Gui, op. cit. p. 140.

[10] Ibid.

[11] Ibid. p. 138. Like Ubertino they cite St. Matthew as an authority for this view (cf. supra, p. 150). Olivi had never really given any definite decision with regard to the time when Christ was pierced by the spear, but had merely suggested as a possible opinion that the incident had happened while He was yet alive. Cf. supra, p. 93, and A.L.K.G. ii. 402.

regarded as the founder of the sect,[1] though in reality there can have been little connection between the moderate and essentially level-headed scholar, with his fine and subtle intelligence, and these poor and bigoted fanatics. Besides Olivi, the Béguins set great store by the memory of the four Spirituals who had been burned at Marseilles, collecting and treasuring their ashes as precious relics, and observing the day of their execution as if it had been the festival of one of the great martyrs of the Church.[2] The roll of their saints was increased rapidly owing to the number of their adherents who fell into the hands of the Inquisition and suffered for their convictions at the stake. Between 1318 and the pontificate of Innocent VI. there were probably not less than 113 victims.[3] Yet certain of the inquisitors discriminated carefully between the different classes of Béguin, for there were some who only adopted the strict manner of life which characterised the sect, and guarded themselves carefully from its errors and exaggerations.[4] Others had accepted only certain of its tenets, and were ready to abandon these if subjected to the persuasions of lawful reasoning and sane counsel.[5] Yet even some of those who did not adhere to all the doctrines of the sect were often not amenable to this form of treatment and held firmly to their former opinions.[6] It is to be feared that in this case the difference between them and the extremists was a matter of mere academic interest to the Holy Office.

The bulk of the Béguins were drawn from the lower classes, but, as in the case of the Fraticelli,[7] they probably had supporters even among men of high rank and assured position. It is only by this supposition that we can explain the proceedings against Adhémar de Mosset, a knight possessing certain fiefs in the county of Rousillon, who was accused by his master, the King of Majorca,

---

[1] Bernard Gui himself never fell into this error, though it is found in Eymerich (*Directorium Inquisitorum*, p. 206) and repeated by Baluze in *Vitae Paparum*, ii. p. 67.

[2] Bernard Gui, *op. cit.* p. 127 s. Cf. *ibid.* pp. 162 and 164, and Vidal, *op. cit.* 582. They compared the four Zealots to St. Vincent and St. Laurence.

[3] This figure is given by Moshiem for Carcassonne, and is taken from a " Martyrologium Spiritualium et Fratricellorum " compiled in 1454. Cf. *De Beghardis et Beguinabus*, p. 499. The same number is given by the English Chronicler, Thomas Burton (*Chronica Monasterii de Melsa* (Rolls Series, 43), ii. p. 323), for the years 1318 and 1330 alone, the victims being drawn not only from southern France but from parts of Italy, Spain, and the Rhineland, and even from England. It is therefore probable that not only the Spirituals and the Provençal Béguins, but the German Beghards and members of kindred sects were included in his list. Cf. *Hist. Litt.* xxxiv. p. 439, *n.* 1.

[4] Bernard Gui, *op. cit.* p. 114.

[5] *Ibid.*

[6] *Ibid.*

[7] Cf. *supra*, pp. 210 and 244.

of sharing in the heresy of the sect.[1] It is not difficult to discover the motives underlying the charge, for Adhémar had been the favourite counsellor of the king's hated uncle and guardian, Philip of Majorca, and had been entrusted by him with the care of his ward.[2] It is possible that in the performance of this duty he had interfered too much with the pleasures of his charge ;[3] and we know that at one time rumours reached the papal court that the boy lacked even the bare necessaries of life,[4] though there is no reason to assume that this was during the period of Adhémar's governorship. At any rate James of Majorca, once his uncle had departed for Naples, was not slow in taking his revenge.[5] The moment was well chosen, for John XXII., freed from the anxieties of his struggle with Louis of Bavaria, had turned his attention to the extirpation of heresy,[6] and his indignation had been aroused by the reports of the intemperate sermon of Philip of Majorca.[7] Moreover, the Bishop of Elne, who would naturally preside at the trial, had already gained a great reputation for his zeal against heretics.[8] The only flaw in the king's carefully laid scheme lay in the fact that his intended victim was personally known to the Pope, and it was largely owing to his influence that the little kingdom of Majorca had loyally supported the Church through the critical years of Louis of Bavaria's presence in Italy.[9] A few days after receiving the summons to appear before the bishop Adhémar presented himself before Jean Cerda, the Commissioner of the Inquisitor of Majorca, and denounced his own confessor, a Franciscan called Guillem Espitalier, as a heretic.[10] His reasons for taking this step are somewhat obscure, for soon afterwards he fled to Avignon in order to plead his cause before the Pope.[11] John XXII. confided the proceedings to Cardinal Jacques Fournier, later to be known as Pope Benedict XII,[12] who as Bishop of Palmiers had had much

---

[1] Vidal, " Procès d'Inquisition contre Adhémar de Mosset, noble Rousillonnais, inculpé de Béguinisme ", *Analecta Gallicana*, i. pp. 555-89, 689-99, 711-22. James II. of Majorca was the principal witness against the accused (p. 722).

[2] *Ibid.* p. 688.

[3] One of the accusations brought against Adhémar was that he regarded hunting as mortal sin (Vidal, *op. cit.* p. 716).

[4] Vidal, *Revue des questions historiques*, lxxxviii. p. 386.

[5] He does not seem immediately to have disgraced Adhémar (Vidal, " Procès," p. 688).

[6] Cf. *B.F.* v. 896, p. 491.   [7] Cf. *supra*, pp. 65 and 186.

[8] Gui Terré. As General of the Carmelites he had been a member of the commissions which sat in judgment on Olivi's " Postilla in Apocalypsim " and on the errors of the Spirituals (*Misc.* ii. 258-70 and 270-71). On receiving special powers against the heretics of his diocese he immediately took proceedings against Adhémar (Vidal, *op. cit.* pp. 685 and 687).   [9] *Ibid.* p. 583.

[10] December 1332. Cf. *ibid.* pp. 571 and 577.

[11] *Ibid.* p. 688 s.   [12] *Ibid.* p. 690.

experience in such matters.[1] The accused appeared before his
tribunal on the 3rd of March 1333,[2] but in spite of the skill of his
examiner very little could be elicited from him,[3] though he was too
wise to deny his connection with certain Béguins during the days
of his intimacy with Philip of Majorca.[4] He protested that he was
a true and faithful Catholic, and declared that he was ready to
submit himself to the judgment of the Pope, using his denunciation
of Guillem Espitalier as a proof of the purity of his intentions.[5] The
cardinal finally determined to await the arrival of the evidence
collected by the Bishop of Elne against Adhémar before proceeding further with the case.[6] This report reached Avignon in the
summer,[7] but it is probable that certain matters connected with the
proceedings were still left in the hands of the local court, for John
XXII. wrote in October to the King of Majorca ordering that
Adhémar should be treated with justice.[8] All through the trial
the scrupulous impartiality displayed at Avignon stands in marked
contrast to the prejudices and intrigues of the tribunal at Majorca.
Many of the accusations in the report sent to the Curia show only
too clearly the determination of James to be revenged on his
uncle's friend, for no serious judge would have taken Adhémar's
disapproval of hunting as a sign of heresy.[9] His loyalty to Philip [10]
and even his former intimacy with Angelo da Clareno could hardly
be accepted as proofs of his guilt, especially as his accusers were
foolish enough to recall the Pope's previous delight in the society
of the latter.[11] The most serious charges appear to have been some

---

[1] He had presided at the trial of Bernard Délicieux. Cf. *supra*, p. 20.

[2] Vidal, *op. cit.* p. 690.

[3] His usual answer was in the negative, and when hard pressed he declared
that he did not remember.

[4] *Ibid.* pp. 574, 576-77.   [5] *Ibid.* p. 577.

[6] The letter directed by the cardinal to the bishop asking for his report of
the case is dated July 4, 1333. Cf. *ibid.* p. 589.

[7] *Ibid.* p. 691. The evidence collected in Majorca is printed (*ibid.* pp. 711-
724).

[8] *Ibid.* p. 695 (from Reg. Vat. 117, 1248).

[9] Cf. *supra*, p. 254, *n.* 3.

[10] Vidal, *op. cit.* p. 714.

[11] *Ibid.* pp. 713 and 716. Adhémar is supposed to have been the friend of
Philip, concerning whom he consulted Angelo. He had been unjustly excommunicated and was unable to be absolved, so that his devout master apparently
had many scruples as to whether he ought to attend Mass. Cf. *A.L.K.G.* i. 564
and *supra*, p. 79. A ridiculous story is given, perhaps taken from some perverted
tradition of the Béguins, which describes how in the days of their intimacy
John XXII. had consulted Angelo as to whether his state was pleasing to God.
While meditating about the matter the former saw in a vision a band of demons
bearing a chalice filled with the poison of iniquity, which they were taking to
the Pope in order that he might drink of it. When they returned again it
was empty (Vidal, *op. cit.* p. 713).

rash words spoken against the clergy [1] and the drowning of two clerks who were guilty of robbery and had been captured in secular dress.[2] Proceedings were recommenced after the arrival of these documents, the proctor of the Bishop of Elne being present at the trial.[3] Unfortunately only part of the record of the last stages of the process has survived, so that it is not certain if Adhémar was finally acquitted.[4] Some four years later, however, Benedict XII. granted him and his wife Bérengère an indulgence "in articulo mortis", a favour not usually conferred on one to whose name the stigma of heresy had been attached.[5]

Perhaps the chief interest in the whole process centres round the first examination held at Avignon. One of the main objects of the judges was naturally to gain information concerning the beliefs professed by Philip of Majorca and his immediate circle.[6] Although the replies of the accused were rarely satisfactory the questions themselves throw much light on the doctrines generally ascribed to the Béguins. Adhémar was asked repeatedly what he believed concerning the age of the Holy Spirit [7] and the new order of evangelists,[8] and if he had heard the Church identified with Babylon the harlot.[9] He was also pressed to state his views on the subject of the future damnation of the clergy, both secular and regular, for the Béguins were purported to hold that only certain of the Franciscans would ultimately be saved.[10] It is from the same source that we learn that the plain of Salsès in the Pyrenees was to be the scene of the final destruction of the Church at the hands of the ten kings of the Saracens,[11] and that Frederick of Sicily was sometimes regarded as the lesser Antichrist.[12] The rôle of his greater successor was assigned either to Philip of Majorca or to Angelo, or Ubertino of Casale.[13] Adhémar was closely questioned also concerning his reverence for the person and the teaching

---

[1] " Si haberet filios magis vellet quod essent suspensi vel mortui quam quod essent episcopi vel sacerdotes " (Vidal, *op. cit.* p. 578. Cf. p. 717). Adhémar's answer was that if he had said this it was " ex lapsu linguae vel aliqua commotione ".

[2] It was in connection with the drowning of these clerks that Adhémar was excommunicated (*ibid.* p. 719 s.). Philip of Majorca ordered him to refrain from hearing Mass as he thought the sentence should be observed in spite of its injustice (*ibid.* p. 724). [3] *Ibid.* p. 724.

[4] The trial was not finished in January 1334, for at that date one of the assessors, the Bishop of Maguelonne, was replaced by Hugues Auger, Canon of Narbonne (*ibid.* p. 676).

[5] April 26, 1336. *Ibid.* p. 697.   [6] *Ibid.* pp. 583-84.

[7] *Ibid.* p. 578.   [8] *Ibid.* p. 579.

[9] *Ibid.* p. 578 and s.

[10] *Ibid.* p. 579. Cf. Bernard Gui, *op. cit.* p. 146.

[11] Vidal, *op. cit.* p. 579. Cf. *supra*, p. 250.

[12] Vidal, *op. cit.* p. 587 s.   [13] *Ibid.* Cf. *supra*, p. 251.

of Olivi,[1] and his judges were particularly anxious to discover whether he possessed any of the writings of the great Spiritual,[2] or had visited or sent candles to his shrine at Narbonne.[3] He was also asked if he revered the memory of the martyrs of Marseilles.[4] Philip of Majorca's famous sermon probably gave rise to certain inquiries connected with the question of the poverty of Christ,[5] and the sanctity of the Franciscan Rule as the completest reflection of the life of the Saviour and His Apostles which had yet been seen upon the earth.[6] Adhémar admitted that before the promulgation of John XXII.'s decretals he had often heard it preached that Christ and His apostles had owned nothing either severally or in common,[7] but that for his part he was quite prepared to accept the papal pronouncements as a final settlement of the question.[8] On the whole the inquiry confirms almost in every particular the account of the doctrines of the Béguins given by Bernard Gui in his *Practica Inquisitionis*.

One of the most difficult and fascinating problems which arises in connection with the Béguins of Provence is the diffusion of the sect in other regions. The similarity between their tenets and those of the Zealots is so marked that it is felt that there must be some close bond of union between them and the Fraticelli. The two names are found together in the decretal " Sancta romana atque universalis ecclesia ", launched by John XXII. against Angelo and his followers,[9] as well as in a much earlier bull of Boniface VIII.,[10] but " Fraticelli de paupere vita " speedily came to

---

[1] Vidal, *op. cit.* p. 585.

[2] *Ibid.* p. 586. In connection with the questions concerning the books of Olivi, Adhémar was asked about his opinions on the subject of the grace conferred by baptism, and the time when Christ had been pierced by the spear.

[3] *Ibid.* Adhémar's answer was that he did not remember.

[4] *Ibid.* p. 582.

[5] *Ibid.* p. 583. He was also questioned as to whether he had rejoiced at the news of the reception of Louis of Bavaria and the antipope at Pisa, and had declared that they would restore the Church to a state of evangelical poverty. Cf. *ibid.* p. 717.

[6] *Ibid.* p. 581.   [7] *Ibid.*

[8] *Ibid.* p. 580. The examiners were somewhat insistent on this point, for they had heard a report that Adhémar, though he secretly disapproved of the papal decretals, was prepared to conceal his views, in the hope that they would be repealed by John XXII.'s successor or by a General Council (p. 584). According to the evidence from Majorca he and the king had differed over the Pope's pronouncements (p. 715).

[9] *B.F.* v. 297, p. 134 (December 30, 1317). Cf. *supra*, p. 63. This bull was reissued in 1322 and again in 1331 (*B.F.* v. 474, pp. 229 and 896, p. 491). In a letter from John XXII. to Robert of Naples (May 1325) the term " Beguini " seems to be used for " Fraticelli " (*A.L.K.G.* iv. 65).

[10] Anagni, October 22, 1296. Cf. *A.L.K.G.* ii. pp. 156-8. Alvaro Paez does not seem to draw much distinction between " Fraticelli " and " Béguins ". Cf. *De Planctu Ecclesie*, L. II. Articulus LI.

be the only term employed to describe the descendants of the old Spiritual party. We gather from Bernard Gui that the Béguins and Spirituals of southern France and the " Fratisselli " of Italy were not only separate but hostile organisations, for the former had serious doubts as to the ultimate salvation of the latter.[1] Another very intricate but interesting problem which still remains to be solved is the connection between the Provençal Béguins and the various communities of the same name which were scattered through Germany and the Netherlands. Unfortunately, as in the case of the " Fraticelli ",[2] the name was often employed as an equivalent for " heretic ",[3] and at present there is little reason to believe that the Béguins of Provence were in any way connected with their namesakes either in the Low Countries or on the Rhine. It is true that one of Clement V.'s reasons for abolishing the Béguinages was the heresy common among their inmates with regard to the divine essence,[4] and perhaps it is more than a mere matter of coincidence that Olivi's views on the same subject were condemned at the same session of the Council of Vienne.[5] Yet all the evidence which we possess would give a definitely Franciscan origin to the Provençal Béguins, while the communities of holy women, later to be called by this title, were in existence in the Netherlands during the actual lifetime of St. Francis, and were not in any way connected with himself or his followers. In Germany, moreover, the Beghards or Béguins seem to have held doctrines similar to those professed by the sect of the Free Spirit condemned by Innocent III. As in the case of many other fascinating historical questions, however, our knowledge of the Béguins is still too hazy for us to do more than arrive at very tentative conclusions concerning the origin and diffusion of the different bodies of men and women who were popularly denoted by that title.

[1] *Op. cit.* p. 146.   [2] Cf. *supra*, p. 210.
[3] Cf. Van Mierlo, *op. cit.* pp. 786 and 790.
[4] John of Winterthur, *op. cit.* p. 74.   Mansi, *Concilia*, xxv. p. 411.
[5] " Fidei Catholicae Fundamento " (*ibid.*).   Cf. *supra*, p. 93, *n.* 3.

CHAPTER VIII

THE SPIRITUALS IN LITERATURE

THE story of the endeavours of the Spiritual party to secure
the true observance of the Rule of St. Francis has been a
subject of great fascination to the imagination not only of
historians but of all who can sympathise with heroic aspirations
towards a noble ideal. Moreover, the struggle between them and
the Conventuals was fraught with momentous implications not only
for the Franciscan Order but for the whole Church, giving rise to
endless speculations on the basis of the claims of religious authority,
which have left their mark on the development of thought. So
much has been written concerning the Zealots that here it is
possible only to mention the more important controversies which
their eventful history occasioned among scholars and name a few
of the writers to whose labours we owe most of our knowledge of a
complicated but enthralling theme.

The survival of many of the writings of the leaders of the
Spirituals is due to the devotion of their followers. Certain of the
manuscripts of Olivi's " Questiones " bear distinct traces of having
belonged to some poor friar, from whom they were probably taken
at the time when the reading of his works was prohibited.[1] The
Dominican inquisitor, Bernard Gui, informs us that the Beguins
in the south of France possessed translations of the commentary
on the Apocalypse and certain other treatises of one whom they
revered as an uncanonized saint, but none of these has yet been
discovered.[2] Our debt to the disciples of Angelo da Clareno is even
greater. We have seen how in the letter in which the broken-
hearted Simon of Cassia announced the death of his beloved friend
and master he ordered the collection and transcription of the letters
and other sayings of the latter, " being unwilling that his memory
should altogether perish ".[3] Perhaps the beautiful manuscript in
the Biblioteca Nazionale [4] at Florence is the result of Brother
Simon's instructions. Certainly if this is the case, his secretary,
John of Salerno, faithfully fulfilled his master's orders with regard
to " fair large letters ". The total absence of all decoration gives
the codex a singular charm, and makes it a worthy memorial to
one whose gracious austerity shines forth from its pages. In his
other writings Angelo has concealed his personality, but in these

[1] Codex Borghesiana, 350. Cf. Ehrle. *A.L.K.G.* iii. p. 471. Another
manuscript in the same collection (C. Borghesiana, 358) was obviously used by
the commission who examined Olivi's writings at the time of the Council of
Vienne. Cf. *A.L.K.G.* iii. p. 473.
[2] Bernard Gui, *op. cit.* p. 142. *Supra,* p. 252.
[3] *A.L.K.G.* i. 536. Cf. *supra,* p. 69.
[4] Codex Magliabecchiana, xxxix. 75. Cf. *A.L.K.G.* i. 536.

letters to his faithful followers, and to those united to him by an even closer bond of friendship, he has poured forth all the deepest feelings of his soul. No letters to Simon himself appear in the collection, for perhaps he felt that these were too sacred to be read by anyone else. Just as the Béguins made vernacular versions of the writings of Olivi, so Angelo's disciples translated his works into their native tongue. A manuscript containing the Prologue to the "Chronicle of the Seven Tribulations" and the first two tribulations has recently been discovered written in the dialect of the March of Abruzzi,[1] a region where he had many followers. The so-called "Leggenda Antiqua", written in the same dialect, bears so close a verbal resemblance to the early part of the Chronicle that many critics have regarded it as the translation of a lost Latin work by Angelo himself. Now Father Lazzeri, the finder of the new codex, has put forward the theory that the Leggenda is a collection of traditions concerning St. Francis, based largely on the "Historia Septem Tribulationum", but with additions from the "Speculum" and the story told by the three companions.[2] Yet Angelo's disciples were not content to preserve only the more popular writings of their master. One codex of his, *Expositio Regulae Fratrum Minorum*, probably came originally from the suppressed Clarenist convent of Stroncone,[3] and the fourteenth-century codex of his translation of the *Scala Paradisi* of the Greek abbot St. John Climacus, now in the Bodleian at Oxford, bears this inscription: "Questo libro sie de li poveri frati di sancto Sebastiano chi stano in la contrata di sancto Raphaelo".[4] The same library, moreover, contains no less than four of the Italian versions of the same book, made by his friend Gentile da Foligno, one of which is late fourteenth century.[5] The three fifteenth-century codices came from monasteries in different parts of Italy, and the poorness of the vellum or paper used, as well as the utter lack of ornamentation,

---

[1] Codex S. Isidore, 1/28. Cf. *A.F.H.* xi. 47-65. Father Lazzeri shows that most of the "Leggenda Antiqua" is identical with the dialect version of the "Historia Septem Tribulationum", while the rest is merely a translation from the "Speculum" and the "Legend of the Three Companions".

[2] The Todi manuscript of the Leggenda, which is incomplete, was discovered and published by Signor Faloci Pulignani in *Miscellanea Franciscana*, viii. The complete manuscript was found later in the Vatican by Signor Minocchi, and has been published by him under the title of "La Leggenda Antiqua, nuova fonte biographica di San Francesco a Assisi" (Florence, 1905). Unfortunately Signor Minocchi's book is now out of print. In reading the version in the *Miscellanea Franciscana* I was much struck by its close resemblance to the first part of the "Chronicle of the Seven Tribulations".

[3] Now at St. Isidore's at Rome (C. 1/92). Cf. Oliger, Intro. to *Expos.* p. xi, and *supra*, p. 225, *n.* 7.

[4] Cod. Can. Lat. Misc. 333.

[5] Cod. Canonici Misc. Ital. 155. Cf. *supra*, 70, *n.* 2.

makes it a possible conjecture that they were originally the property
of Angelo's own community.[1] This work must have been popular
at the end of the fifteenth century, to judge by the numerous
incunables which are still in existence.[2] The Latin version of the
Scala Paradisi was twice printed[3] in the sixteenth century, probably
because of the new version of the same work made by the great
Humanist, Ambrogio Traversari,[4] who in his Introduction commented very unfavourably on Angelo's translation, though he did
not name its author. It is a pity that the Rule of St. Basil and
his other Greek translations have not survived. Still, the men
who took such pains to preserve the *Scala* cannot have been the
ignorant fanatics who appear in the record of the Inquisition processes of the period. Their names, collected from Angelo's letters,
and these translations of his works are unfortunately their sole
memorials.

The foundation of the Osservanti led to a revival of feeling in
favour of the Spirituals amongst a considerable section of the
Franciscan Order, and this has persisted until to-day. Pauluccio
di Trinci and his followers were striving for the same ideal as the
early Zealots—namely, the true observance of the Rule without
gloss—and therefore could not fail to be inspired by the struggles and
misfortunes of their forerunners, even though they regarded their
methods as violent and rash. For Clareno they had an especial
tenderness, for tradition asserted that he had been the spiritual
father of their original founder, Giovanni da Valle.[5] It is just
conceivable that there may have been a considerable influx of
" Fraticelli de paupere vita " into the new Order, and this may

---

[1] (a) Codex Canonici Ital. 249 (vellum). On flyleaf " Opera fatta in
Toscana ", f. 5 *v*., " Iste liber est monasterii sancti Salvatoris et (   ) ".
(b) Codex Canonici Ital. 271. On paper with binding of wood covered with
leather. FIR " Questo libro è dal monasterio della colla 1550 ". F. 135 *v*. " Nel
mile C 500 82 io fra Calisto Anselmi cominciai a (leggere) codesto libro neli 2
jugnio nel monasterio di Sta Maria Madalena di (Treviso) territorio (Leneciario)."
On f. 136 *r*. begins the life of the abbot, " Ysach de Sizia ", written in a very
similar hand to the earlier part of the Codex. On the back of the binding is
found the date 1546.
(c) Canon. Ital. 295 (paper), (incomplete), " Iste liber monasterii (ritatis ?)".
[2] Cf. *supra*, p. 70, *n.* 2.
[3] At Cologne in 1540, and at Venice in 1518. In the Cologne edition it
forms part of the collected works of Dionysius Carthusianus (Leuwis of Rychel),
who used Angelo's version as the text for his " Enarrationes in Scalam Paradisi
S. Ioannis Climaci ". Father Oliger believes the Venetian edition to have been
printed, not from Angelo's version, but from a later one, perhaps of Franciscan
origin, based mainly on his text. Cf. *Intro. ad Expos*. pp. xlv-xlvi.
[4] Traversari certainly meant Clareno because of his reference to his miraculous acquisition of Greek. His introductory letter is quoted by Migne, *P.G.* 88,
615, and by Fr. Oliger in his Introduction to the *Expositio*, p. li.
[5] Cf. *A.L.K.G.* iv. 182, and *supra*, p. 66.

be the basis of the story of the injunction of the dying Angelo to his followers given by Bernardinus Aquilanus.[1] Perhaps the "heretics" whom Gentile da Spoleto, the successor of Giovanni da Valle, was imprisoned for harbouring among his followers, were disciples of Clareno. At any rate it is significant that the best Italian Codex of the " Historia Septem Tribulationum " is still in the Observant Convent of Siena.[2] This was transcribed by a certain *frate*, Girolamo da Siena, in the hermitage of Bel Verde[3] in the year 1405. It would be interesting to know the history of the famous Latin manuscript of the same work now in the Laurenziana.[4] This was transcribed in 1381 by a certain brother Matthew. Cardinal Ehrle, who used it for his edition of the Chronicle,[5] thinks from the Latin that the copyist must have been a German,[6] which makes it less likely that he was connected with the Observants. Certain of the Conventuals appear to have had a great admiration for the Zealots. Bartolommeo da Pisa, in his great " Liber de Conformitate vite Beati Francisci ad vitam domini nostri Jesu Christi ",[7] written in 1385, described Angelo as a great preacher, and very famous both for his holiness and love of poverty, and records his translations from the Greek and his close connection with Simon of Cassia.[8] On the other hand, he entertained a hearty dislike for Ubertino da Casale, perhaps because he regarded him as an apostate from the Franciscan Order,[9] but writes with evident appreciation of Olivi.[10] Moreover, Fra Bartolommeo, perhaps trusting to his position as proctor of the Order at the Curia, made a little book which he probably would not have shown to simple friars. This is now in the Bodleian [11] and contains the Gospels for Lent written very beautifully on one side of the page. On the other, it may be in Bartolommeo's own hand, are relevant extracts taken from the Commentaries of Olivi, while at the bottom of the page are similar passages from Nicolas de Lyra. It is possible that Olivi's works had the same charm for many friars as the tree of knowledge of good and evil had for our first parents. They must have appealed to St. Bernardino of Siena, for he quoted from Olivi's " Summa " in one of his Dialogues.[12] The connection of the

---

[1] B. Bernardini Aquilani, *Chronica Fratrum Minorum Observantiae*, pp. 3-6. This passage is quoted in *A.F.H.* iii. 254. Cf. *supra*, p. 68.

[2] Described by Golubovich, *op. cit.* i. 43 *s*.

[3] Cf. Golubovich, *op. cit.* i. 54.   [4] Cod. *Laurenziana*, Pl. XX. 7.

[5] *A.L.K.G.* ii. pp. 125-55, 256-327.   [6] *Ibid.* p. 124.

[7] Published by the college of St. Bonaventura at Quaracchi in *A.F.* iv. and v.

[8] *A.F.* iv. 340 and 513.   [9] *Ibid.* p. 440.

[10] *Ibid.* pp. 340 and 540.   [11] Codex Canon. Script. Eccl. xxvi.

[12] Dialogus de Sancta Obedientia between Bernardino and his disciple Paul (*Firmamentum Trium Ordinum* (Venice, 1513), f. 164 *r.b*-170 *r.b*. Cited in *A.F.H.* xi. 312). Cf. *supra*, p. 96, *n*. 1.

French Observants with the Spirituals of Provence has not been studied very carefully, but their petition to the General Council of Constance [1] for separation from the Order bears a very close resemblance to a similar petition made by Ubertino di Casale to Pope Clement V. a hundred years earlier. The situation of the reforming party at the beginning of the fifteenth century must have been very similar to that of the Zealots, as can be seen from their complaint of the difficulty of observing the Rule in its original strictness because of the oppression of the chief officials of the Order and the slackness of the majority of the friars. On the whole, the Council was more favourable to their petition than the Pope had been to Ubertino's. It is characteristic of the attitude of the new branch of the Franciscan Order towards the Spirituals that in his collection of the opinions of various early commentators on the Rule, Alexander Ariosti gives extracts both from the writings of St. Bonaventura and from those of Ubertino and Olivi.[2] The change of feeling is still more apparent if we compare the chronicle of the German Observantine, Nicholas of Glassberger,[3] written at the end of the fifteenth century, with that of the *Twenty-four Generals*, written in the middle of the fourteenth,[4] for the later chronicler makes ample allowance for the lofty motives of the Zealots, though he admits that they occasioned grave scandals in the Order, while the earlier one writes with great bitterness, especially against Olivi.[5] Mariano da Firenze, writing almost at the same period as Glassberger, describes with complete impartiality the conflict between the Franciscan Order and John XXII.[6] Even Jacopo della Marchia, the fierce and inveterate enemy of the Fraticelli,[7] was quite ready to acknowledge and rejoice over the fame brought

[1] *Firmamentum Trium Ordinum* (Venice, 1513), f. 151 *r.b*-158 *r.a.* Father Oliger has quoted relevant passages in his article in *A.H.F.* ix. 3-41, to show its close connection with the treatise " Sanctitas vestra " of Ubertino, printed in *A.L.K.G.* iii. pp. 51-89. Cf. *supra*, p. 22.

[2] His treatise " Serena conscientia ", composed between 1455 and 1458 and printed in the *Firmamentum* (Venice, 1513), f. 133 *v.a*-151 *r.b*, is merely a collection of extracts from early Franciscan writers on the subject of the Rule. The quotations from Ubertino are mainly from his treatise " Rotulus iste " (*A.L.K.G.* iii. 93-137), which Alexander obviously regarded rather in the light of an ordinary exposition of the Rule than as a controversial writing.

[3] *A.F.* ii.

[4] *Ibid.* iii. It must be remembered that the writer had had personal experience of the scandal which the lack of discipline of the Zealots had brought upon the Order.

[5] It is noteworthy, however, that the most remarkable testimony concerning Olivi's intellectual powers is found in the *Chronicle of the 24 Generals*, where he is described as " lux in lucem reducens dubia " (*A.F.* iii. 382).

[6] " Compendium Chronicorum Fratrum Minorum " (*A.F.H.* ii. 638-40). On the whole he seems very little interested in the matter.

[7] Cf. *supra*, p. 240 *s.*

to the Franciscan Order by the learning and the other great qualities with which the founders of the sect had been endowed.[1] Perhaps the most widely read of all the writings of the Zealots at the close of the Middle Ages was the *Arbor Vitae*. The numerous manuscripts which exist, not only in Latin but in French, Italian, and Flemish, are a striking testimony to its popularity. In 1404 Martin of Aragon begged Benedict XIII. to send him an example of the book in order that he might have it translated into Catalan,[2] and the Castilian version in the National Library at Madrid was actually made at the command of Isabella the Catholic.[3] In many of the codices the fifth book, containing the author's Joachimite speculations, is considerably mutilated, the eighth chapter being generally altogether omitted, perhaps because of the language used with regard to Boniface VIII. and Benedict XI.[4] In its expurgated form the *Arbor* was apparently regarded as an excellent introduction to the mystic life, and as such was frequently put into the hands of novices.[5] The German Franciscan, Johann Brugman, in his " Speculum Imperfectionis ", complains with great bitterness about the way in which the younger members of the Order were neglecting the old and tried manuals of devotion, which inspired them to pious meditations on the life and passion of Christ, naming among many others both the *Arbor* and the *Imitation*.[6] The Carthusian, Jacques de Gruytrode, Prior of Liége, who also played his part in the religious revival in the Netherlands which is associated with the " brethren of the Common Life ", regarded Ubertino as the most divinely inspired writer of the later Middle Ages.[7] His fellow-Carthusian, Leuwis, the celebrated Abbot of Rychel, however, wrote with strong disapproval of the views on the future state of unbaptized infants expressed by Ubertino in the

---

[1] " Sermo de Excellentia Ordinis Sancti Francisci " preached either at the Chapter-General of Florence in 1449 or at the Congregation of the Observantines held the same year. Among the distinguished Franciscans he mentions : " Franciscus de Marchia " (Francesco d'Ascoli), Michael de Cesena, Magister Petrus Johannis (Olivi), Willelmus Hochanus, Gentilis de Cingulo (Angelo da Clareno), and Ubertinus de Casali. Cf. *A.F.H.* iv. p. 306.

[2] Callaey, " L'Influence et la diffusion de l'*Arbor Vitae* " (*R.H.E.* xvii. p. 535).

[3] *Ibid.*

[4] Callaey, *R.H.E.* xi. p. 723. The fifteenth-century manuscript in the John Rylands Library at Manchester is a very good example of the expurgated version of the *Arbor*.

[5] *Ibid.*

[6] " Speculum Imperfectionis Fratrum Minorum " (*A.F.H.* ii. 617). Brugman was a friend and contemporary of Leuwis of Rychel (Dionysius Carthusianus), and died at Amsterdam in 1473.

[7] The beginning of his treatise on the life of Christ, " Fasciculus myrrhae dilectus meus mihi ", shows his close study of the *Arbor*. Cf. St. Bonaventura, *Opera Omnia*, viii. p. xl, and Callaey, *op. cit.* p. 724, *n.* 2.

Arbor,[1] and Gerson also regarded the book as rash and dangerous, and only fit to be studied by theologians, who were not liable to be led astray by the many errors contained in it.[2] On the other hand, the famous Abbot Trithemius of Spanheim warmly defended both the book and its author, declaring that Ubertino had erred only on matters which in his day had not been definitely decided by the Church.[3] A certain codex in the library of the university at Barcelona places the *Arbor* third in its list of mystic meditations on the life of Christ,[4] and in 1485 an incomplete edition of the work appeared at Venice. Thirty years later extracts from the fifth book were printed under the title of " De Septem Statibus Ecclesiae," and form part of a larger work containing many of the spurious writings of Joachim.[5] It is possible that an age like the Renaissance, which combined a profound scepticism with a surprising amount of superstition and an almost childish belief in sorcery and magic, was far more enthralled by Ubertino's apocalyptic speculations than by the more devotional parts of his great book. Venice can also lay claim to the only editions of Olivi's *Quodlibeta* [6] and his *Expositio super Regulam Fratrum Minorum*, which was printed in 1513 under the auspices of the Observants.[7] The rest of his work was to remain in manuscript until the closing years of the nineteenth century, with the exception of his commentary on the Canticles and the *De Semine Sanctarum Scripturarum*, which were wrongly ascribed to St. Bonaventura, and thus were published in the Tridentine edition of the works of the seraphic doctor.[8] This neglect of the writings of the great Zealot may have been in part due to the suspicion with which he was still regarded by the Franciscan Order,[9] or more probably to a profound lack of interest in the ideas of the lesser theologians and philosophers of the Middle Ages.

The Franciscan writers of the sixteenth century, although they had a sincere and fervent admiration for the Spirituals, seem

[1] Ubertino's view was too stern even for a medieval theologian. Cf. Dionysius Carthusianus, *Opera Omnia* (Tournay, 1903), xxii. p. 451.

[2] " De Susceptione Humanitatis Christi " (De caute legendis quorundam libris), *Opera*, i. (Basle, 1489), p. 573. Cf. *supra*, p. 134, *n*. 4.

[3] *De Scriptoribus Ecclesiasticis*, f. 77.

[4] Cf. St. Bonaventura, *Opera Omnia*, viii. p. xl.

[5] Printed at Venice in 1516. Two copies of this work are in the Bodleian Library.

[6] Cf. *supra*, p. 109.

[7] In *Firmamentum trium Ordinum Seraphici Patris Sancti Francisci* (Venice, 1513), f. 106 r.-124 v. Cf. *supra*, 100, *n*. 1.

[8] Trent, 1772. Cf. *supra*, p. 116.

[9] Although Sixtus IV. had given the friars licence to read the works of Olivi, the Chapter-General of Terni renewed the ban against these in 1500. Cf. *supra*, p. 94.

on the whole to have felt very little inclination to make further researches into their history. A new reformed branch of the Order, the Capuchins, came into being in 1528, and their founder, Louis of Fossombrone, came from Clareno's birthplace. There was a band of Clarenist hermits living in the neighbourhood, so that he may have derived his inspiration from their accounts of their holy founder.[1] It is certain that the members of the new branch of the Order steeped themselves in the writings of the Zealots, and identified themselves with the small body of elect amongst whom the true Franciscan ideal was to survive. One of their number, John of Fano, who had formerly been an Observant, had a great admiration for Ubertino,[2] while another of their early converts, Giovanni da Ventimiglia, had already discovered two copies of the "Chronicle of the Seven Tribulations" at Chiavari. He loved the book so much that he made a transcript of it in " fair large letters ", and this his Superior allowed him to keep as a reward for his labours. In 1530, when he joined the Capuchins, he brought it with him, and it was the source of the whole of the early part of " a simple and devout history " of the Order written by another of the brothers. He was careful to omit anything which he considered unedifying, as for instance the story of the fortunes of the Spiritual party between the pontificates of Boniface VIII. and John XXII. Even the representatives of the Conventual party had lost much of their old prejudice against the Zealots. The learned " Petrus Rodolphus Tossinianensis ", afterwards successively Bishop of Venosa and Sinigaglia, gives a very sympathetic account of their sufferings, which is obviously taken from the "Historia Septem Tribulationum".[3] He also knew the *Arbor Vitae*,[4] and regarded both Ubertino and Olivi as ornaments to the Franciscan Order.[5] The saintly Minister-General, Francesco Gonzaga, writing only a year later,[6] is loud in his praise of Angelo da Clareno, though he seems to have known very little about him, except that

---

[1] Cf. Callaey, " L'Infiltration des idées Franciscaines spirituelles chez les Frères Mineurs Capuchins au XVIᵉ siècle ", in *Miscellanea Francesco Ehrle*, i. p. 389 s.

[2] John of Fano wrote a dialogue on the Franciscan Rule, entitled " Brevis discursus super observantiam paupertatis Fratrum Minorum ", in which he follows Ubertino's opinions very closely with regard to the " usus pauper ". Cf. Callaey, *R.H.E.* xvii. p. 534.

[3] *Historiarum Seraphicae Religionis libri tres* (Venice, 1586), L. II. f. 180 r.- 181 v.

[4] Cf. his account of Ubertino, L. III. f. 334 v. s.

[5] *Ibid.* and L. III. f. 331 r. He is a little more doubtful about Ubertino because of his transference to the " Cistercian " Order.

[6] *De Origine Seraphicæ Religionis* (Rome, 1587), Pt. I. pp. 4-5. The passage in praise of Angelo is quoted in Fr. Ciro da Pesaro's Introduction to *Il Beato Angelo Clareno*, p. lxv.

he was a learned man who had made translations from the Greek, and had founded a new branch of the Order.   The Observant Mark of Lisbon regarded the title of "beato" given him by popular tradition, as a proof of his holiness.[1]   It is not surprising that Angelo's name appears in the Franciscan Martyrology compiled in 1637.   During the same century an ingenious attempt was made to re-establish the reputation of Michael of Cesena by accrediting him with a death-bed repentance.[2]   The tradition is not found earlier than Wadding, and rests on two manuscripts containing a commentary on the Fifty-first Psalm [3] found in the Franciscan Convent at Cesena in the eighteenth century and sent to Muratori.[4]   This is supposed to have been written by Michael during his last hours, but scholars have always had doubts of its genuineness.   No traces of the manuscripts were discovered until recently, when two codices answering the description of the old ones as given in the seventeenth-century catalogue were found in the Municipal Library.   Unfortunately in one of them the commentary is ascribed to Aquinas, while, although the other ends with Michael's recantation, it is written on seventeenth-century paper, and the writing is obviously a later imitation of the medieval hand used in the earlier part of the manuscript.   Moreover, the facts given about the life of the ex-Minister-General are obviously culled from Wadding, and some of them have been disproved by modern research.   Except for the scandal to the Franciscan Order, there is a certain dramatic satisfaction in believing that Michael remained stubborn to the end.

With the exception of the Franciscan writers and Trithemius, very little reference is made to the Spirituals during the fifteenth century.   St. Antoninus, the celebrated Archbishop of Florence, in the third part of his *Historialis* gives a short summary of the negotiations which took place at the time of the Council of Vienne,[5] but is obviously far more interested in the controversy concerning evangelical poverty, since it was from this that the "Fraticelli de opinione" drew their origin.[6]   He gives an account of the later history of the sect, and of the vigorous measures taken against its

---

[1] *Chronica Ordinis a Sancto Francisco instituti*, L. VII. cap. xxiii., cited in Introduction to *Il Beato Angelo Clareno*, p. lxiv.

[2] The fraud was discovered by Signor Carlini. Cf. *A.F.H.* ii. 657-60. *Supra*, p. 196.   As an attempt, however, to re-establish Michael's reputation it was completely successful, for from being the "biforme monstrum" of a mid-seventeenth-century chronicler of Cesena he speedily became the pride and ornament of his native city. Cf. *Fra Michelino e la sua Eresia*, pp. 197-98.

[3] "Miserere mei, Domine."

[4] Muratori, *Rerum Italicarum Scriptores*, iii. Pt. II. pp. 513-27.

[5] *Tertia Pars Hystorialis* (Nuremberg, 1484), f. ccxlviii *r.b.*

[6] *Ibid.* f. cii. *v.a* and ccxlix. *r.a.*

members by Eugenius IV. and Nicholas V., but confesses that they had not yet altogether been exterminated even in his own diocese.[1] It is perhaps for this reason that he devoted a whole chapter of his *Summa Theologica* to an examination of their errors, and the arguments which he uses to refute these show that he had carefully studied the decretals of John XXII.[2] The famous humanist, Platina, however, took the opposite point of view, and declared that the attitude of the Franciscans was more in accordance with the Scriptures than that of the Pope.[3] Probably the interest shown in the struggle was due to the conciliar movement. Gerson and the other thinkers of the century were engaged in proving the supremacy of a General Council over the Pope, and Michael in his treatises had frequently appealed to such an assembly.[4] Yet the case rested on a slightly different footing, for the leader of the Franciscans had regarded John XXII. as a heretic and *ipso facto* deposed,[5] while the theologians at Constance and Basle wished to establish their authority over the Pope as a general principle. D'Ailly's summary of Occam's *Dialogus* is a sign that the works of the fugitives at Munich were being carefully studied,[6] and Gerson in his tract, " An liceat a summo pontifice appellare ",[7] cites an ingenious example taken from the writings of the great Franciscan. If the Pope had prohibited Peter from preaching that Christ was a true prophet, he would have been justified for the sake of the Church in appealing to a General Council. Even at the end of the century all interest in the question was not yet dead, for certain of Michael's appeals and Occam's *Dialogus* were printed at Lyons in 1495.[8]

It is probable, however, that the tendency among Franciscan writers was to dwell rather upon the philosophical renown of the latter than upon his fame as a political thinker.[9]

---

[1] *Tertia Pars Hystorialis* (Nuremberg, 1484), f. cii *v.a* and ccxlix *r.a.*

[2] *Summa Theologica*, Pars IV. Tit. XII. cap. iv., " De errore fraticellorum circa paupertatem Christi et apostolorum ". Father Oliger has pointed out that St. Antoninus, like St. Jacopo della Marchia, was meeting the arguments raised by the " Liber Veritatis ". It is also noteworthy that the *Summa* was composed about 1450, and was therefore almost contemporaneous with the *Dialogus*. Cf. *A.F.H.* vi. pp. 742-45.

[3] *De vitis Romanorum Pontificum* (Cologne, 1568), p. 253.

[4] Appeal from Pisa (*Misc.* iii. 272). Appeal to Louis of Bavaria and other princes (Goldast, *Monarchia*, ii. 1260). Letter to Friars at Chapter-General at Perpignan (*B.F.* v. p. 497, *n.* 7). Cf. *supra*, p. 174 *s*.

[5] Appeal from Pisa, *Misc.* iii. 275-99. Cf. *supra*, p. 176.   [7] Goldast, *Monarchia*, ii. p. 1515.

[6] Little, *op. cit.* p. 231.

[8] The " Opus Nonaginta Dierum " and the " Compendium errorum Johannis Pope XXII." had been already printed at Louvain in 1481. Cf. Little, *op. cit.* 229 and 232.

[9] An Italian translation of Mark of Lisbon (L. VIII. cap. 42), printed at Naples in 1550, describes Occam as the founder of Nominalism. A German

At first sight it appears surprising that, with the exception of Matthias Flacius "Illyricus"[1] hardly any references to the Spirituals are found in the early Protestant writers. This may be due to lack of knowledge or to profound differences in temperament and outlook. The Protestantism of the sixteenth century was on the whole practical and intellectual, and laboured rather for the secularisation of religious life than for union with Christ through complete separation from the world. The passionate mysticism of such men as Ubertino and Angelo would have seemed mere medieval superstition and obscurantism to a man like Calvin, though he would probably have heartily concurred in the former's identification of Boniface VIII. with the mystic Antichrist. On the other hand, except for Olivi, whose speculations were hidden in the papal archives, the Spirituals, like many mystics, had been profoundly uninterested in questions of doctrine, and had been content to accept the dogmas of the Church and to transmute them by the fiery splendour of their fervent imaginations. It is probable, however, that even their very names were unknown in Protestant circles, as they are not even referred to as examples of innocent victims of papal tyranny. Calvin makes no allusion to the controversy between the Minorites and John XXII., although he regarded the errors of the latter with regard to the Beatific Vision as a proof of the fallacy involved in the doctrine of Papal Infallibility.[2] Even those of the Reformers who possessed a somewhat hazy knowledge of the questions at issue in the great conflict make very little use of the writings of the Franciscans at Munich. It is strange that, with the exception of the letter of Charles IX. of France to Pius IV., protesting against the papal treatment of Jeanne de Navarre, Occam

---

version of the same chronicle published at Munich seventy years later goes even further and hails him as the father of Scholasticism itself. Cf. *A.F.H.* vi. p. 224 and *n.* 2, and Mariano da Firenze (*A.F.H.* ii. 636), where, however, certain of Occam's controversial writings are also mentioned. For the early printed editions of Occam's philosophical works cf. Little, *op. cit.* pp. 225-29.

[1] In his *Catalogus Testium Veritatis* he mentions Joachim of Flora, Arnold of Villanova, John of " Rupescissa " together with Occam, Michael of Cesena, and " Petrus Ioannis Minorita " amongst those who had denounced the errors of the Catholic Church. Although he displays very little knowledge of the controversy concerning evangelical poverty it is probable that he had read some of the political writings of Occam, and perhaps also the " Liber veritatis ", which, like Baluze, he regarded as a work of Michael of Cesena. Cf. *supra*, pp. 191 and 231. The seventeenth-century supplement to the *Catalogus* also includes Ubertino da Casale and the Fraticelli among the witnesses to the truth.

Cf. *Catalogus Testium Veritatis Auctarium* (Cattopoli, 1667), pp. 55 and 59. It is interesting that in his youth Matthias Flacius " Illyricus " intended to enter the Minorite Order, but was dissuaded by his uncle, Baldo Lupetino, who, although a Franciscan provincial, was secretly a Lutheran.

[2] *Institutio Christianae Religionis*, cap. viii. p. 133.

is never quoted in support of the doctrine of the independence of Church and State.[1] The German princes in their refusal to attend the Council of Trent merely cite him and Barnes as two English writers who had protested against the errors of the Church.[2] Even so well informed a writer as the famous du Plessis-Mornay, in his *Mysterium Iniquitatis, sive Historia Papatus*, though he gives a comparatively long account of Occam and his treatises,[3] and alludes to some of the arguments contained in them, was more interested in him as a victim of papal tyranny than as a thoughtful writer. He also gives a short summary of the struggle with John XXII., and mentions his decretals, though he suffered under the curious delusion that the Pope was forbidding mendicancy.[4] The Franciscans who disobeyed him and continued to beg for alms from door to door were known as " Fraterculi " and severely punished by the Church. The whole tone of the book can be gathered from the story of the friar who told the Pope to his face that the Roman Church was the harlot of Babylon and her ruler Antichrist, though de Mornay honestly confessed that he knew nothing of the fate of the bold preacher.[5] A more scholarly historian was Melchior Goldast, the Protestant Abbot of Haimingfeld, who collected and published a large number of Catholic treatises to prove that the secular power was independent of the ecclesiastical and that the Emperor derived none of his authority from the Pope.[6] But for his interest many of the political writings of Occam would exist only in manuscript and in the fifteenth-century incunabulae. The great English lawyer, Selden, studied Goldast's book with eager curiosity, though perhaps it was a mistaken patriotism which led him to rate Occam's political speculations even higher than those of Marsiglio of Padua.[7] He seems to have rejoiced exceedingly over the fact that the writings of the former had been placed on the " Index Expurgatorum ", since it furnished him with a further proof of their value.[8] Almost a century earlier Leland, after giving a rather vague account of Occam's conflict with John XXII., prudently refused to come to any decision with regard to the merits

---

[1] Quoted by Goldast in his Introduction to the *Monarchia*. The letter was written in 1563 by Baptiste de Mesnil, one of the councillors and royal advocates in the Parlement de Paris.

[2] *Ibid.* " The Refusal " was written at Nuremberg in 1562.

[3] *Mysterium Iniquitatis*, pp. 447, 449, 451, 460, 465.

[4] Du Plessis-Mornay, *op. cit.* p. 443.

[5] *Ibid.* p. 470. Cf. *supra*, p. 21.

[6] *Monarchia Sanctii Romani Imperii*, 3 vols. The date of the preface of the book is 1611.

[7] Selden, " De synedriis veterum Ebraeorum ", L. I., *Opera Omnia*, vol. i. pp. 1009-10.

[8] " Diu est quod indicibus expurgatoriis prohibita sunt opera Ockhami ejusmodi ; quod mirum, puto, videtur nemini " (*ibid.* p. 1011).

of the questions at issue,[1] and even Bale was wise enough not to allow himself to be carried away by his religious enthusiasm.[2] Pits also is completely impartial,[3] and the impression gained from reading the accounts given of Occam by the three great English antiquarians is that they were interested in him as an illustrious fellow-countryman, and not as the exponent of new and original theories concerning the relations between Church and State. Echoes of the controversy are, however, found in the writings of Cardinal Bellarmine, for in his *De Romanis Pontificibus* he endeavoured to reconcile "Exiit qui seminat" with the decretals of John XXII., thus going back to the original cause of the strife.[4]

The only English writer who collected any treatises either of the Spirituals or of the opponents of John XXII. was the Kentish rector, Edward Brown, who lived at the end of the seventeenth century. The nucleus of the book was a number of literary fragments dating from the ninth to the sixteenth century which had been put together about a century earlier by a German named Gratius, under the title of *Fasciculus Rerum Expetendarum*. Most of these, as Brown related triumphantly in his dedicatory letter to the Bishop of London, had, in spite of their merits, been condemned by the Roman Church. Brown's book was published in 1690 as a warning to Englishmen against the intrigues of the Pope and the Jesuits. The treatise ascribed to Occam was more probably written by some of the Italian Fraticelli towards the close of the fourteenth century.[5] Brown also gave a list of eight of the errors found in John's bull "Quia vir reprobus".[6] This is interesting, as their order is quite different from that generally found in the treatises of Michael and his followers, but unfortunately Brown did not give the source of his information. In the same book he printed the "Vade Mecum in Tribulationem"[7] of "Johannis de Rupescissa". This work is particularly interesting as showing the survival of apocalyptic speculation in the south of France even at the close of the fourteenth century. Brown's prefaces to the different writings in his book show that he was a serious scholar as well as a strong Protestant. The end of his

---

[1] Leland, *Commentarii de scriptoribus Britannicis*, c. cccxxvi. p. 323.

[2] Bale, *Scriptorum illustrium Majoris Brytanniae quam nunc Angliam et Scotiam vocant, Catalogus*, p. 395, xviii. In his accounts of Conyngton and Chatton (*ibid.* 404 and 420) on the other hand Bale gives full vent to his rancour against the friars.

[3] Pits, *De illustribus Angliae scriptoribus*, p. 456.

[4] *De Romanis Pontificibus*, L. IV. c. xiv. Cf. *supra*, p. 200.

[5] "Tractatus Venerabilis Inceptoris Guilelmi Ochami", ii. pp. 436-65. Cf. *supra*, p. 231, *n.* 1.

[6] *Fasc. Rer. Expetend.* ii. p. 42. Cf. *B.F.* v. p. 497.

[7] *Fasc. Rer. Expetend.* ii. 493-508. Cf. *supra*, p. 47.

Introduction to the " Vade Mecum " is worthy of quotation. Having discussed and dismissed its author's claim to be regarded as a prophet, he declared that his readers might equally well consider him endowed with divine inspiration for foretelling that England would soon be freed from the attacks of monks and of her most pernicious enemies the Jesuits.[1]

During the seventeenth century scholars began to make researches into the origin of the Fraticelli, a question which has not been entirely solved to-day, though modern theory is probably correct in believing that their foundation cannot be traced to any one body of men. The Polish Dominican Bzovius, in his continuation of the *Annales Ecclesiastici* [2] of Baronius, caused great scandal by declaring that the Spiritual Franciscans had been the founders of this pernicious sect of heretics. The great Franciscan historian Wadding [3] and his friend and compatriot Anthony Hicquey [4] took up the cudgels in defence of their Order. Modern research has on the whole justified the position of Bzovius, but this does not in any way reflect upon the judgment of the great Franciscan historian. Wadding used the documents known in his day, and especially the papal registers, and many very interesting letters are known to modern scholars only through the medium of his *Annales*.[5] He made great use of Angelo da Clareno's chronicle for writing the history of the Spirituals, and appears to have been very fond of this work, a codex of which he discovered and presented to the Franciscan College of St. Isidore, which he founded at Rome.[6] He admitted that his account was merely an abbreviation of the Historia, but it would perhaps be more just to describe it as a seventeenth-century readaptation which deprives the earlier work of much of its naïve simplicity. For instance in the Chronicle when the Neapolitan inquisitor, terrified by a severe storm, tells Brother Liberato that he is willing to release him immediately, having previously advised him to submit to a formal trial in order to prove his innocence to the world, the latter replies with straightforward directness, " I have decided to be ruled by your former

---

[1] *Fasc. Rer. Expetend.* ii. 493.

[2] Bzovius' continuation was published at Rome in 1617. His work was later continued by Raynaldi.

[3] Cf. *Annales*, vi. 279-90. First edition in 8 vols. (Rome, 1625-1654).

[4] Hicquey wrote under the pseudonym of Dermicius Thadaei. The full title of his book, which was printed at Lyons in 1627, is as follows : *Nitela Franciscanae Religionis et abstersio sordium, quibus eam conspurcare frustra tentavit Abrahamus Bzovius* (*A.L.K.G.* iv. 143).

[5] An example of this is the encyclical letter issued by John of Murrovalle, enforcing the regulations forbidding the friars to receive any property to which an annual rent was attached. Cf. *Annales*, vi. 1302, § i. p. 7. Cf. p. 167, *n.* 2.

[6] Codex S. Isidore, 1/67.

counsel ".[1] In Wadding he makes a much longer and more grandiloquent speech, demanding a trial in order that the slanders of his enemies might be proved groundless.[2] Wadding's verdict on the Spirituals and on Michael of Cesena and his followers was characteristic alike of his moderation and of his submissive attitude to authority. He regarded them as righteous men who had been led by zeal for their Order into the paths of disobedience and presumption, and exhorted his readers to avoid their errors while imitating their virtues.[3] His judgment was generally accepted by the writers of his period. An Observant, Domenico de Gubernatis, writing in 1681,[4] used Wadding as his chief source, while the life of Angelo da Clareno in the *Acta Sanctorum* [5] is composed simply of extracts from the *Annales*. It was the Bollandist Papebroch, however, who discovered the manuscript of Angelo's letters then in the Strozzi collection at Florence. The only part of the codex, however, which he examined at all carefully, was the list of miracles.[6] He notified his discovery to Wadding's nephew, Father Francis Harold,[7] and the letters were examined in connection with the beatification process of John of Parma in 1777.[8] Another scholar of the seventeenth century who was keenly interested in the Spirituals was Colbert's great librarian, Baluze, to whom we owe the publication of the verdict of the judges on Olivi's Postilla in Apocalypsim,[9] and the chronicle of John the Minorite.[10] Unfortunately, Baluze nowhere expressed an opinion on the origin of the Fraticelli, though his contemporary, Raynaldi,[11] had no doubts about their connection with the Franciscan Order, and regarded both the Spirituals and the Michaelists as their founders.[12] His Annals are marred by the bitterness of his prejudice against them, though he made a careful study of their history, and in his book he uses many documents from the Vatican archives. After reading Raynaldi, it is a relief to turn to Mansi's vindication of the Spirituals in his Lucca edition of Baluze's *Miscellanea*.[13] He refused to believe that they were in any way connected with the Fraticelli, and evidently had a great admiration for them, even

---

[1] " Ego deliberavi non recedere a vestro consilio " (*A.L.K.G.* ii. p. 320).
[2] *Annales*, vi. p. 89, 1307, ii.
[3] *Annales*, vi. p. 321, 1318, xxvii. ; vii. p. 86, 1328, xx. Cf. *supra*, p. 201.
[4] *Orbis Seraphicus.*
[5] *Acta Sanctorum* (June 15), vol. ii. p. 1091 *s.*
[6] C. Magliabecchiana, xxxix. *n.* 75, f. 214 *v.*-219 *v.* ; *Acta Sanctorum*, ii. 1100-1102.
[7] Cf. *A.L.K.G.* i. 516. Cf. *supra*, p. 68, *n.* 5.
[8] *A.L.K.G.* i. 516.   [9] *Misc.* ii. pp. 258-70. Cf. *supra*, p. 113.
[10] *Misc.* iii. p. 207 *s.* Cf. *supra*, p. 153 *s.*
[11] The continuer of Baronius and Bzovius.
[12] Cf. *Annales*, xxiv. 1322, L. II. ; 1325, xx. ; 329, xxii.
[13] *Misc.* iii. p. 363 *s.*

T

venturing to declare that it was unjust to condemn Olivi's Postilla merely from the extracts quoted by the judges in their report.[1] However, the last word of the controversy had not been said, and it continued to rage both outside the Order and within. The great edition of the Bullarium Franciscanum, published in 1759, was thought by no less a person than the reigning Pope to be unduly prejudiced against the Spirituals, and a revised version was made by the Observant, Annibali da Latera. He had already shown his partiality for Angelo da Clareno and his party in his Manual of the Friars Minor,[2] a catalogue of the saints of the Franciscan Order, in the appendix of which he defended the Zealots against the attacks of a certain Father Maestro.[3] In his Supplement to the Bullarium he devoted the whole of the eighth " Animadversio " to a defence of Angelo's orthodoxy.[4] His account is especially interesting, as he made use of and printed the famous Epistola Excusatoria, written at the command of John XXII., and selections from some of the other letters to prove his case. He also was the first writer to mention two little treatises by Clareno, the " Breviloquium " and the " Preparantia ",[5] which have only recently been printed,[6] His efforts appear on the whole to have been successful, for, at the beginning of the nineteenth century, an attempt was made to obtain official recognition for Angelo's traditional title of " beato ".[7] This was unsuccessful owing to the lethargy of the cathedral chapter of Cingoli, the town where he probably first was admitted into the Franciscan Order,[8] and also to the difficulty of collecting evidence about the popular devotion paid to his memory. It must be remembered that this was the period following the French Revolution and the Napoleonic invasion of Italy, and probably even the canons belonging to a sleepy little Italian town were too absorbed in the stirring events of their own age, and in their fears with regard to the future of the Church, to have time to spare for researches into the reverence shown by their ancestors for an illustrious fellow-citizen. On the whole, however, with the exception of Mansi, the leading Italian historians took very little interest either in the Spirituals or in Michael of

---

[1] Misc. iii. p. 364.   [2] Manuali de Frati Minori.
[3] Ibid. Appendix, p. 369 s.
[4] Supplementum ad Bullarium Franciscanum, pp. 138-76.
[5] Ibid. p. 172.
[6] By Father Ciro da Pesaro in Il Beato Angelo Clareno, pp. 403-412. Cf. supra, p. 77.
[7] Father Oliger has printed part of the correspondence connected with this attempt in the A.F.H. vii. 556-63. Between 1807 and 1808 no less than fifteen letters were written on the subject of Angelo's canonization. These letters are the private property of " il canone Guglielmo Malazampa " of Cingoli.
[8] Cf. supra, p. 50.

Cesena and his followers. Muratori makes few allusions to them in his writings, and his sympathies were strongly on the side of the Papacy in the great conflict,[1] while Tiraboschi dismisses the writings of Ubertino da Casale and the fugitives of Munich as having nothing to do with the development of Italian literature.[2] On the other hand, Oudin [3] and Fabricius [4] were obviously well informed about them, and possessed considerable knowledge both of the manuscripts and of the early printed editions of their works, and Hélyot, in his great " Histoire des Ordres Religieux ", gives a very sympathetic account of the Zealots.[5] Fleury's *Histoire Ecclésiastique* also deals at some length with the fortunes of Olivi and his disciples and with the controversy between John XXII.[6] and the Franciscan Order, whilst the valuable little treatise, " De Beghardis et Beguinabus ", of the Lutheran historian Mosheim shows that the fate of the Spirituals was not a matter of indifference to Protestant scholars.[7] The next century was to witness a revival of interest, although at first the majority of the historians were content to accept the labours of others, and did not seek to extend their knowledge by further researches into the original documents. The German scholar Giesseler was perhaps the most thorough, for, besides studying the works of Baluze, Raynaldi, and Wadding, he had read parts of the *Arbor Vitae*, and the lives of St. Francis by Thomas of Celano and St. Bonaventura.[8] Hefelè, the learned Bishop of Rotterdam, also devotes a portion of his great book on

---

[1] The names of the Spirituals and of Michael and his followers naturally occur periodically in Muratori's great *Rerum Italicarum Scriptores*, but he does not seem to have had any special desire to edit any writing primarily connected with their history. For his opinion of Michael of Cesena, cf. *Scriptores*, iii. pt. ii. p. 513.

[2] *Storia della letteratura italiana*, v. p. 161. In a sense he was correct, for the *Arbor* and the appeals of Michael and his followers were written in Latin. It was only in the middle of the nineteenth century that certain of the letters of the Fraticelli, which, being in the vernacular, may have influenced the development of the Italian language as a literary medium, were printed in *Scelta di curiosità letterarie* (cf. *supra*, pp. 219, 227, and 232). Tiraboschi also mentions Angelo's translations from the Greek, but obviously only knew of them through the writings of others (*op. cit.* v. pt. ii. p. 423).

[3] *Commentarius de scriptoribus ecclesiasticis*, iii. Cf. pp. 584-89, 748, 788, 888, 904.

[4] *Bibliotheca Latina mediae et Infimae aetatis*. Cf. vol. i. pp. 261, 690, 881, 984 ; vol. iii. pp. 465-67 ; vol. v. p. 774. For Chatton, cf. vol. iii. p. 331.

[5] *Histoire des Ordres Religieux*, vii., pt. v. 5, p. 53. Cf. *supra*, p. 12, *n.* 1.

[6] (Paris, 1759), Livre lxxxvii.-xciii. Fleury relied on Wadding for much of his information, and it is interesting that he believed John XXII.'s decretals to be irreconcilable with " Exiit qui seminat ". Cf. L. XCIII. ch. xv.

[7] (Leipzig, 1790.) This work was edited and revised after the death of its author by George Henry Martini, who enriched it with many valuable appendices containing copies of original documents.

[8] Cf. *Compendium of Ecclesiastical History*, iii. p. 251 *s.* ; vol. iv. pp. 148-56.

the Councils to an account of the Zealots, and of the controversy between the Franciscan Order and the Papacy,[1] while the French historian, Michelet, combined a hatred of medieval obscurantism with a warm admiration for Ubertino da Casale.[2] In England Bishop Creighton refers to the struggle between John XXII. and the Minorites, gaining much of his information on the subject from Goldast.[3] The conflict, however, occurred too early to be dealt with at any length in his book. Dean Milman was possibly more deeply read, especially on the subject of the Spirituals, but his account is marred by modern prejudice, and he makes no effort to understand their aims and aspirations.[4] In the latter half of the century, a considerable amount of research was done in Germany upon the relations between Louis of Bavaria and the Papacy, and the work of such scholars as Müller,[5] Riezler,[6] and Preger[7] gave a considerable impetus to the study of the writings of the Franciscans at Munich, though their main object was to throw light upon the history of their own country. Perhaps of the three Riezler was the most widely read, and his book is cited by Gregorovius in his history of Rome in the Middle Ages.[8] The Zealots were perhaps a little neglected by historians until the end of the century. After 1870, however, there was so great a revival of enthusiasm in their favour as to more than compensate for the former lack of interest.

It is very difficult to discuss the recent researches made by scholars in connection with the Spirituals, for so much work has

---

[1] Cf. Hefelè and Le Clercq, *Histoire des Conciles*, ix. 423 s.

[2] Michelet, *Histoire de France*, iv. pp. 80-82. Cf. *supra*, p. 142.

[3] Introduction to *History of the Papacy* (London, 1897), i. pp. 39-41. Creighton also made use of Riezler's *Die literarischen Widersacher der Päpste zur Zeit Ludwigs des Baiers* for his account of the opinions of Marsiglio of Padua.

[4] *History of Latin Christianity* (London, 1867), vii. bk. xii. ch. vi. pp. 370-80. His unsympathetic account of the Spirituals is preceded by a very highly coloured and laudatory description of Fra Dolcino and his followers, who displayed no greater heroism than the former in the defence of their infinitely wilder religious beliefs. Cf. *ibid*. pp. 358-70.

[5] Müller's greatest contribution to the history of the struggle between Louis of Bavaria and the Papacy is his *Der Kampf Ludwigs des Baiern mit der Römischen Curie* (Tubingen, 1879–1880). Another useful work was his analysis of the documents contained in the Chronicle of Nicolas the Minorite in *Z.K.G.* vi.

[6] *Die literarischen Widersacher der Päpste zur Zeit Ludwigs des Bayers: Vatikanische Akten zur deutschen Geschichte in der Zeit Kaiser Ludwigs des Bayern* (Munich, 1891).

[7] " Der kirchenpolitische Kampf unter Ludwig dem Baier und sein Einfluss " (pp. 1-70). Preger was the first modern historian to question the authenticity of the so-called confession of Michael of Cesena, though he had no documentary evidence on which to base his assumption (*ibid*. pp. 34-35).

[8] Cf. *History of the City of Rome in the Middle Ages* (London, 1895), vi. bk. xi. ch. iii. pp. 115-17, 127-28.

been done and there are so many illustrious names to record. The year 1884 can almost be regarded as an " Annus Mirabilis ", pointing the way to wider and more extended work, for it was then that the French historian Richard, writing in the " Bibliothèque de l'École de Chartes ",[1] drew the attention of scholars to the codex of the " Historia Septem Tribulationum " in the Laurenziana, while Renan gave an account of the Eternal Gospel in his "Nouvelles Études ",[2] and Professor Tocco began his career as a writer on Franciscan subjects by the publication of his " L' Eresia nel medio evo ". It was as if in answer to Richard that the following year Cardinal Ehrle began his labours on the Spirituals with his article in the first volume of "Archiv für Literatur und Kirchengeschichte".[3] Praise of his work is mere impertinence, and all that is possible is to read with reverence and thankfulness the wonderful selection of documents which he has given to the world, and his equally valuable comments upon these. We owe to him the " Epistola Excusatoria "[4] and a fine series of extracts from Angelo's letters,[5] besides the more interesting part of the Seven Tribulations,[6] to wit, the third to the seventh book. He has also given us a very fine and exhaustive study of the life of Olivi, with extracts from his writings,[7] and many of the treatises written at the time of the Council of Vienne,[8] as well as extracts from papal letters and records of Inquisition processes, which throw great light on the after history of the Spirituals [9] and on the origin of the Fraticelli. Unlike earlier writers, Ehrle realised that the name was a general one, used not only to denote many different sects of heretics but also certain orthodox communities not belonging to any definite Order.[10] It is to be regretted that this great historian did not see his way to making a complete edition of the " Chronicle of the Seven Tribulations ". Up to the present only Döllinger's version has appeared. This was published in *Beiträge zur Sektengeschichte des Mittelalters* in 1890,[11] but the text is very faulty and is marred by many omissions. Another great writer on Franciscan subjects, Monsieur Sabatier, felt the need for a new and complete edition of Angelo's great book,[12] but did not undertake the work himself.

[1] *Bibliothèque de l'École de Chartes*, xlv. 523-32.
[2] *Nouvelles Études de l'histoire religieuse*, pp. 217-322.
[3] *A.L.K.G.* i. 509-569.   [4] *Ibid.* 521-33.
[5] *Ibid.* 543-69. A selection from the letters is also given by Tocco (*S.F.* i. 296-310).
[6] *A.L.K.G.* ii. 125-55, 256-327.   [7] *Ibid.* iii. 456 s.
[8] *Ibid.* ii. 365-416, ii. 1-195.
[9] *Ibid.* iv. 1-190.   [10] *Ibid.* iv. 168-80.
[11] *Beiträge zur Sektengeschichte des Mittelalters*, ii. (Munich, 1890), 417-526.
[12] Cf. Intro. to *Speculum*, p. cxxxix. Professor Tocco originally intended to make a complete edition of the Chronicle to be published in the same series as

The deficiency has been in part remedied by Professor Tocco's publication of the first two Tribulations in 1908.[1] The same year saw the appearance of the first volume of the " Archivum Franciscanum Historicum ", the great periodical edited by the Observants of the college of St. Bonaventura at Quaracchi. It is impossible to describe at length the documents published in the different numbers which have contributed so much to our knowledge of an eventful period in the history of a great Order, or to name the writers whose articles have thrown so much light on a thorny and complicated subject. One, however, cannot be passed over in silence, and that is Father Oliger, whose fine collection of documents relating to the history of the Fraticelli appeared in the third, fourth, fifth, and sixth volumes of the *Archivum*,[2] and whose edition of Angelo da Clareno's *Expositio Regulae Fratrum Minorum* was published in 1912.[3] His introduction to this latter work seems to contain the fruit of all previous researches into the life and influence of the great Zealot. Yet the scholars of Quaracchi deserve our gratitude, not only for the *Archivum* but for their fine editions of the works of the Franciscan thinkers [4] and historians [5] of the Middle Ages, and for their courtesy and kindness in lending rotographs of their manuscript treasures to students of the history of their Order.[6] They have also continued the *Bullarium Franciscanum*,[7] which is not only a remarkable collection of the papal letters connected with the Friars, but contains much valuable information in the notes and appendices of Father Eubel. Other names among the many which should be mentioned are those of Father Callaey, who has made a special study of Ubertino of Casale,[8] and the Abbé Vidal, who has given us practically all the information we possess about that strange figure whom Angelo

the *Speculum*, but contented himself finally with a new version of the Prologue and the first two Tribulations.

[1] In *Rendiconti della R. Accademia dei Lincei*, No. xvii. The brothers of the Collegio di San Bonaventura at Quaracchi are contemplating a new version in connection with their great edition of the original sources for the life of S. Francis, to be published in *A.F.* x. So far only the lives by Thomas of Celano have appeared.

[2] " Documenta inedita ad historiam Fraticellorum spectantia." It has now been published as a separate book.

[3] Quaracchi, 1912.

[4] *Biblioteca Franciscana Scholastica Medii Aevi*. Olivi's *Questiones in II. Sententiarum* are published in vols. iv.-vi. Cf. *supra*, p. 106.

[5] *A.F.*

[6] It is to their kindness that I am indebted for the loan of the rotograph of Angelo de Clareno's letters.

[7] Vols. v., vi., vii. have now been published.

[8] *L'Idéalisme franciscain spirituel au XIVme siècle. Étude sur Ubertin de Casale* (Louvain, 1911).

da Clareno loved so well and whose fate is still buried in mystery, the royal ascetic, Philip of Majorca.[1] Another very important study is Dr. Karl Balthazar's *Geschichte des Armutsstreites im Franziskaner Orden*, but unfortunately it ends with the Council of Vienne in 1310. A work of the same character, but even more extended in its scope, is the *Histoire de la fondation et de l'évolution de l'ordre de Frères Mineurs au XIIIᵉ siècle*, of Father Gratien,[2] and Herr Grundmann's recent studies of certain of the pseudo-Joachimite writings have thrown much light on the eschatological speculations of the Spirituals.[3] The feeling of reverence, and yet of fellowship, which the humblest student of Franciscan history entertains for these great scholars may perhaps be compared to the devotion felt by the meanest member of that great Order for its founder and all those who in past ages have laboured to make it glorious.

---

[1] " Un ascète du sang royal : Philippe de Majorque " (*Revue des questions historiques*, lxxxviii. pp. 361-403).

[2] " Die Papstprophetien des Mittelalters ", in *A.K.* xix. pp. 77-139, and " 'Liber de Flore ', eine Schrift der Franziskaner-Spiritualen aus dem Anfang des 14. Jahrhunderts," in *H.J.* 49, pp. 33-91.

ADDITIONS TO NOTES

P. 210, *n.* 7. When my book was already in type, fragments of an inquisition record for 1361, throwing further light on the history of the Fraticelli living in the neighbourhood of Perugia and Città di Castello under the authority of the bishops of that region, were published by Father Oliger in *A.F.H.* xxiv. pp. 63-90. Although professing the rule of St. Augustine, the leader of the sect, " Frater Franciscus Nicolay ", received letters from the Sicilian Fraticelli, and shared their views on evangelical poverty, even asserting that a life of mendicancy was incumbent upon the Pope and the bishops. He refused to recognise Innocent VI. as the lawful Pope, on the ground that he was a Simoniac, and had imprisoned " Johannes de Ruperscissa " lest the preaching of the latter should endanger his own position. The righteous pastor of the new age would be the fratecello, Jacopo di Colonna, whom Rienzo met during his sojourn among the Fraticelli (cf. Puir-Burdach, *op. cit.* p. 309). The chief sign of the former's vocation was apparently his premature baldness, a characteristic which, according to tradition, he shared with St. Peter, the first Pope. The witnesses belonging to the sect are described as offering themselves willingly, and the inquisitor contented himself with allotting them a fixed period in which to unite themselves to some recognized Order, so that it is very probable that they did not approve of the " doctrines " of their leader, or wish to separate themselves from the Church.

P. 223, *n.* 9. Father Oliger's recent article in *A.F.H.* xxiv. pp. 63-90, drew my attention to certain documents published by him in *Z.K.G.* xlv. pp. 215-242. Amongst these is a sixteenth-century transcript of a letter of Nicholas V. in favour of the Clarenists, dated 1447, which he found in the Capucin archives at Rome. This confirms two bulls of Eugenius IV., one protecting the Clarenists in the dioceses of Fermo, Foligno, Camerino, Spoleto, Narni, Amelia, Ascoli, Aquila, and Rieti against the activities of the Inquisition, and another sanctioning their possession of nine hermitages in the three first-mentioned dioceses. Nicholas's letter mentions a priest named Andrea da Fermo as general in the time of Eugenius IV., and Giovanni da Amandola as the present holder of that office. Attached to the transcript is a petition to Clement VII. from an early patroness of the Capucins, Caterina Cybò, Duchess of Camerino, asking that the hermitage of Sta Maria Magdalena, commonly called La Grotta, in the neighbourhood of Camerino, might be transferred from the Clarenists to the new Order, since the lives of the former were unworthy of their profession and a cause of scandal to the surrounding region. Her request was presumably not granted, perhaps because of the protection afforded to the Clarenists by their union with the Observantines in 1517. Cf. *infra*, p. 225.

P. 229, *n.* 4. On July 11, 1328, John XXII. wrote to the Prior of the Dominicans of Carcassonne, permitting him to receive Thomas " de Brancetona " as a member of his own Order in spite of the regulations forbidding such a transference (*B.F.* v. 720, p. 353). I have been unable to find any record of the earlier career of this mysterious individual.

P. 246, *n.* 4. " A questi di scrissi como in Alemagna era scoperta una setta de heretici quasi simili a questi fratizelli de la opinione."—Letter of Bartolomeo de Maraschis to the Marchesa Barbara of Mantua (Rome, Sept., 1466). Pastor, *Geschichte der Päpste*, ii. (Freiburg im Breisgau, 1889), p. 637, § 82. The German sect of Fraticelli appears to have been active in the region round Eger in the year 1466. Its leaders were the two brothers Johann and Livin of Würsberg, the former of whom was regarded as a second Baptist by his followers.

In 1467 Livin died in prison, having renounced his errors, but nothing is known of the fate of Johann (*ibid.* p. 343).   The Observantine chronicler, Nicholas Glassberger, gives a letter from the papal legate Rudolf, Bishop of Lavantino, to Henry of Absperg, Bishop of Ratisbon, drawing his attention to the diffusion of the sect in his diocese.   From Glassberger's account their doctrines seem to have been a somewhat crude recrudescence of Joachimism, but he is more interested in the attempt of the Conventuals to prove a connection between the "heretics" and his own branch of the Order.   Cf. *A.F.* ii. p. 422-26.   Little is known about the later history of the sect, but their connection with the Bohemian Brethren has been established.   Cf. *Z.K.G.* xlv. pp. 231-33.

INDEX

Unless R...
DATE DUE